Comparative industrial relations

D1642688

This is the second edition of a well-established student text giving a thematic and analytical treatment to the comparative and international aspects of industrial relations.

By surveying, integrating and reviewing the expanding body of literature and research findings relating to comparative studies in industrial relations, this volume examines the similarities and differences between countries and institutions around the world. New sections cover the 'individualising' of industrial relations through human resource management, the 1992 EC dimension in relation to multinationals, developments in Eastern European trade unions, and the 'economic democracy' of financial participation by workers in their own companies. In addition, a chapter on industrial relations systems and the macro-economic performance of countries has been added, and all the existing chapters have been updated to include findings of recent research studies. The wide range of differing institutions and practices is set out and emphasis is given to analysing and explaining their similarities and differences. The book looks to incorporate material from Western Europe, North America, Japan and Australasia, as well as examining the conduct of industrial relations in Third World countries.

By enlarging and updating, this new edition seeks to capitalise upon the success of its predecessor and will become essential reading for all those interested in what progress there has been during the last ten years, where this has occurred, and how it compares cross-nationally.

Ron Bean is Senior Lecturer in the Department of Economics and Accounting at the University of Liverpool. He has published widely in the field of labour and industrial relations.

Comparative industrial relations

An introduction to cross-national perspectives

Second edition

Ron Bean

INTERNATIONAL THOMSON BUSINESS PRESS
I ⓉP An International Thomson Publishing Company

London • Bonn • Boston • Johannesburg • Madrid • Melbourne • Mexico City • New York • Paris
Singapore • Tokyo • Toronto • Albany, NY • Belmont, CA • Cincinnati, OH • Detroit, MI

Comparative Industrial Relations

Copyright ©1994 Ron Bean

 A division of International Thomson Publishing Inc.
The ITP logo is a trademark under licence

British Library Cataloguing-in-Publication Data
A catalogue record for this book is available from the British Library

First published by Routledge 1994
Simultaneously published in the USA and Canada by Routledge
Reprinted 1995
Reprinted by International Thomson Business Press 1996 and 1999

Typeset in Times by LaserScript, Mitcham, Surrey
Printed in the UK by T J International Ltd, Padstow, Cornwall

ISBN 1861524951

International Thomson Business Press
Berkshire House
168–173 High Holborn
London WC1V 7AA
UK

http://www.thomson.com/itbp.html

Contents

Figures and tables

FIGURES

TABLES

Preface to the first edition

For some time there has been a developing interest in 'comparative' studies as a sub-teaching area within industrial relations in universities and polytechnics together with a considerable expansion in recent years in the number of industrial relations research studies which are avowedly comparative in their orientation – particularly those relating to socio-political influences on patterns of industrial conflict. Yet there is a notable absence of student texts in this field which are not either dated and/or overly descriptive and factual in the material which they include. Over the past decade the proliferating output of monograph, symposia and journal literature concerned with international and comparative aspects of the subject has been impressive in its volume and breadth, if not always in its depth or quality. A specialised periodical, the *Bulletin of Comparative Labour Relations*, has also appeared on the scene. Moreover, the better studies

> have progressed beyond merely describing country-by-country variations in trade union structure, collective bargaining institutions and public policy frameworks. Attempts are made to provide analytical tools for cross-national comparisons and build theories to account for different patterns of industrial relations.
>
> (Slack 1980: 27)

Thus the aim of this book is to present an introduction to the broad domain of comparative industrial relations via a survey and a drawing together of the recent, more analytic literature – thereby providing some varied (although by no means exhaustive) perspectives on the current state of knowledge in a number of mainstream topics within the field. In consequence, the treatment adopted is both selective, which inevitably involves some arbitrary decisions of inclusion and omission, and thematic. It is organised around a number of central topics rather than in the form of a side-by-side treatment of a number of individual countries, i.e. by focusing on issues across national boundaries it adopts what Blanpain has termed an 'integrated' approach. This avoids a concentration on the domestic minutiae and empirical details of industrial relations practices within particular countries which are readily available elsewhere, and may be of less enduring interest since they can soon become outdated.

The justification for this approach is that, in an attempt to explain systematically uniformities and diversities encountered in cross-national industrial relations, selected countries might usefully be used to provide data for comparative purposes, or as 'ideal types' of particular patterns, but they are not in themselves sufficient. Rather, the focus needs to be directed towards the factors that determine the observed variations – making it necessary to go beyond what Kerr and his colleagues (1962: 11) called 'topographical studies describing the lay of the land in the individual countries':

> to go beyond saying that in Nigeria it was this way and in Turkey that [since] looking at one country at a time each situation appeared historically unique and the totality of the detail was almost incomprehensible.

Dunlop (1972: 102) has described such detailed, institutional comparisons between countries as tending 'to portray an industrial relations zoo' in which form, rather than substance and purpose, are emphasised.

In any case, selections of country-by-country studies often found in 'comparative' volumes, although they may be individually revealing, are frequently repetitious in content as well as tending to be preoccupied with the maze of diverse institutional forms and bargaining arrangements. It has also been pointed out (Kassalow 1969) that many of them are not genuinely comparative at all, since the individual countries could easily stand in their own right as they are largely disconnected, drawing little or nothing from each other and having little in the way of a common, integrating analytical framework. Shalev (1981: 242) regards these sort of studies as displaying what he calls the 'Victorian traveller's approach' since:

> Rather like the Victorian gentleman on his 'grand tour' the reader is presented with a diverse selection of exotic ports of call and left to draw his own conclusions about their relevance to each other and to the traveller himself.

In this book it is not the intention, therefore, to examine in great detail the structure and practices of industrial relations in individual countries as such. It is hoped that the approach which is adopted, by concentrating upon analysis and explanation and drawing together an extensive but scattered literature in this field of enquiry, will prove particularly suitable for the needs of undergraduates in departments of economics, sociology, business and management studies.

In writing the book I have incurred a number of debts. Stan Jones and Tony Lane provided useful suggestions, Alan Gladstone and Keith Sisson kindly allowed me to see prior to publication their studies on employers' organisations and the staff of Liverpool University Library, and the late Mike Jones, were most helpful in obtaining reference material. The text has greatly benefited from the constructive criticisms of the publisher's readers, Peter Sowden of Croom Helm was constantly encouraging from the outset and Vivienne Oakes typed the manuscript most efficiently and uncomplainingly. To all of them, I express my thanks.

Preface to the second edition

Over the past decade, since the first edition of this book was prepared, major changes have taken place in the environment in which industrial relations operate in advanced industrial societies. These have occurred especially as a consequence of growing competition in national or international product markets, together with their rapid change, which has meant that firms have been forced to introduce radical innovations, either technological or organisational, in order to meet the challenge. In some countries, against a background of conservative political victories, privatisation and deregulation, more 'individual' employee relationships are often advocated, with less emphasis upon collectivism. Changes in markets and production systems have resulted generally in greater management initiatives, strong pressures towards decentralisation in industrial relations and the emergence of 'flexibility' as a dominant concept. (At the same time, the collapse of former communist regimes in Eastern Europe, along with the emergence of pluralism and trade unions which are independent of the state, has meant that the industrial relations systems of those countries are also in a process of transition and change.) These developments have been incorporated into the revisions and updating of the original chapters for the second edition, as well as recent research findings for the various topics in the 'thematic' and analytical treatment which has been adopted. A new chapter has also been added on industrial relations systems and economic outcomes in western countries.

I am most grateful to all those who commented on the first edition for their suggestions for improvement, particularly Roy Adams, Phil Beaumont, Howard Gospel and Michael Poole for their advice and help. Once again, Viv Moss has typed the whole of the manuscript both expeditiously and cheerfully and I am greatly indebted to her. Acknowledgement is also made to the publishers of *Employee Relations* and the *Industrial Relations Journal* for permission to reproduce material from two of my articles which first appeared there.

August 1993

1 Introduction: comparative approaches

The academic field of industrial relations is typically defined as being the study of the various aspects of job regulation (Bain and Clegg 1974), with a consequent attendant focus on rule-making in the employment relationship. Alternatively, for those who regard this definition as too restrictive – particularly in its implicit overtones of stability, regularity and mutual accommodation between the parties – the central core of the subject is the 'study of the process of control over work relations' (Hyman 1975: 12). This latter emphasis is intended to highlight the underlying but centrally important issues of control, power and interests[1] together with the generation of conflict, rather than with mechanisms and techniques for its resolution. Such a definition considerably broadens the scope of the subject away from a traditional institutional orientation towards an examination of wider societal influences which affect the character of relations between workers, employers and their respective collective organisations. The primacy of the power relationship has been stressed by Korpi (1981: 190). He maintains that:

> of basic importance for understanding the functioning of the industrial relations system is the distribution of power resources between sellers and buyers of manpower and changes in this distribution. The power resources . . . are, on the one hand, the pattern of ownership of capital and of organisation among employers and, on the other hand, union organisation and political power.

A further, broad conception of the field of study is adopted by Kochan (1980). He sees industrial relations as encompassing the study of all aspects of people at work, including individuals as well as groups of workers (who may or may not organise into a trade union), the behaviour of employer and union organisations, together with the public policy or legal framework governing employment conditions. Such a definition can easily incorporate what some observers detect as a general, structural change in industrial relations in recent years, whereby regularised collective relations via institutional machinery may be increasingly supplemented (and sometimes replaced) by a trend towards more individually based, and more flexible, relations (Fürstenberg 1991).

FRAMES OF REFERENCE IN INDUSTRIAL RELATIONS

A survey of industrial relations research traditions viewed from an international standpoint has suggested that studies tend to cluster around two underlying assumptions. There is firstly the 'pluralist-institutionalist' approach which is especially predominant in Anglo-Saxon countries. Here the discipline is regarded as being of an applied and pragmatic nature and research is empirically oriented, usually with an emphasis on procedural and institutional concerns, towards policy relevance and problem-solving. Second, in contrast, in a country such as Italy the system of stratification and class structure forms an important part of the analysis, which is as much concerned with workers and the working class as with unions and collective bargaining. In class-oriented studies 'politics, political action and the tensions between employers and employees are prominent . . . and less attention is devoted to the actual procedures and practice of industrial relations' (Doeringer 1981: 10–11). These two assumptions are not mutually exclusive, however, and research formulations in France, Japan and Sweden, for instance, have utilised both.

Closely related to these contrasting emphases regarding the nature and parameters of the subject is the question of devising an appropriate conceptual framework of analysis in industrial relations, as well as the extent to which this is explicitly grounded in theory. Doeringer (1981) distinguishes three major divisions: a pragmatic approach in which theory plays little or no role although, as Eldridge (1975: 7) has reminded us, 'the pragmatists in emphasising the need for realistic solutions often carry a good deal of conceptual and theoretical baggage around with them'; second, a Marxist approach stressing class relations and conflict irreconcilability; and, following upon Dunlop's (1958) seminal work, the highly influential 'systems' model focusing upon the rules of industrial relations and their determinants.

In Dunlop's concept of an interdependent industrial relations system three principal actors,[2] namely workers, managers – as well as their representative organisations – together with certain state agencies, all interact to establish a network of rules governing their relationship in the workplace, the rules being the output of the system. The actors, however, are subject to pressures and constraints arising out of the environmental setting in which they operate, assumed to be given and exogenously determined.[3] This background context within which the rules (both substantive and procedural[4]) are developed impinges upon the relationship between the actors and the nature of the rules which they establish. It consists of technological factors, product and labour market determinants, social influences affecting the ideology of the actors, as well as the political environment which, for Dunlop, consists of power relations in the larger society.

A further basic premise of Dunlop's prescription for the advancement of knowledge in industrial relations is the need to break away from the restrictive and myopic confines of problem-solving, institutional studies within individual countries – what has been termed an 'ethno-centric' bias – in favour of broader comparisons over the course of time and across countries. He suggests that the systems model is applicable to the study of comparative industrial relations since, although every country displays special or particularistic industrial relations characteristics because of differences in the environmental settings in which they operate, 'the attention to rule making in industrial relations systems provides a common denominator for the comparative analysis of different forms' (Dunlop 1958: 27). It is probably more valid, however, to argue that its main use is as a means of identifying the relevant variables which help to shape industrial relations outcomes, and of ordering empirical data. His model gives little guidance as to the individual weightings to be attached to explanatory variables for evaluating between them, or the precise ways in which they interact; it is said to lack predictive power (Gill 1969) and it has generated little research which specifically tests hypotheses (Meltz 1991). Furthermore, systems theory fails to explain patterns of industrial relations which have developed in Third World countries (Haworth 1991).

It has also come to be recognised that the environmental constraints identified in Dunlop's theory will not usually be so severe as to predetermine the industrial relations outcomes of any change which takes place within the basic parameters of the system, such as a shift in the competitive product market environment facing firms. Consequently, the concept of 'strategic choice' has been developed as an important and additional, intervening variable. The aim is to attempt to add a dynamic component to systems theory, as industrial relations systems respond to economic, political and social changes whereby the actors (particularly management) will usually have a number of possible responses that they can make. There is therefore some element of discretion in decision-making, which will affect industrial relations in different ways (Kochan *et al.* 1984a). Thus technology, for example, can be viewed not as an outside factor beyond the control of the parties themselves, since there are a variety of alternative technologies which will provide options (Hyman and Streeck 1988).

In fact, it has been argued that international differences in industrial relations can best be explained not by variations in social and economic structure, but rather by historical divergences in institutional development resulting from the strategies and organisation of trade unions, employers and the state (Zeitlin 1987). Certainly, as Roche (1986: 24) has indicated, 'it is conceivable that similar configurations of market, power and technological variables may be consistent with significantly different patterns of industrial relations due to the effects of the institutional systems through which such forces are mediated.' Similarly, choice itself may largely be conditioned by existing institutional arrangements (Streeck 1988).

COMPARATIVE INDUSTRIAL RELATIONS

As regards the nature of comparative investigation within the subject, Sturmthal (1958: 77) defines it as 'research dealing with the same (or similar or related) phenomena in different countries'. A further conceptual distinction may be drawn between 'comparative' industrial relations, and 'international' and 'foreign' studies within the field. International, or transnational, studies deal with those institutions and phenomena which cross national boundaries, such as the industrial relations aspects of multinational companies or the international labour movement. In studies of 'foreign' labour movements in countries other than one's own, the selected countries are usually treated separately with few or no explicit comparisons being made (Meyers 1967). This latter category may form the raw material, or foundation, for comparisons but such studies are to be regarded as preparatory, rather than being fully comparative, since the questions asked of the data are at best implicit and few analytical statements are drawn from them. Essentially, then, 'comparative' industrial relations is a systematic method of investigation relating to two or more countries which has analytic rather than descriptive implications.

Poole (1986a) has advanced four principles for guiding the comparative analysis of industrial relations phenomena: (1) a focus upon environmental influences emanating from societal structures and processes, (2) a multidisciplinary perspective, so as to incorporate economic, political and sociocultural factors, (3) emphasis upon explanatory variables rather than descriptive categories, and (4) the importance of utilising a historical as well as a contemporary dimension.

In addition to the need for identifying appropriate benchmarks and a suitable framework of analysis, we may also ask about the rationale for engaging in work within the field of comparative industrial relations. What can be learned by comparing one system with another? Should comparison be undertaken for its own sake, simply out of intrinsic interest or intellectual curiosity, or should it be directed towards some more closely defined objective? Comparative studies can lead to greater understanding

of the factors and processes which determine industrial relations phenomena since 'the comparative method leads to questions regarding the
reasons for the observed comparisons and contrasts' (Dunlop 1958: vi).
The studies can be illuminating largely because, as Banks (1974) puts it, of
the way in which they reveal differences between systems which in many
other respects are similar, and similarities in systems which otherwise are
different. Hence they throw into relief and bring out the significant aspects
of the phenomenon in question. Used in this way, the comparative
approach can afford a perspective and lead to greater insight into domestic
issues in one's own country, by contrasting its industrial relations institutions and practices with those of other countries, thereby placing the home
country in context; that is to say, the notion that only through comparative
study may one's own system be fully understood (Adams 1991).

There may also be a desire to utilise comparative studies for practical,
policy considerations by attempting to derive lessons from overseas experience, or to use the industrial relations systems of particular countries which
can demonstrate a high success rate within their own society – via a rapid
rate of economic growth or an absence of serious industrial conflict – as
'models' to emulate and possibly adopt (see Chapter 10). Sometimes a case
will be made on the basis of what is known to happen abroad, for the
transfer or importation into a country of particular industrial relations
methods or techniques. In recent years, for instance, some commentators in
the UK have advocated a coordinated pay-bargaining system, on the lines
of those in Belgium and Germany. Also, in the early post-Second World
War period, efforts were made to export American-type trade unions and
collective bargaining arrangements to occupied countries such as Japan.
Yet a regression from those principles soon occurred, after it had become
apparent that the orderly industrial relations which were sought were not
being achieved (Levine 1958; Barkin 1980).

The hazardous nature of any such attempts at over-simplistic inter-
changeability, or piecemeal transplant, forms a recurrent theme in the
literature and has become something of a commonplace. Comparative
industrial relations is not an 'export-import exercise' (Schregle 1981),
since industrial relations phenomena reflect the characteristic features of
the society in which they operate. It follows that because a practice may
work well in one country there is no guarantee that it would continue to do
so should it be transferred elsewhere, especially if it conflicts with indigenous traditions and social values. More generally, it has been contended
that international comparisons can be a trap:

> 'Look how much better the Lilliputians do it', is a tempting cry, but the
> more one looks into it the more one finds that the Lilliputians aren't a

fair comparison with us: they haven't got our antiquated industries . . .
our legal system: and they are less than six inches tall.

(Kahn-Freund and Hepple 1972: 1)

There is therefore a need to proceed cautiously regarding the possibility of
making out-of-context transfers to different social and economic milieux. As
Kahn-Freund (1974) has shown, although transplantation of labour relations
rules relating to individual workers, such as legislative protection against
unfair dismissal, is relatively straightforward, this may not be the case with
provisions of a collective nature. Although it is true that collective bargaining
itself is able to allow for substantial inter-country variations and adapt to a
broad range of economic and political systems (Windmuller 1987), particular
institutions and rules cannot be expected to function adequately if they are
simply wrenched out of their original context and implanted elsewhere without
modification, since they are closely linked with the structure and organisation
of political and social power in their own environment or habitat, and may
reflect specific historical exigencies therein.

It is not necessary to adopt a 'systems' theory approach, interrelating the
background conditions within a social system, in order to recognise that
when some particular aspects of another country's industrial relations are
removed from their social, political and cultural surroundings they may
lose their validity and rationale. In the case of Britain for instance, Wedderburn (1974: 31) noted that the failure of the 1971 Industrial Relations Act,
many of whose legalistic provisions had American antecedents, 'might
serve as a warning against over-simple enthusiasm for the translation of
developments from other countries into the British framework'. With
regard to the codetermination system in Germany, in which a good deal of
interest has also been shown, it is quite possible that the institutional
arrangements which appertain under that system may be a model for other
countries. In Europe the EC has been strongly influenced by German, as
well as Dutch and French, experience in its attempts to devise a common
statute for employee participation within European companies. But it is
necessary to remember that more than institutional factors are involved,
since the German codetermination system is also 'an expression of specific
social and attitudinal characteristics which are not exportable' (Schregle
1978: 97). Thus, it has been claimed that the contribution of the German
system to the debate on workers' participation lies not in its trans-
plantability, but in the additional light it throws on the problems and
consequences of workers' involvement in enterprise decision-making
(Schregle 1987).

Again, in the case of many of the former British territories in Africa,
they had something of a common industrial relations heritage built around

an institutional framework in the British mould which was fostered by colonial administrations. Yet here, too, it was ultimately found to be totally inadequate for the needs of the countries concerned (Gladstone 1980; Kilby 1973). In Nigeria, for instance, the British model did not prove appropriate within a very different social, cultural and economic context, since in that country industrial relations have been strongly influenced by factors such as ethnicity and tribalism, which are very different from the ideologies of the trade union movements in Britain and in the USA (Fashoyin 1980).

These caveats concerning the extent to which industrial relations systems, or parts of them, are directly transposable are not intended, however, to deny the possible relevance of the results of comparative experience as an aid to practitioners and policy-makers, who may hope to utilise ideas, approaches or techniques adopted in other countries. International comparisons can lead us to enquire what each system might usefully learn from others, by way of adaptation and modification of existing systems for instance, so as to remedy weaknesses made visible by comparison. Such studies are frequently problem-oriented as, for example, a recent comparative survey of the problems and substantive policy implications appertaining to statutory union recognition provisions in Britain, the USA and Canada (Beaumont and Townley 1987). A practical and instrumental approach has also dominated the comparative study of Japanese industrial relations, especially in explaining labour's contribution to that country's economic success. In fact, in Britain the innovation of the single-union agreement owes its origin largely to the initiative of Japanese subsidiaries. However, in relation to other features of the Japanese system (see Chapter 4) Dore (1990) has recently concluded that it would be difficult, if not impossible, to have a high-seniority element in pay systems in a society in which every other firm is operating a rate-for-the-job wage system. Also, job security guarantees may not yield the employer payoffs in terms of long-term service and a secure return on training investments if employees have plenty of opportunities to move on to other firms.[5] In short, it may be contended that 'if borrowing becomes too piecemeal and occurs without recognition of the wider context from which elements have to be severed or in which they will have to be implanted, failure or a low rate of success becomes inevitable' (Lane 1989: 294).

THEORETICAL CONSIDERATIONS

Since comparison is one of the most important methods of enquiry within the social sciences[6] a further, and some would argue overriding, purpose of comparative studies is to help promote the development of industrial relations as an academic discipline, by exploring and analysing the determinants of similarities and differences found between national systems (Bean 1987). In this respect, comparisons are directed towards the possibility of making generalisations, about very diverse national situations and exploring the limits of those generalisations by specifying the circumstances under which any variations will occur. Investigation which is directed towards international comparisons should prove more illuminating as an aid to systematic explanation than confining observations to a single national system. Does a certain relationship retain its explanatory power for a number of countries rather than just for one – can it stand up to a comparative analysis? Findings which are replicated throughout a number of countries, or which can be shown to vary under specified conditions, become much more powerful – since 'an explanatory theory of industrial relations cannot be based upon the narrow range of industrial relations processes observable in one, or even a few, countries' (Walker 1967: 108). Findings based upon very limited evidence cannot be regarded as being firmly established and need to be verified by means of additional observations and cases.

By means of a comparative approach, as Galenson (1952: v) expresses it, 'hypotheses that grew out of peculiar conditions in one country can . . . be tested against other bodies of experience, and reconciliation sought in differences among the determining factors'. Thus the aim of comparative analysis is to promote wider understanding of, and foster new insights into, industrial relations either by showing what is unique about any one set of national arrangements or, equally well, reducing what might appear to be acutely specific and distinctive national characteristics by demonstrating their recurrence elsewhere (Rose 1983).

However, in order to make meaningful comparisons more is needed than merely comparative information, since within any field of study theory is necessary both to provide a framework for the systematic analysis and accumulation of the existing stock of knowledge, and to serve as a guide for the selection of research problems. Theoretical studies in this sense might adopt an approach which utilises the findings from a variety of national contexts in order to produce generalisations that attempt 'to distinguish the invariant from the variant, the stable and continuing from the fluctuating and transitory' (Schöllhammer 1973: 24). Alternatively, the studies could begin explicitly with *a priori* hypotheses about the relationship between environmental variables and industrial relations arrangements, and proceed to test their validity – corroborating, refining or rejecting them – via an examination of the experience of a number of different countries. With this latter approach there is a measure of agreement, however, that industrial relations theories themselves need to be built up from observed facts rather than from abstract speculation, and require to be tested and possibly modified in the light of new information. There is thus a reciprocal feedback relationship between theorising and observation (Hill and Thurley 1974; Bain and Clegg 1974).

Whatever the ultimate objectives, a good deal of the existing work within the comparative industrial relations field, although often rich and insightful, has not so far been explicitly theoretical in either its purpose or method (Shalev 1980a). Many studies present empirically derived information arising from cross-national investigations, often relating to institutions and practices, which is then analysed and interpreted with little direct orientation towards theoretical considerations. Yet, as we shall see, recent years have witnessed a remarkable upsurge in research in those areas where quantification is possible, such as strike activity and its determinants (see Chapter 6). In comparison with institutionally oriented studies, this kind of work is much more directed towards the specific testing of hypotheses via the use of multivariate statistical techniques, and it can utilise variables from a number of relevant disciplines. Although the approach raises its own problems of methodology and measurement in attempting to model complex behaviour, it can be useful in sharpening concepts, providing some common ground between different disciplines and isolating the effects of one particular variable while allowing for the influence of the others.

Another strategy which has been suggested is to attempt, at the outset, to ground comparative analysis firmly within the context of explicit and already well-formulated theoretical debate, such as 'convergence' theory (Shalev 1980a). This particular perspective is based on one of the most influential studies in the comparative labour field in the last three decades, Kerr *et al.*, *Industrialism and Industrial Man* (1962). In this book the integrating strand in the analysis of industrial relations within developed (and developing) countries is the universal drive towards industrialisation. The thesis maintains that as technology – seen as the driving force of change – and industrialisation become more uniformly applied, the countries involved will, over an extended period, tend to develop more similar and convergent industrial features, including their industrial relations arrangements, practices and 'web of rules'. Nevertheless, it is recognised that industrial relations will continue to reflect elements of diversity as well as uniformity. Significant national differences will reflect, for instance, the nature of the preindustrial economic and political order whose lingering effects will continue to influence the newly industrialised society, as well as the particular historical periods at which countries began to industrialise in relation to the extent of the role accorded to state regulation.

In a subsequent postscript (Kerr *et al.* 1971) the original convergence thesis itself has become somewhat modified, away from an emphasis on a trend towards uniformity. This restatement holds that no identical systems will emerge and that the convergence of industrial societies is towards a range of alternatives rather than to a particular point. It is now recognised that the industrialisation process is complex and that: 'there are several marked differences in the way that industrialisation has proceeded country-by-country; . . . there is no single logic of industrialisation, though there may only be a few paths' (Hill and Thurley 1974: 154).

Comparative studies by Sorge and Warner (1980) in Britain and West Germany also suggest that although factories in different countries may be very similar in terms of their size, technology and products they can, nevertheless, bring forth distinctly dissimilar forms of organisation and industrial relations. More recently, Goldthorpe (1984) and Streeck (1988) have argued that under the influence of economic pressures stemming from the oil crises and changing world distribution of industry, as well as accelerated technological innovation, *divergent* outcomes have charac-terised advanced capitalist societies themselves, such as a movement towards either a fundamentally contrasting corporatist or free-market model (see Chapter 5).

Yet notwithstanding these criticisms, the notion that one source of difference within cross-national industrial relations may reflect the different stage of development that a society has reached along some continuum – that the stage of industrialisation affects the character of industrial relations – this notion provides one possible (and enduring) focus for inter-country studies. It suggests ideas and implications which can be tested by further research. Dore (1990) used this framework in a comparison of the contrasting employment systems in British and Japanese industry. At the micro-level, a study of airline pilots in Australia, Japan and the USA, found that common technology in the industry had a very significant effect cross-nationally in producing similar institutional forms and union–management relations (Karsh *et al.* 1984). Kobrin (1976) empirically tested the convergence thesis itself using cross-national research for more than ninety countries and found some support for it. He was able to show a reduction in the variance of some selected indicators of convergence (as measured by the standard deviation) at higher levels of industrialisation.

HISTORICAL AND CULTURAL FACTORS

The exposition of the convergence thesis also points to the fact that countries which are alike in other respects would be expected to develop significant differences in their industrial relations if they had industrialised at different historical periods. In fact, it is clear that the main characteristics of national industrial relations, their dominant and distinctive features, seem to be estab-lished at a fairly early stage in the industrial development of a country.

Subsequently, in the absence of major dislocations such as wars or revolution, the provisions appear to show a good deal of tenacity, retaining many of their early characteristics and institutions despite subsequent evolution. Thus, the central and distinctive features of 'voluntarism' in Britain, arbitration courts in Australia and Denmark and the concept of 'exclusive' bargaining representation in the United States emerged early in the formation of those countries' industrial relations (Kerr *et al.* 1962). Britain, as the first industrialised nation, pioneered the development of many industrial relations institutions and arrangements. As a result, its contemporary industrial relations scene has been markedly conditioned by values, conventions and traditions that were established in the past. Hyman (1982b: 108) reiterates the general point that in industrial relations 'the present must be viewed as historically conditioned and historically contingent, and as incomprehensible except by means of historical understanding'.

The consequence of this for a study of comparative industrial relations is that international differences cannot be understood solely in terms of cross-sectional analysis at any one point in time. Instead, longitudinal studies incorporating a time dimension are also required for supplying historical perspective, together with a sharper appreciation of change through time and the conditions which generate it. Fulcher (1991) argues that an explanation of different actual outcomes must also account for those which, although they substantially existed in a society, did not become preponderant, that is the notion of historical 'suppressed alternatives'. An awareness of these may then draw out hidden similarities in apparently very different societies.

Employment relationships have been influenced, not only by the environmental or contextual variables already discussed, together with a country's history, but also in some societies by distinctive value systems and cultural features. An understanding of industrial relations in the Netherlands, for instance, requires an appreciation of the vertical segregation (or 'pillarised' structure) between religiously defined groupings and non-denominational organisations which for so long characterised Dutch society and affected not only unions but also employers. In that country for many years organisation at the social, cultural and political levels was founded upon a system of ideological blocs. Similar cross-cutting divisions of ideological interests are also found in Belgium and there is quasi-pillarisation in Italy (Ferner and Hyman 1992b). More generally, Blum (1981) concluded from an examination of twenty-seven countries that the form which industrial relations take in any one nation does markedly reflect the culture concerned. From a methodological standpoint, however, one problem is that without some analysis of the cultural determinants themselves and their influence on other variables this is something of a non-explanation.[7] 'Culture' can be defined in a myriad ways (Hofstede

1980) and often appears to be used not as an independent, or explanatory, variable but as a residual one representing a variety of unspecified influences.

Nevertheless, a study by Ahiauzu (1982) emphasises that culture[8] is an important environmental factor which cannot be ignored in cross-national studies of industrial relations. It views the connection between culture and job regulation as occurring through the shaping influence of culture upon the attitudinal characteristics of the actors and, therefore, on their behaviour. Thus in societies with different cultures, objective situations may be interpreted in markedly different ways. A further study of British and Norwegian workers and their unions on North Sea oil-rigs, with identical workplaces and technology (Andersen 1988), interprets variations in their institutional behaviour as reflecting the contrasting cultural traditions of the two countries themselves.

METHODOLOGY

In the light of the preceding discussion it is necessary to consider the methodology of comparative industrial relations more fully, since it is clear that to be of value the studies need to be appropriately designed and the cases to be compared require careful selection. In terms of the question of what might usefully be compared, typologies are very important in comparative analysis. They are a classificatory device in the form of a limited number of recognisable patterns into which industrial relations arrangements can be grouped according to their common elements. Since careful attention needs to be given to the economic, political and social setting when analysing industrial relations in various countries it is useful to compare countries with broadly similar characteristics in these respects. 'By looking at industrial relations problems within a given grouping one achieves an "automatic", major reduction in the number of background . . . variables' (Kassalow 1968: 103), since if two or more countries which are chosen for comparison differ in almost every respect, then the researcher has to consider all sources of difference as operative variables. But if the countries have some important conditions in common, these common elements can be treated as parameters and attention then focused on the operation of the other variables.

Broad groupings of this nature are typically based upon the extent of economic development attained and the nature of the political system, such as the distinction between developed market-industrialised societies and developing Third World countries. Other, global taxonomies of industrial relations systems can be constructed based upon institutional-pluralist concepts, or utilising a political economy framework which emphasises the concept of power in the employment relationship (Haworth 1991). We may then wish to compare the categories themselves in order to illuminate particular aspects of industrial relations. For other purposes narrower groupings within the categories may be more appropriate, such as by geographic location, or within the Third World between less developed countries (LDCs) and newly industrialising countries (NICs). Within western market-industrialised countries some years ago among writers in the United States an evolutionist theory of trade union development was popular. It was claimed that unions set out by being radical and militant in their outlook but then went through a 'maturation' process, ultimately becoming pragmatic and less militant. This type of generalisation, however, was based on the assumption that US union development was the norm, and only British, Swedish and German unions were actually included in the comparison. Other European countries, such as France and Italy, were excluded because no such uniform pattern could be found there (von Beyme 1980). Therefore, rather than attempting to generate theories which will hold good for all countries, generalisations may only be possible if 'types' or sub-models (Krislov 1987) can be established. Yet it remains true that unless the typologies are elaborated beyond a mere classificatory and descriptive labelling of different situations, in other words unless an attempt is made to specify the conditions under which each type develops and give them explanatory coherence, they remain at only a very preliminary stage of theorising.

Within any given grouping there is a further need to determine the number of countries to be investigated and also the 'level' at which the comparison should proceed. There are strong grounds for limiting the sample size of the investigation because it is not the number of countries *per se* which is usually important, but rather the range of variation which they provide (Walker 1967). Similarly, a very restricted comparison – perhaps of only two or three cases – permits a more intensive analysis than may be possible with multicountry studies and, if the cases are dealt with in a consistent and systematic way, minimises 'the danger of lapsing into either vacuous description or superficial comparison' (Shalev 1980a: 40). However, a possible limitation of this approach is that industrial relations variables are themselves frequently clustered into national contexts, so that the countries' characteristics are tied together rather than varying independently. Consequently, when the number of countries is small and each very similar, the clustering becomes particularly tight – thereby making it a matter of arbitrary choice to select any one variable for explanatory purposes. In such cases there may be a need to take account of a somewhat larger number of, markedly different, national contexts in order to make possible a more precise isolation of explanatory variables (Sorge 1976).

Once the countries to be compared have been selected, much of the analysis often focuses on the national level, in the form of comparative 'macro' studies, which are sometimes extended to include industry-level comparisons. In contrast, relatively few investigations centre upon the workplace – although there are notable exceptions such as Dore (1990), Gallie (1978), Marsh *et al.* (1981), Burawoy (1983) and Edwards (1986). Marsh's study of the engineering industry in Britain and Germany adopts the standpoint that, whatever the form which industrial relations takes, similar topics for regulation will appear, thus providing a basis for comparison. The structures and activities involved in regulating relations at workplace level, such as wage payment systems, employee hiring and work discipline, are then compared, subject by subject, for five engineering plants in each country.

It has long been recognised, however, that international comparisons of industrial relations which are confined to the national level may produce misleading results because of the possible dominance of one or more particular industries within a given country. Since there are substantial differences between industrial relations across industries, which may be unrelated to the national context in which they operate, what is really an 'industry' effect could be misinterpreted as being a 'national' effect in a comparative study which is confined solely to the national level.[9] To overcome this problem and allow for differences in the industry mix between different countries, industrial relations at industry level also need to be taken into account. That is to say, it is useful to examine the 'double' variation of both national and industry factors. By comparing similar industries across countries the more industry-specific forces of technical and market contexts are held fairly constant. It is then possible to test for any separate impact of environmental forces appertaining to the national level, in terms of broader social and political influences.

This approach was originally utilised by Dunlop (1958) in his examination of available evidence from the coal-mining and building industries across a number of countries. He showed the predominant influence in coal mining of the 'industry' factors of a common technology and similar market or budgetary constraints in shaping certain rules in that industry, including those concerned with safety, layoff procedures and wage structure. The building industry was also found to display common features in many countries. These included highly competitive product markets, with many small-sized enterprises, ease of entry and subcontracting, together with an unstructured labour market typified by short job duration at variable work sites as well as much self-employment. These special characteristics of the industry itself led to an emphasis on rules designed to regulate the forms of product and labour market competition. However, in both industries other rules – relating to the status of the actors and their organisations, bargaining representation and union security (closed shop) arrangements – were largely influenced by features of the national industrial relations environment within each country.

A similar approach integrating the national and industry levels has also been adopted by the Geneva-based International Institute for Labour Studies. Its comparative research programme was designed so that: 'variations between industries in the crucial determinants of industrial relations, and in the relative strength of such determining factors, can be studied against the range of variation provided by international differences' (IILS 1969). The differential impact of national and industry environmental forces upon the structure, processes and outcome of industrial relations have been examined empirically for the important metal-working industry across five countries. The findings suggest that, although there is an interacting effect between the two, many of the fundamental characteristics which are shared by all the cross-national systems investigated for that industry are the result of a common response to modern technological development and mechanised factory production. In contrast, it appears that most of the distinguishing features – especially in the distribution of power – are the result of differences in the national, rather than in the industry, environments (Derber 1976).

More recently, however, Locke (1992) has questioned the whole rationale for treating national systems as the basic unit of analysis and searching for macro-institutional features as the key dimension in constructing comparative typologies of industrial relations systems. He argues that at a time of increasing market fragmentation, together with the opportunity provided by new technologies for firms to develop alternative business strategies, there has resulted a proliferation of diverse industrial relations patterns not simply across nations but within them – and even within the same industries. 'Some of these subnational labour–management arrangements appear to have more in common with their equivalents in other countries than with other industrial relations patterns co-existing within the same national border' (Locke 1992: 230). His suggested approach is, therefore, to focus on micro-level developments, particularly local socio-economic conditions that shape the strategies of unions and management in firms undergoing adjustment, in order to explain the resultant variations within nations.

PROBLEMS IN COMPARATIVE STUDIES

It is apparent from the foregoing discussion that comparative industrial relations is by no means an easy field of study and has considerable inherent problems. It is not only that, as with industrial relations generally, it is multidisciplinary in its dimensions but it also reaches across cultures, thereby exacerbating the difficulties of finding appropriate bases for making inter-country comparisons. There can also be problems in ensuring a measure of concept equivalence across societies, since what are nominally identical practices or institutions may perform varying functions, or have a very different significance. The French use 'participation', for instance, in one sense to mean 'profit sharing', whereas the term is more usually understood in the sense of participation by workers in the management of enterprises (Blanpain 1974). We also know that in a number of countries labour disputes are brought before so-called labour courts for resolution. But in any attempt to compare these institutions on an international basis there are immediate difficulties of terminology, in that bodies with the same name may perform different functions. The German Labour Court, for instance, is empowered to settle labour disputes by means of statutory binding decisions whereas the Irish Labour Court acts only as a conciliation body. In some other countries labour court functions are performed by bodies with different names, such as labour, or industrial, tribunals. Schregle's (1981) approach to this basic problem of what is comparable in cross-national studies is to compare the methods and ways in which particular industrial relations *functions* are carried out in various countries, rather than simply comparing institutions and procedures carrying the same designation. Consequently, a comparative study of the settlement of labour disputes through statutory binding decisions would have to omit the Irish Labour Court (despite its name), but include other bodies such as industrial tribunals in Britain, conciliation and arbitration boards in Mexico and labour tribunals in India.[10]

As well as difficulties arising from terminological variations, Henley (1978) also points to other fundamental issues in this respect. He notes the erroneous conclusions which have been drawn from comparing the functioning of the Kenyan Industrial Court with apparently functionally similar wage-regulating institutions in New Zealand and Australia, in the absence of any consideration of the vast differences in the nature and basis of trade union power as between African countries and industrialised economies. More generally, it is also important to try to avoid the tunnel vision whereby industrial relations arrangements elsewhere are viewed from the particular perspectives and orientations of, say, Anglo-Saxon countries.

Despite the inherent difficulties in comparative work, it has been argued that an international perspective has always been implicit to some extent in the study of industrial relations. For many years this was confined to comparative considerations embracing strong ideological overtones, such as factors which have engendered 'the labour problem' (Weber 1974). Yet, as we have noted, more recent work has adopted a wider focus and a more analytical approach to the subject. The method of enquiry employed in much of the work within the comparative field proceeds at the empirical level[11] and arrives at more general conclusions through a process of inductive reasoning, or more *ad hoc* interpretative insights. Relatively few studies begin with an explicit theory which is then rigorously tested against the data. In large part, this is a reflection of the underdeveloped state of industrial relations theory itself to whose improvement, by way of helping more general theory construction, well-designed comparative studies may be expected to contribute. It is thus a field of considerable potential. As Shalev (1981) points out, comparative analysis not only raises substantively interesting and important questions but also offers a natural and fruitful avenue for the advance of the discipline as a whole. According to Peterson (1986), however, what is particularly required for progress in this field is the development of testable models incorporating key variables and the articulation of hypotheses that allow us to predict future outcomes, rather than relying on after-the-fact explanations for what took place in a given, national industrial relations system.

PLAN OF THE BOOK

In the remainder of the book we survey and discuss the findings of the literature relating to the comparison of national industrial relations systems and particular aspects thereof, in terms of an analysis of the major actors and their organisations together with their activities and interactions. Chapters 2–4 concern workers' trade unions, employers and managements together with collective bargaining – in most western countries still the most important mechanism for determining wages and employment conditions. There follows in Chapter 5 an examination of the role of the state and its agencies as a regulator within the industrial relations field. Chapter 6 deals with strikes and industrial conflict, which is an area where more specific hypothesis testing via quantitative methods is possible. As a result, there has been a recent proliferation of studies seeking to explain international differences in strike activity. Similarly, a good deal of attention has been directed to the important and topical issues of workers' participation in enterprise decision-making, as well as 'international' studies concerned with the operation and labour relations implications of multinational corporations. These matters are discussed in the Chapters 7 and 8.

The first eight chapters concern mainly comparative aspects of industrial relations in advanced, market-type economies in Western Europe, North America, Japan and Australia, although there is also some discussion of the recent changes taking place in the Eastern European (ex-communist) countries towards market-driven systems; it could be argued that these changes appear to reinforce the convergence model. Industrialised countries with a market economy possess at least some basic similarities and common elements of importance so as to permit comparative examination. Chapter 9, however, relates to the special features within a markedly different environment of industrial relations in Third World countries, for whose economies investment by multinational enterprises often plays a decisive role. In these countries not only is the state the largest single employer and the number of wage earners a small part of the economically active population, but in addition the trade unions perform a 'dual' role. As well as the traditional function of protecting and furthering their members' interests, they are also expected to play their part in the country's development effort towards economic growth. This duality presents certain inconsistencies which, as we will show, are not easily reconcilable. Furthermore, much of the available research on developing countries focuses on the wider economic and social context of industrial relations, rather than more exclusively upon the narrower plane of union–management relations (Fashoyin 1991).

Finally, to round off the book, in Chapter 10 we look at the substantive consequences and dependent outcomes of different industrial relations systems in advanced market economies – particularly those which have been regarded as 'models' for others to emulate – in terms of their economic performance, which in recent years has become a topic of increasing interest for comparative consideration.

FURTHER READING

Bamber and Lansbury (1993) have a useful introductory chapter on studying international and comparative industrial relations, although the earlier pieces by Shalev (1980a) and Schregle (1981) are also well worth reading. A major attempt to construct a largely macro-level conceptual model for comparative industrial relations relating the outcomes to environmental conditions, intervening variables and, especially, the strategic choices of the actors, is the book by Poole (1986a).

2 Trade unions

Trade unions are institutional representatives of worker interests both within the labour market and in the wider society, and they accentuate the collective rather than the individual power resources of employees since 'concerted behaviour is the essence of modern trade unionism' (Ulman 1990: 281). However, as well as basic similarities there are also major differences as between trade union movements in advanced industrialised countries, not only in the extent of their membership but also in their role and objectives and the structural divisions that characterise them, which require investigation. In some unions the emphasis is more upon representing the aspirations of the working class as a whole rather than functioning as collective bargaining agencies merely for their own members. In the case of France, it has been said (Kendall 1975) that the workers' decision to join a union represented as much a reflex of class consciousness as any intention to organise practically on their own behalf for enhanced conditions and improved job control, since the traditional bent of French unionism was radical and ideological (Sellier and Silvestre 1986). In contrast, cross-sectional studies in both the UK and the USA have tended to show that, in general, individuals join unions because of instrumental rather than ideological considerations, whereas in Australia individuals who hold a reformist ideology and support socialist, or social democratic, political parties will be more likely to join unions (Deery and De Cieri 1991).

In much of Western Europe a predominant characteristic has been trade union pluralism (and sometimes reluctance to engage in continuous relationships with employers) promoted by ideological, philosophical and religious differences, although in recent years there has been rather less emphasis upon the importance of religious affinity. As a result, the major dividing lines have been less between the craft and industrial unionism dimension than between, on the one hand, secular and confessional (generally Catholic) unionism, and reform-oriented (mainly socialist) or revolutionary (communist or syndicalist) unionism on the other

(Windmuller 1974). Dutch trade unions, for instance, were created by socialist organisers, Catholic priests and Protestant ministers, not by craftsmen or factory workers – which helps to explain the preference for political action (Visser 1992a).

A distinction has been made by Edwards *et al.* (1986) between three types of western-style unionism: (1) unions which act primarily as collective bargaining agents for particular groups of workers (such as those in the United States and the United Kingdom), (2) unions which serve as constituent elements in systems of 'political unionism' (as in France and Italy, together with Spain where union organisation is closely linked to political parties), and (3) unions which operate as partners, even if junior ones, within social-democratic governing arrangements (such as the case of Austria and, for a long period, Sweden). For Poole (1986a), the essential distinction is between union strategies focused by what he terms 'instrumental-rational' concerns (which produce commitments to 'economism', 'pure and simple unionism' and trade unionism under collective bargaining – since they refer to the means to utilitarian ends in the form of material benefits), and those which are dominated by 'value- rational' motives (whereby political, religious or nationalist objectives predominate, involving identification and commitment).

Thus trade unions may seek to achieve their objectives not only by collective bargaining but also by lobbying the legislature, or by a more fundamental form of political action aimed at transforming the employment relationship and society. Moreover, union objectives and orientations are themselves of an extremely diverse nature as between particular countries and require further elucidation.

TRADE UNION OBJECTIVES AND METHODS

In his comparative examination of industrial relations in French and British oil refineries, Gallie (1978: 313) noted the strikingly dissimilar conceptions of the role of unionism and its typical mode of action at the plant level. Broadly, the French unions, as class-oriented organisations viewing contemporary western society in predominantly Marxist terms (particularly the CGT), aspired to promote overall, long-term worker interests rather than to defend particular and narrow craft or job interests.[1] They interpreted their role as being one of heightening the consciousness and awareness of the workforce, seeking to mould perceptions and mobilise workers ideologically towards a far-reaching structural transformation of what was seen as an exploitative and alienating society. Their strategy for the achievement of this objective 'was essentially one of sustained ideological warfare in the context of steadily escalating action over concrete disputes with management'. Conversely, the British unions conceived their role within the factory as being basically one of continuing representation of workforce interests on narrow bargaining issues, that is pressing for objectives which were consciously and explicitly desired by the workers themselves. These aims were to be accomplished by means of negotiation backed up by 'a powerful, well-disciplined and cohesive organisation that would represent such a potential threat in the event of conflict that management was unlikely to risk being unduly unreasonable in negotiation'.

In North America, the particularly distinctive features of unionism which have distinguished it from that found in most continental European countries include 'job consciousness and job control,[2] business unionism, an overwhelming emphasis upon economic struggle and collective bargaining, as opposed to broad political reform of the society and the economy' (Kassalow 1969: 6). The important concept of 'business unionism' relates to the securing of pragmatic, job-related goals in the form of improvements in the economic and social conditions of members, rather than concern with social reorganisation. Unlike most European countries, where a close association between unions and political parties has been a long-standing phenomenon, US unions have had little close or direct connection with political parties and have relied very heavily upon collective bargaining rather than upon political activity as a means of achieving their ends. (The position in Canada, however, is somewhat different since the union movement there – probably because of the different system of government – has developed a broader view of political ideology and has close ties with the New Democratic Party.)

In Germany, on the other hand, there has been greater emphasis by unions upon legislative enactment to further their general objectives since, historically, the unions accepted the republic created after the First World War as being 'their' state and acquired the habit of pressing for government legislation in the social and labour field (Günter and Leminsky 1978). Austrian unions have adopted a distinctive policy based upon long-term cooperation with capital, in order to preserve employment by promoting economic growth – a commitment which was shared by the Social Democratic governments (Traxler 1992). Also in Sweden, from the 1930s to the 1970s unions and managements found common ground in their efforts to increase efficiency under capitalism via self-regulation and, thereby, avoid state intervention in their relationship. In particular, the close links between the Social Democratic party and the union movement provided a two-way channel of discussion and influence between government and the main union confederation, the LO (Kjellberg 1992). By contrast, in Portuguese trade unionism, the predominance of political action has resulted from a number of structural features. These include the historically minor role of societal self-regulation compared to statutory regulation, partisan control of the unions coupled with their prevailing weakness and a chronic bias of employers' associations towards lobbying and reliance upon government (Barreto 1992).

It can be argued, however, that the dichotomy often noted between the more restrictive business union orientation in the United States and European 'welfare' unionism, concerned with wider social objectives as well as the terms and conditions of employment of union members, is somewhat overdrawn. In more recent years US unions have not been inactive in the political sphere and have actually had a large degree of impact on influencing legislation concerned with broader social and economic issues (Lewin 1978). Troy (1986) contends that because of declining membership and smaller gains at the bargaining table, US unions are compensating by markedly increasing their political activity and pressing for greater government intervention in the economy and society. Furthermore, although in European countries some union leaders have undoubtedly regarded trade unions as having a mainly political role, to help change the social and economic order, many rank-and-file members appear to view unions differently – as instrumental agencies concerned with matters arising in the employment relationship. Van de Vall (1970) showed that among Dutch (and German) unionists the most prevalent motive for taking up membership was to secure individual 'conflict insurance', i.e. the provision of legal and material assistance in possible disputes with the employer and protection against arbitrary management decisions. Form's (1973) study of car workers at various skill levels across four countries (USA, Italy, Argentina and India) also showed that they all rejected political unionism in favour of job-related unionism concerned with raising wages and improving working conditions. Similarly, despite the incessant advocacy of the abolition of the private enterprise system by two of the major French unions, a majority of French workers seemed unconvinced and rejected the legitimacy of the unions' attempt to relate 'industrial' and 'political' issues in shopfloor agitation (Gallie 1978). (According to Segrestin (1991), even the leaders of French trade unions have now become politically disillusioned and no longer regard organised labour as a powerful force for social change. Similarly, the former communist-controlled CGIL in Italy effectively abandoned the traditional principle of class struggle at its 1991 congress (Ferner and Hyman 1992b).)

Eastern Europe

Unlike their more autonomous western counterparts, trade unions in Eastern European countries under the Soviet-type communist system until the end of the 1980s were markedly different organisations. Within the context of an ascendant (one-party) state, official ideology proclaimed the unity of individual, group and societal interests, with trade union subordination to the Communist party (and the state) together with integrative union functions which excluded the use of adversarial means (Littler and Palmer 1986).[3] Although unions signed 'collective agreements' at factory, or establishment, level their content was very different from those in western countries – embracing matters such as the fulfilment of state economic plans, the growth of labour productivity, work organisation and administration of state social insurance and pensions. Trade unions did not effectively have the right to strike or negotiate wage levels, which were determined by the administrative centre. But they were required to defend their members from management abuses and bureaucratic excess, including dismissal, as well as from infringements of labour laws. At the same time, unions undertook responsibility for labour discipline, particularly in preventing labour turnover and encouraging the attainment of production targets and work norms. In short, they had a 'dual' role to perform (Ruble 1979), primarily in mobilising workers behind production goals while defending those same workers in job-related grievances against unscrupulous administrators and illegitimate managerial practices. Nevertheless, their interest articulation role was very much qualified in practice in the sense that 'unions [were] asked to act as filters rather than as mouthpieces' (Pravda 1983), passing on shopfloor grievances to management or higher union bodies.

This model of official trade unionism under communism partly explains why, in a country like Poland, worker protest for so long by-passed the trade unions:

> Economic grievances were significant, but the unions served to articulate only minor issues, and spontaneous protest actions took the place of regularised institutional channels of interest articulation. This in turn meant that working class protest in Poland, while emphasising immediate economic demands, had gone beyond the economic sphere to make political claims for new institutions to represent working class interests.
>
> (Millard 1987)

By 1980, at a time of the most severe economic crisis of the postwar period to date, the political expression of workers' interests was through Solidarity and included, *inter alia*, a demand for independent trade unionism.

Subsequent to the collapse of communism in Eastern Europe after 1989, important changes have been taking place in the role of unions, within the context of a greater emphasis on market and political pluralism, away from the former 'transmission belt' model (state-dominated and production-oriented) which prevailed when the Communist party enjoyed a monopoly of power. The former unions were 'organisations with quasi-compulsory membership, often led by geriatric *apparatchiks*, acting both as agents of labour discipline and as channels for allocating social welfare provisions' (Hyman 1991: 633). In Bulgaria, for instance, the former very large unions, structured mainly on industry lines, were disbanded and new ones established. Here plural unionism has emerged in place of the old, highly politicised monistic system, with a growth both in the number of unions and diversity of union types as well as non-compulsory union membership. There was also a proliferation in the number of strikes, arbitration procedures have been established and the first set of enterprise wage bargains was concluded in 1991 (Jones 1992). However, because of the continued predominance of state-owned enterprises (with no real employers' autonomy since the employer function was ill-defined because privatisation had not then proceeded far), there was a lack of employers' organisations which could act as the partners of trade unions in collective bargaining. This also happened in Poland.

Similarly, in Hungary from 1988 to 1990 the traditional trade unions redefined their role, declaring the representation of workers' interests to be their exclusive function, renouncing that of a 'transmission belt'. At the same time, independent trade unions appeared and collective labour disputes (of rights and interests) were legalised (Héthy 1992). The former official trade union movement also continued to be dominant, dwarfing the independents both numerically and financially (Hughes 1992).

The extent of diversity, however, in trade union structure and development since 1989 in these countries is shown by the case of Czechoslovakia. There, although major changes in union outlook and function have occurred, changes to union structure have been surprisingly few. The scope of trade union interests has been narrowed (from incorporating many welfare elements) to a more explicit focus on pay and conditions. But there has been no splitting or disintegration of the national confederation as sometimes occurred elsewhere, no development of 'Solidarity-style' independent unions, and little in the way of competing unions within the enterprises (Brewster 1992). Also, more generally in Eastern Europe, union density remains high despite the breakup of the previous quasi-automatic union membership (OECD 1993). Poland, Hungary and the Czech and Slovak Federal Republics have determined that collective bargaining will be the main method used to establish the terms and conditions of employment; this involves a progressive reduction in the domain of the statutory Labour Code through which the terms were previously determined. In the former East Germany, industrial relations are in the process of being transformed as a result of the adoption of West German laws and institutions across the reunified country (Jürgens *et al.* 1993).

In China by contrast, trade unions, which represent some 90 per cent of workers and employees, still act as 'transmission belts' to put the party's view to workers, they encourage production and engage in political and ideological education. Additionally, they participate in the allocation of the company's profits to be retained for its own disposal, take part in grievance handling and execute numerous welfare and cultural responsibilities (Hoffman 1981; Littler and Lockett 1983; Warner 1991). The trade union is also expected to cooperate with management. Since trade unions reflect features of the society in which they have developed and its political system, it is scarcely surprising to find sharp contrasts between their role and orientation within the communist system, as against those in western countries.

More searching explanation, however, is required for the marked variations in union role and purpose (despite common impulses towards unionism) also found between trade unions in some western, capitalist countries. Although all modern workers' movements have developed strategies comprising both labour market and political components, how can we explain within the European context the greater emphasis upon the achievement of radical change in the structure of society by French and Italian unions – whose thrust (certainly up to the late 1960s) was at least as much ideological and political as industrial – in comparison with German or British unions? Also, at the other end of the scale, why has US unionism traditionally shown a more restricted interest in the political sphere, regarding collective bargaining as being overwhelmingly its major business?

EXPLAINING CROSS-NATIONAL DIFFERENCES IN UNION CHARACTER

Poole (1986a) has observed that, in the genesis of labour strategies, the role of employers, management and the state has been decisive. Militant employer strategies which preclude trade union recognition often promote labour radicalism (see Chapter 3), and a powerful role for the state in the industrial relations system almost invariably promotes politically conscious labour movements. Kendall (1975) draws a contrast between continental European unions and those not only in the United States but also in Britain. He sees Anglo-American unions as being set apart by an emphasis on wage bargaining, together with their greater organisational unity[4] and financial resources. These differences are in turn related to variations in economic and socio-political conditions appertaining during the unions' formative period and in their subsequent historical development. Kendall's explanation concerns the earlier and more vigorous industrialisation process which occurred in Britain and the USA, in comparison with continental Europe, favouring greater popular support for the *laissez-faire* economy and the values which supported it, with a correspondingly reduced role for the state and politics. Equally important, he notes that within these two countries industrialisation proceeded within a context relatively free from the 'trammels of a pre-capitalist past'.

In this latter respect, other authors (Bok and Dunlop 1970) have pointed out that labour movements in continental Europe developed against the backdrop and carry-over of a feudalistic tradition of an earlier age that denied workers access to economic opportunity or political power and which engendered a feeling of isolation and oppression. Throughout the nineteenth century Europe remained predominantly a rural society, particularly in the southern and central parts of the continent (including France, Italy, Spain, Belgium and Austria) where great importance attached to the Catholic church. In feudalistic conditions, where workers lack citizenship rights and where class privileges and distinctions are deeply entrenched, labour movements tend to be highly politicised in order to help effect a radical change in the social order (Kassalow 1969; Shalev and Korpi 1980). In Britain (and also in Sweden), on the other hand, the state controlled the church, feudalism had ended well before it generally disappeared elsewhere in Europe and manhood suffrage had been extended to large sections of the population – unlike most continental countries where it was attained only at a later date, sometimes not until the early part of the present century. (The demand for universal male suffrage had always been high on the agenda of all the continental labour movements.) In the second half of the nineteenth century the British labour movement, in contrast to its continental counterparts, was an industrial movement without at that time the establishment of a political wing. Conversely, 'the simultaneous and combined economic and political struggle of European workers . . . helps account for the more articulated class character of [their] labour movements' (Kassalow 1982: 210), directed against a very visible and expanding bourgeoisie and, in part, a response to a more repressive state apparatus (Geary 1981). Particularly within Italian labour, for instance, the strength of the revolutionary and socialist tradition is partly explained by the late capitalist development of the country, along with a weak democratic tradition whereby universal voting rights for males over 30 were given only in 1912 (Pellegrini 1987).

As for the United States, there was an absence of a feudal past (except in the south) as well as an early attainment of the franchise for white males prior to the rise of the modern labour movement, together with free public education. This absence of a feudalistic social and political structure prior to the onset of industrialisation has been held to help account for American 'exceptionalism', in the form of a weakened socialist consciousness and the lack of strong political party–union ties, although there are undoubtedly other important factors as well. These include the scarcity of manpower and ample employment opportunities for skilled workers, which militated against challenge along political and ideological lines, a complex ethnic (immigrant) labour force composition and radical cleavage which impeded collective action on a class basis, and a political and constitutional structure that discouraged the setting up of third parties (Lipset 1977).

Although one limitation of Kendall's explanation of European and Anglo-American distinctions is that it takes no account of the substantial differences which exist within his two comparison groups (especially those between Britain and the USA), nevertheless it is, as Shalev (1980a) has shown, a useful approach. It links contextual structure to behaviour as a means of explaining the broad contrasts between the greater economism and internal unity of British and US unionism as compared with the politicisation and (outside Britain and Scandinavia) religious/ideological divisions in Western Europe.

The political character of much of the union movement on the European continent also provoked a counter-response by the non-socialist forces in society, particularly the Catholic church, which proceeded to establish rival workers' organisations. In a religiously divided country such as Holland, trade unions had been formed in a period of strong Protestant and Catholic religious revival, when a socialist trade union movement was regarded as implying a secular view of society. Therefore, new Protestant and Catholic trade unions were organised which rejected both the class war concepts and the optimistic socialist utopianism of the secular unions, with the result that three rival trade union centres were created (Albeda 1977). In Germany, a division into socialist, liberal and Christian unions remained until the end of the Weimar Republic in 1993. Even outside Europe, in Canada for instance, Catholic unions were also set up at the beginning of the present century in order to 'protect' French Canadian workers from the more suspect ideological influences of US 'international' (actually binational) unions which were organising there.

In addition to the broad European–American comparisons which have been considered, it is also necessary to explain some of the major variations and country-by-country differences in the characteristics of unionism which exist within the European context itself. In particular, the French union movement differs in a number of important respects from its counterparts in Western Europe. In France membership is very low, unionism has been characterised by weakness and instability and has failed to achieve a mass base comparable to the union movements in Germany, Britain,

Belgium and Scandinavia. Also, it has had somewhat different political perspectives, in terms of a 'persistent leftism' (Adams 1983) rather than pragmatic reformism, and has been more committed to direct political action than elsewhere. This may be attributable, in part, to employer attitudes – in the form of an extreme hostility to trade unionism (Clegg 1976). However, an important structural factor by way of explanation again relates to the nature and pace of industrial development. The slow rate of industrial growth in France and relative lag within an industrialising Europe at the formative period of trade unions meant that they consisted of relatively skilled workers employed in comparatively small-scale enterprises. (As late as 1906 a majority of the industrial workforce were in establishments of less than a hundred employees.) This helped give French unionism an élitist philosophy and strategy, organising a minority of politically conscious and literate workers – in contrast with the more solid and comprehensively organised, dues-paying membership of the British model (Kendall 1975). As Michel (1990: 313) has expressed it, 'French trade unionism embraced only a minority of workers. It was unstable, deeply divided and only asked for low subscriptions because it did not provide any services. . . . In any case, membership was less important than the audience.'

Maurice and Sellier (1979) draw comparisons between what they term the 'charismatic' character of French unionism, appealing to elements of 'emotional commonality' with the accent on class struggle, and the more functional (bureaucratic and professionalised) nature of unions in Germany. They ascribe the difference to factors such as a more socially homogeneous working class in Germany with less diversification in attitudes, in comparison with France. Also, they note the more marked occupational stability of manual workers in Germany as a result of the greater prestige of industrial employment,[5] in contrast to France where the employee's aim upon achieving promotion or becoming successful is typically to leave the ranks of the working class and become an office worker or independent craftsman. These factors help to explain the emergence in Germany of a more unified and organisationally disciplined trade union movement which, unlike French unionism, accepts severe restrictions on the use of militancy within the enterprise (under the co-determination system). In fact, in contrast to those countries in which trade unions form virtually a single channel of representation for workers (as in Britain), in Germany a dual system exists. The enterprise is the domain of the works councils (Jacobs *et al.* 1978) which provide an enterprise-based negotiating partner for management and are restricted by a 'peace obligation', whereas trade unions operate in principle largely outside the workplace (see Chapter 4). We may also note that with the reconstruction of the

German trade unions after the Second World War, following their demise under Hitler, the DGB (central federation) was founded as a unitary organisation to include members of all occupations and political persuasions. This contributed to a formal union neutrality and 'depoliticisation', although in practice there are strong links with the Social Democrats (Günter and Leminsky 1978).

As well as the existence of ideological cleavages between unions on political and religious grounds together with differences of function – as organisations for representation and bargaining, or as a vehicle for mobilising the power resources of the working class – unions also differ as between countries on a structural basis, relating to industry or occupational boundaries. These structural differences will now be examined more closely.

TRADE UNION STRUCTURE

Unions may organise according to 'exclusive' principles, dependent upon their market capacities and resultant ability to erect boundaries, or they may recruit upon an 'inclusive' basis. Thus craft unions in pure form are confined to apprentice-served, skilled workers and are intended to protect and promote a marketable skill. (Sometimes occupational unions, which are not confined to apprentice-served workers, are seen as a form of craft union.) By contrast, industrial unions cover all workers within a particular industry and general unions are completely inclusive in terms of their recruitment, representing a large number of different industries and occupations. Technology is a major explanation for the establishment of these various types of union. The early experience of industrialisation (prior to mechanisation) in both Britain and the USA, and the emergence of skill patterns associated with it, saw the rise and consolidation of craft unions. Because of the early onset of modern economic development in these two countries, workers' experience with industrial capitalism was slower and the transition period longer than was the case in most of northern and central Europe (Kassalow 1982). As a consequence, forms of craft unions with an attendant focus upon occupational solidarity and ideas of job consciousness became well-entrenched over many decades. Complications were, however, introduced into the overall structural pattern with the later growth of unions of other types, such as big competing general unions and white-collar organisations in Britain, along with industrial unions in the USA.

In other countries such as Germany and in Scandinavia, although craft unions were also foremost in the early stages of union development their predominance was more short-lived, with the notable exception of Denmark (Gill 1984). As far as Germany is concerned, the post-1945 reorganisation of the union movement into just sixteen industrial unions made trade union structure in that country the least complex in Europe. In countries where the onset of industrialisation came later (as in Sweden), increasing mechanisation and mass-production techniques, with easily learned and repetitive tasks, did not provide particular occupations with resources to construct powerful unions. Instead, semi-skilled mass-production workers looked to industrial and sometimes general union structures (Clegg 1976). In Sweden, there was an early transition to an industrial union structure via a distinctive ('work material') type of union which organised all workers, skilled and unskilled, who worked with a given material – such as the metalworkers' and woodworkers' unions. This prevented both the craft fragmentation of engineering unionism and the organisation of unskilled metalworkers into a general union, which would have obstructed the development of industrial unionism (Fulcher 1991). In the case of France, Sellier (1973) has suggested that the tendency towards workers' organisations formed on the basis of craft unionism was hampered by the lack of a manpower surplus as a result of an early decline in birth rates. His argument is that the motivation to form strong craft organisations to control entry to the trades will be greater in conditions of labour surplus, which endanger the market position of skilled workers.

Other factors would also appear to be important in explaining the tendency towards organisations along industrial lines. Political influences seem to have been especially important, by way of a facilitating role of socialist ideology, in broadening the structural form of unions away from concern with narrow and particularistic, special interests. A contrast may be drawn in this respect between the highly fragmented union movements in Anglo-Saxon countries, where the historical and ideological connection between socialism and trade unionism was much weaker, and the formation of broad, comprehensive interest organisations on the part of the working class by way of the existence of large industrial unions that were the most conducive to worker unity in those European countries such as Sweden, Austria and Germany with a strong socialist tradition (Streeck 1981; Slomp 1990). As von Beyme (1980: 32–3) has explained:

> The industry principle was realised best in countries where there was a close co-operation between a big Social Democrat Party and a relatively central-
> ised union movement. Whether there was a direct organisation link between the Party and the unions (Denmark, Norway and Sweden) or only an informal relation (Germany and Austria) was only of secondary importance.

In France, unions have long been organised predominantly along industrial lines. National unions exist in each industry for each of several main confederations (national groupings of trade unions), they recruit across all trades and across all categories of employees and thereby compete with each other. These sorts of divisions create a markedly different system, however, from the 'multi-unionism' which exists in Britain. Within any given plant French workers have a choice as between several unions differentiated on political and ideological grounds, rather than by means of any structural principles of organisation. Similarly, Italian unions have never been organised on a craft or occupational basis, apart from a few exceptional cases. They are, nevertheless, complex organisations comprising national vertical unions which organise all workers of the same branch of the economy (with provincial, regional and local sections), together with horizontal structures aggregating all workers and/or vertical structures within each geographic area. Horizontal linkages have been particularly important in Italy, probably more than in any other European country, as a result of a number of factors. These include:

> the late development of Italian industry and the fragmented character of the labour market, the traditionally high level of unemployment, the very political orientation of the Italian labour movement, particularly of CGIL [the major federation], giving great importance to the unity of the working class. . . . and to the pursuit of general goals by the unions.
>
> (Treu 1981: 114)

The prevalent structural form of a country's trade union movement also has a number of important consequences. A predominance of occupational unions leads to highly fragmented unionism, and ideological and religious divisions also make for duplication of union organisation, thereby weakening bargaining potential and often making for difficulties in promoting effective representation of workers in individual establishments. By contrast, the presence of a relatively small number of unions – even if not entirely structured according to the principle of one per industry, at least covering large sections of industry – appears to be associated with markedly fewer inter-union jurisdictional disputes. This may be illustrated by the contrast between Britain and the United States, *vis-à-vis* Sweden and Germany (Windmuller 1981). A further comparison between railway workers' unions in Britain and Germany (Seglow *et al.* 1982) showed that the cleavages between the three railway unions in Britain, arising because of the occupational exclusiveness of the drivers and the separate footplatemen's 'line of promotion' (unlike Germany[6]), has been a notable restraining influence upon the attainment of an integrated approach to pay bargaining to promote the interests of railway workers.

Outside Europe and the United States, however, the structural features (and consequences) of trade unions in Japan and Australia are of particular interest and will now be considered more fully.

As compared with other advanced economies, a notable feature of the structure of labour organisation in Japan is the prevalence of comprehensive unions at the level of the individual enterprise. Enterprise unions generally group all regular workers, including white-collar staff, who are employed in an undertaking operated by a single management, but they are not 'company' unions and are basically independent of management. In 1985 there were more than 34,000 unions of this kind, some 80–90 per cent of the total, covering more than twelve million members. Because of the lack of a pervasive craft history, since Japan incorporated advanced mechanisation and new technologies at a comparatively early stage in its development, the unions which were formed were unable to make a sharp separation among job groups a basis for organisation. Indeed, because job distinctions and jurisdictions within largely self-contained, internal labour markets are very weak, and in the absence of an (external) market-based wage system, it was probably inevitable that unions would be established on an enterprise basis. Within any given industry:

> Wages and conditions of work varied from firm to firm. The employer sought to establish a paternalistic relationship with his workers and would not tolerate attempts by outsiders (e.g. trade union officials) to participate in negotiations. The workers, for their part, were not conscious of sharing a common interest with the body of employees in the whole industry, and their conditions of employment were hostile to the appearance of any such consciousness. Such attitudes were conducive to the development of enterprise unions rather than occupational or industrial unions.
>
> (Allen 1981: 84)

This particular form of unionism does not create distinct organisations of craft and professional employees and is therefore associated with an absence of demarcation problems. A single enterprise-based union structure also reduces the transaction costs of negotiations within an undertaking and, by tying the workers' and union leaders' interests to those of the firm, the enterprise union has been a strong force in ensuing labour–management harmony (Sakoh 1990). A further consequence of enterprise-based unions, however, is that although they permit a high degree of rank-and-file participation in decision-making, they nevertheless fail to organise large proportions of workers in smaller firms where unionism is discouraged by paternalistic employment relationships. As Levine (1981) points out, the decentralisation, exclusiveness and high degree of autonomy of enterprise unions (despite their affiliation to industry-wide federations) means sacrificing a high degree of labour movement solidarity and leaves them open to at least the possibility of employer influence.

In comparison with the countries so far considered, some rather different distinguishing characteristics typify the trade union movement in

Australia. Its trade unions have a structural complexity similar to that in Britain as a result of 'the movement's craft origins, the subsequent grafting on of semi-skilled and unskilled employees [and] flirtation with industry unionism' (Cupper and Hearn 1981: 25). However, the development of Australian unions has been markedly and uniquely influenced by the institutional support given to the unions by the federal arbitration system which has long played a fundamental role in wage determination and the settlement of disputes (see Chapter 5). Arbitration not only led to centralised wage-fixing and a high degree of centralised decision making by both employers and unions, as well as inhibiting the development of a strong shop steward movement, it also fostered a fragmented union movement (Lansbury 1978a). Arbitration bestowed legitimacy upon the early trade unions, they were explicitly recognised and the system depended for its effectiveness upon their participation. Unions became registered, thereby conferring access to an arbitration tribunal, and once registered, they were largely protected from the emergence of new, rival organisations.[7] As a result, the system of registration led to the early establishment and subsequent continuation of a large number of small unions and, as a secondary consequence, helped to impede amalgamation and union rationalisation. In 1986 there was a multiplicity of 326, mainly small, unions organising a total union membership of some three million employees. Many Australian unions have therefore lacked the industrial strength to be able to achieve their industrial aims outside the framework of the arbitration system (Martin 1975).

Having now examined the objectives and formal structural characteristics of trade unions, it is also necessary to consider their more informal organisation at workplace level since, in many Western European countries during the post-Second World War period, there has been a notable growth of bargaining at plant level – often outside official union channels – along with a progressive enlargement of its scope (see Chapter 4). This has been one reason for the increasing prominence of work groups at local level often demanding greater autonomy and a more active role in policy formulation than that provided by the official union structure.

WORKPLACE ORGANISATION

Statutory, or voluntary, machinery for workplace employee representation is a well-established part of most European systems of industrial relations. In the UK and the Nordic countries, trade union workplace organisations such as shop steward committees are the dominant form of worker representation at workplace level, whereas in Germany, the Netherlands and other continental countries works councils (formally independent of the trade union) are the predominant form of workplace institutions. In Austria, for instance, the works councils perform union representative functions on the shopfloor, and alternative channels of union workplace representation such as shop stewards do not exist. Nevertheless, works councils in that country are said to be the backbone of the unions, since they not only recruit members but also collect dues, explain union policy and relate information on shopfloor opinion back to union officials. In particular, when performing functions on the unions' behalf, 'works councils can make use of their legally privileged position, and their protection from discriminatory treatment by the employer' (Traxler 1992: 281).

Similarly in Germany, since most works councillors are members of the trade union concerned, the works council can be considered as a channel through which trade unions exert influence on firms (Berghahn and Karsten 1987). Most German unions also have their own representatives (stewards) alongside the works councils, but their functions are limited. In many cases, they are both messengers of the works council and the mouthpiece of their work groups (Jacobi *et al.* 1992). The strength and professionalism of Dutch works councils is also related to the position of union members within them, since trade unions are the main support system for works councillors – although that has never guaranteed union control over the councils (Visser 1987, 1992). Also, in Spain, the unions' organisation at the workplace is generally linked closely with the works council (Lucio 1992). In a number of countries, in recent years, there has been some reciprocal penetration of areas which were formerly kept more or less separate, since 'unions at workplace level are taking on works council functions while works councils are becoming engaged in work that unions have hitherto regarded as their sole prerogative' (Windmuller 1987: 34).

In Switzerland, the main vehicle for employee interest representation at company level is the works committee. These committees are voluntary institutions with information and consultation rights laid down under the terms of the collective agreements and, unlike Germany or Austria, there is no legal framework requiring their establishment. At the same time, however, as in Germany the existence of such committees gives rise to a dual system of interest representation, with the union being responsible for collective bargaining above the level of the company, while the committee has jurisdiction over workplace issues. 'The latter is meant to be accountable to the employees rather than the union, although in practice the unionised members of the committees usually maintain close contact with the local branches and officials' (Hotz-Hart 1992: 310).

By contrast, in Britain there is no such dual system of representation since there is no clear-cut distinction between collective bargaining and the role played by trade unions in some countries outside the workplace. There is, however, a strong tradition of shop steward bargaining with management over the regulation of work, early craft unions having laid the groundwork for a continuing emphasis on sectional workplace bargaining. In much of British industry, the absence of exclusive bargaining jurisdiction for any one union created a hiatus in the lines of authority and communication between shop stewards and national union organisations. As a result, shop stewards have been more closely tied to their work groups and in several industries were able to create spontaneous, coordinated organisations at factory level to take advantage of increased bargaining opportunities during a period of relatively 'soft' product markets prior to the mid-1970s. They also operated to a great extent independently of official union hierarchies (unlike union workplace 'clubs' and representatives in the Nordic countries which are wholly integrated into the national unions and their local branches). More recently, along with a formalisation of the machinery of plant-level representation by management, some unions have established new policy-making bodies at company and industry level in order to increase shop stewards' integration into their official structures (Edwards *et al.* 1992).

Similarly, in the Netherlands the unions made structural adaptations to their own organisations so as to meet the needs of the rank and file. They retained their existing geographically based, local structures but supplemented them with official plant-based groupings and union plant representatives became recognised. In this way, their organisational structure reflected and incorporated the shifting focus of trade union activity from national, regional and local interests down to the plant (Albeda 1977). Also, in Sweden, the unions attempted to accommodate work group aspirations by allowing local unions a greater say in employment practices and – via legislation – expanding the role and powers of shop stewards, including the right of safety stewards to order a work stoppage in certain circumstances (Forsebäck 1980). In fact, such legislative support for union workplace organisation (which also occurred in Italy in the 1970s) has helped to cushion trade unions against the impact of pressures emanating from the more adverse economic climate of the 1980s.

As well as workplace organisation, a further level at which cross-national comparisons may be directed is the 'internal' government of trade unions and the extent of democratic control by their membership, as opposed to oligarchic domination by the leadership, since unions are formally democratic institutions based upon the consent of their members.

INTERNAL UNION DEMOCRACY

Von Beyme (1980) has pointed to the potential influence of union size and pluralistic divisions upon the degree of union democracy. The pressures of bureaucracy are seen as being greater within large, comprehensive unions so that fragmented, ideological unions (as in the 'Latin' countries) do not possess specialised staff resources to the same extent as more pragmatically based general unions, and they therefore leave greater room for local and plant initiatives by the membership.

In Western European countries, some recent comparative analyses have attempted to evaluate the relationship between union leaders and their base, in terms of the responsiveness of the former to the latter as regards the ability to influence decisions. It is contended that the potential for responsiveness should be greater where members can use a combination of 'exit' and 'voice' mechanisms, and the cost of those mechanisms is relatively low (Lange 1983). For French unions, the best existing guarantees of democratic operation are said to be the purely voluntary character of membership, so that members may exert a strong pressure on union officials by threatening to leave the union, and the pluralistic structure of the trade union movement which, in the absence of any monopoly, may oblige unions to appear more receptive to their members' demands (Blanc-Jouvain 1988).

Clegg (1976: 54) maintains that power within unions is concentrated at the level at which bargaining is typically conducted (although this is not the only influence), so that 'industry bargaining concentrates power at the centre [and promotes integrated, bureaucratic union government], whereas bargaining at lower levels disperses it to the regions or branches'. In Sweden, where industry or higher-level bargaining predominates, although there are variations as between unions within individual industries the unions are generally strongly organised and their officials have considerable power. The central union federation (LO) has also been very strong, largely because it played a significant and continuing role in collective bargaining. Conversely, in the United States where collective bargaining takes place mainly at plant level union government is also very much decentralised and the branches ('locals') have considerable independence. In Britain, the development of informal, workplace-level bargaining and shopfloor activism since the 1950s led to some, although by no means universal, decentralisation of union government in some of the public service unions, for instance, but most notably in the transport workers union (TGWU). In the latter union these changes 'were less a surrender of power to the shopfloor than a formal accommodation to the reality of decentralisation which had occurred during the post-war years' (Hyman 1983: 42).

A contrasting perspective, however, which makes little allowance for the effects of collective bargaining arrangements is the study of democracy in British and North American unions by Edelstein and Warner (1975), and that for Mexico by Thompson and Roxborough (1982). The so-called 'structural' approach adopted by these studies concentrates upon the organisational structure of unions rather than focusing upon the activities of their membership. It looks for formal arrangements such as size and frequency of union conventions or conferences, selection and voting methods for the union executives and the existence of intermediate union-governing bodies, i.e. devices which can facilitate, when full advantage is taken of them, the development of power bases independent of union leaders. The studies tentatively suggest that such union organisational factors are more important influences in promoting internal democracy than are national, contextual characteristics such as the political and industrial relations systems, or the existence of competing union federations. However, this remains an open question since the research needs to be replicated for a considerably increased range of countries.

In many countries, the issue of democracy in trade unions has not been a matter for government intervention because unions have been viewed as private organisations which workers join voluntarily. In Scandinavia and Germany, for instance, forms of external regulation are generally absent since they have strong, recognised, unitary union movements with long traditions of universalistic practice, of organising and representing diffuse interests even beyond the sphere of their members – without recourse to methods of 'union security' such as the closed shop. Resistance to external regulation has been less successful, however, in countries such as the USA and Britain where union movements are decentralised and divided by sectoral representation of workers, with a strong presence of craft unionism (and with 'union security' mechanisms) – leading to conflictual competition between unions (Treu 1987a).

In addition to those dimensions of trade union activity which have already been discussed, a further important aspect relates to the significant cross-national variations which exist in the extent of trade union membership. Despite the fact that many advanced western economies have similar characteristics, in terms of a high degree of industrialisation, urbanisation and technological development, they nevertheless display markedly different degrees of labour force unionisation. Also, the size of union membership is an important consideration in its own right since it is one of the main indices of unions' industrial power.[8]

LEVELS OF TRADE UNION MEMBERSHIP

Some indication of the disparities to be explained is contained in Table 2.1. This shows, for twelve countries in rank order, overall union membership 'density' (members as a percentage of the number of potential members –

the domain of the latter being taken to approximate to the size of civilian wage and salary employment). For some countries, however, retired and self-employed persons who belong to unions are included, whereas they are excluded in others. Similarly, unemployed union members are more likely to remain in membership, and consequently will be included in the figures, in those particular countries (as in Scandinavia) where unions are responsible for administering unemployment insurance benefits. In order, therefore, to facilitate international comparisons the data are also shown on an adjusted basis, to focus on those union members who are most directly influenced by union activities, by excluding union members who are unemployed, self-employed or retired.

Table 2.1 Trade union density in selected OECD countries, 1989/90

	Unadjusted data, 1990 (%)		Adjusted data, 1989 (%)	
Sweden	95	(1989)	84	
Denmark	88		75	
Italy	65	(1988)	47	
UK	46	(1988)	41	(1988)
Australia	43		34	(1988)
Germany	39	(1989)	33	
Canada	36		33	
Switzerland	31		28	(1986)
Netherlands	28		28	
Japan	25		26	
USA	16		16	
France	11	(1989)	11	

Source: C. Chang and C. Sorrentino, 'Union membership statistics in 12 countries', *Monthly Labor Review* 114, 12, 1991

There are also problems with measuring (and interpreting) trade union membership itself, since in the United States, for example, some employee associations may not call themselves trade unions although they engage in bargaining activities. In France, the only source of such statistics is the unions themselves (or, indirectly, via the support given to the various unions in elections for enterprise committees), so that trade union pluralism and rivalry result in membership figures which are over-inflated (Bridgford 1990). Again, in countries such as Germany and the Netherlands – despite their fairly low union densities – a higher proportion of workers are covered by the terms of the union-negotiated collective agreements as a result of the legislative provision for the 'extension' of agreements throughout an industry (principally in order to protect employers from the effects of low wage competition). Furthermore, at a disaggregated level corresponding to where collective bargaining is actually conducted in most countries, unions may be well organised in spite of an overall low average density.

In France (and also in Spain), the importance and influence of unions is certainly much greater than the low membership figures would imply. French membership statistics are not a very satisfactory index of the status of trade unions, since their strength depends more on their social and political influence than on organisational membership. Furthermore, the quasi-monopoly of the five main national union federations (which are automatically considered to be 'representative' and therefore given bargaining rights) gives them an institutional strength largely independent of their actual strength in terms of members (Sellier and Silvestre 1986). Such qualifications notwithstanding, an explanation is required for the major inter-country differences in density which are depicted in Table 2.1. In particular, we need to explain the contrast between the 'high' Scandinavian figures and the 'low' levels of unionisation found in the United States and France.

Clegg (1976: 27) has put forward a theory of union density for those countries which rely predominantly upon collective bargaining to regulate employment terms. Inter-country divergences 'are explained by variations in the extent and depth of collective bargaining and in support for union [membership] security, either directly from employers or through collective agreements'. Therefore, the greater the 'depth' of bargaining (in terms of the involvement of local union officers and shop stewards) and union support, then the higher the density, since members will be attracted if workplace benefits are secured and workplace services provided.

In this approach, the high level of unionisation in Sweden is not the result of any cultural propensity on the part of the Swedish population (because of its ethnic homogeneity) to seek objectives by way of interest group organisations, a factor which Adams (1975) notes has sometimes been suggested by way of explanation. Rather, not only does Sweden have the widest coverage of collective bargaining for manual and white-collar employees, along with well-developed workplace organisations, but most importantly member firms of the centralised employers' body support trade union membership and encourage employees to join and remain in the union. As early as 1906, after a period of intensive industrial conflict, an agreement was reached (the 'December Compromise') on the membership issue between the union and employer central federations. In return for the unions' consent to formally acknowledge managements' prerogatives of decision-making at plant level, employers would recognise the right of workers to join unions and would not discriminate against them for doing so. Yet employers were not prepared to give similar support to organisations of white-collar and professional employees. Indeed, they vigorously opposed their unionism. Therefore, the catalyst helping to promote high density among salaried staffs was government support in the form of legislation since 1936 guaranteeing the right of association and negotiation to white-collar, as well as manual, employees. Kjellberg (1992) emphasises the combination of centralisation and decentralisation, bringing workers directly into contact with the union at the workplace, in promoting high union density.

Scandinavian experience would suggest that a further facilitating factor in sustaining high membership has been the unions' special role in administering the unemployment insurance scheme, which provides one of the strongest incentives for union membership. Rothstein (1990) has observed that in the five countries with the highest levels of membership in the western world (Sweden, Denmark, Finland, Iceland and Belgium), all have union-controlled unemployment insurance funds.

In contrast to Sweden, at the bottom end of the union membership table a country with a comparatively low (and declining) overall density is the United States. Once again, the dimensions of collective bargaining would seem to be important as contributory factors, by way of a narrower extent of bargaining in the USA as well as employer hostility to trade unionism (especially in the south). Moreover, to achieve recognition in the legalistic and decentralised bargaining system in the United States a union needs to win a majority vote in a ballot; although perhaps 40 or 45 per cent of the employees in a given enterprise may desire union services the union fails to achieve recognition because of the unwillingness of a majority of their colleagues to opt for unionisation. Consequently, because non-recognised unions are of little benefit to employees, there is less incentive to join (whereas in European countries with industry-wide or regional agreements, it is not uncommon for a union to represent less than a majority of workers within any given enterprise).

In relation to the marked relative decline which has occurred in more recent years in US union membership, however, one sort of explanation emphasises the importance of structural changes in the economy and in the composition of employment (a movement away from a goods-producing economy and manufacturing employment to a service-dominated economy which is more difficult for unions to organise). Although such shifts in employment have also taken place in other countries, in the USA they began sooner, proceeded more rapidly and their scope was more extensive than in Canada or Western Europe – particularly since the US labour movement is essentially a private-sector movement (Troy 1990). By contrast, some observers point to sharply increased employer opposition to union recognition since the 1970s, as managements have instituted a retreat from collective bargaining in favour of a slow but steady growth of non-union human-resource management systems (Kochan *et al.* 1984b; Miller 1987). In part, this has been a consequence of the need to cut costs arising from exposure of product markets to international competition and the effects of deregulation, together with a much larger union-relative wage effect (differential) in the USA as compared with the wage premiums paid in other OECD countries (Blanchflower and Freeman 1992).

· In the case of France, also at the foot of the table, the low level of union membership may be explained partly by the deep-rooted ideological divisions within the fragmented trade union movement which has hampered the recruitment and retention of members, but more importantly, according to Clegg, because of the late development and lack of depth of collective bargaining whose regulatory effect has been relatively limited. (Indeed, a specific intention of the Auroux laws of the early 1980s was to redirect the institutionalisation of the unions towards the company (Segrestin 1991). Not only has there been a history of strong opposition to trade unionism and lack of support for union security at enterprise level by employers (particularly those in small, paternalistic firms) and more recently a greater emphasis upon direct forms of communication and increased individualisation of the employment relationship, but trade unions have also not regarded the negotiation of agreements and protection of immediate job interests – certainly at plant level – as their central concern. Rather, a contestative stance towards the employer and political action have ranked highly in their strategy. All this no doubt limited the perceived usefulness of union membership to workers, particularly since few individual benefits accrue from union membership and under the *erga omnes* principle, all workers receive any collectively bargained benefits in any event (Sellier and Silvestre 1986). Similarly, social legislation has provided workers directly with benefits which unions have been unable to obtain via collective bargaining – which has been a further disincentive for workers to unionise (Goetschy and Rozenblatt 1992).

Other factors may also have been important in France. The low capitalisation of industry together with its subordinate place to agriculture until fairly recently (and an early development of the service sector of the economy[9]) have tended to limit workers' bargaining power, and diversification made for greater difficulties of organisation. It has also been pointed out by Kendall (1975) that the original, 1936, legislation on union rights within the enterprise gave the 'most representative' unions in the plant the right to bargain,[10] not necessarily the majority union. The allocation of bargaining rights to minority unions in some cases (thereby institutionalising union pluralism) may also help to explain the chronic weaknesses of union organisation in France. In fact, paradoxically some authors regard the weakness of unionism in France as largely a state-created one (Sellier and Silvestre 1986).

More generally, Visser (1988) has shown, by means of correlation analysis across ten European countries, that unified (or non-competitive) trade union systems are associated with higher levels of unionisation. (Hence, the more integrated Scandinavian unions and national federations do much better in this respect than those in France where union factionalism has predominated.) Three reasons are put forward for this relationship: (1) unified and concentrated unions are better able to economise their resources and, by being more cost-efficient in delivering services, are thereby more attractive to members, (2) members find it easier to identify with an undivided union movement, (3) employers and governments also find it easier to recognise and give institutional support to a unified and more representative union.

In a recent study, Bean and Holden (1992a) have examined variations in trade union membership across sixteen OECD countries in the 1980s. The influence of collective bargaining structure upon membership is supported in relation to the 'extent' of bargaining, since a positive association is found between union membership and the percentage of employees covered by collective agreements, together also with the degree of centralisation of wage bargaining (see Chapter 4). Furthermore, previous studies have shown that, within the public sector, the large size of the employing unit and the high degree of bureaucratisation have fostered a general awareness among employees of their collective interests and the need to advance them through collective organisation. These influences also appear to have made public-sector employers more willing to recognise unions, and governments have sometimes encouraged union membership for their own employees as a matter of policy. Thus, in those OECD countries with a large public sector there is found to be a higher overall percentage of trade union members within the labour force. (Moreover, the importance of the public sector for unionisation seems to have increased over the past two decades.) Since government policies on union recognition and security can also exert a more general influence upon levels and stability of union membership, via legislative and institutional support, Bean and Holden find that countries in which Social Democratic or Labour governments have frequently been in office since the 1960s tend also to have high levels of union membership. Conversely, it has been claimed that in the case of Britain, much of the marked decline in union density experienced during the 1980s is directly attributable to the unfavourable industrial relations legislation introduced by the Conservative government (Freeman and Pelletier 1990).

As well as the influence of collective bargaining and government policy, a further thesis put forward to help explain inter-country membership differences relates to the effects of concentration of capital. Stephens (1979) claims that in the Scandinavian countries, whose industrial structure (in contrast to the United States and, especially, France and Germany) is characterised by a small number of highly-concentrated oligopolistic employers, to be able to operate effectively unions must organise a higher proportion of the labour force. Under these conditions, it is necessary to organise all employers operating within the same market in order to preclude the possibility of a wage increase secured at one firm adversely affecting its competitive position, and therefore employment. In a recent empirical study of twenty countries Wallerstein (1989) has concluded that the size of the labour force itself, i.e. potential union membership, is also a major explanation of cross-national variations in union density. A negative relationship between union density and potential membership is found, because in smaller (national) labour markets unions can achieve higher levels of unionisation more cheaply in terms of recruitment costs, which depend partly on the numbers being recruited. In contrast, unions in larger labour markets will accept lower levels of unionisation.

Having considered possible explanations for some of the major inter-country differences between the levels of union organisation at a particular point in time, it is also useful to examine the related question of the factors which help to explain the year-to-year fluctuations in union membership over the course of time. Especially during the 1980s, in many countries membership has declined and the trade union movement has been in retreat. But this decline has been experienced more sharply in some countries (such as France and the UK) than others, and in the Nordic countries density has tended to increase. Unlike the 1970s, when union membership generally increased, this period was marked by very high unemployment levels and lower rates of price inflation.

UNION GROWTH

Much of the work in this area has been done by economists whose approach is based upon the hypothesis that workers will join unions if the expected benefits and returns from the services which unions can provide – in the form of relative wage gains, taking up grievances, access to specialised information and the like – exceed the expected costs. These costs comprise not simply membership dues, but also such factors as the possibility of employer hostility and retaliation (in the form of job loss or victimisation) as a result of taking up membership. Most of the early studies on the causes of union growth related it primarily to the influence of the business cycle and its key components, including employment, industrial production and price changes. It was claimed that union growth was positively correlated with business prosperity, increasing when it was good and falling when it was bad. A notable early study of union growth which employed data relating to changes in general business conditions for France, Germany, England and the USA over the period from the 1890s to the 1930s was that of Davis (1941: 627). He was able to show that fluctuations in union membership appeared to be determined, at least in part, by fluctuations in economic conditions. Nevertheless, he emphasised that 'a mere analysis of economic conditions does not suffice for an adequate understanding of the ups-and-downs of unionism'. In addition, he pointed to the influence of union leadership which can have a decisive impact on union membership growth via the policies and organising techniques which are adopted, and governmental encouragement which may also become a major factor in promoting union growth.

The main contemporary study of union growth which utilises inter-national comparisons is the model devised by Bain and Elsheikh (1976). This is tested against empirical data from four countries: the UK, USA, Sweden and Australia. The general form of the model employs the rate of change of prices (ΔP), the rate of change of wages (ΔW), the level and/or rate of change of unemployment (U or ΔU), together with the (lagged) level of union density (D_{t-1}) as determinants of the proportional rate of change of union membership (ΔT). Thus,

$$\Delta T = f(+\Delta P, +\Delta W, -U, -D_{t-1})$$

with the anticipated positive and negative influences being as shown. It is contended that for union growth to take place workers require both a 'propensity' to join a union and the 'opportunity' to become a member. The explanatory variables which are utilised are expected to have an impact upon union growth because they affect the opportunity and/or the pro-pensity of workers to join a trade union. Briefly, the rationalisation for their inclusion is as follows. Rising prices are perceived as a threat to living standards, so that the faster prices are increasing the more likely are workers to wish to join a union in order to maintain their standard of living. Also, in so far as price rises are a reflection of business prosperity, they may favourably affect the opportunity to organise. This is because employers may be more willing to concede worker demands and grant trade union recognition when any resultant higher labour costs can be passed on to their customers in the form of price increases. Second, a wage change variable is included in addition to a price variable, since it is hypothesised that workers may seek to unionise not only to defend an existing standard of living but also to attempt to improve upon it. 'Hence, when money wages are rising, workers may, rightly or wrongly, credit such rises to unions and hope that by beginning or continuing to support them they will do as well or even better in the future' (Bain and Elsheikh 1976: 64).

A further variable, unemployment, is presumed to influence both the opportunity and the propensity to unionise. In conditions of high unemployment employers, having relatively increased bargaining strength, may be in a better position and may be more willing to oppose trade unionism. At the same time, unemployment is likely to reduce the propensity of unorganised workers who are in a job to become unionised, for fear of antagonising their employer. It may also affect the propensity of workers who become unemployed to remain union members, since the cost of membership becomes relatively more expensive and any collective bargaining advance which the union secures will have little relevance for them. Finally, it is anticipated that union membership growth will also be affected (negatively) by the existing level of union density because of the 'saturation', or upper-limit, effect. Union organisation tends to take place first among groups of workers who are the easiest to organise; as union density rises, the greater the difficulty of increasing membership still further.

Although it might be thought that it would be difficult to capture the phenomenon of union growth across a number of countries on the basis of a single behavioural equation of this kind, without making allowance for additional socio-political factors, or resorting to *ad hoc* explanations for individual countries, in fact the model performs surprisingly well. When tested initially for UK data over an eighty-year period (1893–1970) all the explanatory variables are statistically significant and have the expected (positive or negative) signs and the model is stable over time, i.e. the same factors 'explain' union growth in various sub-periods. For the entire period, it accounts for some 70 per cent of the year-to-year variation in the rate of change of aggregate union membership. However, in attempting to ascertain the applicability of the model to other countries, in order to strengthen confidence in the results, it is recognised that instead of simply applying it to them mechanically some account needs to be taken of prevailing differences in industrial relations systems.

Nevertheless, it was found that only one modification to the basic specification of the model was required. Allowances have to be made in the USA and Australia (though not in Sweden) for the impact on union growth of government action. In the United States, union membership from the mid-1930s to 1947 was undoubtedly stimulated first by the Wagner Act and later by the actions of the War Labor Board in promoting collective bargaining and union recognition (see Chapter 5). Therefore, an additional variable is added to the equation to take account of this influence.[11] The results of testing the model, over a period from the late 1890s to 1970, are satisfactory for all the variables employed, and the government's impact upon union growth is shown to be highly significant. Also, as we noted earlier, in the case of Australia government arbitration directly promoted the formation and growth of unions. Indeed, in the three decades from the turn of the century when the compulsory arbitration system was introduced, the proportion of union members in the workforce increased sevenfold – from 6 per cent in 1900 to 47 per cent by 1927. This was a figure unmatched anywhere else in the world at that time (Martin 1975). Allowance for this favourable influence from the early introduction of arbitration is included in the equation, and it is further anticipated (correctly) that in the case of Australia the price change variable will be statistically insignificant in accounting for union growth. The reason is that the arbitration system to a large degree adjusts wages in line with the cost of living, thereby reducing the 'threat' effect which rising prices would otherwise pose to workers' living standards.[12]

Similarly, for Sweden, three of the four variables are found to be significant although the results generally for that country are less satisfactory than for the other three. In Sweden, as in the USA and Australia, the government also attempted to foster union growth by legislation. The major intention of the 1936 Act, however, was specifically to encourage white-collar unionisation and Bain and Elsheikh (1976) find no evidence that it had a significant impact upon aggregate union growth. Therefore, in applying the model to Swedish data (as with union growth in Britain) it was not felt necessary to take account of government promotion of unionism. Of the four basic variables utilised, the rate of change of wages is not significant and has the wrong (negative) sign. The authors speculate that this may be because with a centralised collective bargaining system which is fairly remote from the workers, 'the less conscious they will be of the gains achieved, and hence the less likely they are to be credited to union activity' (Bain and Elsheikh 1976: 109). This explanation is not entirely convincing, however, since it overlooks the important industry and workplace negotiations which also take place. In addition, the model employing Swedish data is not stable over time, so that the relationships pre- and post-1939 are significantly different, again it is suggested because of the way in which the Swedish bargaining system became more centralised after 1939.

A more recent analysis of German union growth (Schnabel 1987) also concludes that wages and prices have a positive influence and (lagged) unemployment a negative influence upon union growth, while for the Netherlands (Visser 1987) price changes, unemployment and union density explain 60 per cent of the total variation in union membership over the period 1913–85. In the case of Canada, a model which incorporates structural changes (by industry and sex) in the composition of the labour force, in addition to macroeconomic variables, explains almost 90 per cent of the variation in aggregate union membership (Kumar and Dow 1986). In Australia, also, probably at least a half of the decline in union density during the 1980s was the result of the influence of structural change in the mix of industries, sectors and occupations (Peetz 1990). However, although such external, explanatory factors constrain outcomes, they still leave room for strategic choice by the actors. Furthermore, the impact of (universal) changes in the sectoral and occupational composition of employment on labour movements is mediated by an array of nationally specific factors (Hyman 1992).

More generally, we may conclude that the Bain-Elsheikh study provides support from several countries for the effects of economic conditions (and the influence of public policy) upon union growth. The model does not claim to include all the possible determinants of union growth and because it is concerned with the rate of change (rather than the level) of union membership influences such as the structure of the labour force which exhibit little annual variation are excluded. There are, however, various criticisms which can be made of the Bain-Elsheikh model itself. These include conceptual problems such as the lack of theoretical explanation for the assumed 'credit' effect of money wage increases to trade unions by potential members, the 'free-rider' problem[13] and the possibility of a two-way relationship between wage increases and union growth which, unless allowed for, could limit confidence in the results. Furthermore, Price (1991) has argued that, over the longer term, economic variables are likely to be much more influential in explaining membership changes in periods of relative stability or institutional consolidation, particularly in those countries where unions have an essentially economistic character. By contrast, periods of accelerated socio-political change (paradigm shifts) and the associated development of the trade union movement via a fundamental system change, need to be analysed 'qualitatively'. Although Bain and Elsheikh do not deny the importance of the social and political environment in which unions operate, as well as the effects of economic forces, these influences are dealt with in only a limited way. Little is said about workers' consciousness (awareness and interpretation of their situation), or the social and political impulses towards joining the labour 'movement' which have undoubtedly been important in Western Europe. At particular historical periods, political ideology helped provide a unifying force for labour, instilling a sense of perspective and purpose beyond the mere rectification of current grievances. In France for instance, a country not included in the comparison, the bursts of activity and membership growth – interspersed with long periods of relative dormancy – seem to have depended more on political events (as in 1936, 1947 and post-1968) than upon changing economic circumstances (Sellier 1978). From this perspective, a later study across eight OECD countries since 1960 (Ng 1987) has shown that the annual growth of aggregate trade union membership is enhanced when either (pro-labour) socialist or liberal parties are in government, although the effect of the particular political party on union growth is not constant over time (Bean and Holden 1989).

SUMMARY

This chapter has examined from a comparative standpoint a number of important characteristics of trade unions, mainly in relation to industrialised, market-type economies. In these countries unionisation emphasises the (collective) situation of employees as sellers of labour power, counteracting the bargaining strength of the owners of capital who direct their labour. Beyond such common features, however, it has been shown that there are marked diversities between national labour movements as well as within them, in relation to their goals and objectives (broader or narrower conceptions), structural features, size and membership densities. These differences have multiple causes, since trade unions are responses of workers to the varying economic and political features of the environments in which they operate. Ideology has been one major determining factor in the strategic approach adopted by unions. In some continental European countries where workers were confronted with deep-seated social and political inequities, unions have been markedly political in orientation, seeing themselves as committed and class-oriented agents of social change on behalf of all workers and not merely union members. By contrast, in the United States (and some would argue in Britain) greater emphasis has been placed upon the attainment of shorter-term economic gains for their own members, although broader considerations of social justice and 'movement' are not entirely absent.

The importance of the formative states of unionism in determining structural features (which are themselves closely related to function and objectives) and in giving direction to subsequent developments has also been emphasised. In countries where industrialisation and the establishment of the trade union movement came somewhat later, this facilitated the organisation of industrial rather than craft unions and, in turn, often contributed to a strongly socialist influence over the labour movement. Also, in Western European countries, social and political impulses towards joining a trade union have been important, as well as any individualistic evaluations of the relative economic benefits and costs of membership. This may help to explain why, in models of the historical determinants of trade union growth which concentrate solely upon economic variables, up to 30 per cent of membership growth typically remains unexplained.

Changes which have occurred in the occupational, sectoral and social composition of the labour force in recent years have been largely detrimental to union organisation. In particular, the growth of new occupational groups with scarce skills (which may lead to a preference for individual, rather than collective, labour market strategies) makes it difficult for unions to recruit such workers, while the growing numbers of employees in private services with low-paid and insecure jobs may lack the resources and cohesion to undertake collective action. Visser (1992b) sees such structural changes in employment as portending further social and organisational fragmentation of unions, a decline of trade unions as 'movements', together also with a weakening of the central peak federations. (In nearly all countries the only consistently growing or stable unions are those of public-sector employees, and even here the potential for growth appears to be narrowing (Cella and Treu 1990).[14])

We have also shown that opportune environmental conditions for unionisation can include not only economic factors and the composition of employment, but also government encouragement and the willingness of employers to recognise and negotiate with unions. In this respect, US experience of 'union busting' by employers has not generally been replicated in Europe in the 1980s, probably as a result of the greater flexibility of collective bargaining and often statutory supports for union representation (Hyman 1992). It may be the case that the unions which have adapted better to the crisis of the 1980s are those which have expanded their function beyond economic unionism, such as towards the enterprise by way of some type of employee participation, or towards political action including some sort of concertation with the state (Cella and Treu 1990). Similarly, Turner (1991) maintains that where union integration into the process of managerial decision-making, together with appropriate laws or corporatist bargaining arrangements, prevails, union influence remains more stable. Where, however, the opposite institutional attributes pertain, unions have declined substantially in influence since the late 1970s.

Employer policies in relation to trade unions, together with the more general role of employers in industrial relations, are considered in the next chapter.

FURTHER READING

There is a stimulating chapter on diversities within national trade union movements by Cella and Treu (1990), while a general introductory survey of unions, which includes comparative material, is Jackson (1982). A recent study of various theories of trade union purpose and cross-national trade union movements is Martin (1989). Country-by-country studies which include extensive material on unions are Ferner and Hyman (1992c) and Bamber and Lansbury (1993). For a survey of union growth models across countries, see Bean and Holden (1994). Many of the issues raised in this chapter are dealt with at greater length in Strauss *et al.* (1991).

3 Employers and managements

Employer interests in industrial relations may be promoted by individual firms or undertakings acting singly, by a group of enterprises acting together via an *ad hoc* body, or by a permanent association of employers to represent their collective interests. In the United States, although associations for multi-employer bargaining purposes exist in a number of key areas and industries, there are none with the membership density or authoritative stature possessed by many of their European counterparts (Adams 1981). In fact, as we will show, employers in North America – particularly in the manufacturing sector where enterprise-level bargaining and large corporations predominate – have felt less need of association with other employers for negotiating purposes. Also in Britain over the past two decades there has been a trend towards the adoption of company-centred industrial relations policies rather than continued adherence to the norms laid down by an association. This tendency has been especially marked within large establishments in the engineering and chemical industries, although multi-employer bargaining by means of an employers' organisation still remains the predominant pattern in highly competitive industries with low capitalisation and high ease of entry such as clothing and construction (Sisson 1987).

It is therefore necessary to consider on a cross-national basis for industrialised market economies the genesis and evolution of employers' associations, external to the firm or enterprise, which have typified collective bargaining arrangements with unions in most Western European countries. Equally, as in North America and Japan especially, where bargaining is conducted mainly inside the undertaking and employers negotiate separately with union representatives, we will need to consider aspects of industrial relations management within the individual undertaking itself. Even in these countries, however, although employers' organisations may not be direct bargaining institutions they can still play an important role in industrial relations by helping to achieve a degree of cohesion among employers through their coordinating and advisory functions. In Japan the influential Federation of Employers' Associations (Nikkeiren) draws up wage bargaining guidelines which are often worked out by bodies where the major undertakings that will apply them are represented.

We will show that employers are key actors within industrial relations and that they possess a considerable margin for defining their own policies which are not wholly determined in response to the actions of unions, or to economic and political pressures. Indeed, Tolliday and Zeitlin (1991a) maintain that the decisions of firms and employers' associations are the product of internal political pressures as well as external pressures, and that their substantive choices can modify as well as reflect, their environment.

EMPLOYERS' ASSOCIATIONS

Where the main impetus towards collective action on the part of employers related to the regulation of trading and commercial matters, what are now called 'trade associations' were set up. If, however, a clear distinction could be established between such economic interests and social and labour policy matters then 'employers' associations' came to be formed – as in the Nordic countries, Germany and Switzerland. They would undertake responsibility for all aspects of the employment relationship including trade unions and government legislation relating to labour matters.[1] Sometimes the two functional concerns were closely linked:

> [since] the aim of achieving a strong competitive position in international markets, or at least the concern not to be at a disadvantage in comparison with competitors in other countries, was one of the chief arguments advanced by some of the first employers' associations against proposals for social reforms through protective labour and social legislation.
>
> (Windmuller 1984: 2)

In France, trade associations dealt both with 'economic' and 'social' matters – although, as far as industry-wide relations with trade unions were concerned, organisation among employers remained greatly underdeveloped until well after the First World War. At confederal level the central (peak) organisation, the CNPF, also combined the functions both of an employers' and a trade association from the time of its establishment in 1919 – as did the Confindustria in Italy. By contrast, the central bodies in Sweden and Germany (the SAF and BDA) are exclusively employers' associations.

For individual industry organisations a further important consideration in this respect concerns the nature and characteristics of the particular industry itself. In the building industry, not only in France but also in Sweden, Germany and Italy, as well as in Britain, the main body was (and still is) both an employers' and a trade association since it is not easy to separate the negotiation of wages from matters such as agreed arrangements for contract tendering. Conversely, in the case of the metalworking industry in all the above five countries the main body is exclusively an employers' association – since the great diversity and heterogeneous product range of the industry (basic steel, cars, electrical equipment, etc.) precluded representation via a single trade association. Although dual employer structuring may be common, nevertheless our main concern is more specifically with the origins and development of employers' associations themselves.

The historical development of associations concerned with the employment relationship during the late nineteenth and early twentieth centuries may be explained, as a negative response on the part of employers to accommodate the external challenges which confronted them, on the basis of three broad sets of factors. The objectives were, first, to counter the rapid growth of trade unionism which was taking place with the acceleration of the industrialisation process. Second, employer alliances might be stimulated for purposes of market regulation, especially in those industries with competitive, domestic product markets, as a means of regulating wages and thereby helping to stabilise market conditions. A third influence in some countries was the inducement for employers to come together in federations as a result of actual or threatened state intervention in the employment relationship, or sometimes because of the growing complexities of the legislative framework under which employers had to operate. Each of these factors will be examined below.

There is no doubt that the early growth of trade unionism was a major influence in establishing the possibility of a cohesive bond between undertakings which otherwise would have been difficult because of their commercial rivalry. Thus in France, a quickening movement favouring *patronal* (employers) associations in the 1890s was, in part, a defensive response to a trade union movement which was about to adopt an ideology of radical syndicalism that appeared more threatening. There was also a felt need for mutual protection against the changing nature of strikes, which were becoming organised and coordinated rather than being spontaneous reactions (Oechslin 1972). A central employers' body in Austria was similarly formed to resist working-class agitation, after the ground had been prepared by a manufacturers' strike indemnity association. In Sweden, employers' associations were set up as a counter-mobilisation to the growing organisational strength of the trade union movement. In particular, the 1902 general strike accelerated the creation of a central employers' organisation to provide financial assistance to strike-bound firms (Forsebäck 1980). Further, in the case of Australia employers' associations were established partly to counter and present a united front against the rapid expansion of trade unions (Ford 1980). In Britain, also, the intention was 'to establish a countervailing power to the growing effectiveness of unionism' (Yarmie 1980: 212).

The genesis of employers' associations, however, was not only as a response to trade union growth and militancy because to some degree it was, in addition, a reaction to economic pressures. The impetus for employers to associate was particularly marked for those undertakings which operated in highly (and often increasingly) competitive product and factor markets, provided that most of the market could be covered.[2] Association bargaining could prove a means of enhancing market control in labour-intensive industries, since wages could be 'taken out of competition' as between employers themselves. Thus in Israel, associations were formed on an industry-wide basis which usually coincided with product and labour markets (Shirom and Jacobsen 1975). In the Japanese textile industry long-standing employers' organisations were equally active in regulating employer competition for labour and in fixing labour standards – even at a time when the supply side of the market was little affected by trade unions (Taira 1973). It has been argued by Johnston (1962) that in Sweden, however, it was not so much the benefits of having uniform wage levels which were the major attraction of association. Rather, it was the negative purpose of employers being able to present a united front so as to prevent the unions from 'whipsawing' individual firms (see Chapter 4). More generally under association bargaining it has been shown that:

> the employer is not only provided with maximum assurance that his competitors will make the same settlement that he does; he is also assured that his competitors will be shut down ... when he is shut down, so that he need not reckon on a permanent reduction in market share when calculating the costs of a strike.
>
> (Ulman 1974a: 104)

These considerations have been used to help explain the prevalence of multi-employer (association) bargaining in non-manufacturing industries in the USA such as trucking, construction and retailing which are characterised by a large number of small and medium-sized firms operating within highly competitive and often localised markets, conditions which favour common settlements (Derber 1984). Where competing firms are small they may wish not only to help regulate competition in the product market by joining together, but also to protect themselves against a marked inequality in bargaining power, since they are too small to be able to deal effectively with trade unions unaided.

Conversely, although employers' associations are not restricted to competitive industries, it is often claimed that large establishments in oligopolistic situations may be reluctant to join, since they will be more self-sufficient for bargaining purposes, and less dependent upon the services and support which an association can offer. They may also wish to avoid the possible constraints of association membership if they enjoy lower unit costs as a result of scale economies or capital intensity, so that they can make wage concessions which might jeopardise the existence of smaller enterprises. Therefore, very large firms which have secured a degree of market dominance may often prefer independence, or, where they do retain formal employers' association membership, may have 'non-conforming' status whereby they are not required to follow the terms of a national agreement and disputes procedure (such as occurred with a number of firms in the Chemical Industries Association in Britain, including ICI and Glaxo).

Yet it can be contended that large size and a high degree of industrial concentration of capital tend to assist the organisation of employers by making agreements between them easier to secure and enforce. 'Oligopolists and other small groups have a greater likelihood of being able to organise for collective action, and can usually organise with less delay, than large groups' (Olson 1982: 41). Ingham (1974) maintains that this was the case in Sweden where strong, centralised employers' associations could develop (arguably) as a consequence of the domination of a narrow and specialised export market by a small number of large-scale employers who had common interests. Also in Germany, it has been claimed that cartellisation (reflecting the later date, and a particular mode, of industrialisation) gave rise to strongly structured employers' organisations which attained an authority over their members that was never to exist in the smaller, diversified and under-capitalised industrial enterprises in France (Maurice and Sellier 1979). It would appear, therefore, that although large size may reduce the propensity of firms to organise into associations, it enhances their opportunity to do so should they wish. They could find it easier to come to an agreement to support each other during a lockout for example, because they will have sufficient financial resources to enable them to survive periods of inactivity.

Furthermore, given that such firms will wish to attain stable parameters for future planning within the undertaking, in order to reduce uncertainty, the need to secure market regulation will not be the only motivation to associate. There may also be a need for more predictable and controlled behaviour on the part of the labour force particularly in relation to the calling of strikes, i.e. a desire for labour, as well as for market, regulation and control. In this respect, the associations can try to ensure that disputes are processed in an orderly way through the imposition of an industry procedure agreement.[3] In the case of Germany, for instance, it has been noted that: 'Because multi-employer bargaining guarantees industrial peace during the currency of the industry-wide agreement, large firms have a strong incentive to join their employers' association and observe its disciplines' (Jacobi *et al.* 1992). Sisson (1990) has also observed that although the great majority of the members of employers' organisations are small companies, nevertheless the key participants are the large, and increasingly multinational, companies such as Electrolux, Bayer, Fiat, Hoechst, Peugeot-Talbot, Philips, Unilever and Volvo. It is the decision of these large companies to remain in membership which explains the dominance of multi-employer bargaining in most European countries (see below, p. 60).

In addition to the factors already discussed, the main stimulus to employer organisation in a number of countries appears to have been less that of a counter to growing union power, or an attempt to achieve market (or labour force) regulation, and more a response to what was perceived as a threat to common employer interests arising from increasing state intervention. This was true to some extent in France where, by the turn of the century, it was necessary to articulate more forcefully to the government employer opposition to labour legislation, in view of 'the apparent receptivity of lawmakers to demands from Socialists and organised labour for assistance' (Kuisel 1981: 20). It was especially notable in the case of the Netherlands, where early employer alliances had been forged for pressure group purposes with a view to opposing the introduction of new social policies and labour legislation (van Voorden 1984). With the advent of such legislation after the First World War, the creation of a central employers' association fulfilled the need for an authoritative spokesman to represent employer interests before the legislature. At industry level there was also a demand by individual firms for association services and technical assistance in applying and interpreting the legislation, since 'most employers had neither the economic strength nor the managerial skills . . . to cope by themselves – and simultaneously – with the unions and government apparatus' (Windmuller 1967: 49).

In Japan, during the 1920s, expanding employers' associations also became active in opposing government labour policy. They delayed revisions of the Factory Law which were aimed at strengthening protective measures for workers and they effectively opposed government attempts to grant legal recognition to trade unions at that time (Taira 1973). At an even earlier date in Australia, the state – rather than the unions – appeared to be the major impetus for employer organisation (Plowman 1987), since the development of employers' associations had been facilitated by government intervention and by the increasing complexity of the legislative labour–management framework (see Chapter 5). In that country the original intention was to oppose the compulsory arbitration system which employers had regarded as a fundamental challenge to management rights, and subsequently to disseminate information and advice to association members 'in interpreting the maze of awards, classifications and legislation that the system was producing' (Plowman 1980: 253).

It is apparent from the above discussion that although it is sometimes assumed (by drawing on the basis of United States experience, for instance) that the main driving force behind the establishment and growth of employers' associations is related to market or 'economic' factors, wider international evidence suggests that a more eclectic explanation is required. Jackson and Sisson (1976: 319) have warned against ignoring 'the processes which mediate the effects of economic forces upon actual behaviour'. For one thing, employers' behaviour both in the USA and Sweden was profoundly influenced by what they perceived as the threat posed by unions upon their ability to manage. Furthermore, the juxtaposition of particular historical, political events with economic forces often seems to have been decisive in stimulating defensive reactions by employers. In Sweden there was the 1902 political general strike for manhood suffrage and in Germany, during a period of anarchist violence, the 1904 Crimmitschau strike had a critical influence on employers and accelerated the trend towards their organisation (Puységur 1951). Certainly, it was the effects of such rising social tensions and widespread industrial conflict which motivated the giant Siemens company in the electrical engineering industry to join the metalworking employers' association (Homburg 1983). In France, Sellier (1978) has pointed out that the (late) appearance of employers' organisations, oriented towards labour rather than commercial interests, in 1919 and again in 1936, corresponded to two periods of social crisis and state intervention towards resolving it. A confederated employers' organisation was set up in 1919 at the behest of the state which wanted a partner for the application of the new law on collective wage agreements.

European–North American contrasts

The role of political pressures such as these as a major influence upon the development of employers' associations has been emphasised by Adams (1981). He puts forward a theory to account for the broad differences as between Western Europe and North America, both in the extent of organisation among employers themselves and in their behaviour towards trade unions. He notes that in Europe employers generally have formed associations and have been willing to accept trade unions, whereas in North

American industries, especially in manufacturing, employers have pursued more independent policies and their attitude towards unions remained, at best, one of grudging tolerance, if not of open hostility. Adams maintains that these observed variations may be traced historically to differences in government action.

After the 1880s European unions expanded their membership among the ranks of the unskilled. Many of these worker organisations also embraced a class philosophy, were centralised in structure and had links with Labour or Socialist parties. In Germany, for instance, important unions initially grew out of the socialist political movement itself. But they failed to achieve recognition in heavy industry because of employer resistance to the whole idea of joint regulation of employment, which was interpreted as a political challenge to employer power and authority. The position in other European countries was similar and, with exceptions such as Sweden and Britain, the unions were unable by their own devices to force employers to seek an accommodation with them.

At the same time, however, in response to the growing political power of labour, governments began to pursue a more conciliatory approach towards the labour movement. Instead of openly siding with employers, they instituted a rather more evenhanded policy intended to bring labour and management together to regularise their relations. Pressures began to be put on employers to recognise and negotiate with unions. As a result, employers came to reappraise their previous tactics of attempting to contain unions by means of active opposition, since that was more likely to result in increased government intervention to facilitate recognition. In any case, as has been shown elsewhere, 'total suppression of trade union activity without the help of the state was impossible' (Jackson and Sisson 1976: 311). Thus employers came together for mutual support since labour's (political) goals posed a threat not merely to individual employers, but collectively to employers as a class. Moreover, in view of the government's stance, their new associations began to recognise and establish ongoing relations with unions on an industry or regional basis – although they continued strongly to oppose a union presence within the enterprise, in order to maximise their own control.

By way of contrast, the situation in North America was quite different. There, the mainstream of the labour movement was content to confine its challenge to employers to the economic sphere and, in the absence of any socialist party alliance, no serious political challenge was posed. Employers therefore had less reason to associate for defensive purposes since although trade unionism did represent a challenge to managements' power to manage, 'it was manifest as a threat to specific employers in specific industries at specific times and places rather than as a general threat to employers as a class' (Adams 1981: 286). It is true, however, that for United States employers direct control of the workplace was crucial[4] and many of them fought unionism with every weapon at their command. The difference in their market situation was also important in explaining opposition to unionism, since US manufacturing employers concentrated upon standardised products sold on price – which had to be kept down (Phelps Brown 1983).

In industrial relations within the major industry of steel, the most striking difference between the United States and Britain in the late nineteenth and early twentieth centuries was undoubtedly the behaviour of employers (Holt 1977). As in other US industries technical change was more extensive and rapid than in Britain, so that the importance of introducing technical innovation also helps to explain the greater hostility of American employers to (craft-type) unions. In the US steel industry, not only did employers control a rapidly changing technology but the small number of very large firms which existed possessed vast financial resources. Also, employers were uninhibited by political constraints unlike their counterparts in Britain, a country in which the working class was politically more potent. As a result, US employers were adamant in their determination to resist efforts to unionise their mills. In fact, more generally it has been shown that the most important single cause of violence in labour disputes in the USA during the early years of the present century, involving at least 700 deaths and several thousand serious injuries, was the denial of union recognition for purposes of collective bargaining (Taft and Ross 1979). A further, recent comparative study of the British and American machine trades (Haydu 1988) has also shown how the pace of change in technology, union growth and market structure shaped employers' policies – with the timing of changes in technology and industrial structure relative to union growth, determining which (different) solutions for common labour problems would be followed by employers.

In the United States, government support for organised labour came at a later date than in Europe, only in the mid-1930s, and even then it still remained open to employers to try to persuade their own workers (short of using overt coercion) not to vote for union bargaining rights; i.e. they still maintained 'an ethical mandate to continue with their belligerent behaviour towards unions' (Adams 1981: 287). Thus, employers in North America – unlike those in much of Europe – were not required by government to recognise unions as the legitimate representatives of the working class. Certainly, employers were not propelled into joining associations, since by the time they were required by legislation to bargain with unions US manufacturing was itself organised into company units large enough for employers to be self-sufficient and not to require association bargaining

(Thomson 1981). Also, in several European countries legislation had been passed to 'extend' agreements to employers who were not a party to the negotiations (see Chapter 5). This, too, encouraged the growth of employers' associations because non-members would then join in order to have a voice in determining bargaining outcomes which affected them. In the USA such extension provisions were virtually non-existent. Finally, independent single-employer (rather than association) bargaining meant that the large US firms could still continue to deal with their own employees – even if they were now organised into trade unions – rather than be faced with an external trade union body against which they had fought for so long (Sisson 1987).

In Western European countries, however, by the time of the First World War, well-developed and stable associations of employers had become established both at national (confederal) and at industry levels, with the notable exception of France. Their role and legitimation were further strengthened during the war, since governments tended to incorporate the associations in order to assist in wartime economic administration. As Windmuller (1984) has shown, employers' associations were then further consolidated and entrenched during the inter-war period (although there were some notable exceptions[5]) since collective bargaining became institutionalised in this period in many countries. Similarly, in the post-Second World War period more interventionist governments wished to deal with authoritative employers' representatives, sometimes with the aim of promoting greater centralisation in collective bargaining. Since association (or multi-employer) bargaining became a major part of the industrial relations systems of these countries, the specific collective bargaining role of employers' associations now requires more detailed analysis.

Collective bargaining via associations

There is no doubt that the growth and authority of employers' associations has had a major influence upon both the development and direction of collective bargaining in many countries (although in Australia employers' associations were not the principal architect of bargaining structures, since it was union initiatives which metamorphosed compulsory arbitration into arbitration bargaining (Plowman 1988)). In Britain, once employers' federa- tions had been established, albeit often in response to trade union expan- sion and activity, they then proceeded to assume the initiative by redesigning the existing system of industrial relations to their own wishes. This involved the introduction of centralised procedural agreements for dispute settlement, and the associations were also a very significant influence upon the adoption of industry-wide agreements on pay and hours

(Clegg 1979). Conversely, where employers' associations remained weak and underdeveloped – as in France up to the inter-war period – collective bargaining played a negligible role in setting the terms and conditions of employment, with the result that legislative provisions assumed relatively greater importance.

In Sweden, the reaction of employers to the rise of trade unions was also vital in determining the level at which collective bargaining would be conducted. The fact that employers were organised by industry had a feedback effect on the structure of manual workers' trade unions. Employers demanded that unions bargain with them on an industry-wide basis and their pressure was critical for the eventual securing of the industrial union principle of organisation. In more recent times, the functioning of Swedish industrial relations has been as much, if not more, dependent upon the centralisation of power within the employers' confederation as upon the unions' peak organisations. Similarly in the pre-1914 period in Germany, the authority of employers' organisations over their members helped the attainment of an earlier recognition of collective bargaining (outside manufacturing industry),[6] in contrast to its much later acceptance in France. The tight organisational structure of employers' associations in both Sweden and Germany has also helped to make the lockout (which rarely occurs in most other countries) a potent weapon in contemporary industrial relations to be used, on occasion, against the unions. In the case of Portugal, employers' associations 'have consistently opposed regular and formal company level bargaining, so as to discourage union activity within the enterprise and maximise employer control over employment conditions' (Barreto 1992: 472).

In addition, the structure of collective bargaining is an important influence upon the role and locus of decision-making within employers' organisations themselves. In Germany where industry-wide bargaining on a regional basis is the most prevalent, industry-based employers' associations and their regional sub-groupings are the important bodies which carry out the major bargaining activities. In fact, the employers' central confederation (BDA) does not engage in collective bargaining and although it does provide information and guidance to its affiliates, via its Collective Bargaining Coordination Committee, its pronouncements on wages take the form of non-binding recommendations. In the building industry in France, Sweden, Britain and Germany the fact that the respective employers' organisations are essentially federations is also tied up with the structure of collective bargaining, since in most cases the local or regional organisation was – or is – a bargaining agent (Sisson 1987).

Although the central confederations of employers' associations are usually much less involved in collective bargaining than are the industry associations, nevertheless in a few countries the peak organisations do play a major role. In Sweden the negotiation of economy-wide agreements on wages by the union and employer confederations reinforced the prominent position of the Swedish Employers' Confederation (SAF). In the Netherlands, as a result of a long history of legislative enactment in social–economic affairs and close involvement of unions and employers with government in this area, the two national employers' confederations (denominational and non-denominational) also carry somewhat greater weight than their member associations. This is a consequence of the fact that 'a central body, like a national federation, is best suited and equipped to represent the employers' view on any proposed legislative or administrative action' (Bomers 1976: 78). In Australia under the compulsory arbitration system, the peak employers' confederation (CAI) made representations before the wage hearings of the federal Arbitration Commission, and in Israel the central body represents its member firms before the labour courts.

At industry level, multi-employer bargaining under the auspices of employers' associations continues to play an important role in Western European countries such as Germany, France, Sweden and Italy, although, in the case of Switzerland, a number of individual firms have recently left their employers' association to secure independence in order to facilitate restructuring – or because the associations are dominated by smaller firms which are in a majority (Hotz-Hart 1992). The most notable decline of multi-employer bargaining in manufacturing, however, in favour of single-employer (enterprise-specific) negotiations, has occurred in Britain during the last twenty years. In fact, 'employers in Britain are unusual within Europe in having so fully turned their backs on multi-employer bargaining as the means of regulating basic terms and conditions' (Edwards *et al.* 1992: 17).

The reasons for this contrast have recently been investigated by Sisson (1987). His explanation is not the fact that in Britain multi-employer agreements failed to determine actual earnings levels in the workplace, nor that firms simply wished to retain their bargaining independence. (In the motor vehicle industry, for instance, although Ford is not a member of an association in Britain, it is nevertheless in Germany an active member of the metalworking employers' association and follows the terms of its negotiated agreements. Similarly, Massey-Ferguson is not an association member in Britain, but is a member in France.) Sisson maintains that the real reason for the difference is that in Britain multi-employer bargaining has increasingly been found to be incapable of performing what employers regard as its major function, namely the neutralisation of the workplace from the activities of trade unions. He therefore views multi-employer (association) bargaining as being principally a political institution – via a system of control that defines the nature and extent of trade union involvement in the rule-making process – rather than an economic one to achieve market regulation. This contention now requires further elucidation.

For the important group of metalworking industries in all of the five European countries which Sisson investigates, multi-employer bargaining was established, as a 'historical compromise', by the parties themselves in Britain and Sweden and underwritten by legislative enactment in the other three countries (France, Italy and Germany), but in response to a somewhat differing challenge from the trade unions. In Britain it came from the craft unions which, due to the early date of industrialisation, were already well-established in the workplace. The emphasis in agreements was therefore placed upon procedural rather than substantive rules designed to uphold the employers' right to manage in the face of attempted unilateral imposition of working rules by craft unions. In continental Europe, however, the union assault came not from workplace-based craft organisations but from more centralised (and politicised) industrial trade unions. Multi-employer bargaining outside the establishment at regional and industry level – whose comprehensive and detailed substantive agreements were backed by law and left less scope for further negotiation in the workplace – could therefore be a means of continuing to exclude trade unions from the workplace or, at the very least, to set limits to the role they could play there. In Sweden, for instance, a strong employers' confederation enforced managerial prerogatives from the early years of the present century, prerogatives which were also supported by the legal framework until the law was changed in 1977 (see Chapter 7).

In Britain, however, worker attempts in the 1950s and 1960s to improve upon the minimum substantive terms of employment in more favourable labour market conditions, together with the lack of legally binding disputes procedures, stimulated the expansion of (fragmented) workplace bargaining over pay and a high proportion of shopfloor strikes. All of this transcended the frontier of control and undermined the employers' ability to manage. The result was that in order to regain control over industrial relations, particularly as product markets hardened and competitive pressures increased in the 1970s and 1980s, a restructuring and formalisation of 'domestic' bargaining, especially wage payment systems, was needed. But this reform could only feasibly be carried out within companies and plants by single employers, rather than by multi-employer associations.[7] Consequently, the move towards single-employer bargaining in Britain became more firmly established, especially in large firms which had the necessary managerial expertise to undertake such reforms. An accompanying development was that from the 1960s employers' associations in some important industries changed the emphasis of their role. From being a central coordinator, determining a common line to be followed by all member firms, they became more a centre to which their members might turn for advice and industrial relations services, particularly those relating to the expanding field of labour law and other consequences of government action such as incomes policy requirements. Although there was no mass exodus of member firms from employer bodies, nevertheless 'employers have used their associations more as advisers than negotiators and have increasingly looked after negotiations for themselves' (Brown 1981: 24).

In continental Europe, employers have been able to meet recent pressures for greater bargaining decentralisation (see Chapter 4) without having to abandon multi-employer bargaining – whose agreements still leave considerable flexibility for large firms to develop their own 'organisation-based' employment systems. The danger with a total decentralisation of negotiations for the larger companies is that they would then have to deal directly with trade unions, rather than with company-based works councils (Sisson 1990). Thus in the Netherlands, for instance, multinational firms such as Philips remain prominent members in employers' associations, but they negotiate their own separate, sectoral agreements (Visser 1992a).

A trend towards the internalisation of negotiating activity has not only been apparent in Britain (and continental Europe); in countries such as the United States and Japan, where enterprise-level bargaining has pre-dominated, labour relations issues have also long been handled by the managements of individual undertakings themselves. Because employers can increase their profits and accumulate more capital when they have greater control over the labour process ('the process wherein workers' capacity to labour is translated into actual work' (Edwards 1986: 1) – or, the transformation of labour power into labour) – it is claimed that in the USA, in the pre-Depression period, mechanisation and subsequent reorganisation of the labour process were the prime mechanisms used in the 'transfer of skills' (production knowledge) from craftsmen to manager – whereby craftsmen lost the very basis of their union organisation and subsequent collective action (Griffin *et al.* 1986). Also internal 'job ladders' of promotion and wage benefits were developed by managements within some large firms as a deliberate control strategy to counter unionism and increase the dependence of workers on their companies.

Similarly, the emphasis in large-scale Japanese companies has been on the creation of organisation-oriented, bureaucratic policies emphasising job security, seniority-based promotion and incremental pay scales. In Japan one of the most salient characteristics of post-Second World War industrial relations has been the development of control by professional managements in the larger enterprises. Also, in Germany some firms such as Siemens originally joined employers' associations, yet never fully relied upon them as a collective means of defending managerial prerogatives and curtailing union activities in the workplace. The association was not a substitute for, but rather a supplement to, internal company means of labour control (e.g. via a company union) (Homburg 1983).

Some discussion is therefore needed from the available comparative literature of internal labour control mechanisms at the level of individual enterprises and the strategies of managements towards employment relations.[8] The term 'strategy', as a way of conceptualising management actions, refers to long-term policies pursued by management and it implies, according to one common approach, that management has a choice between alternative possibilities with respect to the best ways of attaining its labour relations objectives within the constraints set by the external environment. Thus boundaries to strategic choices will be set *inter alia* by political and economic forces. Moreover, as Poole (1980: 40) has observed:

> the implication of strategies will in themselves depend greatly upon a series of further conditioning variables such as managerial organisation, patterns of authority within the management hierarchy and, above all, upon the power of oppositional groups (especially trade unions).

MANAGEMENT STRATEGIES

Many typologies of strategies towards industrial relations have been suggested with the objectives of securing managerial control over the work process, obtaining the allegiance of the workforce and negating trade union influence within the enterprise. On the basis of United States experience Edwards (1979) identified a progression of employer strategies from 'simple' (direct) control in small firms, whereby arbitrary power to issue instructions and discipline employees is accorded to foremen and supervisors,[9] through 'technical' control in which machines set the pace of work, especially in mass-production industries, to a 'bureaucratic' stage where work becomes highly stratified and employers develop a system of impersonal rules to control workers. Also, a range of managerial devices designed to enhance worker satisfaction and exclude or counter trade union influence in the undertaking may be introduced, including company unions, welfare policies and paternalism. Much of the literature in this area has been of US origin and the more general applicability of such managerial strategies to other countries needs, therefore, to be considered in the light of evidence from cross-national studies.

The comparative study of oil refineries in France and Britain by Gallie (1978: 314) highlights important differences in managerial strategies. In broad terms it was found that British managements had adopted a control system which relied little upon direct managerial intervention and allowed the workforce a greater say in decision-making, essentially as a recognition of the *de facto* power of trade unions and shopfloor organisation within the industry at that time. Management could be faced 'with severe economic losses if it failed to take into account their views, or to win their consent on issues which were felt to be of major importance by the workforce'. In contrast, trade unions in France had too little organisational strength at the workplace to be able to inflict major economic losses on the firm, and they were considered to be too ideologically radical to be permitted a higher degree of participation. French managements were able to exercise a much tighter system of control, involving a higher ratio of supervisors to workers together with the imposition of more disciplinary sanctions. At the same time, there was an emphasis upon paternalism to enhance worker motivation and promote effective work performance which might otherwise have been impaired by this control strategy.

Gallie concludes that the relatively greater emphasis upon authoritarian and paternalistic practices within the French context was not solely a reflection of managerial attitudes engendered by the structural characteristics of industry, as typified by a long predominance of small family firms in which the employer regarded himself as having a right to exclusive control. In fact, similar managerial characteristics have continued to prevail in larger, technologically advanced firms. Thus in both the French and British refineries industrial relations became 'firmly locked into the wider institutional patterns of their societies', reflecting the historical development of their social structures and the differing cultural orientations of the actors. Even within highly automated, and almost identical, sectors of the refining industry no process towards similarity or 'convergence' in managerial strategies in the two countries appears to have occurred.

In addition to direct, or personal, control it has also become usual to distinguish a form of control which is incorporated within (impersonal) technological structures. Such technical control first began to be developed in the mechanised, mass-production industries in the United States during the 1890s and early years of the present century, as epitomised in the steel mills. Because expensive capital equipment and the attainment of a rapid 'through-put' of production were central to this development, 'the craft skill and judgement of the workers had to be as much as possible superseded, as did the control of workers over the pace of work' (Lazonick 1983: 112). Profitable mass production necessitated not only employer control over the planning and organisation of work but also reliable, attentive and loyal workers to perform it. One management response in the USA was therefore to introduce a range of welfare policies, and employee representation plans, generally known as 'company unions'. Similarly, in some of the large industrial enterprises in Germany during the inter-war period with the introduction of standardised mass-production techniques a parallel emphasis was placed upon welfare measures (company housing, provision of leisure activities, etc.) as a means of motivation, promoting integration and worker commitment to the company.

However, in contrast to the situation in the United States and Germany, comparative research has shown that both technical control and corporate paternalism failed to become important long-term strategies in much of British industry in the early part of the present century because of a predominant small-firm structure, together with the opposition of well-entrenched unions. In the engineering industry, for example, employers were unable completely to transform work relations towards de-skilling and standardised mass production, mainly because they were not prepared to undertake the major capital investment which would have been required (Zeitlin 1983). In the car industry, control of the labour process through machine-pacing was also not generally regarded as a viable strategy by British management in the context of the existence of powerful labour organisations at the point of production and a desire to reduce the perceived increasing antagonism of labour to capital. Instead, productivity improvements and more cooperative attitudes were to be attained by other devices such as wage incentive schemes (Lewchuk 1983).

A third strategy used to manage and motivate employees as the size of industrial enterprises increased has been the development of bureaucratic personnel policies. These are characterised by internal company training and promotion systems, complex wage hierarchies, as well as greater job security, since most jobs are insulated from the direct effects of competitive forces in the external labour market. In the United States during the 1920s, job security and internal job ladders (i.e. promotion from within the firm) began to be introduced, it has been claimed, partly in order to differentiate the (semi-skilled) labour force and break up the sense of solidarity that united a firm's workers in collective opposition to their employer – and they were to prove particularly effective in forestalling unionism (Edwards 1979). In the case of the steel industry, Stone (1974) contends that the restructuring of job hierarchies, the creation of internal job ladders and accompanying wage payments did not, in fact, reflect the attainment of technical skills derived from on-the-job training. Instead, employee loyalty and dependability could be the major factors in securing promotion through the hierarchies. With this line of argument, however, it is possible to exaggerate the extent to which the hierarchical division of labour – fostering divisiveness among workers – was primarily a result of deliberate employer labour strategy, rather than being more an unintended consequence of technological advance.

A similar strategy of bureaucratisation emerged during the inter-war period among Japanese employers, which was to some extent directly influenced by developments in the United States (Taira 1973) and by the early rise of monopolies in Japan – which could provide secure employment under conditions of product market stability (Koike 1988). In order to absorb growing labour militancy, maintain and prevent turnover among their (mobile) key workers and strengthen their right to manage, employers' labour strategy in the larger enterprises turned to establishing their own training schools and internal promotion ladders (Littler 1982). Where necessary they were also prepared to set up enterprise works committees with employees' representatives, while at the same time strongly opposing external industrial or national unions. Thus: 'By differentiating in a complex fashion its own workforce management from the practices of all other firms, each firm hoped to balkanise the labour market and to tie the well-being of employees to the success of the firm' (Taira 1973: 174).

In the heavy engineering industry, as well as internal labour markets Japanese employers also chose paternalistic practices and employee welfare provisions, rather than accept the threat to their power posed by trade unions and collective bargaining (Okayama 1983). Nevertheless, the different reward and promotion systems appertaining in Japanese industry, founded in part upon an acceptance by management of the need to enhance the welfare of all permanent employees, reflect quite different values to those of US management. 'The example of Japan, therefore, indicates the importance of general social and cultural factors in influencing the thrust and direction of strategic managerial thinking' (Thurley and Wood 1983: 213).

In the postwar period, by the early 1980s it had become apparent that new developments in the organisation of production were taking place in some advanced industrial societies as a reaction to world-wide economic changes.

> The most important of these has been a shift in the international division of labour and world trade. The emergence of industrial economies in low-wage. . . . countries which can produce standardised goods cheaper than the advanced industrial countries, has forced the latter to reconsider their role in the international division of labour and to look for alternative markets. The production of specialised/customised and/or high-quality goods . . . suggested itself as a new strategy. This applied also to home markets where the demand for standardised goods was often saturated and where the development of more sophisticated tastes required more individualised goods as well as more frequent changes in product.
>
> (Lane 1989: 163)

Thus in product markets which are both fast changing and often dependent upon rapid technological innovation, employers needed to find ways of managing 'an unprecedented degree of economic uncertainty' (Streeck 1987: 285). A new mode of management thinking and practice in relation to industrial production organisation, 'flexible specialisation' (Piore and Sabel 1984), challenges the Taylorist (scientific management) view of labour as 'a factor disruptive of production, to be substituted as far as possible by machines and restricted and controlled as much as possible' (Lane 1989: 179). Instead, labour is seen as a valuable resource whose skills and initiatives should be fully utilised. In some countries these more recent developments have also been associated with the adoption of what is now termed 'human resource management' (HRM), which requires further discussion.

Human resource management

HRM has been described as 'strictly speaking more a bundle of over-lapping notions than a concept in its own right' (Brewster and Bournois 1991: 4). A central tenet, however, is its link with the strategic management of business organisations; this reflects *inter alia* a concern over the moti-vation, commitment and training of employees as a result of a changing environment of increasingly open markets, major technological changes necessitating rapid alteration in required skills and aptitudes, along with the vital importance of quality in international competition and the role of employees in bringing this into effect (Poole 1990). Human resource management regards people as the most important single asset of the organisation, it is concerned with the long term and it seeks to enhance company performance.[10]

As regards industrial relations implications, for Guest (1987: 503) the values underlying the HRM approach are firmly rooted in a unitarist/individualistic view of the employment relationship in terms of: 'a set of policies designed to maximise organisational integration, employee commitment, flexibility and quality of work. Within this model, collective industrial relations have, at best, only a minor role.'

The origins of HRM can be traced to the USA where, since the 1960s, there has been a non-union (as well as union) system for organising employment relationships – a system which has drawn heavily on concepts of human resource management (McKersie 1987). In the United States, the approach has therefore come to be associated particularly with a strategy of union avoidance, by means of an emphasis upon relations with individual employees intended to undermine the 'collectivism' on which trade unions and collective bargaining depend. Also in Canada, where HRM has been implemented in a unionised workplace, managers can use HRM to exacerbate union weakness by expanding collaboration between managers and workers in ways that are not mediated by unions (Wells 1993). The available empirical evidence, however, suggests that there are appreciable differences between US-style human resource management and the forms which are being adopted in Europe.

In the British context, although in recent years there have been a range of management-led initiatives which have brought about some marked changes (including employee appraisal and performance-related pay systems, together with direct communication systems such as team briefings and sometimes 'quality circles'), there is little evidence to suggest that these initiatives constitute a widespread adoption of an integrated HRM approach, rather than more piecemeal and *ad hoc* reactions to economic pressures. Storey and Sisson (1990) cite four factors which help to explain the (so far) very limited degree of strategic transformation in HRM policy and practice in this country:

1 The underprovision of management education and training, whereby few British managers have had the chance to be seriously exposed to formal planning processes. In this respect, a key aspect would appear to be the relatively early growth of the diversified form of business organisation, and yet the relatively late adoption of the rigours of the managerial control and planning system which are regarded as appropriate for the divisionalised form.

2 Organisational strategies have tended to focus on traditional domestic markets and on short-run profit indicators rather than (longer-run) market share, i.e. an emphasis upon 'short-termism' which militates against the adoption of strategic planning in much of British industry.

3 The predominance of the finance function and associated ways of thought in British management, in contrast to countries like Japan and Germany where the production function has been predominant. A consequence has been a tendency to treat people as commodities rather than as assets, and to regard training as a cost rather than an investment.

4 The ownership of corporate assets mainly by institutions such as investment trusts and pension funds (in contrast to Germany and Japan where banks are the major shareholders). The fund managers again tend to have primary regard to maximising returns over the short term.

A recent study in Britain (McLoughlin and Gourlay 1992) of non-union establishments in high-technology industries, often regarded as exemplars of new human resource management techniques designed to substitute for unions, provided some support for the existence of HRM-type approaches in terms of individualised modes of job regulation. But, at the same time, it also found that HRM is only one, and by no means the dominant, approach to managing employee relations in high-tech establishments. Furthermore, there was also evidence for HRM being developed in the context of a trade union presence.

For other European countries, in contrast to the United States where HRM has often been accompanied by a marginalisation of the unions, or the creation of union-free enterprises, the evidence indicates that 'it has operated in parallel, usually accepting the constraints imposed by a union presence, sometimes actively involving the unions in its operation' (Ferner and Hyman 1992a: xxii). Additionally, given that the notion of organ-isational independence and autonomy is central to the HRM concept, a further difference is that managements in Europe have less autonomy and freedom of action than those in the USA – because, for example, of legal constraints on the employment contract and the establishment of pay levels outside the organisation itself (Brewster and Bournois 1991). It has also been shown in a ten-country European study (Brewster and Larsen 1992) that in terms of integration between HRM and corporate strategy, and the degree of devolution of responsibility for HRM to line management (which is also emphasised in the human resource approach), there are clear national differences throughout Europe. Sweden and Switzerland, and to a lesser extent Norway and Denmark, approximate most closely in these respects to a 'pivotal' model of the HR function. More generally, the evidence suggests that the US-based concept may not fit comfortably with the reality of human resource management in Europe, particularly in relation to a non-union orientation.

A survey of Japanese subsidiary firms in six EC countries also discerned a pattern in their industrial relations and human resource management practices which involves careful selection, continuous vocational training, motivation through involvement and pay on the basis of performance, combined with a high degree of job security (EJILB, 1992).

CONCLUSIONS

In this chapter we have examined comparative aspects of the nature and development of collective employers' associations together with the management strategies of individual firms. In many countries employers' organisations originated, often in periods of cyclical upswing in economic activity, with the intention of providing protection against onslaughts upon the position of employers and the undermining of their prerogatives, especially from trade unions. Although mainly reactive bodies at the outset, they were not slow to initiate new patterns of industrial relations in countries like Britain and Sweden. As Crouch (1993: 114) has observed, although historically employer organisation has often followed that of labour, nevertheless 'once goaded into action by labour, employers often set the pace for subsequent organisational development'.

However, although it is possible to identify a number of common facilitating factors in the development of employers' associations in various countries there are also some important differences both between and within countries, particularly in the extent to which these bodies engage in direct negotiating activities on behalf of their members. To some extent this has been influenced by the economic structure and market factors in the particular country or industry concerned. But it also appears to depend upon the extent to which employer control over the workplace is enhanced by multi-employer bargaining rather than by independent, single-firm action. From the evidence of a ten-country study, Gladstone (1984) notes that the activities, structure and functions of employers' associations do show a good deal of inter-country variation, often a reflection of distinctive historical experiences and a particular course of industrialisation – with resultant differences in the environment in which a country's industrial relations system has to operate.

Similar observations can be made in relation to the development of management strategies in industrial relations at the level of the individual enterprise. We have noted similarities in company labour strategies in the USA, Germany and Japan during the inter-war period by way of the introduction of enterprise career structures and bureaucratic internal promotion systems. Britain was something of an exception, however, not only because of the slow development of the large corporation and mass-production techniques, but also because of the effects of a long-established, powerful and horizontally structured trade union movement which opposed such firm-specific practices and internal labour market systems.

In sum, employers are highly significant as actors in their own right, they have initiatory power and their activities are a critically important variable affecting the direction and development of industrial relations. Not least, as we have shown, an analysis of the role of employers and their organisations leads to important insights into the structure and dimensions of collective bargaining. It is this topic which will be considered in the next chapter.

FURTHER READING

The most comprehensive international surveys of the functions and policies of employers' associations are Windmuller and Gladstone (1984) and Sadowski and Jacobi (1991). Employer organisation and policies in a number of countries, particularly in the metal industries, are examined in Tolliday and Zeitlin (1991b). Differences in management styles in

Germany, Britain and France are discussed in Lane (1989), while for a survey of human resource management practices in the EC member countries there are two special issues of *Employee Relations*, vol. 14, nos 4 and 5, 1992.

4   Collective bargaining

Collective bargaining is a decision-making process between parties representing employer and employee interests, whose purpose is 'the negotiation and continuous application of an agreed set of rules to govern the substantive and procedural terms of the employment relationship, as well as to define the relationship between the parties to the process' (Windmuller 1987: 3). Hence, it can be regarded not only as a mechanism for setting wages and other terms of employment, but also more generally as a means of regulating labour–management relations. In many industrialised market economies collective bargaining became so firmly established that it has often been regarded as virtually synonymous with the prevailing system of industrial relations. Windmuller (1987), however, claims that in recent years, along with some decline in the number of employees covered by collective agreements, there has also occurred a subtle weakening in the position of collective bargaining as a decision-making process. At the same time, there has also taken place in a number of countries since the late 1970s a substantial increase in organised consultative relations between employers and employees. Joint consultation differs from collective bargaining in that it is intended to be advisory to management, rather than a decision-making process. It does not imply the threat of collective sanctions, since it emphasises a cooperative approach to labour–management relations,[1] and it is not necessarily carried out with trade union involvement.

NATURE AND FUNCTIONS

Although it is perhaps the single most prevalent aspect of postwar industrial relations systems in advanced capitalist societies (Crouch 1982a) collective bargaining is in fact a multifaceted institution which, on an international basis, has diverse meanings and functions. In addition to rule-making, thereby reducing the degree of uncertainty confronting workers and management, it can also be a vehicle for resolving disputes, a power relationship,[2] a form of joint industrial government and, by channelling and reducing conflict, a central integrating mechanism of capitalist society (Müller-Jentsch 1985). By providing for rules that are jointly made, collective bargaining is held to contribute to managerial control by legitimating rules and institutionalising industrial conflict (Sisson 1987). Where it is conducted at enterprise or plant level, it may also be regarded as a form of participation for workers or their representatives (see Chapter 7). Thus in Norway, employers have viewed collective bargaining as a mechanism providing for industrial peace, whereas according to the CGT in France it has been seen as a form of class struggle (Schregle 1981). In the USA, collective bargaining is considered almost as 'the alpha and omega of trade unionism' (Reynaud 1975).

National industrial relations systems also differ significantly in the extent to which bargaining relationships between management and unions are themselves predominantly of either an adversarial, or a more co-operative, character. Adversarial bargaining refers to distributive, or zero-sum, bargaining in which one party's gain is the other's loss:

> This type of bargaining assumes that there is a pervasive conflict of interest between the parties on fundamental issues and entails a short-term, low-trust perspective in which each side's strategies and tactics depend on the changing balance of power resulting from fluctuations in the business and political cycles.
>
> (Zeitlin 1990: 406)

By contrast, cooperative bargaining refers to integrative, or positive-sum, bargaining as a method of joint conflict resolution and problem solving. It assumes an underlying common interest between the parties which overrides particular conflicts, entailing a long-term and high-trust perspective.

No national system corresponds fully to either of these 'ideal types', however, since both conflict and cooperation are structural features of all industrial relations systems. Nevertheless, adversarial bargaining is said to be broadly characteristic of the USA, the United Kingdom and other Anglo-Saxon countries together with France, Italy and other Latin countries. Cooperative bargaining (social partnership approach) predominates mainly in the Nordic countries, Germany, Austria, Switzerland and Japan. The strategies adopted by the actors are clearly important in explaining such international differences and are themselves influenced by cultural and ideological attitudes, as well as institutional structures in terms of trade union organisation, the strength of employers' associations and the level at which collective bargaining takes place. In France, for instance, bargaining external to the firm long predominated because of employer and union preferences. Employers wished to neutralise the firm as a place for bargaining and the unions, seeking to avoid becoming 'incorporated', were led to favour a strategy based on confrontation rather than upon agreement (Eyraud and Tchobanian 1985).

Further differences between countries relate to the status and scope of collective bargaining agreements:

> In most continental European countries, collective agreements have the force of a legal contract, often with a peace clause for its duration and with the possibility of extension to non-union employees. By contrast, in British law a collective agreement is no more than a gentleman's agreement, a compromise for as long as neither of the parties wants to withdraw from it.
>
> (Visser 1991: 97).

In the case of Japan, collective agreements tend to be notably more general and abstract than their western counterparts, a characteristic – so it is claimed – of the nature of Japanese personal relations in which there is reluctance to have one's rights and obligations closely defined (Hanami 1979). The 'extension' of the terms of an agreement, by law, to all non-signatories within a given industry or region, to prevent wage undercutting and employers therefore operating at a competitive advantage, prevails in France, Belgium, Germany, Italy, the Netherlands and Switzerland – although not in Scandinavia, where there is already very high collective bargaining coverage anyway, nor in North America, since it is not so readily adaptable to systems based chiefly on enterprise-level collective bargaining (Windmuller 1987).

In countries where there is a large degree of regulation of the terms of employment by the state, the role of collective bargaining may be correspondingly reduced. For instance, in many Latin American countries collective bargaining is only a secondary source of rights and obligations in labour relations after legislation (Bronstein 1978). Among European countries, in the historical development of French industrial relations the frequent intervention by public authorities gave union struggles a decidedly political flavour. Instead of bilateral employer–union agreements there developed belatedly a protective labour law which, by the very functions it fulfilled, was a hindrance to the emergence of collective bargaining (Maurice and Sellier 1979). Nevertheless, over the past thirty years statutory regulation has diminished somewhat in importance in France and collective bargaining has developed considerably, doing much more than filling the gaps left by legislation. Collective bargaining is a flexible instrument and can build upon the minimum standards which the law lays down. Sometimes it has played a pioneering role in bringing about new developments, such as the Renault agreement on the duration of holidays which then became generalised by legislation (Despax and Rojot 1979).

Similarly, in Germany collective agreements have on occasion introduced new labour norms which subsequently became generalised minimum, statutory standards. An example is the 'social plan' package of protective and compensating measures for workers made redundant, originally negotiated in the coal and steel industries (Günter and Leminsky 1978). In that country legislation also maintains an important position in the setting of norms for industrial relations and working conditions, covering many fringe benefits that could be collective bargaining issues elsewhere. Moreover, some topics are placed by law within the (codetermination) jurisdiction of the works council, a formally union-independent system of interest representation in which all eligible employees may vote and stand for election regardless of union membership. The distinction between codetermination and collective bargaining is important in that works councils, as agents of codetermination, are legally forbidden to call a strike whereas unions, as collective bargaining agents, are not (Streeck 1981). Works councils have been particularly important in securing improvements in working conditions and other non-wage elements since many of these are so specific to individual workplaces that they cannot be regulated by means of a general, industry-wide agreement.

In Belgium it has been argued that there is so much social and labour legislation that there is less room for collective bargaining. Although it is true that the iegal provisions are mostly protective minimum standards which can be improved upon via collective bargaining, the fact remains that collective bargaining itself does not have the same range as might be the case if legal provisions were fewer (Blanpain 1982). It may also appear that the scope for collective bargaining would be more severely curtailed in Australia where the state-operated system of conciliation and compulsory arbitration has shaped labour–management relations since the turn of the century (see Chapter 5). Nevertheless, such third-party regulation has often incorporated and consolidated employment terms which have already been agreed via prior negotiations between unions and employers. In this sense, the Australian compulsory arbitration system, although a form of statutory regulation, may also be regarded as part of a collective bargaining system (Clegg 1976). The compulsory arbitration system in fact emphasises conciliation, with arbitration by tribunals in the event of failed negotiations.

Coverage

The number of employees to whom a collective agreement applies will usually be larger than the number of trade union members, particularly where negotiations are conducted on a multi-employer, or industry-wide, basis since employers typically apply collective agreements to all their employees, whether unionised or not, and because of the legal extension of collective agreements in some countries. The gap between the two will be substantial in a country such as France where union membership is relatively very low, but quite narrow in the USA, Canada and Japan where union recognition and collective bargaining is contingent upon the attainment of a demonstrable majority of union members among the employees. Table 4.1 presents estimates of comparative union membership density and collective bargaining coverage for a number of countries.

Table 4.1 Estimates of union density and bargaining coverage, early 1990s

Country	Union density (%)	Bargaining coverage (%)
Australia	35–40	85
Denmark	85–90	95
Sweden	90+	90+
Germany	35	90
Netherlands	25–30	80
Italy	65	80+
United Kingdom	40–45	55
Switzerland	30–40	65
France	10	70–80
Canada	35–40	40–45
USA	13–18	20+
Japan	20–25	20–25

Source: R. J. Adams, *Industrial Relations under Liberal Democracy: North America in Comparative Perspective* (forthcoming)

In terms of the overall coverage of collective agreements Windmuller (1987) has observed that in contrast to an upward trend in the 1970s (with the exception of the USA and possibly Japan), the changes during the 1980s were generally downwards. Part of the explanation for this relates to the changing structure of employment in that manufacturing industry, where collective bargaining has been strongly entrenched, has been declining whereas the less well-organised service sectors have been increasing. At the same time, although the public sector as a proportion of total employment and collective bargaining coverage continued to increase, these were usually insufficient to offset the sharp decline in manufacturing industry.

BARGAINING STRUCTURES

The regularised patterns of union–management interaction, or the network of institutionalised bargained relationships, is referred to as the 'bargaining structure'. Although it may be contended that it is the actual process of collective bargaining, as an ongoing activity, which is at the heart of industrial relations, the negotiating process itself has received little attention in international studies – although exceptions are Smith and Turkington (1981) and Shirom *et al.* (1992). Greater interest has been generated by bargaining structures which, as will be shown, establish the framework for the exercise of power within the labour market. A number of different dimensions of bargaining structure have been identified. These include the one or more 'levels' at which negotiations take place, the 'extent' or coverage of the resultant collective agreement across different sectors of employment and groupings of employees and employers (often termed the 'bargaining units'), and the 'scope' of bargaining in relation to the range of subjects included therein. How do these structural arrangements vary across countries, what are the determinants of the variations and what are their consequences for industrial relations systems? These questions will now be considered in turn.

Bargaining structures within the international context, although extremely heterogeneous rather than conforming to any simple and tidy pattern, may be broadly classified in terms of the level at which negotiations are mainly conducted. Three modal types can be distinguished: *industry-wide*, multi-employer bargaining which is external to the firm, as practised in much of Western Europe on wage-related issues; *single-enterprise* or firm bargaining, as typically found in North America and Japan; and *economy-wide* systems between trade union and employer central confederations which have been characteristic of several countries including Norway, Sweden, Finland, Denmark and, at one time, the Netherlands. In many countries the terms and conditions of employment are the result of agreements made at two or more different levels. In Italy, for example, three basic levels of collective bargaining – national (inter-confederal) together with industry and company, or plant, levels – have played a major role, with the prominence attached to each of them differing over the course of time.

How, then, may such differences in bargaining structures between national industrial relations systems be explained? Why do some countries have a structure which is characterised predominantly by either highly centralised or industry-wide agreements, whereas others have far more decentralised arrangements? There is a large measure of agreement within the literature that the structure of bargaining which becomes associated with a particular country's industrial relations system is not simply the result of chance occurrence or historical accident, but develops instead because of identifiable forces. In this respect it would appear that the preferences and relative power of the parties are especially important in shaping structure – that either unions or employers, or in some cases the government, want (and if necessary can make) it that way. Therefore, we now need to examine the explanatory factors which help determine on an inter-country basis each of the three major types of bargaining structure which have been identified. It needs to be remembered, however, that in categorising collective bargaining arrangements there are marked differences not only as between countries but within each national context as well.

Industry bargaining

Industry-wide wage bargaining between national trade unions and employers' associations, whether conducted across an entire industry, or as in Germany more partially for the regional subdivisions of an industry, has been the prevailing practice in most Western European countries. This broadly based, or as Windmuller (1977) terms it 'macro-oriented', European bargaining structure eschewed formal negotiations at the level of the individual enterprise, in marked contrast to the enterprise-centred bargaining structures in North America and Japan. Industry-level bargaining would seem to have corresponded most closely to the preferences of employers and their capacity to organise themselves with a view to protecting market shares and strengthening their own bargaining power. Contemporary bargaining structures are, to some degree, a reflection of bargaining patterns established at a fairly early stage of industrial development. In most European countries collective bargaining, whether conducted at the regional or district level, involved a group of enterprises rather than individual firms or plants.

This early development can often be related to the competitive dimensions (ease of entry and relatively low degrees of concentration) within the product market, together with labour market considerations. Certainly, in Britain much of the impetus for joint action came from employers who were close competitors with each other in the sale of their product. They were anxious to help regulate competition throughout the product market by establishing uniform rates of pay and standard conditions. This interest in wage regulation, standardising and setting a floor to wage costs – thereby limiting competitive wage and price cutting – was especially prevalent in labour-intensive industries where labour costs formed a relatively high proportion of total costs.[3]

As well as the extent of product market concentration, a further influence concerned the spatial or geographical concentration found in a number of important industries in Britain. This also favoured multi-employer bargaining arrangements because, since the workforces of geographically concentrated industries are likely to be subject to less variation in local labour market pressures, it was possible to establish and more easily maintain a meaningful wage structure for district, or higher-level, employer groupings (Beaumont *et al.* 1980). Moreover, by the time of the First World War a widening in the geographical scope of product markets themselves and a desire to eliminate competition from low-wage districts – together with government setting of many wage awards during wartime – all these influences tended to extend the area of collective bargaining still further to the industry level.

Similar considerations were also applicable in some continental European countries. In France before the First World War collective bargaining existed only in mining and printing, both geographically highly concentrated industries in which employers had an obvious interest in getting themselves organised, in this case in order to avoid 'whipsawing'[4] by the union. In fact, Sellier (1978) attributes the generally late establishment of collective agreements in France (only since the mid-1950s for the bulk of the private sector) partly to the association by employers of workers and unions with revolutionary ideologies, but also to the marked weakness and slow development of employer organisations, the state long remaining the main partner of the unions.

Moreover, if employers had to bargain with trade unions their preference was for multi-employer bargaining at regional or industry level, instead of engaging in direct enterprise dealings. In the Netherlands and several other continental countries, the union's rightful place was very much regarded as being 'not inside the plant but beyond the gates' (Windmuller 1967). In France 'unions were kept at a distance by the system of industry-wide bargaining which dealt with limited subjects and did not endanger the day-to-day power of management to make operating decisions' (Meyers 1981: 191) – although a union presence in the plant was later forced upon management by legislation as one of the consequences of the 1968 strikes and plant-level bargaining was boosted by the Auroux laws in the 1980s. Industry bargaining was also preferable to employers in Italy since it allowed their associations to maintain a tight control on bargaining activities, while at the same time freeing the individual employer from direct impact with the union – yet giving the employer ample leeway to influence his employees from outside union channels (Treu 1981). Even in Britain Phelps Brown (1959) has shown that employers did not want to work in 'double harness' with their own men, that is to say they would strongly resent their own workmen claiming to argue as unionists with them in their own works. Especially in continental European countries, Sisson (1987) has shown that the main employer motivation for preferring multi-employer bargaining was to help neutralise the workplace from trade union activity – so as to enable the maintenance of managerial control.

A preference by employers that bargaining relationships should follow the contours of an entire industry, or relate to some other multiple of firms, was often matched by similar union attitudes towards bargaining structure. They, too, wished to expand the size of the bargaining unit to reduce the possibilities of substitution within product and labour markets. For those unions organised on a comprehensive, industrial basis it is easy to see that they would be likely to seek bargaining arrangements founded upon the extent of the product market. According to Chamberlain (1961: 4–5):

> Here the interests of the workers cross occupational lines . . . [and] if their product must enter into competition with a substitute product made under cheaper working conditions, they will find it difficult to maintain or improve their own circumstances. If a common agreement blankets all competitors, however, none can secure an unfair advantage by under-cutting the labour standards.

By ensuring the general application of minimum wage standards industry-wide bargaining could also prevent workers from competing with one another by offering to work for less. For Italian unions in this respect, industry bargaining corresponded originally to a need to unite their scarce resources in order to guarantee uniform, minimum conditions of work 'to an impoverished, fragmented and still mostly agricultural working class, privileging the weak sectors thereof with respect to the elite' (Treu 1981: 135).

For the more numerous, horizontally structured unions in Britain – of the craft type which crossed industry lines – their interest during the nineteenth century lay in obtaining uniformity of conditions for the particular occupation throughout the labour market. Although, on the face of it, this would not appear to have been conducive to the development of industry-wide bargaining, paradoxically such 'division by occupation promoted bargaining by industry' (Phelps Brown 1959: 362). Because the various occupations in any one employment would monitor and compare their respective rates of pay, and given that the ability to pay of the employer was the same for all of them, they tended to negotiate a common bargain. It was more practicable to do this for a district or industry, since firm-by-firm bargaining was precluded for want of suitable union organisation to bring together all employees at the workplace. In this way the structure of British unions themselves contributed to the growth of industry-type bargaining. It is true that these original objectives and policies of particular types of union concerning the labour and product markets of the relevant occupation and industry have subsequently been modified, as the unions amalgamated or became more diversified in terms of their recruitment. Yet they did have an important influence on the evolution of bargaining structure and the characteristic form which it assumed.

In addition to such economic influences, it has been observed that there was also an ideological basis for continental European trade unions' preference for broadly based, industrial bargaining. As we noted in Chapter 2, many unions have regarded themselves as being part of a socialist-oriented labour movement, directed towards a fundamental reconstruction of society. From this viewpoint, any highly segmented representation of worker interests in relation to employers, such as via individual enterprise bargaining, had little appeal. Instead, the unions looked towards wider structures which would advance the interests of all workers in an entire industry, or a territorial subdivision of it, and promote as large a degree of solidarity as possible (Windmuller 1987). Consequently:

> the employer tendency to favour the industry type of bargaining was reinforced by the broad socialist, class consciousness of major European unions which probably led them to favour this approach, since it would engage 'employers through mass class action', and also extend protection to a larger part of the workforce.
>
> (Kassalow 1982: 216)

In contrast to this first basic pattern of bargaining which has been delineated, industry-wide and multi-employer agreements, we now turn to an analysis of the rationale of single-employer bargaining at the level of the enterprise or plant (not necessarily coterminous) which is typically found in the United States, Canada and Japan. In the USA it is estimated that about 80 per cent of collective agreements are confined to employees of a single company and about two-thirds are limited to a single plant.

Enterprise bargaining in North America

In the United States multi-employer, or association, bargaining at district or regional level was by no means unknown, primarily in industries exemplified once again by highly competitive product markets. There, the large number of small employers might combine together as a defence against an otherwise predominantly unilateral, union imposition of terms. For the union, also, multi-employer bargaining was probably the only administratively feasible form in many local product markets consisting of numerous small-scale undertakings. Multi-employer bargaining makes for simplification of effort in that separate contracts do not have to be negotiated with each individual employer. Similarly, in industries with casual employment such as building – in which employees lacked permanent attachment to a given employer – the union's focus of organisation was the product or labour market rather than the individual firm. This tendency became even more pronounced as the market widened with improved means of transportation. For all these reasons multi-employer bargaining came to predominate in non-manufacturing industries and, more exceptionally, elsewhere in the concentrated industries of basic steel and the railways where government intervention seems to have been a decisive factor in shaping the bargaining process (Livernash 1963).

On the whole, however, the trend in the USA was decidedly against broad industry bargaining arrangements, particularly in the dominant manufacturing sector where single-employer bargaining units became the norm. On the employers' side: 'the competitive spirit and the trust in the superiority of individual initiative [were] so strong that there was not even the required minimum of willingness to co-operate with other employers for the common benefit' (Windmuller 1987: 85). Moreover, the rise of giant firms in some of the basic industries conferred on the employers a high degree of self-sufficiency in any dealings with combinations of employees. Once more employer influences in favour of a restricted bargaining base were reinforced by congruent considerations on the union side. Livernash (1963) would even claim that the structure of bargaining in the United States has been primarily determined by union preferences and, unlike the situation in some European countries, employers appear to have exerted only minimum, positive influence. Unions might favour single-employer bargaining as a deliberate strategy since it would enhance their relative bargaining power in terms of a potential ability to whipsaw individual employers. In other instances this form of bargaining structure might prevail only as a second-best option because of the union's inability to organise the total product market, a necessary condition for the enforcement of industry-wide bargaining. Also, in terms of their aims and philosophy most US unions concentrated their attention on practical, 'business unionism' improvements in the terms and conditions of employment. These:

> could be attained only by organisations that had gained secure positions inside the enterprise. [Thus] North American unions, unlike their counterparts in European countries, insisted with remarkable success on entrenching their presence at the work site itself and not merely outside the plant gates.
>
> (Windmuller 1987: 86).

As well as the interests and objectives of the bargaining parties themselves, an additional influence favouring single-employer bargaining structures in the USA relates to the role of state policy. Certain kinds of employer combination seem to have been hindered by anti-trust legislation and this may help explain the generally low level of organisation among employers. A more important factor, however, has been the provision of government support for collective bargaining. In the United States the 1935 Wagner Act was the watershed for trade union recognition and protection of employee collective bargaining rights, particularly in the mass-production industries of automobiles, steel and rubber. One feature of the Act was the principle of majority rule for electing the employees' bargaining representative, which would then be granted exclusive jurisdiction as the negotiating agent for all the employees in the bargaining unit. The important point in this respect is that the legislative rules introduced into industrial relations emphasised the establishment of bargaining relationships plant by plant and enterprise by enterprise rather than on any wider basis. In the case of Canada the 1944 legislation[5] was patterned upon the Wagner Act and introduced certification processes compelling employers to engage in collective bargaining. Furthermore, Labour Relations Boards would usually confine certification orders to single-plant or single-location bargaining units (Herman 1966).

Enterprise bargaining in Japan

Having examined the main reasons which explain the predominance of localised, single-employer bargaining on the North American continent we now consider the case of Japan, the other major country in which collective bargaining is normally conducted on an enterprise basis rather than in the form of industry-wide agreements. Japanese industrial relations display a number of important characteristics relating to the three so-called 'pillars' of the system, appertaining particularly to larger firms:[6] single-enterprise trade unions, lifetime (or, more strictly, career) employment and seniority-related wages. The enterprise-based bargaining structure is closely inter-twined with the structure of workers' trade unions. In Japan each union caters for workers employed within a particular enterprise and it concludes agreements with the management of that same enterprise. The emergence of the enterprise union form of organisation after the Second World War and the importance attaching to its role in the industrial relations system has its economic basis in the practice of lifetime employment for key employees.

One sort of explanation sees such practices as permanent employment and seniority wage systems as being related to Japan's unique cultural traditions and the carry-over to modern industry of patterns of social relationships and obligations which characterised feudal Japan.[7] Other, perhaps more convincing, approaches see them as an employer response to the exigencies of the labour market and as a control device to elicit and reward loyal workforce behaviour (Jacoby 1979), since lifetime employment is not a practice of very long standing in Japan. In fact, the system developed during the transition to industrialisation in the early part of the present century. In order to alleviate bottlenecks in the supply of skilled labour at that time each enterprise or factory assumed the responsibility for training recruits for the emerging mass-production industries. Therefore, training became internalised within the structured organisation of the firm itself and to reduce turnover an internal labour market system of workforce allocation and promotion, along with a wage structure, was developed (see Chapter 3). Moreover, because employees were typically trained as single-skill operatives for a particular type of (often) enterprise-specific technology, their acquired skills were largely non-transferable. Employees therefore had a vested interest in remaining with their firm since job mobility was restricted, and employers wished to retain skilled labour so as to recoup their investment in training costs. Koike (1988) also dismisses the unique culturalist explanation, since he points out that the seniority wages and permanent employment characteristics of Japanese employees in large companies, although more widespread across the workforce, are similar to those enjoyed by many European white-collar workers.

In explaining the shape of the bargaining structure in Japan, as with the industry-wide structures in Europe and the decentralised arrangements in the United States, the wishes and expressed policies of the bargaining parties themselves would appear to have been a predominant factor. Unionised workers sought employment security and income advancement primarily within their respective enterprises. Similarly, Japanese employers have tended to favour enterprise bargaining. They did not want outside intervention in the collective bargaining process from representatives of more broadly based trade unions, since such interference could be inimical to the preservation of paternalistic employee relations within the undertaking (Okochi *et al.* 1973). Also, in parallel with the United States, the influence of public policy seems to have been an additional factor of some importance, since it has been observed that the policy of the occupying powers after 1947 probably strengthened the tendency to form enterprise-based unions rather than alternate structures for bargaining purposes (Levine 1981). Collective bargaining in the public sector in Japan, however, remains more underdeveloped and problematic (Hanami 1989).

Economy-wide bargaining

We now turn to an examination of the third identifiable category of bargaining structure, economy-wide agreements in certain European countries. Their outstanding feature is the conduct of negotiations not initially through the individual trade unions and employers' associations themselves but rather via the central confederations to which they are affiliated. The major agreements are drawn up between a small number of tightly controlled organisations and the outcome of their central negotiations sets guidelines and limits to the industry-wide negotiations which subsequently take place.

This sort of system was operative in the Netherlands from the end of the Second World War until the early 1960s. It resulted from government initiatives which centralised the process of wage fixing so as to keep down labour costs and promote savings, in an attempt to accelerate the modernisation of industry and foster economic growth. Henceforth, key negotiations on changes in the basic terms of employment took place between the union and employer confederations in close consultation with the government agencies concerned. Until its eventual collapse under the weight of accumulated economic pressures, the system operated successfully for almost twenty years. It was administratively feasible because Dutch industrial relations had always been characterised by a relatively high degree of centralised control over the bargaining process, together with a weak position of the trade unions at shopfloor level.[8] Also, in that particular period, the country had been ruled by governments which by virtue of their composition and policies were able to secure trade union cooperation (Albeda 1971).

Within the Scandinavian countries the predominant role of central organisations of employers and workers in negotiating collective agreements is best known in Sweden. The evolution of Swedish collective bargaining into a system of 'economy-wide' agreements was greatly dependent upon the presence on both the employer and employee sides of a small number of organisations, each large enough to bring crucial influences to bear on the development of bargaining issues across the whole labour market. Certainly, on the union side, the major central trade union body (LO) attained much greater power and authority than either the TUC in Britain or the AFL-CIO in the United States and the Swedish Employers' Confederation (SAF) had tightly controlled powers over its affiliates since its inception.

Before the Second World War and in the immediate postwar period industry-wide collective agreements continued to be negotiated in Sweden between individual employers' associations and trade unions, with little intervention from their respective central organisations. During the 1950s, however, employers began to press successfully for coordinated, central wage bargaining which continued subsequently to the 1980s. Centralised negotiations between the union and employer confederations led to 'frame agreements' which then provided guidelines for industry-wide negotiations between the national unions and employers' organisations. As a final step, the agreements were adjusted to local conditions via negotiations between managements and the workplace union organisations. Swedish employers believed that the greater coordination of negotiations by means of central bargaining could reduce the incidence of industrial conflict. A further consideration was that it would increase their own bargaining power since wage settlements made under the previously more decentralised system were proving increasingly expensive for employers. The unions would use the early settlements made in annual negotiations as a precedent to obtain leverage in their own bargaining and would attempt to improve upon them still further. The leapfrogging process which resulted meant that, as a wage round progressed, later settlements tended to be more favourable to the unions and also more costly to the employers. In addition, unions would often delay settling in the hope of securing improvement, thus protracting wage bargaining. It was further claimed that the wage determination mechanism conducted on this basis gave a strong impetus to inflation.

For the unions, one of the main inducements in favour of centralised negotiations was that they offered a better prospect for promoting the labour movement's specific policy of 'wage solidarity'. This had originally been introduced in the 1930s with the aim of reducing what were regarded as unwarranted differentials in wages, in particular as a means of improving the position of the lowest-paid workers. Since the main differences in wage levels were to be found between, rather than within, unions an expanded role for the LO in wage negotiations had also been deemed necessary. With a central, unified system of negotiations there would be greater opportunity to reduce the wage 'spread' between industries, not least because then no bargaining group would be relatively disadvantaged for having settled in advance of the others.

The development of economy-wide agreements for both Scandinavia and the Netherlands reflects, however, not only those influences which are specific to the various countries themselves but also more general factors. Country size, for instance, appears to be related to the propensity to centralise collective bargaining authority within national confederations. As Weber (1963) points out, Sweden, Holland and Denmark are small nations with limited-sized labour forces and only a few industries of major importance. Consequently, economy-wide bargaining units were more organisationally practicable and easier to establish. In addition, the economies of the Netherlands and the Scandinavian countries are especially sensitive to international trade influences, which may also have encouraged a broad approach to wage determination. In this latter respect, government policy (or the threat of intervention) would seem to be the most significant factor tending to remove authority over collective bargaining to the national confederations. Fulcher (1991: 218) maintains that in Sweden 'central bargaining had functioned initially as a covert form of state regulation'. Attempts to align the outcome of wage negotiations with macroeconomic policy objectives have been one factor which tended to raise the level of bargaining and it also played a significant role at certain periods in countries such as Holland, Norway and Austria.

In summary, it is apparent from the preceding discussion of industry-wide, enterprise and centralised (or confederal) collective bargaining arrangements that in focusing upon determinants of the main forms of bargaining structure a number of diverse factors are important in explaining the marked differentiation found between countries. Their early bargaining patterns and nature of product markets at the time bargaining developed, the willingness or otherwise of employers to form bargaining coalitions in dealing with unions, the form of divisions between unions themselves, together with the role of state policy – these have been the major, identifiable forces. In attempting to weight the relative importance of these individual variables, some observers, despite the countervailing evidence, would maintain that on a world-wide basis economic forces have had only a limited influence in shaping bargaining structures (Beaumont *et al.* 1980). However, it is generally recognised that economic considerations are undoubtedly important in helping to shape the changes which have occurred within existing structures over the course of time, since collective bargaining itself is an evolving social institution. These changes also require discussion.

Changes in bargaining structures

It is true that, once established, the main elements of bargaining structures tend to persist and remain relatively stable. They do not usually break out suddenly from their traditional framework and veer off in some new direction. Yet the structures are by no means completely static. Shifts in market and technological factors, government policy and worker aspirations have been incorporated and bargaining structures gradually modified, sometimes substantially.

Notwithstanding certain exceptional cases such as Australia, where the government resorted in the early 1980s to a centralised system of wage determination via the Accord (voluntary incomes policy), as well as Switzerland or Austria where there has been continuity in the structures and levels of collective bargaining, the general trend in recent years has been towards greater decentralisation in collective bargaining structures. Yet as Windmuller (1987: 114–15) has emphasised, such decentralisation has not taken place everywhere in identical terms and it can have quite different meanings.

In systems traditionally emphasising industry-wide collective bargaining, as in Great Britain, it may refer to the development of negotiations at plant and enterprise levels. In countries with highly centralised structures . . . such as Sweden, it may involve the assertion of greater independence from the restraints of national central authority by employers' and workers' organisations at individual industry levels. And in situations traditionally characterised by pattern-setting (or coordinated) bargaining, as in the steel industry of the United States, it may mean a shift from bargaining over master agreements to negotiations based essentially on the competitive circumstances of the individual enterprise.

These more recent decentralising pressures, however, contrast with earlier episodes in that they come almost exclusively from the requirements and strategies of employers, rather than – as in the late 1960s in, say, Britain or Italy – being an expression of enhanced workplace union power (Ferner and Hyman 1992a; Treu 1987a). Such centrifugal tendencies can be explained by a number of factors. The changing world distribution of industry, together with the product market crisis in advanced industrialised economies induced by widespread economic recession, has required improved international competitiveness by firms. (In the USA, the UK and New Zealand governments have also emphasised the deregulation of product markets and the introduction of competition into areas which were previously the monopoly of public-sector organisations.) This has forced companies to seek not only to reduce costs, including labour costs, but also to be able to adapt more quickly and flexibly to changing market conditions particularly since, with the trend in most advanced industrial societies towards a service and information economy, consumers require more diversified and frequently changing products. The introduction of new technology (which has become more essential to managements' competitive strategy in terms of achieving greater flexibility in the production process), and accompanying changes in the organisation of work, have also led employers to move towards a more decentralised and enterprise-based approach (Bamber and Lansbury 1989), since it is at that level where the specifics of work reorganisation are located. At the same time, in many countries there has been an increasing differentiation of occupational groupings within the labour force, such as the divisions within manufacturing enterprises between skilled 'core' workers and less skilled (and often temporary) 'peripheral' workers, together with an accompanying greater labour market fragmentation (Lash and Urry 1987).

Many of these newer industrial relations issues, particularly those relating to labour flexibility, new forms of work organisation and technological change, are thought to be more amenable to discussion and negotiation at enterprise, plant and shop level, rather than at industry or national level (Gladstone 1989). Moreover, the trend towards the decentralisation of collective bargaining seems likely to survive the economic recession, since it is due primarily to structural rather than to cyclical influences (Windolf 1989).

In some countries a further impetus towards decentralisation of the bargaining structure has also come from government policies, in addition to the influence of product market factors, technological advance and changes in the labour process. In France, the Netherlands and Sweden it became an explicit objective of government to encourage more local decision-making and bargaining at the level of the individual firm and plant. Furthermore, 'governments have also provided the framework for greater employer flexibility by labour market deregulation notably in Spain and Portugal – but also in Britain, Italy and many other countries' (Ferner and Hyman 1992a: xx).

The effects of these recent changes upon collective bargaining structures should not, however, be overstated – especially not those changes which may appear to produce convergent systems. Certainly in the USA, bargaining which has traditionally been decentralised appears to have become even more fragmented over recent years. Also in Britain there has been an accelerating change away from multi-employer bargaining towards more 'enterprise oriented' forms (Brown 1986); this was already well under way in the 1970s and appeared virtually completed by the early 1990s. At the same time in most European countries, although decentralised bargaining has taken on an appreciably larger role, multi-employer negotiations covering industry sectors remain the predominant mode of collective bargaining. Thus in France, despite greater institutionalisation of collective bargaining under the stimulus of a new legislative framework, aimed particularly at the level of the enterprise, collective bargaining at industry level remains essential – setting the basic framework and rules within which plant-level bargaining evolves (Goetschy and Rozenblatt 1992). Similarly in the Netherlands, industry agreements have not disappeared under the pressures towards greater decentralisation, but the application of the agreements has been made more flexible so as to allow tailoring to the needs of individual firms (Visser 1992a). In Germany, although sectoral multi-employer bargaining still prevails, nevertheless the scope of negotiations between management and works councils at establishment and enterprise level has increased. Streeck (1988: 24) has observed that 'such decentralisation of collective bargaining may afford firms more internal flexibility for adjustment and restructuring and may thus help contain pressures for neo-liberal de-regulation of the external labour market.'

For the Nordic countries, decentralising tendencies away from economy-wide agreements have also become apparent. In the case of Finland, centralised agreements between the peak organisations both of employers and employees, together with the government, have for the most part continued to prevail – although in practice they have become diluted, with some unions breaking away from the centralised agreements to try to obtain improved terms at industry level (Lilja 1992). Denmark has also been moving away from the truly centralised bargaining which prevailed from 1961 to 1981 towards decentralisation to the sector level (yet with highly synchronised bargaining outcomes), with metalworking often being the most influential pace-setting industry. In Norway, employers have come to favour decentralised bargaining so as to relate pay more closely to labour market conditions and because centralisation has blocked adjustments to pay structures. 'Industrial restructuring and work reorganization require the development of new skills and strategies of worker participation, often linked to more differentiated rewards systems' (Dølvik and Stokland 1992: 161).

The recent disintegration of centralised bargaining is, however, best known in the case of Sweden. Here, the demand for decentralised negotiations came chiefly from industries such as metalworking which have a large export volume and are highly dependent upon the international market. The need for firms to restructure in order to remain competitive, together with high profits in many firms along with shortages of skilled labour, created the need to adjust remuneration to fit market conditions (particularly by establishing wider differentials than were provided for in central agreements), while encouraging greater productivity (Ahlén 1989). At the same time, however, those employers outside the tradable goods sector preferred to retain LO–SAF central negotiations. The result has been a broad tendency to decentralise private-sector bargaining, but with periodic and partial recentralisation, as in 1986 and 1989. The recent decision of the SAF to withdraw from corporatist arrangements and national negotiations would appear to reduce the likelihood of any permanent return to the centralised negotiations of the classic 'Swedish model'.

Consequences of bargaining structures

Having explored, at some length, the categorisation and determinants of inter-country bargaining structures, it is also necessary to look at some of the implications of these structures for the conduct of industrial relations. In fact, cross-national differences in bargaining structures have been shown to produce a very significant impact upon a country's entire industrial relations system. As we discuss below, these include the degree of centralisation of union and employer bodies, the level of trade union density and strike patterns. (Some of the economic consequences which also appertain to bargaining structures are considered in Chapter 10.)

There is a relationship between the level at which bargaining takes place and two other variables. Bargaining levels are related to the structure of the parties themselves in collective bargaining, particularly the extent to which their own respective organisations are strongly centralised (federated) at national level, and second to the extent or density of unionisation of a country's labour force (Clegg 1976). The relationship between degree of centralisation[9] and level of bargaining has been explored empirically by Blyth (1979) who found a broad correspondence between the two variables for a number of countries. Highly centralised employer and union federated organisations were shown to be related to the prevalence of national or economy-wide bargaining, whereas decentralised structures were associated with enterprise- or workplace-level negotiations. It has been argued by Clegg (1976) that, in terms of the causal direction of the relationship, it is the level of bargaining which determines the degree of centralisation, with the result that power is decentralised within organisations when bargaining takes place at a decentralised level and vice versa. A relationship between the bargaining level and the extent of union and employer organisational centralisation may be expected, since appropriately structured organisations are likely to be established so as to meet the requirements of a particular level of decision-making in the bargaining process. Blyth also noted a tendency for bargaining at the national (or at local) level to be associated with a correspondingly high (or a low) density of unionisation. The explanation put forward is that where nation-wide collective bargaining is carried out, union recruitment is facilitated by the favourable public exposure of union negotiations, since the benefits secured by bargaining then accrue to large numbers of workers. In contrast, in a country like the USA with mainly enterprise-level bargaining, unionisation must precede collective bargaining and each individual extension has to be fought for at plant or company level.

In their study of bargaining structure and macroeconomic performance across countries Calmfors and Driffill (1988) developed an index of the extent to which wage-bargaining structures are centralised within OECD countries. They define centralisation as 'the extent of inter-union and inter-employer cooperation in wage bargaining with the other side', thus focusing upon the extent to which coalitions are formed, both among and between union and employer central organisations. Their definition relates not only to the level at which bargaining occurs, since it is more concerned with the behavioural (rather than simply the formal) content of wage setting. The index itself is made up of the sum of two components: the number (if any) of existing central union and employer confederations[10] and the extent of their cooperation, together with the various levels of coordination within the organisations for bargaining purposes (3 = national level, 2 = industry level and 1 = enterprise level). Thus, in France, Italy and Switzerland, for instance, union federations are split along political and religious lines, and in Canada and the USA there is no tradition of involvement by the central organisations in bargaining. In the Nordic countries central wage agreements between powerful national employers' and union confederations have been characteristic, whereas in Germany, the Netherlands and Belgium the main negotiations occur at industry level, and they take place predominantly at enterprise level in Canada, the USA, Japan, Switzerland and the UK.

This measure of centralisation of bargaining is related in Figure 4.1 to trade union densities for the sixteen countries for which both measures are available. It is apparent that there is a positive relationship, such that countries with highly centralised bargaining arrangements tend also to have high union densities, and vice versa. The correlation coefficient between the two variables is high and statistically significant, $r = 0.71$. This would appear to reflect both the level at which bargaining is conducted, and the effects of a unified and concentrated (rather than fragmented) trade union movement. Moreover, to the extent that trade union recognition has been associated with government pressure, this has frequently been exerted through the medium of employers' associations, which typify more centralised bargaining structures (Beaumont 1987).

The influence of collective bargaining structure upon union membership is also supported in relation to what Clegg calls the 'extent' of bargaining, i.e. the proportion of workers covered by collective agreements, hypothesising that the greater the extent of bargaining the higher will be the membership density. Utilising the ILO's approximate estimates for percentage of employees covered by collective bargaining, which are available for only twelve countries,[11] the scattergraph of the relationship is shown in Figure 4.2. The correlation between bargaining coverage and union density is 0.76.

In his study of collective bargaining in an international context, Clegg (1976) regards differences in the level at which agreements are concluded as an important determinant not only of membership density but also of a number of other aspects of union behaviour, at least in those countries where collective bargaining is the main method of trade union action. As we have seen, he argues that trade union government will be relatively centralised where agreements are drawn up for an industry or an entire country, and will be relatively decentralised where they are regionally- or plant-based. Accordingly, the level of bargaining influences the

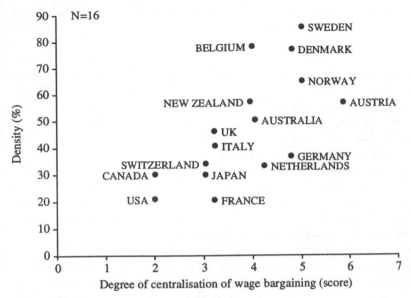

Figure 4.1 Union density and bargaining structure, 1980–5
Source: Bean and Holden (1992a)

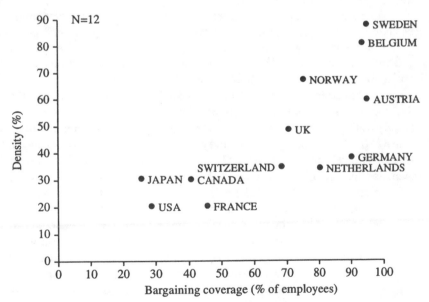

Figure 4.2 Union density and collective bargaining coverage, 1980–5
Source: Bean and Holden (1992a)

distribution of internal union power. In turn, this affects the extent to which union workplace organisations have independent authority to negotiate over a wide range of issues.

Furthermore, Clegg maintains that the pattern of strikes is closely associated with the structure of collective bargaining (see Chapter 6). He expresses the view that strikes will be few in number where collective bargaining is conducted at higher levels and more numerous where there is plant bargaining, largely because in the latter case the stakes are less high and strikes can be called at much less cost to the membership as a whole. Thus the relative cost and consequences of a strike to the parties concerned will vary with the type of bargaining structure. An empirical investigation of the relationship between bargaining structure and strike activity has been carried out by Hibbs (1976) for fifteen advanced industrial economies over the period 1950–69. He shows that mean man-days lost per 1,000 workers were highest in decentralised systems characterised by firm-level bargaining and lowest in highly centralised systems typified by economy-wide bargaining arrangements, that is to say an apparently negative relationship between degree of centralisation and strike activity. However, when the analysis was extended from consideration of only a single variable relationship to a multiple regression model which was controlled for other possible influences on strikes, such as unemployment, profits and real wages, it was then found that bargaining structures did not have a statistically significant influence.[12]

The explanatory approach of Clegg, relating differences in trade union behaviour to variations in the dimensions of collective bargaining, is penetrating and wide-ranging in its integrating of contemporary international evidence and historical determinants, but it has also been subjected to criticism. In the case of particular countries such as Sweden his interpretation has been challenged. Korpi and Shalev (1979) maintain that the development and pattern of collective bargaining in Sweden must be seen largely as a consequence rather than as the cause of changes in trade union density. Increasing union strength and a changing (political) power balance forced Swedish employers to deal with workers as a collectivity rather than, as Clegg suggests, the support given by employers being decisive for union recruitment. In Italy, Cella and Treu (1990) maintain that the structure and initiatives of employers' associations have tended to be a response to, rather than a determinant of, those of trade unions. More generally, it may be asked, to what extent is it appropriate to regard collective bargaining – the explanatory variable in Clegg's theory – as an independent and primary determinant in its own right, rather than as a transmission mechanism for other forces? Although Clegg identifies the structure and attitudes of employers' associations and managements as the main direct influences upon the dimensions of bargaining themselves, in fact the determinants of collective bargaining receive little detailed attention in his work. It may be that bargaining structures and processes can be more usefully approached within a broader framework as secondary, or intervening, variables which are themselves dependent upon more basic socio-economic forces within modern industrial societies (Shalev 1980a).

Industry level and workplace studies

So far in this chapter we have been concerned with the determinants and consequences of collective bargaining structures as they appertain on an inter-country basis at national level. However, bargaining structures may also be compared at the disaggregated industry or workplace levels and they vary greatly within countries as well as between them. We therefore conclude with a brief examination of a number of studies which either explicitly compare bargaining structures of different countries at a sub-national level, or those which seek to identify systematically by means of quantitative methods inter-industry determinants within a single, national industrial relations system – the results of which may then be compared as between countries.

In an interesting comparative study of the US and British steel industries (Elbaum and Wilkinson 1979) explanations are sought in the historical development of the two industries for their pronounced industrial relations differences: a long period of violent conflict in the United States, in contrast with more orderly procedures and fewer strikes in Britain. From the common starting point of an industrial structure typified by similarities in basic technology, fragmented and competitive product markets, with subcontracting to organise production and the labour process, marked divergencies occurred in subsequent developments. In both countries collective bargaining had emerged in a form strongly influenced by product market considerations. Demand was unstable and in the highly competitive market prices fluctuated widely, thus requiring firms to be able to reduce costs quickly in a recession in order to avoid losses. Sliding-scale arrangements provided the solution since:

> by joining with the skilled workers in agreements linking wages and prices, employers could hope to regulate competitive wage cutting amongst themselves in recession and end costly stoppages as the workers recouped these losses in booms. Such arrangements suited the mutual interests firms shared both with each other and with skilled workers.
>
> (Elbaum and Wilkinson 1979: 286)

A transformation took place, however, in the US industry in the late nineteenth century, from that of a small-scale, competitive structure towards a large-scale and increasingly concentrated one, controlled ultimately by a handful of firms. The main influences were innovations in steel-making technology whose production indivisibilities meant that the minimum efficient scale of operations was greatly increased. Also, an expansion in the level of demand occurred, particularly for steel rails – within a market well-protected by tariffs from the effects of foreign competition. In Britain, on the other hand, technical change was slower, plants remained relatively small scale and demand conditions were far less favourable in competition with foreign steel industries. As a result, the early system of collective bargaining continued intact. In contrast, in the United States the development of large-scale steel production both weakened the craft basis of unionism and correspondingly enhanced the power of individual firms in relation both to the unions and product market. 'The large firm could, by securing more effective control of its labour costs, use its massive productive resources to capture larger and larger shares of the market and consequently the benefits of collusion with rival producers and trade unions rapidly declined' (Elbaum and Wilkinson 1979: 301). Therefore, in the USA, the methods of collective bargaining associated with the heyday of competitive capitalism were outmoded and eventually destroyed, along with the breaking by employers of union control of the labour process. (In Britain, the exercise of control over the organisation of work at the plant level was of particular importance in enabling the trade union system to survive the impact of major economic, technical and organisational changes.)

In an investigation of industrial relations arrangements at workplace level Marsh *et al.* (1981) compared a number of plants in the engineering industry in Britain and Germany. Although there are important internal variations within each country, on a cross-national comparison two principal structural differences are noted. First, in Britain the primary basis of relationships is centred upon the workplace itself where unions and managements function largely autonomously with no substantive external, regulative framework. This is attributed mainly to historical reasons whereby the function of external agreements in the UK has been largely procedural, rather than substantive. In contrast, in Germany workplace relations are essentially dependent upon external regulation in the form of regional agreements. Although informal plant bargaining does take place the additions and amendments are not regarded as being competitive with external agreements. A second difference concerns the single union–management channel for handling regulative issues in Britain as opposed to the dual, but clearly differentiated, system in Germany between the works council structure and that provided by the union and employer.

As a consequence of these differing structures of job regulation notable differences in the behaviour of workplace representatives are apparent. Shop stewards in the UK enjoy greater freedom in pursuing their own domestic negotiating relationships with their managements, especially since there is no alternative workplace structure to provide a competing focus of authority or regulation. In Germany, workplace representatives in this industry see themselves as part of the administrative framework for the smooth conduct of industrial relations and work within given administrative and legal constraints. By way of contrast, the British shop steward reacts to, and is more prepared to challenge, management decisions, regarding himself 'less as an agent of regulation than as a tactician in pursuit of tangible, if elusive improvements for the rank and file' (Marsh *et al.* 1981: 185).

A further analysis of workplace bargaining in the metalworking industry, but in this case as between Britain and Sweden, has been carried out by Korpi (1978b). He emphasises the actual similarities in the pattern of bargaining, despite the differences which exist in the formal structures. Although the scope of workplace negotiations had been more restricted (by law) in Sweden than in Britain, in both countries the bargaining which occurs relies largely upon informal agreements and tacit understandings. Similarly, although the works clubs which are in charge of workplace negotiations in Sweden are sub-organisations of the branches of the national unions, and less loosely linked to union organisation than the equivalent shop steward system in Britain (at least before the expansion of single-employer bargaining), nevertheless they act independently of the branch and national union headquarters. In both countries the high levels of unionisation and low unemployment rates for much of the earlier postwar period gave workers significant leverage in workplace negotiations. Korpi concludes that workplace bargaining is not more under the control of the central union organs in Swedish manufacturing industry than has been the case with its British counterpart.

In addition to such single-industry, cross-country studies the recent availability of quantitative survey data in Britain and the United States has now made it possible to test some explanatory hypotheses of bargaining structures more systematically across a much broader cross-section of industries. In the absence of a fully developed theoretical model, Deaton and Beaumont (1980) use a number of *ad hoc* explanatory variables, derived from the case study literature of bargaining structure, in an examination of almost 1,000 establishments in the manufacturing sector in Britain. The objective is to identify the determinants of multi-employer or single-employer structures. Utilising the statistical technique of discriminant analysis they find that high regional concentration, high union density,[13] and multi-unionism are associated with multi-employer bargaining, whereas larger establishments, multi-plant firms, foreign-owned firms, high [product market] concentration industries and firms with industrial relations management tend to have single-employer bargaining.

(Deaton and Beaumont 1980: 210)

Within each industry group high labour cost was associated with multi-employer bargaining, although as between industries no such relationship between labour cost and bargaining level was apparent. Broadly similar findings emerge from an empirical study of US manufacturing industries (Hendricks and Kahn 1982). Their results indicate that bargaining structure is systematically related to product and labour market considerations and that high concentration and large plant size are found to be strongly associated with single-firm, as opposed to multi-firm, agreements. The authors conclude that their findings support the hypothesis that 'unions and management consider choices of bargaining structure in a systematic way that reflects the basic environment in which negotiations take place' (Hendricks and Kahn 1982: 182).

SUMMARY

Throughout this chapter the emphasis has been directed towards the determinants and consequences of bargaining structure, since this is a concept which has been accorded a considerable role in explaining a number of important collective bargaining phenomena, both within and between national industrial relations systems. It has been shown that the structural dimensions of collective bargaining vary greatly as between industrialised countries since they reflect the distinctive economic and social contexts in which they are embedded. Although many aspects of collective bargaining are usually discussed within the confines of specific national contexts, comparative analysis can provide important insights into the operation of collective bargaining and the ways in which different systems respond and adapt, both in convergent and divergent ways, to the environmental changes generated within modern societies.

In all countries there has been pressure in recent years for greater flexibility and adaptation to rapid productive changes, which appear to be one of the basic driving forces towards bargaining decentralisation (although the extent of the resultant changes in bargaining structure varies as between countries). Despite the changes which have taken place in the external environment, however, unlike the position in the United States, in many European countries there is no evidence that a radical or irreversible decline of collective bargaining itself has taken place (Baglioni 1989). At the same time, collective bargaining faces major obstacles because of the weakening of union organisational power, the resurgence of employers' initiative, as well as the push to return to market regulation and to allow for a flexible organisation of work (Cella and Treu 1990). What is also apparent is the importance of government policy, of encouragement or discouragement, for the practice of collective bargaining (Adams 1993). In the next chapter, the role of the state itself in industrial relations is considered more systematically within the international context.

FURTHER READING

The standard general work on collective bargaining in developed market economies is Windmuller (1987), while an excellent seven-country analysis is Sisson (1987). For Western Europe a detailed recent exposition of bargaining structures and changes in seventeen countries is contained in Ferner and Hyman (1992c).

5   The role of the state

In this chapter we consider the role of the state in industrial relations, primarily from the standpoint of the approach and involvement of government. Although the 'state' also includes parliament and the judiciary, as well as the police and military, it is government which is now the most significant element in determining the legal environment within which industrial relations operate. The government can be regarded as an actor within industrial relations performing a number of distinct roles. A primary purpose has been to act as a third-party regulator promoting a legal framework which establishes general ground rules for union–management interaction, particularly in the procedures for collective bargaining. 'All modern states try to fix the rules of the game by, at a minimum, specifying tactics which are not permitted and by facilitating the coming together of the parties for negotiation' (Shorter and Tilly 1974: 24). Second, and additionally, as a means of supporting and underpinning collective bargaining – or as a supplement to it – governments make statutory provisions relating to minimum conditions of employment including health and safety and in some countries wages and working hours. In relation to these substantive conditions of employment Clegg (1976: 101) notes that:

> the law can be used to establish minimum standards while collective bargaining exploits particular advantages to secure higher standards wherever it can. . . . The law can also be used to generalise concessions gained through collective bargaining and to enforce them on recalcitrant employers.

A third, well-established function in many countries is the provision of state services for conciliation, mediation and arbitration[1] with a view to facilitating the settlement of industrial disputes. In Britain and the United States there is a wide variety of public peace-making machinery, whereas in France and Germany institutional provision of government assistance in dispute resolution has been minimal.

More latterly, a fourth aspect of the role of the state became increasingly important – that of a direct and primary participant as a major employer within the public sector. In this respect, the greater the importance of government as an employer the more pervasive is its influence likely to be on bargaining developments and the content of agreements, since it may then influence the pattern of industrial relations by its own behaviour and example. In fact, the enlarged role of government as employer in the postwar period, together with the greater responsibility which it came to accept for overall economic management, led to increased concern for the substantive outcomes of collective bargaining as well as for the smooth functioning of the bargaining machinery. In this respect we may also identify a fifth role of government, as a regulator of incomes. In many countries incomes policies have been used in an attempt to modify or neutralise the results of collective agreements, and public-sector workers, whose wage increases are highly visible, were required to conform to the government's pay guidelines in order to influence private-sector wage settlements. During the 1980s, however, in many European countries the expansion of the state sector came to be curtailed and the growth of government employment was halted, along with a sharp decline in public enterprise employment. This occurred within the context of an emphasis on policies for the control of public expenditure together with a 'roll back' of the state from intervention in the economy and, in some countries, the deregulation of labour markets.

Industrial countries differ, however, in the extent to which they rely on government legislation to determine the procedures of collective bargaining, to fix the substantive terms of employment and to settle disputes. In the United States, the law has been markedly influential in shaping the industrial relations system, particularly in regulating the contours and tactics of bargaining, although less reliance has been placed on legislation to fix substantive employment conditions. In Germany, also, the law has assumed a central importance and extensive influence in the relations between capital and labour – partly as a result of pressure from the collective bargaining parties. In France, the Collective Agreements Act of 1950 similarly provided a comprehensive legal framework for collective bargaining. By contrast, in Britain until the 1970s industrial relations were less regulated by law than other western countries since there was an enduring tradition of 'voluntarism' and self-determination by the parties which had become a part of the British cultural heritage. In the case of Australia, an industrial relations mechanism in the form of a government arbitration tribunals system was set up at an early stage in the country's industrial development. The main intention was to institutionalise industrial conflict and thereby protect society from the effect of large-scale industrial struggles. As a consequence of such heavy dependence upon state intervention for more than three-quarters of a century, it might be argued that 'by international standards Australia . . . is the most legal and legalistic system in the western developed world' (Niland 1978: 79).

Given such marked diversities in the nature and scope of government involvement, we need to analyse more fully some of the major cross-national differences within the various areas of government activity in industrial relations which have been identified. We begin with the development of public policy towards collective bargaining.

REGULATION OF COLLECTIVE BARGAINING

In attempting to explain the extent of legal intervention in the bargaining process on a cross-national basis the degree to which collective bargaining was accepted and well-established at an early stage, or else remained underdeveloped, is an important factor. This is because, in historical terms, the intention of government intervention – once unions had been conceded lawful status – was typically to promote collective bargaining. Since any appearance of formal symmetry in the individual employment contract conceals a real inequality of bargaining power between the parties,[2] collective worker action came to be seen as necessary to countervail superior employer power and thereby establish a rough equilibrium of forces. It was only later legislation aimed at reforming and conditioning, rather than being enabling and supportive, which has taken the view that collective bargaining and union activities require to be curbed rather than encouraged (Clegg 1976).

Rimlinger (1977) in a comparative analysis of Britain, the United States and France has argued that government relations with the labour movement have undergone a similar historical evolution, going from an initial phase of suppression of workers' organisations and collective action at the onset of industrialisation, to one of toleration and encouragement, followed by a later period of more detailed regulation of workers' rights by the state. (More recently, Jacobs (1986) reached a similar conclusion utilising a broader sample of European countries.) However, because of differences in prevailing social and economic conditions, as well as the extent and pace of industrialisation, this common evolution has taken a markedly distinctive form within each of the three countries that Rimlinger investigated, which requires closer examination.

Britain

In comparison with other countries, industrial relations in Britain – the first nation to experience an industrial revolution – developed on the basis of arrangements that relied little upon the intervention of law as a regulatory device. The special and peculiar situation of Britain in respect of a very extensive period of government abstentionism from detailed involvement in collective bargaining has been attributed to the influence of the prevailing economic and social philosophy during the formative years of trade unionism in the early nineteenth century. The establishment of unions coincided with a period in which the ideas of *laissez-faire* liberalism were predominant in economic life. Initially, the application of this doctrine meant that the law was used in various degrees to persecute unions. Collective organisations of workpeople for economic purposes were against the interests of property owners, since they restricted competition and freedom of individual contract within the labour market. (At the same time, they were also seen as a potential political threat to the incumbent regime itself.) Because at this period the role of the state was that of enforcing a legal structure necessary for the functioning of the market, specific pieces of statutory legislation such as the Combination Acts were used to repress unionism, and the common law – made and interpreted by judges – was usually implacably opposed to union activities.

However, the application of legal penalties by no means prevented the continuation of trade unions and after the 1820s the state no longer contemplated serious attempts at further suppression. Not only was it ultimately conceded that trade unions would no longer be unlawful bodies but, equally importantly, a growing number of employers had come to be prepared to deal with them. Unlike the situation in, say, the Scandinavian countries[3] where the later development of industrialisation had precluded the long-term predominance of autonomous craft unionism, in Britain trade unions acquired and maintained substantial bargaining power at an early date in important sectors of the economy. However, they never mounted a sustained campaign in favour of legal, procedural intervention as a means of promoting collective bargaining. The main reason appears to be that in large parts of industry, particularly the skilled trades and coal mining, the union movement had developed substantial industrial strength and already achieved bargaining status prior to the extension of the franchise in the second half of the nineteenth century and the subsequent growth of union political influence. Once the more repressive restrictions on workers' organisations and collective labour actions had been removed, the unions then had the basis and capability to promote and further extend collective bargaining by their own efforts. During the last quarter of the nineteenth century collective bargaining spread even to the unskilled in the service and transport industries.

There can also be little doubt that their long history of struggle for legal recognition – in contrast to Swedish unions, for instance, where the resources of the state were not used to impede their development[4] and which did not have to endure long periods in which the courts treated them as conspiracies (Johnston 1962) – had made British trade unions deeply suspicious of any attempts to interfere with collective bargaining. The same was true of Germany where unions also had relied on autonomous action and voluntary organisation, opposing the introduction of a positive collective bargaining law because of the belief that an inescapable corollary of such legislation would be legal regulation of their activities (Kahn-Freund 1981). Unlike British unions, however, they had failed in the pre-1914 period to achieve recognition in heavy industry because of determined employer resistance. Consequently, many of them were then prepared to relinquish reliance upon their own organisational autonomy when the state promised, at the beginning of the Weimar period, to deliver recognition through legal guarantees.

It was Kahn-Freund who pointed out that the organic relationship between law and industrial relations in the 'formative period' in Britain (1850–1906) was unique because of a combination of three circumstances found in no other comparable labour movements in the formative period of their labour laws:

> First the labour movement was relatively strong. Trade unions achieved bargaining status without legal assistance at a relatively early stage. Secondly, this was achieved without the aid of a working-class political party. Pressure was applied on the bourgeois parties in Parliament. The Labour Party was born only in 1906. Thirdly, the basic trade union laws were established before universal male franchise.
>
> (Wedderburn 1983: 37)

One important consequence was that the legal form of collective trade union rights consisted largely of negative statutory protection, or what have come to be called 'immunities', from the sanctions that would otherwise attach in law, rather than positive legal rights to associate, to bargain and to strike as in many comparable countries. As a result of all these factors Hyman (1975) has suggested that in Britain the *laissez-faire* doctrine itself came to be reinterpreted, certainly by the 1890s, to imply that unions and employers should carry on their relations with a minimum of state interference. It was not so much that the government was averse to regulation in principle. Rather, the problem was the practical one of finding appropriate measures which could be enforced and which would not do more harm than good (Phelps Brown 1959). Until the 1970s therefore, when more stringent and detailed government intervention was introduced, the industrial relations system in Britain continued to be conducted predominantly on the basis of voluntary collective bargaining without legal compulsion on either side, and implemented through unenforceable agreements.

USA

In the United States collective bargaining had experienced an early development somewhat parallel to that in Britain. Both countries had entered into modern economic development at least several decades ahead of Western Europe and in the USA unionism not only remained confined largely to skilled workers for an even more extensive period of time than was the case in Britain but it also continued as a purely industrial force without any serious ties to political parties. The narrow craft foundation of American unionism and its failure to penetrate the basic manufacturing industries was a major reason why, apart from a brief spurt in the First World War, membership never rose much above 10 per cent of non-agricultural employment until the late 1930s (Reynolds 1978). Although unions favoured voluntary collective bargaining, their weakness in major sections of the economy made any extension a slow process since employers were far more reluctant to engage in it than their European counterparts, for reasons which have already been examined (see Chapter 3). Indeed, employer resistance was the major force in accounting for the long years of union failure in the mass-production sector and the fact that by the early 1930s American organised labour could be described as an 'arrested' movement in that it: 'had not breached the industries charac-terised by the giant firm, by multiplant operations for a national market; by an advanced technology involving mechanization and division of labour; and by a work-force composed primarily of unskilled and semi-skilled men' (Brody 1980: 82).

Employers had again been assisted in the suppression of unionism by a sympathetic judiciary and in the United States, in contrast to much of Europe, it was predominantly the common law rather than the legislature which defined the rights of workers. In Britain, parliament would intervene at crucial times (under political pressure) to restate the rights of workers after conservative court rulings had undermined them, whereas in the USA statutory laws bearing upon industrial relations were more sparse. Before the 1930s, when Congress took charge of public policy in this area, labour's rights had been decided mainly by court decisions which were much less liberal than those in Britain (Rimlinger 1977). Before 1931, the courts had issued some 10,000 anti-labour injunctions to prevent unions from committing specific acts of interference with employers' business and property rights. So-called 'yellow-dog' contracts, whereby an employee undertook not to join a union as a condition of employment, were enforceable in the federal courts as well.

The Depression of the 1930s was to have a major impact in altering the climate of public opinion and in promoting state intervention in support of union organisation and collective bargaining, to redress a serious and continuing imbalance of power. An important underlying assumption of the 'New Deal' was that unequal bargaining power between employers and unorganised workers (or weak unions) had not only encouraged labour unrest but actually aggravated the Depression, by reducing and destabilising wage rates and thereby restricting purchasing power. As a consequence of these changing public policy orientations, the first major and comprehensive piece of federal legislation to be applied to collective bargaining, the Norris–La Guardia Act (1932), gave protection to unions against court injunctions and yellow-dog contracts and a further 'balancing' law, the National Labour Relations (Wagner) Act of 1935, became the most important landmark in this field of American regulatory legislation. The law was henceforth to be used as a positive force in shaping bargaining relations between labour and employers such that the latter were required to bargain over specific subject areas. The extensive legal framework introduced by the Wagner Act established and protected employee rights to organise and bargain collectively by means of the banning of certain forms of management conduct as 'unfair labour practices' and it laid down the principle of exclusive representation,[5] whereby one union would serve as the sole representative for all employees in the designated bargaining unit, and 'majority rule' for selecting the representative.

The need to take administrative decisions on the selection of exclusive bargaining agents is partly a reflection of the fact that in North America competition and jurisdictional rivalries within the union movement have been heightened by the uneasy coexistence of craft and (later) industrial unions. Whereas, in those European countries where the main emphasis centres upon industrial unions the potential for inter-union conflict has been less. Even in Britain, where craft and general unions have coexisted, the willingness of unions to be jointly represented in collective bargaining has obviated the need for such decisions to select exclusive bargaining agents. In fact, the more general emphasis on detailed procedural regulation and administration of collective bargaining in the USA[6] than exists elsewhere may also be explained in terms of structural factors, in the form of a predominance of bargaining at the enterprise level. Regulation was required because the specific items of negotiation characteristic of this arrangement – determining effective employment conditions and involving a union presence within the enterprise – are more likely to produce disputes than European industry-wide bargaining on more general issues and minimum standards.

The fact that enterprise bargaining also takes place in Japan, yet largely without such external procedural regulation, does not invalidate this observation of an apparent relationship between decentralised bargaining and a high degree of state intervention. Japanese collective bargaining displays unusual characteristics as regards its late development in comparison with its western counterparts. Other notable features (as we saw in the last chapter) relate to the internalisation of skill acquisition within large firms and lack of entrenched and sharp occupational differentiation, together with the enterprise form of union organisation whereby most union officers are regular employees of the enterprise, or 'insiders', who are assigned to union business. Since most collective agreements are negotiated between an enterprise union and its responding enterprise, there was little cause to necessitate the involvement of government agencies (Shirai and Shimada 1978). Furthermore, because in this kind of decentralised structure – unlike that of the USA – issues were negotiated relating to enterprise workforces as single entities, such as general wage increases rather than wage structures as between sectional job groupings, there was less need for administering detailed collective agreements via external control (Levine 1980).

Finally in relation to the USA, and unlike some European countries (although not Britain), the absence of statutory authority to 'extend' collective bargaining agreements to non-signatory parties is also rooted in the US industrial relations structure. It is relatively easy to extend an agreement containing a limited number of minimum terms and conditions to encompass employers and workers at the economic and geographical limits of the industry, especially where such an agreement has been negotiated by an employers' association broadly representative of a large number of firms:

> In the United States, however, where rival unions may coexist in a single industry, where contract terms set actual rather than minimum requirements, and where provisions are highly complex and often vary from one firm to another, it would be very difficult to find a single set of terms that would be suitable in the industry.
>
> (Dunlop 1976: 238)

France

In contrast to both Britain and (more latterly) the United States, collective bargaining in continental Europe before the Second World War was less developed; and in France, certainly before 1914, it played a negligible role in the determination of wages and working conditions. In that country state action towards labour was especially repressive during the nineteenth century. Legislation forbidding worker combination, such as the Chapelier Act, although different in philosophical conception was similar in substance to British and American doctrines of common law conspiracy. But even when French labour laws were relaxed after the 1860s, recognition was accorded only to the right of association and not to the right (with an implicit obligation upon the employer) to bargain. Concurrently, however, state intervention began to appear at times of serious industrial conflict so that state agents in local areas (*préfets*) would not only seek to promote arbitration but also induce employers to negotiate. Moreover, in the big social crises, 'the [national] government intervened in order to settle conflicts whose intensity and violence could have had serious political consequences' (Sellier 1978: 218). Notably in 1936, after the election of a Popular Front government and widespread strikes for the right to organise and bargain collectively, the Matignon Agreement resulted in the promotion and extensive state regulation of collective bargaining and union rights in the enterprise. In effect, the government became the major party to collec- tive bargaining since it could convoke unions, and more particularly employers, to the bargaining table and it prescribed much of the subject matter of collective agreements.

Although the new legislation gave the 'most representative' unions at plant level the right to bargain (thereby tending to prevent the organisation of non-independent, company unions), it was actually the government – rather than the workers via a ballot, as in the USA – that determined which organisations were the most representative. Again, unlike US practice, the legislation on union recognition did not adopt the rule of the majority, since the most representative union might have only a minority of the organised workforce. Nor did it adopt the principle of exclusive union representation, largely because of ideological differences within the labour movement. Yet, for the first time, the coverage of agreements could be 'extended' to include companies not represented at the bargaining table. It would thereby compensate for the organisational weakness of employers' associations in sectors such as agriculture, commerce and textiles where – in a country whose economic development had been marked by slowness of industrial concentration – there were many small, non-affiliated establishments over which employers' organisations could exercise little authority. By means of this device, the terms of negotiated agreements could be elevated by government sanction from private contract to public regulation (Meyers 1981).

It has been contended by Sewell (1977) that the origins of the distinctive French interventionist and regulatory attitude by the state towards industrial relations may be partially ascribed to the Revolution and its attack on any form of private privilege. Since that time the state has retained an abhorrence for publicly recognised, voluntary associations which were unregulated because within the French context this necessarily smacked of privilege: 'In short, the French interventionist approach to labour relations reflects peculiarly French definitions of the limits of private and public spheres, definitions that automatically made the state a potential party to any agreements negotiated between employers and unions' (Sewell 1977: 229).

It is apparent from the above discussion that the distinctive methods developed for regulating industrial relations in Britain, the United States and France reflect basic social and economic differences and the respective power positions and strategic choices of the parties, together with a particular historical conjuncture of events. Similar influences may also be delineated in the very different regulatory approach which has evolved in Australia. The industrial relations system in that country (along with a similar, and even earlier, pioneering innovation in New Zealand) is unique within developed, market economies in that it has utilised conciliation and compulsory arbitration over an extensive time period as the major form of conflict resolution, with a government body as a direct participant in industrial relations rule-making processes. This applies not only to dispute settlements but also to the fixing of wages and working conditions by means of legally enforceable awards. We now turn to an analysis of the determinants of this particular form of state regulation.

COMPULSORY ARBITRATION IN AUSTRALIA

The Australian arbitration system employs third-party decision-making in the adjudication of substantive issues – unlike US labour law which, although it sets out detailed procedural rules for the conduct of bargaining and establishes the right to union recognition, does not usually prescribe what the results of those bargains should be. However, compulsory arbitration in Australia does not exclude, nor is it incompatible with, collective bargaining. On the contrary, its founders hoped that it would help to achieve the recognition of collective bargaining. As Walker (1970: 15) has expressed it, compulsory arbitration 'in effect granted the unions' demand for collective bargaining, but at the same time placed a check upon their power by restricting strikes'. In practical terms, where the parties arrived at agreement prior to a dispute being referred to arbitration, 'consent' awards could be applied for in order to give effect to the agreement.[7] As a result, agreements directly negotiated by unions might co-exist with, or take the place of, arbitration awards in a hybrid form of quasi-collective bargaining (Lansbury 1978a). Certainly, it would be wrong to characterise the Australian system as purely one of compulsory arbitration (Blain *et al.* 1987).

The historical determinants of this system relate particularly to the great strikes which occurred during the 1890s concerning the right of unions to bargain collectively in the face of a concerted attempt by employers to replace newly developing agreements in certain sectors of the economy, such as the pastoral (sheep-raising) industry as well as shipping and docks, with individually negotiated (non-union) contracts. Although compulsory arbitration had been under discussion for some years prior to these particular events, the savagery of the ensuing conflicts and utter defeat of the unions provided a backdrop for the introduction of a legalistic framework for handling industrial relations. As a direct heritage of its formative years this was to reflect 'an inordinate preoccupation with strike prevention and settlement' (Niland 1978: 27). One of the main objectives in establishing compulsory arbitration in Australia was to make strikes unnecessary, with the intention of protecting the public by avoiding a repetition of the dislocations to the economy occasioned by lengthy industrial stoppages. At the same time, with the unions' power to force employers to bargain collectively virtually eliminated, as a result of events which from their viewpoint 'epitomised desperation, defeat and disillusionment' (Cupper and Hearn 1981: 15), they recognised that political action in the form of government intervention would be needed to secure the benefits which industrial weakness had denied them.

The vital significance of these early conflictual events in giving a particular and distinctive direction to the Australian system[8] has been stressed by Isaac (1973). He speculates that had the strikes not occurred and collective bargaining been allowed to continue to establish itself, then the course of Australian industrial relations might well have developed more closely upon the lines of the British pattern. On the other hand, Phelps Brown (1959: 189) has suggested that although it had been decided by the late 1890s not to adopt compulsory arbitration in Britain, mainly because of the practical difficulty of enforcement where the unions were strong and might not accept its awards, nevertheless 'if disputes had been more costly in the 1890s, or the international outlook more threatening, or the unions passing through a phase of weakness, Britain might have come to it then'.

As regards Australia and New Zealand, however, it is worth noting the importance of environmental conditioning factors, as well as particular events, in facilitating the introduction of governmental arbitration. Both countries had small populations together with large agricultural and pastoral sectors which were at the heart of the economy. In New Zealand the predominance of small-scale industries and scattered and isolated communities were hardly conducive to the development of strong, well-organised unions. It was not surprising that the unions 'dissolved like snowflakes' in the face of a serious employer offensive, so that the labour movement then turned to political action (Roth 1974). In Australia, too, a pragmatic labour movement concerned with securing practical results was quite sympathetic to social reform via state action. Also, as Omaji (1993) has argued, compulsory arbitration in Australia institutionalised an already existing dependency of the industrial relations actors upon the state.

Arbitration as a method of centralised wage-fixing was also to utilise social and equity criteria in terms of setting a structure of basic wages providing for minimum needs together with a superstructure of largely historically determined differential margins for skills. It was the favourable economic circumstances of these countries which helped to ensure the viability of such a system. New Zealand had no industries manufacturing for export (except those processing agricultural produce) and therefore in competition with other manufacturers in foreign markets, and its home industries also had tariff protection against competition from imports (Hare 1946). Similarly, in Australia manufacturing employers were sheltered by tariffs from foreign competition and sometimes would be given full tariff protection only if the Commonwealth Arbitration Commission certified that their industries paid 'fair and reasonable' wages (Walker 1970). As a result, wage levels could be set broadly by the government with less regard to the profitability, or external competitive position, of the individual industries concerned.

It is clear from this consideration of the early development of public policy in a number of countries that some common features may be discerned in relation to its objectives, notably a desire to maintain industrial peace and the support of collective bargaining directed towards that end – with the timing of the measures frequently being determined by the occurrence of national crises. In this respect, the traditional concept of a public stake in industrial relations was a procedural one, to reduce the level of strike activity and the scope of industrial disputes 'lest an amalgamation of issues conflate into uncontrollable conflict that might damage at least the government's own standing and possibly civil peace as well' (Crouch 1991: 332). Strinati (1982) maintains, however, that fundamentally state intervention in industrial relations derives from the logic of capitalist development, in terms of the need to provide for the maintenance and continuity of production and capital accumulation, which in turn necessitates state intervention in the management of industrial conflict. Yet, as has been shown, considerable national variations are to be found in the ways in which the attainment of these objectives has been sought, according to the particular circumstances of individual countries.

Moreover, although the historical origins of government intervention were important in helping to determine the subsequent shape of cross-national industrial relations, including the structure of collective bargaining itself (Clegg 1976), the course of public policy in this area has been characterised by significant shifts of direction and, in some cases, a certain volatility over time, rather than following a unilinear course from suppression, to toleration, to encouragement. It has been particularly influenced by changing economic conditions which affect the balance of power in collective labour market relations, as well as by the political complexion of governments. Thus, on the basis of an examination of the evidence from a wide range of countries, Adams (1993) concludes, it appears likely that governments will choose to encourage unionisation and bargaining, for example, where: (1) a Social Democratic or Labour Party controls the government, (2) collective bargaining is considered to have positive consequences for economic growth, (3) bargaining is regarded as an effective and necessary means of conflict control, and (4) organised labour has a great deal of political influence. Also, to some extent, policy has been a reaction to the (sometimes unforseen) consequences of earlier government intervention. Some of these policy changes which have been introduced will now be examined.

CONSEQUENCES AND EVOLUTION OF PUBLIC POLICY MEASURES

In both the USA and Australia, two countries with extensive regulation where it had been decided that collective bargaining was underdeveloped, the objective of bringing the parties together via legislative measures and thereby forcing employer–union interaction and dealings was attained. Also, the expectation of a consequential marked increase in trade union growth proved to be well-founded. In the United States, the legal protection accorded to trade unions under the Wagner Act was undoubtedly a crucial factor in hastening trade union growth, with total membership increasing almost threefold between 1934 and 1939. The legislation was successful in encouraging collective bargaining and it underwrote the decentralised structure of agreements made at plant level.

In contrast, however, to government endorsement of private-sector unions during the period from 1935 to the 1950s (and of public-sector unions in the 1960s and 1970s), by the 1980s – in conditions of very high unemployment and increased international competition, particularly from Japan and the newly industrialising Asian countries – policy in the USA continued to move away from active encouragement of unionisation and collective bargaining, thus accentuating the trend towards more management power in industrial relations. Although the nominal policy of support was still retained, and there was no new suppressive legislation,[9] in reality the government neglected to enforce laws protecting workers from victimisation and dismissal when employers increasingly broke the law in order to escape from the strictures of collective bargaining. A conservative national government also effectively encouraged aggressive anti-union employer behaviour by breaking a strike of air traffic controllers and outlawing their union (Adams 1992a), it deregulated the transport industry (thereby increasing competition, and resulting in downward pressure on wages), and its appointees to the agency responsible for ensuring workers the right to organise – the National Labor Relations Board – instituted major policy changes that were unfavourable to unions (Wheeler 1987). Yet in Canada, the government has continued to give strong support to collective bargaining. Adams (1989) attributes the difference between the two countries to the differing nature of their political systems. In Canada, a viable political strategy adopted by the labour movement, in terms of its strong ties with the New Democratic Party, has forced the government to continue with support of favourable labour legislation – whereas the resistance of the Republican Party and (conservative) southern Democrats was sufficient to impede it in the USA.

In Australia, the regularisation of industrial relations together with the according of legitimacy to organisations of workers was also greatly facilitated by the introduction of the government-operated arbitration system. Since dealing with large numbers of employees who were not well organised might have swamped the federal or state arbitration tribunals with business, a first step was to require employees to be organised so that their representative body could be covered by a single award (Howard 1980). In this way the arbitration system created an institutional need for unions so as to promote administrative efficiency. Since it depended upon unions for its operation it was to prove a major stimulus to union growth (as shown in Chapter 2).

In terms of the level at which bargaining was conducted, unlike United States procedural legislation, Australian arbitration also helped to widen the bargaining unit and extend it even to an economy-wide basis in the case of federal awards on minimum wages and standard hours of work. Furthermore, as with the supportive legislation in the USA whereby what had previously been non-negotiable matters could be designated as 'bargaining issues', it also extended (although to a more limited extent) the scope and subject areas of collective bargaining, since the tribunals determined which claims were appropriate and therefore acceptable.

In the USA, favourable experience of legal support measures in terms of the results obtained had helped convert unions, including most of the older craft organisations, from a belief in the virtues of unbridled voluntarism (Flanders 1974). In Australia, however, the unions' attitude to the arbitration system remained more ambivalent. With around 300 employees' organisations covering a workforce of some six million, Australian unions are highly fragmented and the weaker ones (originally in the pastoral and manufacturing sectors) supported arbitration since they had much to gain. Unwilling employers could be taken to a tribunal whose award could be legally enforced. Yet some unions with strong bargaining power, due either to their strategic position or to more favourable economic circumstances consequent on a rising market, came to support a greater emphasis upon directly negotiated agreements. The object was to secure better wages and conditions from particular employers than could be obtained from tribunal awards. In fact, from the 1960s until the mid-1970s the relative importance of such direct agreements increased substantially, there was a movement away from centralisation, and more generally the tribunals themselves adopted a pragmatic approach in making awards which would prove acceptable by reflecting the unions' enhanced bargaining power under full employment (Isaac 1973).

Subsequently, the prominence and authority of the arbitration system became reasserted once more, against a changed background of large-scale unemployment and inflation in which privately negotiated 'over-awards' became more difficult to obtain from employers. In a country dependent upon foreign trade and investment, the economic crisis also prompted a changed government after 1975 to institute a shift from encouraging collective bargaining, to more stringent legislation penalising failures to abide by compulsory arbitration awards. Centralisation in wage setting was subsequently strengthened by the negotiation in 1983, between a new Labour government and the central trade union body of the Accord, similar to the social contract forms of incomes policy which have been developed in several European countries (see p. 126). In Australia, the policy was later modified, however, under economic pressures, towards a more decentralised basis and enterprise bargaining, in which additional wage increases became linked to greater workplace efficiency, i.e. a productivity-oriented policy. (Also, the Australian system of industrial relations is currently undergoing major changes towards fewer unions, organised along industry lines.)

Interestingly, in New Zealand the system of compulsory conciliation and arbitration introduced in the 1890s as the primary mechanism of industrial relations continued down to the 1970s without any significant change in philosophy or structure. In 1987, however, compulsory arbitration in the processing of disputes of interest was abandoned and a commitment made to a political philosophy of seeking to eliminate, or at least minimise, direct government involvement in disputes. These changes were introduced during a period of radical economic reform, on market-oriented principles, by a Labour government. Subsequent legislation by a

Conservative administration has withdrawn all exclusive rights previously accorded to unions, as well as encouraging the development of non-union bargaining agents and individual employment contracts (Hince and Vranken 1991). In fact, the 1991 Employment Contracts Act reverses almost a century of legislative development and attempts to reduce significantly the role played by collective organisation and union–employer negotiations.

Significant shifts over time in public policy towards collective bargaining have taken place, however, not only in the United States and in Australasia – in countries with a tradition of extensive state regulation – but also at the other end of the continuum, including Sweden after the unofficial strike wave in the 1960s. Most notably in Britain, a view shared by all the actors – that industrial relations are conducted most effectively and peacefully when unions and employers make their own voluntary arrangements – was not inviolate for all time. Although it set a pattern of continuity which was enduring for many decades it became modified in the early 1970s, largely under the exigencies of a relatively deteriorating national economic performance, towards a much more interventionist government strategy. In terms of underlying economic conditions, as Crouch (1991: 348) has observed:

> While organized labour was building new rigidities into the labour market, employers were seeking a new degree of flexibility to cope with unstable product markets. While unions were trying to protect declining industries, new patterns of international trade and the growth of the newly industrialized countries in the Pacific were rendering these industries hopelessly uncompetitive.

Following the election of a new and radical Conservative government in 1979, an abrupt shift in state policy occurred,[10] the implementation of which was made possible by union weakness within a context of a subsequent collapse of employment levels and much of manufacturing industry. This policy introduced a tough legal framework for restricting union freedoms and marked the final end of the 'voluntarist' tradition in Britain. Large parts of the public sector became privatised, and action was taken to reduce the institutional regulation of the labour market (by imposing minimum articulated conditions) in order to expose industrial relations more directly to market forces. Moreover, there was a gradual abandonment of the doctrine that union recognition by employers and the elaboration of bargaining procedures constitute 'good' industrial relations (Crouch 1991). Thus, the long-standing public policy of support for collective bargaining itself and the use of the law to bolster it were ended. Indeed, the new policy of 'market individualism' put the accent not upon the attainment of a 'balance' in industrial relations, but upon 'the individual' (Wedderburn 1988, 1989).

The redefinition of the role of the public sector together with greater control of public expenditure in Britain and other European countries has also put pressure on the state's own employees, via the restraint of public-sector pay levels for instance which have, on the whole in most OECD countries, fallen behind those of the private sector. This helps to explain the increased importance of public-sector issues in industrial relations in recent times. In Germany public employers are no longer 'model' employers guaranteeing stable and life-long employment (Jacobi *et al.* 1992) and in Belgium civil servants have been the main victims of the austerity policies of government (Vilrokx and Leemput 1992). Between 1984 and 1990 in New Zealand the Labour government undertook, as part of a wider programme of sweeping economic liberalisation, a programme of state restructuring 'that was remarkable for its scope, its speed and its ideological consistency' (Walsh and Wetzel 1993: 58). State agencies were privatised and a highly centralised, legalistic public-sector industrial relations regime was ended. Similarly, a traditional consensual and pluralist approach to industrial relations in this sector became largely discarded. More generally in the 1980s:

> The traditional notion of the state enterprise based on the public service employment model . . . with its exemplary wages and conditions and benign attitude to unions has been seriously challenged. . . . Governments are encouraging the development of more autonomous, commercially-oriented organisations in which a role for unions is no longer assured.
>
> (Frenkel 1990: 39)

An interesting example, however, of the unintended consequences which have sometimes resulted from government policy initiatives, together with the limitations of state intervention designed to make effective a previously weak and underdeveloped system of private-sector collective bargaining, is the case of France. Collective bargaining was initiated in that country with great difficulty because of employer resistance, partly in response to the radicalism of trade unions such as the CGT (Sellier 1978), and although legal intervention in the form of successive statutes took place over many years French collective bargaining continued to remain stunted. In the early 1980s, the new Socialist government therefore attempted to encourage the spread of collective bargaining, as the main means of regulation in industrial relations, as well as a greater commitment to it. Legislation was introduced (the Auroux laws) which included a requirement on employers to negotiate annually on pay levels with employee representatives at the enterprise level,[11] as well as enhanced powers for worker representatives. The aim was to institutionalise bargaining at the company level and revive unionisation by giving the unions an opportunity to obtain negotiated agreements and thereby enlarge their recruitment platform.

In the event, however, although the effect was to produce a big revival of company-level bargaining, 'accompanied by a new recognition of the legitimacy of union action on the shop floor' (Segrestin 1991), nevertheless union membership continued its precipitate decline. The failure of union membership to respond to such potentially positive influences of government policy may be attributable to a number of factors. As well as the offsetting, negative effects of high unemployment, because bargaining is now mandatory it will occur whether or not workers support unions and, within the French context of unionism with a markedly ideological orientation, a government mandate to bargain is not as beneficial for them as would be the case in the UK or USA where collective bargaining is the primary function of unions (Adams 1993).

Having examined the role of the state in establishing ground rules for the collective bargaining process we now consider a second major function, in the form of legislative provisions concerning the terms and conditions of employment.

REGULATION OF EMPLOYMENT TERMS

As well as legislation relating to procedural aspects of collective bargaining negotiations there are also cross-national differences in the extent to which countries provide statutory regulation of the substantive terms of the employment relationship. In all countries the state sets certain minimum standards in relation to areas such as occupational safety and health, but regulative legislation dealing with wages, hours and other major conditions is more uneven. In Britain and more especially in the USA, a greater reliance has traditionally been placed on collective bargaining than on legal enactment. In the latter country, substantive norms such as length of the working week, paid holidays, fringe benefits and health insurance, which elsewhere are often handled by legislation, are regularly dealt with through collective bargaining. Originally, in both countries, well-entrenched and self-centred craft unions relied upon autonomous employment regulations and opposed state intervention, fearing that it would weaken their strength and solidarity (Clegg 1976). Such attitudes have, however, long since been eroded and Lewis (1976) notes that in the case of Britain the unions had campaigned unsuccessfully up to the early years of the present century for the introduction of a legal minimum wage and maximum daily hours of work.[12] Yet statutory protection was not extended more widely than safety, health and welfare measures, largely because the unions themselves ceased to press for it. Instead, they came to rely increasingly upon the domain of collective bargaining as the single most important method for regulating their members' terms of employment since

> over a period of time employers were prepared to concede what Parliament denied, and consequently through experience unions became deeply attached to the efficacy of industrial negotiations over the method of legal enactment [although the two] were never regarded as mutually exclusive.
>
> (Lewis 1976: 8)

In the United States, the preference for collective bargaining over legislative enactment was also enhanced by its high payoff, in part as a result of a long-run scarcity of labour, strengthening workers' market power, together with rising productivity and real wages. At the same time, a split between federal and state levels under the US political system, as well as the willingness of the courts to declare unconstitutional legislation which was felt to hinder inter-state commerce, made it more difficult to obtain effective protective legislation (Edwards 1978). In contrast, in more recent years a good deal of regulatory legislation in the areas of equal pay, employment discrimination and pensions has been actively sought by unions and enacted. It would appear that as a means of obtaining their objectives the focus of US unions may now be shifting away from an overwhelming reliance upon collective bargaining, with its restricted and diminishing coverage, towards increasing support for the method of legal enactment. In this respect, the introduction of government wage controls in 1971 seems to have been a significant event since the unions 'learned the importance of a political counterpart to bargaining effectiveness' (Rosen 1975).

In continental European countries state regulation has played a greater part in determining wages, working conditions and fringe benefits than in either Britain or the USA and therefore the political process has assumed a critical role. This greater statutory emphasis ('juridification') derives in part from the close linkage of continental European labour movements with political parties, whereby legislation was seen as being able to provide universal benefits common to the working class as a whole. There was also an old tradition of state intervention and regulation in economic life. In the case of Germany, for instance, although the state had opposed the development of collective labour organisations, the social security policies of Bismarck (on insurance for health, accidents and old age), along with their sequel in the Weimar republic, created a system of protective legislation and welfare provisions for individual workers then unknown in other countries. At the present time, statutory norms provide a floor of minimum standards for German workers including wages, hours, vacations, job security and safety provisions which the unions have come to regard as a body of irreversible social rights (Günter and Leminsky 1978).

Kahn-Freund (1972) made the broad generalisation that regulatory legislation concerning the terms of employment has tended to prevail over collective bargaining where the political power pressure of workers exceeds their industrial power pressure, that is on issues which the unions have felt unable to resolve on their own account. Thus in the relatively favourable market conditions of pre-1914 Germany, the economic power of the unions was greater than their political power, whereas in the new political democracy established after 1918 the reverse was the case-so that they then relied to a greater degree upon legislative measures. Similarly, for France, Lange *et al.* (1982) notes the duality of focus of French unions which, having achieved only modest success in relation to their labour market objectives because of industrial weakness, looked to the political process through pressure on the state. Questions which might elsewhere become matters for collective bargaining have therefore been the object of politics, legislation and state regulation. Nevertheless, this contrast should not be overdrawn since the more recent growth of French collective bargaining implied that less was expected from government legislation and more from direct negotiations (Reynaud 1975). Also, the view that employment legislation and collective bargaining are necessarily alternative and competing routes to the achievement of labour's objectives often seems nowadays to be misplaced. They can be more usefully regarded as supplementary and mutually reinforcing since, as in both Germany and France, collective bargaining achievements may be incorporated into law, extended and passed on to labour as a whole.

As well as provisions concerning the substantive conditions of employment a further well-developed function of the state has been the establishment of procedures to assist in the resolution of industrial disputes, to which we now turn.

DISPUTE SETTLEMENT MECHANISMS

Negotiations of employment conditions presuppose the possibility of disagreements occurring. Even where an agreement has been concluded and relations between management and workers regularised at the level of the undertaking, grievances are inevitable. It therefore became recognised that third-party peace-keeping procedures would be both useful and necessary to help resolve disputes with a view to the avoidance of industrial actions. This could take place by means of judicial settlement via courts of law in the case of those agreements with legally binding rules, or by government-sponsored conciliation, mediation and voluntary arbitration for these and other categories of labour dispute.

In a number of European countries (Austria, Germany, Luxembourg, Switzerland and Scandinavia) the right to strike is circumscribed by the legally binding obligation to keep the peace during the life of a collective agreement whose terms are legally binding. In these countries an important distinction is drawn between disputes of 'right' and disputes of 'interest'. These are considered to be of a different order, in the belief that the problems arising in the negotiation and the application of a collective agreement – although closely related – are distinct processes requiring different procedures of settlement. 'Rights' disputes relate to the interpretation of the existing collective agreement and the parties may not resort to pressure tactics such as strikes and lockouts for resolving the issues. Instead, they must do so through negotiations or, in the last resort, by the binding decision of a specialist labour court which exists in most European countries (Aaron 1971). In contrast, interest disputes concern matters as yet ungoverned by law or contract, such as the negotiation of a new agreement or the renewal of an existing one. In these cases the parties may resort to industrial action once the old agreement has expired.[13] The issues involved here are regarded as being inappropriate for judicial settlement, whereas the making available of third-party conciliation or mediation devices are principal means to help ensure their peaceful settlement. Thus the 'peace obligation' during the term of the contract is central to this distinction between disputes of right and disputes of interest (Elvander 1974).

In the USA and Canada, although a similar distinction is observed, with conciliation and mediation procedures being used for helping to settle economic or interest disputes, the institution of the labour court does not exist. Instead, as a means of resolving rights disputes under the collective agreement there has evolved a unique system of private grievance arbitration – informal, yet binding, industrial jurisprudence – in which the arbitrators are jointly selected and paid for by the parties. This was a logical development since, unlike industry-wide bargaining arrangements in European countries, in North America the parties were immediately and closely involved in the administration and application of the collective agreement at local level. By way of contrast, in Britain no such rights/interest distinction is made. Indeed, it would scarcely be possible since the parties do not usually intend their agreements to be legally binding contracts and informal (unwritten) 'custom and practice' has often governed their more detailed terms. A further impediment relates to the unspecified and indefinite duration of many agreements, which made collective bargaining something of a continuous process in which differences relating to the interpretation of an agreement merge imperceptibly into differences concerning claims to change its effects (Donovan 1968).

A comparative study of dispute settlement mechanisms within the Nordic group of countries (Elvander 1974) maintains that the particular pattern of the state's conflict-resolving function is largely determined by a combination of historical factors of a political and economic nature (concerning the date and character of the industrialisation process), together with the resultant structure and power position of labour market organisations. In Finland the 1918 civil war helped to weaken and politically split the labour movement which, because of its reduced ability to participate constructively in conflict resolution, in turn facilitated state intervention. In contrast, Sweden differs from its Scandinavian neighbours in that the Basic (Saltsjöbaden) Agreement of 1938 between the central union and employer federations, whereby the negotiation of disputes became obligatory and the responsibility for preserving industrial peace rested with the parties themselves, had the effect (as was the intention) of obviating the need for extensive interventionist state legislation for conflict resolution. The defeat of the Swedish unions in the 1909 general strike was an event which had made them particularly hostile to all forms of state intervention in labour disputes, in contrast to the labour movements in Norway and Denmark which never experienced a setback of such proportions. However, the feasibility of reliance upon their own system of regulation was only possible because of the strongly centralising tendencies of the union and employer federations facilitated by the earlier development of large-scale, concentrated industry in that country.

Later industrialisation in Norway, which thereafter developed at a faster pace, led not only to industrial unrest but was also a factor in the labour movement's assumption of a more radical character and greater factional tendencies than occurred in Sweden and Denmark. This helps to explain the more active role of subsequent state intervention in disputes in that country (often in the form of compulsory arbitration), as compared with other Nordic countries. In the case of Denmark, a consequence of early and slowly developing industrialisation, with small-scale production units, was that the organisational structure of the labour movement assumed an aspect of a guild tradition expressed in the form of only a limited concentration of centralised power within the LO. In contrast with the other Nordic countries, there was a predominance of horizontal craft unions whose locus of internal power also resided less at the centre. Once again, the resultant splintered organisational structure impeded the achievement of self-regulation and helped promote the conferring of substantial powers upon the state's mediation system.

Although this particular comparative study is highly perceptive in its analysis of the effects of industrialisation and political factors, it neglects somewhat the consideration of possible market factor determinants, such as differing degrees of export-dependence among the various Scandinavian countries. These may also have been important variables in their own right in helping to shape industrial infrastructure and therefore the extent to which this facilitated the development of more, or less, powerful employers' organisations capable of assuming regulatory functions.

As well as the traditional 'background' role performed by the state in making provisions to assist dispute resolution in the bargaining process we have also noted that governments themselves have become increasingly involved in the outcomes of (particularly wage) bargaining, which we now need to consider.

GOVERNMENT INTERVENTION IN THE ECONOMY

Miliband (1969) has argued that in those instances where governments have felt it incumbent to intervene directly in disputes between employers and wage earners the result has tended to be to the disadvantage of the latter rather than the former, even though it may well have been done ostensibly in the name of the 'national interest'. This view strongly challenges pluralist interpretations of the role of the state which is seen as being by-and-large neutral in relation to the various (and competing) interest groups in society, merely holding the ring around them (Giles 1989).[14] In particular, the approach maintains that there is no third, separate element at the bargaining table representing the 'national' interest – according to which the interests of society as a whole are claimed to transcend narrow, sectional interests – since behind its everyday usage lurk distinctive material interests and, more precisely, class interests (Hyman 1982a).[15] The thrust of this standpoint is that the growth rates of western capitalist economies have deteriorated in more recent years, thereby reducing the margin for a 'positive-sum' resolution of industrial conflicts by means of the granting of economic concessions. Greater state intervention in indus- trial relations (especially in wage bargaining) has therefore appeared more attractive where governments became increasingly and actively involved in the management of economic affairs. Edwards (1986) takes the view, however, that the state itself is a 'relatively autonomous' actor in that it cannot be directly tied to the interests of capital, since it has to manage contradictory pressures (as well as conflicting demands from groups within the ranks of both capital and labour).

A major problem for governments in the earlier post-Second World War period was that the increased industrial strength of workers' organisations, consequent upon a long period of full employment, had given them more power to raise money wages. If these were passed on in price increases then foreign competitiveness would be impaired, and if they were not then profits (the source of capital accumulation) would tend to be squeezed. It was this problem which provided the spur to state action directed towards inducing, or compelling, trade unions to cooperate in a voluntary (or statutory) incomes policy so as to restrain money wage demands in collective bargaining (Panitch 1977).

One response of the state in dealing with the economic behaviour of trade unions was to develop a 'corporatist' or 'neo-corporatist' strategy, which 'integrates organised socioeconomic producer groups through a system of representation and cooperative mutual interaction at the leadership level and mobilisation and social control at the mass level' (Panitch 1980: 173). This typically involved the non-conflictual integration of central trade union and business organisations into tripartite economic planning bodies, directed particularly towards agreement on incomes policy programmes in which the unions became involved in the support and administration of wage restraint to their members. Propitious institutional conditions for such neo-corporatist concertation, as in Holland, Austria and Scandinavia, include a largely unified and centralised trade union movement with industrial unionism as the dominating organisational principle over more fragmented union structures. They also include Labour or Social Democratic governments with their typical institutional links, strong personal ties and ideological affiliation with the trade union movement (Keller 1991).

Corporatist structures can most clearly be identified in early postwar Holland (and to a lesser extent in Belgium) where the unions became integrated into incomes policy institutions for the formulation of national economic policy, and later in Germany where there was a long tradition of a corporatist legal framework aimed at checking conflicts of interests. In the latter country, a programme of 'concerted action' was instituted in the mid-1960s, concerned in principle with achieving congruence between the macroeconomic goals of state policy and those of the major collective organisations. In practice, the emphasis was upon moderating wage settlements to pay guidelines and with cooperation rather than conflict in industrial relations. Concerted action at the macro-level, seeking to harmonise socio-economic interests to help stem inflation and stabilise conflict, also became a key feature of industrial relations at certain periods in countries like Italy and Spain, as well as in Portugal, whose characteristics were not particularly conducive to this type of practice (Treu 1987b, 1989). It is also primarily a European phenomenon, although it has aroused interest and a limited development in some Latin American countries (Cordova 1987).

Corporatist arrangements were, however, characterised by instability, partly because union leaderships tended to be insulated from the rank-and-file and membership pressures at plant level therefore caused them on occasion to withdraw their cooperation – as in Holland and Germany. Also, where unions at national level became too strong for consensual policies with the state to be achieved then a form of 'bargained corporatism' (Crouch 1979) might be introduced. Here, union support for wage restraint requires that the government makes bargained concessions by way of improvements in items such as hours of work together with non-work issues relating to pensions and other social benefits. The best illustrations of this approach are the 'social contracts' negotiated in Britain and in the Netherlands during the 1970s, although there were also parallels in the Scandinavian countries, as well as in Austria, Ireland and Finland. The *quid pro quo* for restraint in nominal wage increases usually focused, by way of obtaining resources on the political market, on tax reductions, price controls and subsidies together with social policy measures and employment schemes (OECD 1979a).

Where, however, governments are not prepared to bargain with the trade union movement a policy alternative for the ordering of government–union relations is what has been termed 'neo-*laissez-faire*', or market liberalism. With this alternative, as characterised for instance by the Conservative governments in Britain after 1979 with an avowedly anti-corporatist ideology, trade union strength is pushed back and the outcomes of collective bargaining controlled not by compromises and agreements but by macro-economic measures such as strict money supply control and the level of unemployment, buttressed by selective pieces of industrial relations legislation (to restrict picketing, strikes and the closed shop, etc.).

In fact, corporatist arrangements have declined generally in Europe over the past decade and there is now far less convergence between countries in this respect. Although concertation has endured in Austria and in Sweden (until 1992) and there are still (qualified) corporatist tendencies in Ireland – as well as the new system of national consultation linking industrial relations and economic policy continuing into the early 1990s in Australia – concertation has declined in Belgium, Denmark, the Netherlands and Germany, and it is decidedly absent in Britain (Baglioni 1991). Part of the explanation for the decline has been the replacement in government of Labour and Social Democratic parties by Liberal–Conservative ones[16] 'which mistrust any sort of corporatist solutions since these are based on political mediation of interest rather than their preferred mode of regulation – the market' (Keller 1991: 85). Since corporatism thrives during periods of economic boom, persistent and much higher unemployment has significantly weakened unions' bargaining power so that there may be less need for governments to seek their cooperation in the macroeconomic sphere, i.e. pay restraint could be imposed through the market rather than negotiated through 'political exchange'. Structural factors also appear to have been important (Lash and Urry 1987), and include growing differentiation and fragmentation in the labour market and the associated economic pressures for decentralised flexibility, together with increasing internationalisation of the economy which, *inter alia*, tends to put pressure on national states to reduce deficit spending. Thus the state itself now has less resources than in the past to spend on supporting social pacts (Treu 1989). In the case of Spain, the dropping of social concertation by the mid-1980s occurred, in part, because it was believed to help maintain labour market rigidities, and thus impede rationalisation towards enhanced competitiveness.

In some cases, the tripartite macro-corporatist arrangements at national level have given way, under Liberal–Conservative programmes which concentrate upon the level of the firm, to what have been termed 'micro-corporatism' or 'productivity coalitions'. With this arrangement, 'cooperation with management and commitment to the firm's central goals are exchanged for greater job security and participation in strategic decision making' (Windolf 1989: 2). It is argued that these schemes may become increasingly important in the future, particularly at times of prolonged economic deterioration.

SUMMARY Conclust essay?

In this chapter we have examined the role of the state in providing a more, or less, comprehensive legal framework for industrial relations (dependent in part upon a country's own history and its national traditions) and in many cases making limited provisions relating to minimum wages, hours and working conditions. It has been shown that in the post-Second World War period the state became increasingly and actively involved in regulating the conduct of industrial relations, particularly with a view to influencing the outcome of negotiations. However, this trend towards increasing regulatory policies together with the management of the economy by an interventionist state now appears to be ending, although major cross-national diversities remain (Keller 1991). In many countries, the state has initiated policies towards the deregulation of parts of the existing industrial relations system, especially labour market deregulation, thereby opening it up to the free play of market forces, as in Britain, Belgium, Spain and, to a more limited degree, in both Germany and Italy. This has been in response both to pressure from employers for greater flexibility in forms of employment contract and with a view to creating more jobs – in the belief that greater employment will be created if real wages and employers' labour costs are allowed to fall without impediment. Although the long-term trend may be described as a movement towards more encompassing substantive rules, frequently imposed by the state in terms of legal intervention, at the same time it is also contended that the new industrial relations of the 1990s will likely be characterised by an increasing importance of procedural rules and regulations which permit greater 'flexibility' to managerial decision-makers (Keller 1991).

To the extent that governments follow strategies of deregulation and de-institutionalisation of the labour market, thereby emphasising greater individualisation of employment relations, it would appear that strong and highly centralised trade unions with legally formulated rights of collective bargaining, participation and codetermination (as in Germany, Austria and Sweden) are better able to resist such attacks than decentralised and weaker organisations with fewer formalised rights, as in the United States (Keller 1991). Existing legislation can be a 'relatively effective buffer against attempts drastically to change the [industrial relations] system' (Jacobi *et al.* 1992: 230). In the case of Italy, also, it is contended that the unions' position in the enterprise was protected (more than in, say, Britain), by the higher-level framework of legislation and central agreements which defined a structure of workplace representation (Ferner and Hyman 1992b). A further factor in the Italian case was the weakness of the state itself, which precluded a British-type Thatcherite legislative and political programme for curbing union power and bolstering managerial prerogative – with the result that more cooperative enterprise relations have been instituted since the late 1970s.

It has also been suggested that in general terms the role of the state in industrial relations may be viewed within the context of the need to permit the process of capital accumulation to continue, without disruption from industrial conflict, in order to promote the successful operation of the economy. However, the extent of state intervention as directed towards this end has varied considerably among countries, reflecting diversities in their own economic and political developments. In relation to the procedural aspects of collective bargaining, the degree of state regulation tends to increase as the prevailing level of negotiations moves closer to the workplace. This has been particularly apparent in the USA and Canada, but there has also been relatively detailed procedural regulation of relations between works councils and managements in Germany and the Netherlands.

In Britain during the earlier postwar period, the growth in militancy of powerful groups of shopfloor workers who were 'estranged from the control, influence and policies of the leadership of their official union hierarchies' (Strinati 1982: 203) was much more marked than in most other

European countries and it took place against the background of a weakening and undercapitalised economy. Thus state regulation increased in an effort to promote a more orderly system of industrial relations in which industrial conflict could more readily be contained.

The incidence and determinants of industrial conflict itself, as expressed mainly in strike activity, are examined from a comparative perspective in the next chapter.

FURTHER READING

There are useful general chapters on the state's role in Windmuller (1987) and Keller (1991), and on theoretical approaches in Adams (1992a) and Giles (1989). A recent analytical historical study across fifteen West European countries is Crouch (1993). Concertation practices in various countries are analysed in the special issue of *Labour and Society*, 12, 1987.

6 Industrial conflict and strikes

Some observers would contend that conflict, latent or manifest, is the essence of industrial relations (Barbash 1979) or, at least, most would agree that it is deeply rooted, enduring and an essential feature of the employment relationship:

> Conflict of interest between management and workers is an inevitable ingredient of the workplace – conflict between those who pay and those who are being paid; between those who give orders and those who are expected to obey; between those who make decisions and those who must live by them.
>
> (Summers 1991: 165)

Within the shifting complex of economic and technical forces in market economies, job security, the price of labour and control of its uses – power relations as exemplified in command and subordination – the conditions of production as well as its results, all these are sources of tension and latent conflict. In given circumstances they become manifest in one or more forms of overt conflict. In fact, the conflict universe encompasses both collective and individual responses, including not only strikes (concerted, temporary cessations of work) but sabotage, work slowdowns and boycotts as well as individual actions such as absenteeism and quitting. In Japan, for instance, the diverse, demonstrative forms of conflict incorporate 'sick-outs, leave taking . . . rallies, billboards, flyers, armbands, headbands [displaying union demands and other slogans]' (Levine and Taira 1980: 68). There are also distinctive patterns of industrial conflict found in Greece where, in the main, strikes are not used to apply sustained pressure upon employers during collective bargaining. Since Greek unions do not have the resources for such a trial of economic strength, they resort to a variety of 'cut-price' sanctions including short workplace stoppages, go-slows, working to rule, refusal to perform specific duties and sit-ins (Kritsantonis 1992).

In consequence, although strikes are usually the most visible and conspicuous expressions of industrial conflict, and in a country like the United States have dominated other forms of protest, they are not the only medium through which conflict of interests and values can be expressed.

CROSS-NATIONAL STRIKE DIFFERENCES

Despite their partial nature, strikes are frequently used in comparative studies as an index of conflict for which statistical data are readily available. In addition, the quantitative analysis of strike activity which proceeds via model building and testing techniques is sometimes regarded as being a particularly fruitful area for the development of theory, since it lends itself most readily to the use of formalised data (von Beyme 1980). An immediate problem, however, in the cross-national comparative analysis of strikes is not only that it may be of limited value, if industrial conflict takes diverse and uncorrelated forms between countries, but also the fact that the strike itself is not a homogeneous phenomenon. It can have different meanings and significance in different parts of the world, as well as fulfilling varying functions over the course of time. As Dunlop (1978: 7) has observed, it may be used 'as an organising device, a means of general protest, as a political demonstration, or it may be regarded as an integral part of the collective bargaining process used to induce agreement'.

In the United States, for instance, the strike, as the most typical form of labour dispute, is a pivotal aspect of the union–management relationship and a major component of the collective bargaining process when an impasse has been reached (although this is not true in the public sector where strikes have generally been prohibited in favour of third-party procedures to resolve a negotiating impasse). Because, in an unorganised plant, a union has to win an election contest in order to gain recognition rights from the (often unwilling) employer an adversary position is encouraged from the outset, so that 'in a real sense a conflict situation is the midwife of almost all new American unions' (Kassalow 1977: 120). In Germany, unlike the position in Belgium or Italy (until the 1990 law on disputes in essential services) where in principle the strike has been subject to no legal regulation, only strikes called by unions within the collective bargaining context (upon the expiry of a collective agreement) are legalised. 'Political', as well as solidarity and sympathetic strikes, are generally illegal. Thus, Maurice and Sellier (1979) have characterised the strike in Germany as being a 'legal bureaucratic phenomenon' called upon the authoritative decision of the union to set it in motion and support it financially. In the case of Japan, however, the strike performs a somewhat different role and is not the final weapon in collective bargaining, or the most usual form of labour dispute. Frequently, it will be called at the onset rather than the breakdown of negotiations (before any bargaining has taken place) to warn employers and demonstrate the union's seriousness about its demands, as well as the extent of union membership support and solidarity. It will typically be carried out with the employees remaining at the work-site, and thus resembles the sit-down strikes found in some western countries (Hanami 1979).

In contrast to such purely collective bargaining orientations of the strike, the situation in countries such as France and Italy may be distinguished. Here, capital–labour interactions have often been determined more by 'raw' power relations than in the more mediated, institutionalised systems (Ferner and Hyman 1992a), with the strike fulfilling other additional functions. It has been contended that, in France strikes are a 'charismatic' phenomenon (Maurice and Sellier 1979) and that more generally within the Latin countries, as manifestations of worker protest, they often possess a 'mystical quality' (von Beyme 1980). The right to strike has been enshrined in the constitution both in France and Italy, being a human right belonging to a political tradition and comparable to freedom of speech and association. In the pre-Second World War period in France, when employers would not generally accept unions for bargaining purposes, one prime objective of strikes appears to have been to compel public intervention in order to make recalcitrant employers more pliable (Shorter and Tilly 1974). In the postwar period strikes in that country could also assume an enlarged role as a symbolic protest, as 'displays of power and organisational ability' (Crouch 1978), to impress the strikers' case upon decision-makers in the legislature. Similarly, in Italy strikes were often regarded less as a means of winning specific economic demands than as an exercise in mass mobilisation and propaganda (Kendall 1975) – given the complex interconnections between politics and industrial relations in that country and where the general strike has been a traditional vehicle of political protest.

Instead of treating strikes as an incident in the bargaining process, the orientation of this kind of approach views them within a wider context as having an important role in broader societal struggles for power, whereby industrial conflict itself assumes a larger, socio-political significance. Nevertheless, as we will show, this interpretation within the French context is more applicable to certain kinds of strike undertaken at particular periods of time, rather than to all strike activity. It would, perhaps, be more accurate to say that in France a 'strike' covers a whole range of different phenomena. It can be a symbolic expression of protest, as with political strikes directed against unfavourable government decisions for instance, whereupon union members have frequently marched and demonstrated in the streets of Paris. But equally, in more recent years, it has also been concerned with enterprise-related issues such as wages and conditions. Similarly, in Italy some recent stoppages have been interpreted as reflecting a change in the character of the strike, from a vehicle of popular mobilisation to an instrument of competitive inter-group conflict, by way of restoring pay differentials for craft and professional workers (Ferner and Hyman 1992b).

As well as such differences in the functions and significance of strikes, viewed from a comparative perspective, there are also marked variations between countries in the forms which they assume, as well as their levels and trends over both the short and longer terms. These require an appreciation of the complexities and limitations of published strike data, since strike statistics can be used to develop different kinds of argument:

> as indicators of social and industrial change, as an attempt to test theories – of corporatism, of the labour movement, of the role of the economic environment . . . and as part of a political debate about the state of a country's industrial relations compared with others.
>
> (Eldridge *et al.* 1991: 133)

INTERNATIONAL STRIKE STATISTICS

Because strikes are a highly complex social phenomenon, there are not only problems in adequately explaining their causes, but also in measuring their magnitude. Strike activity may be measured in various ways, although most countries record three basic series of data on industrial disputes, namely the number of strikes (and lockouts), the number of workers involved and the number of working days lost (i.e. number of workers involved times duration of the strikes in working days). Significant differences exist, however, between countries in the criteria which are used to determine whether a particular work stoppage will be included in their officially recorded statistics. Considerable caution is therefore required in making detailed international comparisons since the differences in coverage vary enormously and may, in part, explain why a given country appears to have a better, or worse, record than another country (Bird 1991). For instance, the minimum size criterion for inclusion in the strike statistics varies on an inter-country basis from Austria, Italy, the Netherlands and Japan, where there are no restrictions on size, to the United States where not only has the duration of a dispute to last for more than one day (as is also the case in Sweden, France and Switzerland), but also – since 1981 – the dispute needs to involve more than 1,000 workers.[1] Some countries, such as Germany and Canada, exclude working time lost by those workers who are indirectly involved in a work stoppage, that is those unable to work because others at their own workplace are on strike, whereas other countries attempt to include such workers, for instance the Netherlands, New Zealand and the USA. 'Political' strikes are not included in the figures for the UK and the USA. Furthermore, some countries exclude the effects of disputes in specific industrial sectors. Thus in France, Portugal and Belgium, public-sector strikes are omitted (resulting in increased un-reliability of the official statistics as an indicator of strike trends, given the growing importance of public-sector disputes in recent years), and Japan also excludes working time lost in unofficial disputes.

With these observations in mind, Table 6.1 shows a comparison of industrial disputes for a number of OECD countries for which data are available, recorded according to the countries' own definitions, using ten-year averages (to smooth the effects of any particular, extreme years) for the decades of the 1970s and 1980s. Because differences in industrial structures within countries may also explain, in part, variations in their strike incidence, in order to reduce this effect the table shows cross-country comparisons for a group of selected industries which are especially dispute-prone. The measure used is the number of working days lost per 1,000 employees (standardised to take account of the number of workers in each country), since this measure is the least vulnerable to problems of reliability and validity, as it is less sensitive than the number of strikes to variation among different countries in criteria for inclusion (Jackson 1987). It is less likely to be distorted, since it is principally affected by large-scale stoppages which are more likely to be recorded whatever the statistical system used.

It is clear that there are marked differences in the incidence of industrial disputes as between countries, with the Netherlands, Germany, Sweden and Norway experiencing a relatively low incidence of working days lost, whereas Greece, Canada, Finland, Australia and Spain had a high incidence. In the case of Greece and Spain, Ferner and Hyman (1992a: xxix) comment that 'the heritage of authoritarian dictatorship remains relevant, with weakly institutionalised bargaining institutions and a con-tinuing tradition of politicized mobilisation and contestation'. In com-parison with the 1970s, however, as Table 6.1 indicates, there was a general decrease in the incidence of working days lost in most countries during the 1980s (albeit by differing proportions), although in Norway and Sweden it was somewhat higher. Not only may strike activity have been generally dampened by the effects of a harsher and more competitive economic environment, which reduced union bargaining power, along with the effects of increasing unemployment and declining unionisation and in some countries the policies of Conservative governments, but also possibly

Table 6.1 Industrial disputes: working days lost per 1,000 employees in selected industries,* 1970–9 and 1982–91 (annual averages)

	1970–9	1982–91
Greece	na	4,470
Canada	1,840	850
Australia	1,300	570
Spain	1,240	650
Finland	1,150	470
UK	1,090	610
Denmark	580	330
Norway	90	170
Germany (FR)	90	50
Netherlands	80	40
Sweden	40	90

Source: *Employment Gazette*, December 1991: 656; December 1992: 611. (Since 1987 strike data for Canada have had a threshold of 500 workers.)

*Mining and quarrying, manufacturing, construction, transport and communication

as a result of new institutions of dispute resolution. These include, particularly, new structures of workplace representation whose effect could be to reduce discontent arising from intra-firm restructuring of production (Ferner and Hyman 1992a).

At the same time, however, there was also a significant increase in the 1980s of labour disputes in the public sector in a number of countries (Shalev 1992), as in France, Spain and Britain (although not in Germany). Government restraints on public-sector pay in the interests of reducing public expenditure, together with attempted rationalisation of the public sector itself and its existing work organisation, as part of the drive towards greater efficiency and flexibility, have created new scope for conflict. The resultant sectional grievances of particular groups of the workforce have been exploited, in Italy and France especially, but also in Britain and elsewhere, by the development of rank-and-file organisations, and in Spain and Italy by the growth of autonomous unions among groups such as airline pilots and train drivers (Ferner 1991). Furthermore, a relatively slow development of dispute procedures within the public services generally may also help to explain the increased incidence of labour disputes in that sector (Ozaki 1987).

As a further basis for the international comparison of work stoppages, particularly where the strike 'profiles' of countries differ as between the three basic measures themselves, a number of additional, derivative

Table 6.2 Strike profiles, 1961–85* (annual averages)

	Frequency	Breadth	Duration
Belgium	4.9	19.4	10.3
Netherlands	0.7	4.8	4.2
UK	9.8	80.0	4.9
Ireland	15.8	49.1	12.5
Italy	24.1	492.7	2.5
France	18.1	110.6	1.7
Norway	0.9	5.5	11.4
Sweden	2.1	14.9	5.9
Denmark	7.0	41.3	5.5
Canada	8.9	44.6	15.5
USA	6.2	27.0	16.6
Australia	44.1	210.7	2.3

Source: ILO, *Year Book of Labour Statistics* (Geneva, 1962–86), for industrial disputes and number of wage and salary earners

*For Belgium the measures are calculated up to 1979, for the USA to 1980, and for France and Italy to 1982, since the compilation of the series changes in subsequent years, or data are unavailable. (There are also no officially recorded statistics for the number of strikes in Germany.)

statistics are often calculated. *Frequency* is the number of work stoppages per 100,000 employees, *breadth* (or participation) is the number of workers involved in disputes per 1,000 employees and a proxy measure for *duration* (or length) is the number of working days lost per worker involved. These measures, calculated over a twenty-five-year period for a number of advanced industrial economies, are shown in Table 6.2.

Utilising these sort of measures, von Beyme (1980) has distinguished three broad typologies of conflict behaviour within capitalist countries. (Some disaggregation within the categories may be necessary, however, because particular countries can display divergent traits.) The 'West European' type is distinguished by a large number of relatively short, although widespread, strikes. It is recognised, however, that this type requires further differentiation, as is clearly indicated in Table 6.2. It is also argued that within this category political motivation often plays an important part, in addition to questions relating to income distribution, since strikes may be symbolic or undertaken to exert pressure upon political bodies. Second, a 'North European' type has been delineated. There the number of strikes tends to be low, although they are of short duration. Also, Social Democratic parties have been influential and there is a long tradition of negotiation by the labour movement with political bodies, as in the Scandinavian countries and to some extent in Germany. Finally with the 'North American' type, strikes are relatively frequent and notably long-lasting, but are used predominantly for economic purposes (with political influence being exerted mainly via organised lobbying). They are also mostly constitutional and official.

Not only are there cross-national differences in the level and patterns of work stoppages, but also divergences in the trend of strikes over the longer term. From 1900 to 1972, for instance, strike activity in Canada, France, Italy and the United States either increased or fluctuated around a constant mean level. Yet it decreased to negligible amounts in Denmark, the Netherlands, Norway and Sweden (Hibbs 1978).

In the light of these preliminary considerations, we may ask what accounts for such differential levels and cross-national patterns of strike activity in western countries? A number of general explanations have been put forward which, although they include several variants, may conveniently be grouped into four major categories. These comprise, first, institutional approaches, which relate particularly to collective bargaining arrangements, in terms of structural dimensions and the efficiency of procedures for dispute resolution in different countries. Second, there are 'organisational-political' theories, emphasising the capacity of labour to mount strike action, together with an insistence that collective bargaining must be seen as an intervening variable within the context of wider and longer-term societal changes in the political power relationship. A third and more recent approach centres upon the workplace level and may be termed a (micro) 'politics of production' approach. It concentrates on the struggle for control at the workplace and suggests that 'the tools used to generate and resolve day-to-day disputes between unions and employers in different countries may hold a hitherto untapped power to explain different patterns of industrial conflict' (Haiven 1991). Fourth, there are explanations embedded in prevailing economic conditions and primarily applicable to short-run variations in the frequency of strikes. The salient features of each of these perspectives need to be considered in turn.

We begin with the approach which maintains that strike activity is not independent of institutional arrangements in that, although conflict may be inevitable, 'the particular structure and process of bargaining play a major role in determining the extent to which this conflict can be settled short of strike action' (Kaufman 1982: 482).

INSTITUTIONAL EXPLANATIONS

A general link has been postulated between the nature of the industrialisation process and patterns of worker protest and reaction, as manifested in strike action. Strikes are expected to peak during the early stages of industrialisation as a result of protests against the difficult adjustments required of the labour force in moving from traditional society to the discipline and pace of industrial production (Kerr *et al.* 1962). Thereafter, as industrialisation evolves, the amount of worker protest tends to decline. Emerging worker organisations control spontaneous protest expressions and they themselves become accommodated within the system. Institutional mechanisms of negotiation, such as collective bargaining and grievance procedures, are set up to resolve industrial relations differences so that, although conflict continues to exist within the employment relationship, its magnitude is reduced and it assumes a less open form.

There are, however, severe doubts about some aspects of this particular line of argument. It cannot explain why heightened strike activity is marked by discontinuous phases, and strikes may not peak in the early stages of industrialism if workers are insufficiently mobilised for collective action. Moreover, at the empirical level, it has been shown that in the United States and a number of other countries there has been no tendency for strike activity to decline. Instead, the outstanding feature of American strike levels has been their 'long term constancy with measures of worker involvement and duration showing no general upward or downward trend' (Edwards 1981: 51). Nevertheless, the 'institutionalisation' thesis itself has remained an important strand in the comparative literature on strike activity. It was originally used by Ross and Hartman (1960) who sought the determining influences on relative strike activity, within fifteen countries over half a century, in aspects of their industrial relations systems. They emphasised the reduction in organisational, and to some extent economic, influences on conflict as a consequence of the acceptance of trade unions by employers, mutual accommodation and the resultant institutionalisation of collective bargaining. Centralised bargaining systems, in particular, would contain or reduce the level of industrial conflict, since worker and employer organisations are enabled to impose real behavioural constraints upon their respective memberships. In essence, it was postulated that countries with stable and unified union movements, accepted by employers and locked into centralised and well-developed collective bargaining machinery, were those which would enjoy the greatest peace in industry. High strike activity in Italy and France (Mediterranean pattern), therefore, could be explained largely in terms of low levels of unionisation, a union movement riven by disunity and internal factions and one mainly un-recognised by employers – resulting in weak and unstable labour–management relations. By way of contrast, the much lower strike propensities in Scandinavian countries (northern European pattern) were attributed to the facts that their labour movements had firm and stable memberships and that collective bargaining, which became institutionalised early in the present century, had become well consolidated and centralised.

More generally, the greater incidence of industrial conflict in the United States (North American pattern), in broad comparison to that in many European countries, has also been explained as a function of the level and scope of collective bargaining (Kassalow 1977). The wide coverage of collective agreements in Europe is seen as encouraging more consensual tendencies. Bargaining along a broad industry front lowers the negotiating stakes in line with the ability to pay of marginal producers, thus reducing the potential resistance of many firms. In addition, less of a direct challenge to job control and managerial prerogatives at plant level is involved. The very extensiveness of industry- (or region-)wide negotiations may inhibit bargainers from allowing bargaining to break down because of the more widespread effects of any ensuing strike, particularly where negotiations are economy-wide as has been the case in Sweden. In the United States, on the other hand, conflict becomes exacerbated by decentralised bargaining since strikes involve crucial and fundamental battles over the control of the workplace (Edwards 1981). In consequence, employers have been more hostile to unions which have frequently been unable to establish a permanent and stable position (i.e. the thrust of this position is that industrial relations in the USA have been less than fully institutionalised).

Furthermore, Kassalow argues that generally in Western Europe because of a considerable dependence upon international trade the parties have always appreciated the importance of exports for their economies' well-being, a fact which is also used as one explanation for the lower strike propensity of many European countries in comparison with the United States. Streeck (1988) has pointed out that Germany, for instance, is the world's largest exporter of manufactured goods and, in consequence, its economy is highly exposed to world market pressures. Hence, it is only against this background that the high degree of stability and mutual co-operation in German industrial relations can be understood. Yet the importance of this particular factor can be overstated, since severe export dependence did not prevent rising levels of industrial conflict in a country like New Zealand, which were actually concentrated in the export-related sectors of the economy (Korpi and Shalev 1979).

Clegg (1976) has also put forward an institutional theory to account for the varying status and dimensions of strikes, based upon evidence from six major industrial countries (Australia, France, West Germany, Sweden, the UK and the USA). He contends that strike patterns are closely associated with the structure of collective bargaining in each country in terms of the bargaining level and disputes procedures, together with the indirect effect of the level of bargaining through factional competition within trade unions. Thus the relatively high proportion of union-sanctioned, 'official' strikes in the United States is explained by the predominance of plant-level bargaining. With this form of bargaining structure a strike can be called at relatively little cost to the membership as a whole in terms of the payment of strike benefit, because only a limited number of workers need be called out. Thus strikes can be called in particular plants without bringing out all the workers from an entire industry (as in, say, the Netherlands) or region (as in Germany). Clegg also regards the extent and development of disputes mechanisms and procedural norms within a country as important dampening influences, especially in reducing the number of unofficial strikes, since these devices function as an alternative to striking during the currency of the agreement. Comprehensive procedural arrangements in Sweden are seen as helping to explain the relative infrequency of strikes in that country,[2] whereas their absence in France have been associated with a high strike incidence. In Italy, increased institutionalisation and a trend towards greater 'proceduralisation' over the last decade appear to have contributed to a reduction in conflict (Ferner and Hyman 1992b). In the case of Germany, the substitution of the works council (with a statutory peace obligation) for union 'in-plant' bargaining may also have helped reduce the level of stoppages – although possibly at the price of reducing the employees' degree of job control at the point of production (Kendall 1975). Finally, high strike activity can, according to Clegg, be partially related to factional competition both within and between trade unions, being particularly marked in the USA but not in Sweden or Germany. For internal political reasons, a successful strike is a means of impressing sections of the union's membership, or potential membership, and securing their allegiance. In Clegg's theory, therefore, differences in strike levels and patterns across countries are related mainly to the institutional structure and characteristics of collective bargaining.

Infrastructural variations

A somewhat different institutionalist line of approach is that adopted by Ingham (1974) in his comparative study of industrial conflict in Britain and Scandinavia, of which Sweden is taken as the main example. His analysis goes beyond identifying and relating salient differences in bargaining structures between countries to their respective levels of conflict, since he attempts to explain the detailed origins of the institutional arrangements themselves. His thesis is that institutional variations in industrial relations systems depend primarily upon differences in the industrial infrastructure, that is to say economic structure and mode of production of the countries concerned. The dominant features of contemporary industrial relations are seen as being crucially influenced by the yearly stages of the course of industrialisation in the countries investigated. Three particular dimensions of infrastructure are selected as being the most relevant to the development of industrial relations systems: the extent of industrial concentration, the degree of product differentiation and specialisation, and the complexity of technical and organisational structure.

The first determinant, a high degree of industrial concentration in which output in the major sectors of the economy comes to be dominated by a small number of large concerns, is particularly apparent in the case of Sweden. In that country the small size of its own domestic market meant that, in the late nineteenth century, expansion had necessarily to be geared to foreign demand in export markets. The highly competitive nature of the export sector tended to force out smaller, inefficient firms, leaving a markedly concentrated industrial structure. This particular aspect of infrastructure, in turn, affected industrial relations. Since the various industrial sectors had become dominated by a small number of large firms operating within oligopolistic market structures, characterised by low levels of price competition within and between the sectors, Ingham argues that collective organisation among employers was facilitated. Strong, centralised employers' organisations could be established leading to the growth of formal institutions for the regulation of conflict since, if necessary, the employers' body was sufficiently powerful to be able to impose such regulation. In this exposition, therefore, a crucial role in the development of institutional regulation in industrial relations is attributed to employers. By way of contrast with Sweden, in nineteenth-century Britain there existed a large, diversified and highly competitive home, as well as overseas, market which was supplied by a preponderance of smaller and medium-sized firms. The result was less commonality of interest among (more fragmented) employers, so that combination to form strong, centralised institutions was far less possible than in Scandinavia.

As well as the effects of industrial concentration, a second, and related, source of infrastructural variation concerns the degree of product specialisation within an economy. In this respect, Ingham (1974: 42) suggests that:

> those societies which were among the first to industrialise and which possess large domestic markets have tended to produce a wider range of goods than smaller countries which successfully industrialised later to a large extent through the export of highly specialised products.

This particular dimension also helps determine the capacity of a society for developing centralised institutions for the regulation of conflict. In Sweden, the crucial significance of exports dictated the production of a small range of products (ballbearings and other specialist engineering products) for highly specialised markets, and therefore a relatively un-differentiated industrial structure. In the case of Britain, product diversity and differentiation – by producing a vast range of goods for both domestic and foreign markets – were added to the industrial infrastructure during the last century, thereby inhibiting the development of formal and centralised regulatory organisations.

A third important feature of industrial infrastructure is the complexity of the production system itself, which affects the structure of the trade union movement. A country such as Britain, which was the first to industrialise, tends to have a complex production system. It has passed through and incorporated a number of different technological and organisational phases, beginning with a craft and workshop technology, moving through mass production and ultimately on to automated systems. The effect of this structural development upon the labour force is to produce a vast range of occupational skills and specialisms and, correspondingly, a large number of highly differentiated trade unions organised along occupational lines in order to cater for them. Such a structure precipitates sectionalism and conflicts of interest within the labour movement, thus reducing cohesive-ness, solidarity and the growth of powerful central union bodies.

As a contrasting development, industrialisation took place in Sweden at a later date and could therefore take immediate advantage of factory production technology. Because craft-based workshop technology never became predominant in its manufacturing industry the Swedish labour movement developed a more unified and homogeneous structure, and workers soon became organised principally on an industrial union basis. These factors made it easier for the central union organisation (LO) ulti-mately to assume a strong degree of control over its affiliated unions. The authority of the LO was also reinforced since its permission has been required before major strikes can be called (in order to secure access to the central strike fund), and it has the right to be present at industry-level negotiations. (More recently, however, Fulcher (1988) has argued that Sweden's late industrialisation made possible the emergence of a unified labour movement not because technical development had undermined skill divisions, but because of political influences, in that a unifying socialist ideology was available by that time. By contrast, in Britain labour became organised, on the basis of strong craft unionism, before a socialist move-ment had emerged.)

In Ingham's exposition these structural tendencies within the labour movement complement the centralisation achieved on the employers' side and further reinforce the institutionalisation of conflict. It would appear, however, that the main credit for the greater adherence to agreements in Sweden belongs to the employers' side (Clegg 1976). Employers have been less prepared than their British counterparts to make concessions at local level which overrode agreements, because of the stronger discipline within Swedish employers' bodies. As a result of these factors, open conflict is more inhibited in Sweden because it becomes channelled through the highly developed and formalised institutional framework.

A subsequent study by Waters (1982), along similar lines, contends that the mode of production and accompanying structure of industrial society are the main generators of different patterns, or 'shapes', of strikes in capitalist societies. His model, which focuses upon the identification of a number of historical phases (accompanied by particular patterns of conflict) in the process of industrialisation, is developed against the background of Australian experience, although its general outlines are also applied to Sweden, the USA, Britain and France. He distinguishes craft, mechanised factory, assembly line, and service and automated production phases, each of which is characterised by a specific mode of production organisation, and with strikes increasing at the opening of each of the four production phases. Franzosi (1985) has observed, however, that if strike activity is mainly related to modes of production, internal to any given country and corresponding to successive stages of economic development and industrialisation, there would be no reason to expect peaks in strike activity in Australia to coincide with similar peaks in other countries at very different stages of economic development. Yet the timing of these does overlap with the major strike waves of other western countries.

In fact, theories which purport to account for variations in particular dimensions of strike activity as between countries by means of differences in the social organisation of production, have been subjected to some further criticism. In particular, Ingham's explanation of the institutional contrasts between Britain and Sweden, in terms of differences between their economic substructures, is somewhat problematic in relating these divergences to trends in industrial conflict. It can be misleading to draw too sharp a contrast between the flourishing of the strike in postwar Britain and its decline in Sweden, since in the latter country the frequency of unofficial strikes increased significantly after the late 1960s (Korpi and Shalev 1979). It may be the case that strike reduction in Scandinavia has been of a cyclical, rather than secular, nature. That Ingham exaggerates the amount of control over wage negotiations exercised by the central institutions in Sweden is also evidenced by the amount of 'wage drift' which occurs at plant level, outside the control of the central organisations. Furthermore, the analysis is essentially in terms of an assumed mechanistic relationship, with no account of the processes which may mediate the effect of infrastructural considerations upon actual behaviour (Jackson and Sisson 1976). It has also been pointed out by von Beyme (1980) that this approach – if extended beyond Britain and Scandinavia – does not explain for instance why Canada, with a similar level of concentration to Swedish industry, has a high strike incidence[3] whereas Germany, towards the lower end of the concentration scale, has been relatively strike-free.

As regards Sweden, the main difficulty, however, for the thesis relating changes in the long-term number of disputes to the growth of institutions for the regulation of conflict concerns the timing of the respective changes. Korpi (1980) has shown that as early as the first decade of the present century Sweden had some well-developed institutions for containing and regulating conflict, yet the level of disputes was not reduced at that period. Rather, along with Norway, man-days lost continued to be the highest in the western world. The dramatic change to very low relative dispute levels came suddenly in the mid-1930s. Korpi contends that although institutions are significant, they must not be taken as being the primary cause of any substantial decrease in manifest conflict. In the case of Sweden the decisive changes in the level of conflict manifestations appear to lie elsewhere, outside the orbit of the industrial relations institutions themselves. He claims that the explanation is to be found in political changes, in the coming to power of the Social Democrats in 1932 and their remaining in office for many years subsequently. This gave the unions political options in the form of access to political and legislative power, with the result that there was then less need to fight costly battles in the industrial sphere. Political means had become available for securing a more favourable distribution of economic rewards since 'to the extent that labour is successful in acquiring control over political institutions it can exercise its power through these means and will not be limited to the industrial arena' (Korpi and Shalev 1979: 170). At the same time, the political power resources of Swedish employers became correspondingly depleted in that they could no longer rely on having a friendly government to intervene on their behalf, as and when necessary. Thus, as with the labour movement, a change also took place in the employers' conflict strategy. It was decided to seek an accommodation with the LO with a view to promoting economic growth. By renegotiating their interrelations in this way, conflict of interest might be converted from a 'zero-sum' to a 'positive-sum' type, to enable both parties to improve their positions – even if their relative shares did not change very much.

In summary, critics of the institutionalisation of conflict thesis would maintain that although it can be a valid explanation of the form and type of conflict as expressed through strikes, it overstates the role and importance of industrial relations institutions themselves in accounting for inter-country diversities in the levels of industrial conflict. On this view, institutional arrangements for conflict resolution should be seen more as intervening, than as independent, variables affecting the level of conflict. It is too facile to identify the institutional framework as the major cause of any decrease in overt conflict levels. Rather, the institutional arrangements themselves reflect, and are dependent upon, the power structure of society, as well as on changes therein. Therefore, for Korpi the development of such institutions, together with any accompanying decline in conflict levels, are jointly attributable to a third variable – the underlying differences in power resources between the contending parties. That is to say:

> the extent of dissatisfaction with inequalities in work-related rewards will depend on the aspiration level of the workers, which in turn can be expected to reflect their power position in relation to the employers. If the power position of the workers continues to improve, this can be expected to affect their social consciousness and to generate a desire for improvements.
>
> (Korpi 1978a: 47)

In this respect, it is widely recognised that an emphasis solely upon structural determinants of industrial conflict is insufficient, since it is also necessary to consider attitudes and consciousness. Workers respond not simply to the objective features of a situation, but to their own perceptions and interpretations of it. In addition, the labour force needs to be mobilised for the undertaking of collective action. It is therefore claimed that the political process approach to industrial conflict is particularly valuable since the workers' power position can also affect their social consciousness and their will to mobilise.

We will now examine on a cross-national basis the broad category of organisational-political theories, in which strikes are seen as being determined by wider social and political forces, as a contrasting approach to those which stress the primacy of conflict-regulating institutions.

ORGANISATIONAL AND POLITICAL THEORIES

The work of Shorter and Tilly (1974) for France is particularly notable for its emphasis on the organisational and political position of labour as factors influencing the level of strike activity. Trade unions are viewed as a mediating influence between workers' dissatisfactions and the translation of those grievances into overt protest, since prior organisation is regarded as a precondition of strike activity. For Shorter and Tilly, each of the periodic waves of strike activity in France reflected an increase in the organisational capacities of the labour movement, with the timing of the waves being determined so as to take advantage of crises at critical junctures of French political history. They portray the strike as an instrument of political action, a means of putting pressure on the political centre when the industrial working class, as a contender for power, has not yet been admitted into the polity and does not participate in the government process. In this sense the strike becomes a means of involving workers in political processes – and not only by compelling government action on behalf of the strikers in the dispute itself.[4] At particular periods of political crisis, such as 1936, 1947 and 1968, it was a method of impressing upon the public the force and vigour of demands from a temporarily highly mobilised labour movement for a greater share of national production and a louder voice for a working class 'avid for representation within the magic circle of centre stage politics' (Shorter and Tilly 1974: 74).

This approach is best seen, however, as a partial rather than universal explanation of strike activity in France. In that country not only have strikes been undertaken by unorganised workers but also, by way of determining factors, it is important to distinguish between 'waves' of strikes and 'ordinary' strikes. Strike waves[5] within particular years represent an exceptional spread of strikes to many companies throughout all regions and industries, their timing coinciding with political events. By contrast, economic factors are the precipitating cause of ordinary strikes directed at the employer and have a set of demands related to the subject of bargaining (on wages, employment, etc.). Especially since the late 1960s, some long strikes during phases of economic recession have been undertaken in order to protect employment, thus making 'a transition from the symbolic or admonitory strike [at low average cost per striker] to the resistance strike' (Sellier 1978: 226). In addition, short strikes have been geared not only to symbolic political protest but have also been used in the collective bargaining process, for example for the reopening of agreements (of indefinite duration) where employers have been unwilling to take the initiative to renew them.

Shorter and Tilly's analysis of the more political character of many strikes in France leads them to ask whether it is possible to explain broader trends in international conflict patterns on a similar basis. They recognise that in examining the complex phenomenon of strike differences among nations, other influences as well as political factors will need consideration. Yet they claim to be able to discern aspects of French strikes which reflect universal trends, running parallel in all western countries in the past century. They point to an essential comparability of conflict patterns among countries with similar modes of worker representation in the central polity. Before the Depression of the 1930s, the strike profiles of most countries in Western Europe were very similar in terms of frequency, extent of worker involvement and duration, as the working classes mobilised themselves for political action. Subsequently, in the postwar period a divergence occurred and in countries where the working class had succeeded to political power, such as Scandinavia, the strike underwent a transformation. The strike rate became negligible, since it was no longer necessary to attempt to affect political decision-making through the medium of strikes.

In contrast, where such changes did not take place, as in France, it is claimed that strikes continued to be a vehicle for political protest, with wage demands being merely a mobilising device in a push towards broader objectives. Hence, the finding that, after 1945, French strikes (at least until the mid-1970s) became shorter in duration – since only a brief stoppage was required to make a symbolic political point – but large in terms of the number of workers involved. In short, politicised unions were 'able to interest a wide range of workers in limited commitments of time and energy for collective enterprises' (Shorter and Tilly 1974: 307). It is worth reiterating, however, that somewhat different interpretations of the frequency of short strikes as a dominant characteristic of industrial conflict in France are possible – such as relating this type of stoppage to features of the prevailing system of collective bargaining, together with an inability on the part of the unions to finance lengthy strikes (Goetschy and Rozenblatt 1992).

Korpi and Shalev (1979) have extended and developed the line of approach in which strike trends are grounded in a political explanation towards further comparative perspectives. For them the wider relevance of the political interpretation evolves out of an original analysis of the Swedish case, rather than that of France. They view industrial conflict as an important symptom of societal change, with a central role being assigned to changes in the distribution of power resources between the contending parties. As we have indicated, in the case of Sweden after the coming to power of the Social Democrats in the 1930s: 'The unions had . . . access to a relatively efficient, political alternative [to strikes] which they could use to achieve important goals, primarily through changes in employment, fiscal and social policies' (Korpi 1978a: 99).

Thus, via what has been termed a process of 'political exchange' (Pizzorno 1978), the centre of gravity of distributional conflict moved from the industrial to the political sphere. Swedish labour practically renounced the strike weapon so as to pursue more effectively, and at less cost, its long-term class interests in the latter arena. For such an exchange to be possible, however, the power of labour within government has to be secure and likely to be enduring for an extended period, not only so that the unions may be convinced of the benefits of a less militant industrial policy, but also to persuade employers to reach a lasting accommodation with them. Similarly, in order to be able to 'deliver' its part of the bargain, the labour movement requires a good deal of organisational unity between, and within, its industrial and political wings, together with internal control and discipline over its constituents. In effect, the emphasis of these institutional prerequisites is upon a high degree of coordination and organisational centralisation.

In seeking to substantiate this thesis on the basis of wider, international comparisons Korpi and Shalev look for parallels and contrasts to the Swedish case in which Social Democratic governments have achieved durable power, the labour movement is united and organisationally strong and the level of industrial conflict has declined. A number of variant groups of countries are then identified, the first consisting of Austria and Norway which most closely follow the Swedish model. Since the Second World War both these countries have had Social Democratic rule, or at least a strong Social Democratic presence in government, centralised and unified labour movements and a marked decline in the level of industrial conflict. At the opposite extreme are the USA, Canada and Ireland where socialist parties enjoyed little electoral support and have not played a significant role in national politics. Furthermore, their labour movements are not highly coordinated or organisationally centralised, and levels of conflict have remained high post-1945, as well as being largely retained within the employment context.

There are also a number of intermediate countries such as France (up to 1981 when the Socialists came to power), Italy and Japan where, although the labour movement enjoyed significant electoral support and was relatively highly mobilised, it remained excluded from the executive branch of government and totally lacked the prerequisites for political exchange. It is argued that with these conditions the effect is actually to increase the level of industrial conflict. Finally, there is a group of 'exceptional' countries including Germany, the Netherlands and Switzerland (both of the latter two countries having somewhat weak labour movements and yet also low levels of industrial conflict) whose experience does not easily seem to fit the hypothesis. Germany, for instance, is a country in which it is readily conceded that although the Social Democrats remained outside the government until the mid-1960s, nevertheless the level of industrial disputes remained very low – among the lowest in the industrialised world.

A further, related approach towards explaining long-run comparative trends in industrial conflict, and one which also views strike activity in terms of political factors, is the general comparative study of eleven countries by Hibbs (1978). His explanation for the differential strike trend experience of these countries concerns the 'political economy of distribution' of the national product. In countries in which a major reduction in the volume (man-days lost) of industrial conflict has taken place, such as Norway and Sweden, this is explained largely by the effectiveness of

Social Democratic and Labour governments in socialising the consumption and final distribution of national income. The crucial factor is not the coming to power of Social Democratic regimes *per se*, but the change in the locus of the distribution of national income produced by their welfare state policies. In these countries, governments have created a large public sector and a high proportion of the national income has become socialised, so that there is collective consumption in the form of extensive provision of public services and a high 'social wage'. Thus the political process dominates the shaping of the final allocation of the national product. In these circumstances it is argued that the distributional struggle thereby becomes removed from the private market place, where allocation takes place through collective bargaining and industrial conflict and where labour's economic well-being is determined predominantly by market outcomes. Instead, the struggle is shifted to the political arena where labour and capital now compete through political negotiation and electoral mobilisation. On the other hand, those countries which have experienced little change in average strike volume over the twentieth century (or where strike activity increased) – France, Italy, USA and Canada – are those in which centre and right governments have predominated.

Cameron (1984) has also shown, in a quantitative study for eighteen advanced capitalist countries over the period 1965–81, that countries in which 'leftist' parties most frequently controlled government tended to experience an infrequent use of the strike, and that a low level of strike activity was also associated with a high 'social wage'. He contends that the trade-off of industrial militancy by workers and their unions depends not simply on access to political power by Labour parties, but on the payoffs which such governments can then institute – especially low unemployment and a high social wage. Also, where the labour movement is highly inclusive in membership, highly unified in the sense of having a small number of industry-wide unions and delegating considerable power to the confederation (i.e. some of the organisational attributes of 'corporatism'), then the parties linked to that movement are likely to control government for much of the time.

Although political theories insist that the system of industrial relations 'is placed firmly in the context of the political economy, the class system and the power structure of society' (Korpi 1981: 209), political interpretations themselves are not immune to criticism. Edwards (1981), for instance, suggests that in playing down the role of collective bargaining as a means of resolving disputes – in favour of broader socio-political variables – they are too dogmatic, replacing one overarching explanation for another. His position is that although the political environment needs to be taken into account, the effect of that environment on strikes is usually mediated through the bargaining system. Fulcher (1991) also argues that in the case of Sweden, it was not the accession to power by a Social Democratic government in the 1930s which then produced industrial peace, via influencing the strategy of the labour movement. Rather, the critical influence was a shift in employer strategy to minimise, by means of promoting joint central regulation through employer and union confederations, the threat of Socialist state regulation.

Particular problems arise in sustaining the Korpi and Shalev thesis for the 1980s, in terms of the typologies presented, since a substantial decline in labour disputes took place in France (which began even before the accession to power of the Socialists), as well as a notable increase in disputes in Social Democratic Sweden. Furthermore, their study gives little attention to either the nature of the state within a capitalist society, or to the importance of the production process itself and changes therein, as a source of industrial conflict. In the latter respect, Batstone (1985: 52) has argued:

> It would seem reasonable to expect that greater attention be paid to the way in which political action either reduces issues of conflict at the point of production or shapes the resolution of disputes so as to reduce resort to industrial action.

Similarly, it is necessary to focus attention on the workplace level in order to ascertain the extent to which there are systematic variations in the ways in which work is organised, and the conflicting divisions of interest created by the labour process and its control.

THE 'POLITICS OF PRODUCTION'

A third approach towards the comparative explanation of conflict generation and resolution therefore focuses upon the workplace 'politics of production'. For Burawoy (1985) production politics relate to the institutions and 'struggles'[6] that control the labour process at the workplace level. Managements' freedom to discipline workers may be constrained by, say, collective bargaining. But the state itself is also involved in the regulation of the labour process, restricting (via legislation on hours of work, employee dismissals, etc.) employers' freedom to use the labour power which they have bought. Certainly for the USA, Edwards (1986) has shown that the practice of workplace relations was shaped by state activities and cannot be understood outside them.

Haiven (1990) has employed these ideas to compare the generation, resolution and resulting differential levels of conflict at the workplace in Canada and Britain. In explaining why the Canadian system may generate more conflict than the British, a number of key substantive issues of workplace struggle between management and labour are identified – such as discipline and job control. Although the power to discipline is an essential employer tool, it cannot now be used on an arbitrary basis partly because in Canada there is a system of arbitrated review of discipline, and in Britain the provision of industrial tribunals. However, tribunals are rarely used by unions. Instead, disciplinary outcomes are bargained, and conflict on this issue thereby mollified, in the more strongly unionised workplaces. By contrast, in Canada, because of the predominance of arbitration, the workplace participation of unions in disciplinary outcomes is limited, so that worker frustration may therefore remain unventilated. But probably the most contentious issue in both countries around which shopfloor conflict centres is job control, including effort-bargaining, the pace of work and manning levels. In Canada, job control is an exclusive management right and there is no formal mechanism for its regulation, whereas in Britain, although conflict occurs over this issue, it has long been a legitimate area for negotiation at shopfloor level. By being forced underground in Canada, job control issues may then become manifest in indiscipline and wildcat strikes.

Although the institutional and (macro-)organisational-political theories which have been considered may help to explain longer-term comparative strike characteristics and trends they will not explain year-by-year variations in strike activity. Instead, these strike fluctuations need to be related to variables which themselves fluctuate markedly on a short-term basis, those of an economic nature.

ECONOMIC DETERMINANTS

Few aspects of strike activity have received greater attention than the relationship between changing economic conditions, particularly unemployment, and changes in the number of strikes. Numerous individual country studies, based upon the prototype Ashenfelter and Johnson (1969) model for the USA, have examined the relationship between strike frequency (number of stoppages) and some indicator of changes in economic activity or business cycle influences over relatively short time-periods. They have generally (though not invariably) found that there is a significant, positive association between the two, with the number of strikes moving pro-cyclically. The role of economic influences is developed within a collective bargaining framework in terms of variables which will lead to a changed propensity of workers' organisations to undertake strike action, and of firms being prepared to incur a strike. It is assumed that strikes occur over wage or similarly related issues, thereby abstracting from the multidimensional nature of collective bargaining by concentrating upon only a single aspect of the wide range of bargaining issues, as well as doing scant justice to the strikers' complexities of motivation.

Rees (1952) originally pointed out that economic conditions in the form of business prosperity, especially of tight labour markets, would affect the timing of strikes – assuming some given, existing stock of grievances. Unions are more likely to press their demands in prosperous periods when the costs for their members will be reduced. As a later researcher has expressed it:

> The success of a strike depends on the extent to which workers can minimise costs to themselves while imposing large costs on the employer. Periods of low unemployment increase the bargaining power of workers on both counts: employees have greater alternative sources of work while the costs to the firm both in the form of profits foregone and of difficulty of attracting substitute workers are increased.
>
> (Kaufman 1982: 479)

In contrast to traditional bargaining power theory, which contends that strikes are more likely to occur when workers are in a strong economic position in relation to management, more recent quantitative studies of strike frequency in the USA (Mauro 1982) and Canada (Cousineau and Lacroix 1986) relate strikes to imperfect information held by all the bargaining parties involved. This new literature maintains that rapid fluctuations in economic conditions will lower the predictability of strike results, thus removing the capacity of each side to make pre-emptive concessions and therefore increasing the likelihood of negotiations ending in a strike (Cohn and Eaton 1989). In particular, inflation is an important predictor of strike frequency since it increases uncertainty about future price changes and wage levels.

An economic explanation has also been proffered to account for the fact that in most western countries strike 'waves' have occurred at the same particular historical junctures. From the evidence of five countries (USA, France, Germany, Italy and the UK) over a period of more than a century, Screpanti (1987) has concluded that major international upheavals in the form of strike waves tend to explode around the upper turning points of long (Kondratieff) economic cycles at fifty-year intervals, and Mandel (1980) points to favourable labour market conditions at the cyclical peak of economic growth and prosperity as inducing the outbreak of these strike waves. Although their precipitating causes may be economic, to the extent that strike waves heighten tension both within the workplace and in society as a whole about authority, control and power, their meaning is often deeply political (Franzosi 1989b; Haimson 1989).

Having identified a number of perspectives which seek to explain the longer-term patterns and changes in strike activity on a cross-national basis, together with short-term, year-to-year fluctuations, we can also examine the translation of these approaches into testable models for empirical evaluation via quantitative techniques.

EMPIRICAL STUDIES

A number of statistical studies of the time-pattern of strikes on an international basis have been carried out utilising the economic, institutional and political-organisational perspectives which we have examined. Creigh *et al.* (1984) tested, across twenty OECD countries over the period 1962–81, a number of explanatory variables to account for differences in stoppage incidence (number of working days lost), rather than strike frequency. The most important single explanatory variable was found to be standardised unemployment rates across the countries. A similarly ambitious study investigating the relationship between macroeconomic variables and aggregate strike activity across a broad data base for seventeen countries was undertaken by Paldam and Pederson (1982). They employed annual observations for a twenty-year, postwar period into the 1970s, and in this case the dependent variable is specified as the number of strikes. It was found that for a majority of countries previous increases in money (and to a lesser extent real) wages were positively and significantly related to strike frequency. The unemployment variable was less successful in that only a third of the countries were found to have significant coefficients and the sign (direction of influence) on the variable also differed among countries. Interestingly, when the seventeen countries themselves are broadly grouped into 'low-conflict' countries, such as those in Scandinavia with strong, centralised and unified labour movements whose party is frequently in office, and 'high-conflict' countries with weaker and decentralised labour movements (including North America, Australia, France and Italy) the economic variables perform consistently poorly for the low-conflict countries. The authors also suggest that although the unemployment and wage change variables are found to be 'correctly' (negatively) signed and significant for the USA, in fact the Ashenfelter and Johnson-type bargaining model, which had dominated the construction of economic strike models, appears to be inapplicable to many of the other countries in the sample. This model was developed within the context of the US industrial relations system and might therefore be less directly applicable to other national industrial relations environments.

Snyder (1975) has put forward the view that the economic models of strike fluctuations which have been tested within individual countries are theoretically incomplete and empirically misspecified since they neglect, as potentially important determinants, the organisational capacity of the labour movement to press its demands, the institutional setting and the influence of the political environment. Although this criticism is undoubtedly overstated, it is true that the data for most longitudinal studies comprise only a relatively limited and homogenous time-span (usually of less than two decades). Snyder therefore contends that the findings will be valid only for the particular institutional context within which a country's industrial relations are conducted, and furthermore a context which can be considered to be constant over such a restricted period. Conversely, it is hypothesised that variations in the institutional setting over the longer term will produce marked variations in the determinants of strike activity – which can be demonstrated empirically using both international and inter-temporal data. Thus, for Snyder, the institutional contexts themselves must be placed at the centre of the analysis.

Snyder's model

In his formulation, he distinguishes between two types of institutional setting. The first is where union membership is large and relatively stable, the political position of labour firmly established and collective bargaining itself is well institutionalised. Under these conditions he maintains that the assumptions underlying the economic bargaining model will hold well, in terms of calculations by the parties of short-run gains and costs. The second type of setting, however, reverses these conditions: union membership is low and unstable, labour organisations are not legitimate interest groups with regular influence over political decision-making in resource allo-cation, and collective bargaining is underdeveloped. Within these parti-cular arrangements the assumptions of the 'economic' model will not hold and Snyder believes that longer-run political objectives, such as national polity membership, become more important to labour than short-run eco-nomic costs and benefits. Equally, the organisational strength of labour is problematic under these conditions in that although low unemployment, for example, may increase the propensity of workers to take strike action their opportunity to do so may be impaired by insufficient prior organisation. Following Shorter and Tilly (1974) Snyder therefore maintains that in uninstitutionalised settings the strike is a political, more than economic, weapon and that it will fluctuate with political changes and labour's organ-isational strength.

The hypothesis is then tested intertemporally, using both strike frequency and size as dependent variables for three countries, France (1876–1937 and 1946–66), Italy (1901–24, and 1947–70) and the United States (1900–48 and 1949–70). The large break in the series for Italy (1925–46) is a consequence of the absence of reliable strike information for the fascist period when strikes were illegal and were systematically suppressed by Mussolini. It does mean, however, that for Italy the sample size of the earlier period is somewhat small and it also includes the (probably distorting) effects of a world war. The orientation of Snyder's approach is that in France and Italy it is expected that because industrial relations had remained relatively less institutionalised, political and organisational factors will be of predominant importance in explaining fluctuations in strike activity in both periods. In the United States, however, there have been substantial changes over the course of time in the institutional parameters affecting industrial relations structure, from an uninstitutionalised environment in the pre-Second World War period to a more institutionalised setting thereafter. Consequently, in terms of his dichotomy, there should be a corresponding and observable shift in the determinants of strikes as between the two periods.

The empirical results obtained for the United States appear to be consistent with the hypothesis. For the earlier period the economic variables utilised – unemployment, as an indicator of labour market tightness, and the (lagged) percentage change in real wages – are both found to be statistically insignificant and the latter variable also manifests the 'wrong' (positive) sign. Conversely, a unionisation variable is significant, as are two political variables, namely the percentage of Democrats in Congress and a 'dummy' variable to represent the years of Democratic presidents.[7] The rationale for the inclusion of the political party affiliation variables is that governments which are favourable to labour may have the (unintended) effect of encouraging labour demands, possibly because of the greater likelihood of success. Also, in uninstitutionalised conditions, by lacking an 'inside track' to the state legislature, labour's collective demands find expression through the strike.

The major finding of the study for the USA is that, for the postwar period, the regression coefficients change markedly from those of earlier years. After 1949 both economic variables are statistically significant and in the expected direction, whereas the effects of unionisation and the political indicators become insignificant and are incorrectly signed. Thus in the postwar years the effect of organisational and political influences on fluctuations in strike activity do not seem to be important. Snyder's explanation for the lack of impact of the political variables is not that Democrat officials had by then become less sympathetic to labour but that, with improved political representation of labour's interest, political demands were no longer channelled through strikes. If it is true, however, that these changes have occurred over time in the parameters affecting industrial conflict, it is difficult to see why there has not been a corresponding shift in the overall volume of strikes over the long term, and in their composition in terms of size and duration.

Although Snyder's evidence for the United States appears consistent with the institutionalisation hypothesis, his empirical results for France and Italy, with less well institutionalised relations throughout both time periods, are more mixed. Because of the different political systems in Europe, as well as data limitations, for these countries some of the explanatory variables are changed. National income rather than unemployment is used as a measure of economic activity, since reliable unemployment statistics for France and Italy were not available for the whole of the earlier period. The political variables also represent a different dimension to those representing political 'attitudes' employed in the analysis for the USA. Following Shorter and Tilly, a dummy variable is included for election years throughout the period, together with a second variable relating to the number of cabinet changes which have taken place. The basis of the argument is that political crisis or change, which these measures are intended to represent, will increase the vulnerability of government to labour demands which are themselves expressed through strike action.

The results obtained for France are consistent with Snyder's explanation for the pre-1938 period. As anticipated, the economic determinants of strikes perform poorly whereas the election year (political) variable and, especially, the organisational (union membership) variable are significant. Similarly, in Italy (given the data limitations) there is no significant influence of economic factors, but there is a significant, positive relationship between strikes and union membership. For the postwar period, however, the explanatory power of the model is far less satisfactory. Although there are no substantial changes in the economic parameters – which still remain insignificant, as expected – in postwar France both the political and organisational variables then also become insignificant. In the case of Italy, union membership remains, as in the prewar period, the only significant predictor of fluctuations in strike activity. Snyder concludes that his findings are, nevertheless, broadly consistent with the hypothesis concerning the impact of institutional setting upon the determinants of strike activity.

Although the results of this study are interesting, there are a number of criticisms which can be directed at the specification of the model itself and also the interpretation of the results.[8] As Edwards (1978) points out, there are obvious problems in attempting to measure satisfactorily the political components of industrial conflict. To use the frequency of cabinet changes as an indicator of alterations in the national political position of labour has been described by one critic as 'downright silly' (Gallie 1975), since formal government changes need not necessarily involve heightened conflict. For the USA, however, Snyder uses a somewhat different political measure in terms of the actual composition of the political centre itself. In consequence, any direct comparison between the results for the three countries must be somewhat suspect. Also, an underlying relationship between the composition of the political centre and strike activity is by no means easy to rationalise in a convincing way. 'There are obvious reasons why the level of unemployment should affect workers' willingness and ability to strike, but the influence of such things as political upheaval and the party of the President is much less clear' (Edwards 1978: 325). A further possible limitation is that the level of trade union membership might also be mainly determined by the economic influences incorporated in the model, rather than having (as assumed) an independent effect.[9] Similarly, although the model presupposes that strike activity depends partly upon the extent of trade union membership, there could well be simultaneous determination between strikes and unionisation. In other words, greater strike activity which is successful might itself also give rise to an increased density of trade union membership.[10]

To test for these sorts of possibilities, two further studies relating to strike determination in the United States have been carried out by Kaufman (1982) and Skeels (1982). Their results throw doubt on some of Snyder's conclusions for that country. For the 1900–48 period, it is found that both economic factors (at least as measured by unemployment together with price changes) and organisational factors do seem to affect the level of strike frequency, and that political factors appear unimportant. In the post-1948 period, however, fluctuations in union organisation ceased to be important in explaining annual movements in strike activity and economic factors did become relatively more important – as Snyder originally showed. Skeels employs a two-equation model in order to overcome the difficulties caused by any mutual determination of strikes and union membership by economic factors. He finds that, in the prewar period, strikes were not a significant determinant of union membership growth but that a good deal of the union growth can be explained by the same economic factors which influence strike activity. Nevertheless, when he estimates the residual proportion of union organisation which can only be explained by non-economic factors, this residual variable is found to be positively and significantly related to strike frequency. Thus it appears that the union organisation variable does more than merely pass on the influence of economic forces to strike activity without adding any additional explanation in its own right.

CONCLUSIONS

It is hardly surprising that some of the evidence from quantitative, empirical strike studies is conflicting. With this research methodology there are problems in selecting appropriate empirical counterparts for theoretical constructs, as well as a considerable distance between the occurrence of strike behaviour at the micro-level and testing its determinants (usually) by means of aggregative data.[11] Also, when using very highly aggregated strike data what is being ascribed to, say, political changes might be due in part to secular structural changes in the economies concerned – such as relative changes in industrial structure as between traditionally high-conflict, and low-conflict industries (Paldam and Pederson 1984). Moreover, while the empirical results may be consistent with the causal hypothesis advanced, the fact remains that often 'an infinite number of hypotheses may "fit" any given set of observations with equally good results' (Evans 1976: 74).

An even more telling criticism of the validity of this methodology, when employed on a comparative basis in the form of undifferentiated multi-country studies, is that of Dunlop (1978). He believes that such studies are not likely to produce important findings because not only does the role of the strike differ as between various countries – and a strike which has a political purpose is not likely to have the same determinants as one designed to secure immediate economic improvements – but also, with respect to longitudinal studies, sample periods incorporating several decades often reflect industrial relations systems at various stages of development and are therefore qualitatively different. The causes and meaning of strikes can shift over the course of time, as we have noted. In short, 'the logic of industrial conflict is conditioned by nation- and time-specific institutional settings [so that] we should be wary of attempts to apply a fixed explanatory model to multinational data sets' (Shalev 1983: 428).

However, one of the major benefits of studies such as Snyder's (in which the countries to be compared are not only more carefully focused but the sample periods themselves subdivided and differentiated), and the ensuing debate which has been generated, is the reorientation of analytical work on strike activity away from one-dimensional theories towards a fuller appreciation of the total environment in which industrial relations take place. This incorporates not only economic conditions but also the institutional framework of collective bargaining, the parties' organisational strength, power resources and attitudinal characteristics, together with political events and the broader political 'climate'. Recent empirical work on postwar Italian strikes, for instance (Franzosi 1989b), incorporates business cycle and bargaining structure as explanatory influences, together with the underlying political processes at particular significant time periods. A similarly eclectic approach in testing the determinants of the variation in median days lost through strikes for eighteen OECD countries from 1960 to 1975 was adopted by Batstone (1985). His model includes measures of some of the substantive as well as procedural aspects of industrial relations and work organisations, the structure of collective bargaining and the nature of both trade union and confederation organisation, along with the extent of division among Social Democratic parties. Robertson (1990) also regards industrial conflict as a product not only of changes in wages, prices and profits but of particular institutional structures, including those within the political arena, which facilitate compromise, exchange and coordination among otherwise antagonistic groups in society. Using a framework based on transaction-cost economics, within the context of limited information, he finds empirical evidence across nineteen countries over a period of two decades that strike volume is a function of market and institutionally based transaction-cost efficiencies.

It remains true, however, that although the various theories which have been discussed in this chapter may explain conflict behaviour in certain countries and at particular time periods they do not amount to 'general' theories which are universally valid in all national settings. In attempting to understand the complex changes which have occurred in the manifestations, trends and counter-trends of industrial conflict in western countries during the twentieth century there remains considerable potential for further research.

FURTHER READING

A useful, book-length survey of strikes and industrial conflict covering much of the ground in this chapter, and with particular reference to the UK, USA and Australia, is Jackson (1987). The paper by Franzosi (1989a) provides a good critical and comprehensible assessment of quantitative strike research methodology, as well as various theoretical standpoints. A detailed critique of 'political-economy' approaches is Batstone (1984, 1985), the 1985 article also being a first-rate empirical study of international variations in strike activity. A recent survey article of the whole field is Edwards (1992).

7 Workers' participation in decision-making

It is generally conceded in the liberal democratic world that working people should have a right to participate in the making of decisions which critically affect their working lives (Adams 1986). Certainly, during the 1970s, there was a widespread and increasing preoccupation with various schemes for employees' participation in decisions within undertakings, especially in Western Europe where it achieved major social, economic and political significance.[1] One important development which occurred at that time was the strengthening of participatory mechanisms in legislation in countries such as Germany, Sweden, Norway and the Netherlands. The world recession of the early 1980s, however, severely reduced the power of labour and appeared to restrict or curtail, even if it did not reverse, many of the initiatives underway in developing more participative forms of organisation, since in a situation of high unemployment managements were able to reassert a high degree of control over the labour process. At the same time, in a number of countries there was also less political pressure to accommodate labour through participation in decision-making (Poole 1989). Other observers, however, maintain that, although some organisations took advantage of reduced union power to dismantle or neutralise certain participative mechanisms (Hardy 1985), there is hardly any evidence of an overall tendency towards the breaking down of the democratising process in western work organisations (Lammers and Széll 1989) and some of them, in fact, launched various types of worker participation programmes as the only viable solution to their economic difficulties (Long and Warner 1987).

In this chapter it is intended to attempt to explain the objectives and rationale of participation as between countries where they differ, why its structural forms may vary and, on the basis of cross-national evidence, to elucidate some of the influences which determine the outcomes and effectiveness of participation.

It is true that there are a variety of definitions, terminological variations and differing views as to precisely what the concept of 'participation' entails. Schregle (1976: 2) regards the related term, 'industrial democracy', which is often used (interchangeably) in the literature as being of 'an emotive and ill-defined nature' having political and ideological overtones. According to Walker (1974: 6), 'workers' participation in management occurs when those at the bottom of an enterprise hierarchy take part in the authority and managerial functions of the enterprise', so that employees become involved in extended areas of decision-making and control which had previously been reserved exclusively as management prerogatives. Thus, institutionalised workers' participation emphasises changing the balance of decision-making within the firm.

COLLECTIVE BARGAINING

On this definition, collective bargaining at the level of the undertaking is undoubtedly a form of participation, since it implies not only informing and consulting workers but also negotiating with them on matters which otherwise would be the subject of unilateral decisions (ILO 1981b). As Schregle (1981) has emphasised, the concept of participation should not be too closely identified with the existence of specific participative machinery. The important point is whether, and to what extent, workers normally acting through their representatives have an influence on the decision-making process within the firm. This may be achieved through collective bargaining, which can be said to remain the major form of workers' participation in North America, Britain and to a significant extent Japan, as well as most of the countries in English-speaking Africa. The overwhelming reliance by unions in the United States on collective bargaining, *ex post* reaction to management initiatives and the use of countervailing power, means that the line of interest conflict between labour and management does not become blurred. This avoids possible role conflict for the office-holder, and the problem of double representation for the employee which may occur with formalised schemes for participation in management (Herding 1972). In Australia, also, unions have preferred to rely upon negotiation along with the regulation of employment conditions through the industrial (arbitration) tribunals.

Where more formalised and explicit arrangements for employees' participation have been introduced, they assume a wide diversity of forms of either a legalistic or voluntary nature. These include codetermination and worker directors (employee representatives on corporate policy-making boards), works councils or similar bodies at plant level,[2] joint consultation and communications, together with workers' self-management systems and individual producer cooperatives. Yet, as the ILO (1981b) has shown, in countries such as India and Pakistan the introduction of other types of machinery has generally not slowed down the development of collective bargaining, which continues to remain the fundamental element of worker participation within undertakings.[3] Also, in the well-known case of Germany, participation in enterprise decisions has not destroyed collective bargaining. Rather, research findings suggest a certain division of responsibility for the protection of workers' interests between collective bargaining and codetermination. In this respect, 'collective bargaining provides the basic pattern of working conditions on a regional and/or industry wide level; co-determination fills out this pattern on the plant and firm level' (Adams and Rummel 1977: 20). A comparison is sometimes made between British shop stewards' committees and German works councils, since they carry out many of the same activities, such as negotiating the application of wage payment systems, job grading, short-time working and redundancies. Such parallels should not, however, be overdrawn since there are some important differences. Not only has the works council no right to strike but also, as Kahn-Freund (1979: 12) observed some years ago:

> It is carefully regulated, protected and restrained, and lives behind a formidable high fence of elaborate and minute statutes and a gigantic wall of case law, whilst the shop-stewards' committee thrives in the open country of 'custom and practice'.

FORMALISED PARTICIPATION SCHEMES

Because workers' participation is a multidimensional concept rather than a single coherent entity (Ackers *et al.* 1992), there are a number of ways in which its various forms may be distinguished from each other and classified. Formal schemes of participation may incorporate either the *direct* involvement of employees at workplace level, via production conferences, workers' assemblies and similar arrangements, as for instance have been common in Hungary and some other Eastern European countries, or be *indirect* by means of the representatives of workers on decision-making bodies within the enterprise – as in the German codetermination scheme. Indirect (or representative) forms of participation may advance democracy within work organisations without sacrificing modern administrative structures and practices (Poole 1986b).

At the lowest (shopfloor) level, participation may take the form of semi-autonomous work groups being given a large element of responsibility for the organisation, supervision (and sometimes redesign) of their jobs. These sorts of programmes were initiated in a number of western countries in the late 1960s largely in response to labour market shortages combined with certain long-term social/demographic trends, which resulted in problems of excessive turnover, lack of motivation and inability to recruit workers for some low-level tasks (Long and Warner 1987). In more recent years, intensified international product market competition and new technologies have created additional managerial imperatives to reorganise production and work processes. In the Swedish car industry, for instance, employers who were under pressure to achieve flexibility as well as reduce costs, increasingly concluded that Fordist and Taylorist concepts of work organisation were ineffective (Kjellberg 1992). They therefore resorted to autonomous work groups and no traditional first line supervisors. Poole (1979) maintains, however, that it is doubtful whether such programmes (which have also become popular in the USA and Canada) constitute genuine participatory institutions, rather than a series of *ad hoc* experiments. Also, in the case of Italy, advanced electronics did not always lead to 'post-Taylorist' forms of flexible work organisation, and in some cases there has been a return to assembly-line operations following experiments with teamworking (Ferner and Hyman 1992b).

A further, recent participation mechanism that allows employees at plant level direct involvement in decisions which affect them is that of 'quality circles'. These involve regular meetings between a supervisor and department members, with the objective of identifying ways of enhancing productivity and product quality, together with improving morale and managing the implementation of accepted ideas. Quality circles can now be found in most Western European countries including Britain and, especially, France; in Germany by the mid-1980s 45 per cent of the hundred largest firms had introduced the device (Jacobi and Müller-Jentsch 1991). In Britain, they have been particularly associated with foreign-owned firms as methods to gain employee loyalty and commitment (Purcell *et al.* 1987). These new models of direct employee involvement can be seen as part of human-resource management, promoting participation of an instrumental character whose object is to mobilise employees' productive and motivational resources – especially to supplement and support flexibility strategies. In France, it has been claimed that: 'the employers are aiming to improve the quality of working life by various means including quality circles and the individualisation of the employment relationship, in order to reduce the number of issues that are confronted by collective action' (Goetschy and Rojot 1987: 148).

In the case of Norway, new forms of work organisation have tended to by-pass unions and focus more upon individual employees (Dølvik and Stokland 1992), while in Britain the Conservative government also has an ideological preference for direct forms of individual employee involvement rather than indirect, institutionalised procedures involving employee representatives. By contrast, such direct employee involvement – circumventing unions – has been rare in Italian firms (Ferner and Hyman 1992b) and in Germany human-resource, participatory management is intended to complement institutionalised employee representation rather than to displace it (Jacobi *et al.* 1992). Similarly, in a multinational car plant in Austria, the union was able to enforce its right to be fully involved, via its unionised works councillors, in new forms of work organisation (Traxler 1992). There is, however, some evidence that shopfloor initiatives such as quality circles may deflect workers' desires away from participation at the managerial level in strategic decisions (Drago and Wooden 1991).

A further dimension of participation relates to its 'depth', regarding the extent of decision-making powers that are transferred to workers – which may be negative (vetoing management decisions), or positive and initiating. Strauss (1979) makes a basic distinction between three major participation models in terms of the degree of workers' influence or control over management along an implicit scale, namely consultative participation, co-management or decision-making, and workers' self-management. In both industrialised and developing countries joint consultation committees, or works councils, are by far the most common bodies for associating workers with decisions in undertakings. With joint consultation, management makes the final decision, but workers have the right to information and can offer advice and objections. In most European countries works councils originally developed along the lines of this model, although they have since acquired decision-making powers on certain matters (requiring their prior agreement) such as hours of work, vocational training and safety and welfare, as well as rights to information and consultation.

Second, joint decision-making bodies may be distinguished in the pure form of which the parties have equality of power and the consent of each side is required before action can be taken. Codetermination schemes follow this model and collective bargaining, although it is 'disjunctive' – emphasising the distinctiveness rather than the commonality of management and worker interest – may, as we have observed, also be viewed as a meaningful form of workers' participation, by way of influencing the exercise of managerial power and achieving a measure of joint regulation over workplace decisions.

The third and most far-reaching category is that of workers' control, as typified (in principle) by the former Yugoslav self-management system, introduced in 1950 and maintained until 1989, within a framework of social ownership in which the assets of an enterprise were owned, not by the state or private owners, but by society as a whole. There is also the communal kibbutz organisation in Israel, as well as producer cooperatives in Western Europe in which workers or their representatives have final authority. Self-management (on the Yugoslav model) has also been introduced in certain enterprises in Algeria, Madagascar, Malta, Tanzania and elsewhere – although similar experiments carried out in some countries of Latin America have been practically abandoned (ILO 1985).

Objectives

There are important and related differences in the purposes which the particular type of participation is intended to promote and from which its institutionalised forms cannot be abstracted. In Germany, although the concept itself has a long history, special considerations were applicable in that 'control over capital' was one important reason for union pressure towards codetermination in the iron and steel industries immediately after the Second World War, 'to make certain that German industrialists would never again finance an extremist party' (Hartman 1975: 55). More generally, some observers have attributed either an 'integrative' or a 'transformative' function to the objectives of workers' participation schemes.

The integrative function, premised upon the basis of unitary or pluralist conceptualisations of the enterprise, attempts to foster an identification of workers with their own particular firm so as to secure 'more compliant and supportive responses from employees to managerially defined purposes and achievement of managerially defined goals' (Ogden 1982: 547). From this managerial standpoint the rationale for encouraging participation is directed towards the realisation of a number of pragmatic ends, such as the achievement of greater organisational effectiveness and a reduction in industrial conflict, or more generally as part of the managerial control system in getting decisions accepted by employees. From this perspective, Ramsay (1977, 1983) has pointed to the cyclical appearance of workers' participation schemes at particular times as a management-induced method of securing greater labour force compliance during periods of challenge from labour to the legitimacy of capital and the authority of its agents, such as occur in conditions of tight labour markets and rising industrial militancy. This cyclical analysis begins from the presumption that industrial relations are essentially relations of conflict, over the control of the labour process and over the distribution of the value created through that process. Thus for Ramsay (1983: 220), participation is 'a child of managerial crisis', when control over labour is in some way perceived to be under pressure. The need for management to respond to labour's demands via focusing on such schemes will thereafter recede, once the requisite conditions have passed, until the next periodic upsurge.

Alternatively, participation may be viewed as an important objective in its own right as a means of promoting individual worker satisfaction, or extending the rights or benefits of political democracy to the industrial sphere. In Germany, for instance, 'the federal legal code encapsulates the concept of citizenship in all areas of social life' (Loveridge 1980: 305). For the labour movement, participatory schemes may be part of a transformative strategy either towards promoting a more generally participative society as was the case in the former Yugoslavia, or Chile in the early 1970s, or by mobilising workers to demand a radical expansion of influence towards full control – thereby generating pressures for a transformation of the existing social order (Stephens 1980). In the case of India, the introduction of participation in industry was seen as a prerequisite for the establishment of a socialist society (ILO 1981b).

In developing countries, unlike some in the West, the drive for associating workers with enterprise decision-making has been largely a government initiative. Here participation is often viewed as an important tool for assisting economic development, in mobilising support for modernisation and attainment of the objectives of national development plans. It was for this reason that workers' self-management was assigned an important role by socialist and nationalist governments in countries such as Chile, Peru and Algeria (Strauss 1979; Zeffane 1981).

In Eastern European countries over the forty-year period of communist rule, a host of direct and indirect forms of participation were introduced to which four major functions were attributed (Héthy 1991): (1) legitimation of the socialist political system, (2) promotion of economic performance, (3) conflict-solving, and (4) the realisation of social values such as collectivism – although the emphasis accorded to participation in general, and to each of the objectives, varied from country to country as well as over the course of time. In some of the countries greater enterprise democracy became more predominant as a response during periods of labour crisis. For instance in the case of Poland, self-management was accorded a high priority at historical turning points when there was heightened political activity and weakness on the part of the central authorities, and it ultimately became viewed as an instrument for the mobilisation of political support for societal reform (Szul 1986; Bielasiak 1989). In Czechoslovakia, the brigade system of workers' organisation, introduced in the 1980s, embodied aspects of the autonomous, or semi-autonomous, working group. 'Its principal goal [was] the improvement of production and work organisation with the direct participation of all members of the collective' (Cziria 1992: 188).

EXPLANATIONS OF CROSS-NATIONAL DIFFERENCES

We now turn to a more detailed analysis of the origins of similarity and diversity in the national institutions for workers' participation in developed market economies. Several comparative perspectives may be delineated in this respect. As discussed below, these include cultural and ideological influences, collective bargaining structures and power relations between the industrial relations actors themselves.

Specific cultural and ideological factors have been widely employed as important explanatory devices in national comparisons. In the United States, it has been argued that the importance which has traditionally been accorded to property rights has tended to militate against the development of participation in general since, outside the range of issues subject to collective bargaining, a widespread acceptance of the legitimacy of management authority has continued to prevail (Lodge and Henderson 1979). The workers' self-management system in Yugoslavia also reflected a social and ideological background which is distinctively significant. Historically, the ethnically differentiated peasant population of Yugoslavia had evinced a deep distrust of central authority which, together with the political instability and poor communications of the country, resulted in a good deal of local self-sufficiency and autonomy (Riddell 1968). During the Second World War, the pluralist and decentralised partisan movement also formed part of a pattern of resistance to mistrusted central authority. Thus, although the political and economic system set up after 1945 was patterned on that of the Soviet Union, after the break with the USSR there was a switch from administrative centralism back to more traditional decentralisation. In this respect, the new self-management system could be viewed as being: 'not only the voluntary act of the political élite ... but at the same time a transformation of the [wartime] liberation movement, based on political participation, into a labour movement which was henceforth based on the economic participation of those employed' (IDE 1981a: 219).

The German participation system in many ways assumes a harmony of interest between management and labour and has been described as 'basically a strategy of cooperative unionism' (Fürstenberg 1980). It is marked by concern for consensus; its important legal characteristics include an integrating element according to which the (purely employee-constituted) works councils are required to collaborate with management, have no right to resort to strike action and indeed are forbidden to encourage strikes. These features have also been interpreted as a reflection of cultural and ideological influences in which not only is there a preference for statutory regulation enforced by the courts but also 'accommodation and integration, as well as order and authority, occupy an important place in the [German] system of national values' (Schregle 1978: 88). Dahrendorf (1968) views the emergence of codetermination as a consequence of the German tradition of avoiding and abolishing conflict at its roots rather than containing it by institutionalisation, a preference which may be traced back to German socio-philosophical thought in the nineteenth century.[4]

This view, however, appears somewhat oversimplified since, although in the last few decades German trade unions have become well-integrated into society, prior to the First World War they were as radical and Marxist-oriented as those in France, Italy and Belgium (Sorge 1976).[5]

Fox (1978) also sees the origins of German codetermination as being rooted historically in (somewhat different) features of the culture and social relations of that country. In particular, industrialisation and the factory system developed within a society which, because of its late development in the closing decades of the nineteenth century, still retained the structure of 'vertical bonding' between employer and employed. This became carried over into industry and was facilitated by the early emergence of large economic units, leaving no room for an infrastructure of medium-sized enterprises and bourgeois entrepreneurs. Whereas in contrast:

> in Britain the rising class of bourgeois entrepreneurs were creatures of a society and culture in which feudal and manorial vertical bondings, underpinned by paternalist dependence relations and ideology, had been undermined and corroded for a period of two centuries or more.
>
> (Fox 1978: 22)

A further illustration of the importance which is accorded to 'special factors' of this kind is the commercial success of the Mondragon producer cooperatives in the Basque region of northern Spain. This group of enterprises was established in 1956 and produces a wide range of manufactured, and some agricultural, products. A number of studies have noted the importance of Basque nationalism and its distinctive culture as a binding force encouraging mutual cooperation between capital and labour, directed against a repressive Spanish central government (Thomas and Logan 1982). A further significant feature, that is often claimed to provide a foundation which is receptive to the economic requirements of self-management, is a relatively high propensity to save on the part of the Basque population. However, the relevance of such ethnic considerations as a major determining factor in Mondragon's success has been questioned by Bradley and Gelb (1982). Their empirical work points to the greater significance of other influences. In particular, the limited labour mobility which exists partially insulates the cooperatives from competitive pressures of the external labour market. This permits more compressed wage differentials and, since workers are required to contribute to the financing of the enterprises, helps ensure economic viability by retaining savings and equity capital intact to sustain growth and accommodate technical change.

In a broader comparative analysis of the United States and continental Western Europe Kassalow (1982) again suggests that the different forms taken by workers' participation can be partially explained by differences in the ideological background of their respective labour movements. The demands of American unions have usually been expressed in terms of the strengthening of collective bargaining, in contrast to the wider social thrust of European union policies whereby democratisation of the enterprise has often been regarded as a step towards the broader transformation of authority and power within society. Kassalow traces the origins of this difference, and the direct identification of European labour movements with the democratisation of the political process, to the fact that the rise of trade unionism in Europe in the latter part of the nineteenth century was itself an important part of the struggle for political democracy – especially the attainment of universal suffrage. By way of contrast, the US union movement came into being several decades after universal male suffrage had already been established.

As well as cultural and ideological influences, a second comparative perspective points to differences in collective bargaining structures within the different countries as an important explanatory variable affecting the kinds of participatory mechanisms which develop. Clegg (1976) sees the level at which bargaining is conducted – either plant- or industry-wide – as a vital factor in explaining the differences between the attitudes of US and continental European unions towards workers' participation schemes. Industry bargaining can regulate only general matters common to all the enterprises which it encompasses. Detailed topics which are specific to each undertaking require regulation at plant level. As a result, in the absence of such bargaining, alternative machinery needs to be introduced if unions are to exercise a degree of control over these matters. In Germany, for instance, some of the topics which in other countries would be processed through collective bargaining agreements are handled by works councils. According to this line of argument therefore:

> so long as adequate arrangements are made for collective bargaining within the plant, collective bargaining may be regarded as a satisfactory form of industrial democracy. But where regional or industry agreements fail to provide for plant bargaining, there are demands for alternative arrangements to allow workers to exercise some influence over those matters which concern them and which cannot be adequately regulated in regional or industry agreements.

(Clegg 1976: 97)

Windmuller (1977) adopts a similar approach by stating that institutionalised workers' participation in Europe is a reasonable facsimile of the United States pattern of decentralised collective bargaining (although much more universal in its coverage), as adapted to the historically different circumstances of Western European countries. In other words, some of the main purposes of workers' participation have been achieved in the USA through an enterprise-centred system of collective bargaining with a wide range of negotiable issues, which may include the location of new plants, automation and changes in work processes (Willman 1983). Procedures for dealing with grievances in the typical US collective agreement also give workers considerable influence over the regulation of their employment conditions. That is to say, participation via collective bargaining occurs not only in the original negotiation of the agreement, but in the continuing role of the union in administering the agreement during its lifetime. More latterly, however, the decline of collective bargaining in the USA has led some commentators to suggest that policy-makers should consider requiring the institution of works councils, or even worker representation on company boards of directors (Kochan and McKersie 1989).

In the case of Japan, the opportunities for workers' participation have also been primarily conditioned by the extent, enterprise-based structure and influence of trade unions. The opportunities have been expanded by a widening in the scope of collective bargaining as well as by more formally prescribed methods such as joint consultation committees. In practice, the latter are usually set up under the terms of the collective agreement and may therefore be regarded in varying degrees as pre-negotiating bodies (Okamoto 1979). Where negotiating matters such as wages and conditions are discussed in joint consultation, it is an established practice that unions will not exercise their right to strike over them. In this respect, the joint consultation systems of enterprise unions and German works councils are similar in the way they operate (Shirai 1983).

In continental Europe, there is no doubt that workers' participation schemes may be regarded in some essential respects as an extension of collective bargaining to the individual enterprise. They tend to promote the integration of statutory works councils into the bargaining structure by allocating them explicit bargaining rights in certain subject areas, and sometimes according them responsibility for overseeing the implementation at plant level of the industry agreement. In Germany works councils, in practice the major codetermination institution, may also use their right to exercise veto powers over issues such as overtime working, as a counter to get concessions on particular collective bargaining matters where they have weak powers or none at all (Crouch 1982b). Conversely, in Britain, the importance of joint consultative machinery declined in the 1950s and 1960s mainly as a consequence of the growth of collective bargaining at workplace level. There is evidence, however, of its more recent revival as a result of a number of factors, including a weakening of the market basis for local shop stewards' organisations due to the economic recession – although frequently the joint consultative committees exist alongside collective bargaining, rather than serving as an alternative to it.

In any case, although consultation was supposed to be restricted to matters of common rather than of conflicting interests, such as safety and welfare, these could also become issues for negotiation – thereby making it difficult to draw a firm dividing line between them.

The level at which collective bargaining is conducted also affects the extent to which trade union power is centralised. This is an important consideration because one prerequisite for the institutionalisation of participation appears to be the existence of a unified rather than a fragmented trade union structure whose central body occupies a dominant position, as in Scandinavia where it was established prior to the Second World War and in both Germany and Austria where a single union centre emerged in the postwar period. In Germany, the relative centralisation of bargaining functions has been held to be conducive to the evolution of works councils and board-level codetermination. In the Netherlands, a further result of a high degree of centralisation was the tendency, before 1960, to prefer forms of participation which operated at the national or industry, rather than enterprise, level (Albeda 1977). By contrast, in Britain, the presence of powerful and semi-independent organisations of workers at local level tended to render works and consultative machinery ineffective, unless it was formally integrated into the union channel. In the case of India, government sponsored workers' participation was weakened by the long-standing conflicts between rival organisations concerning rights to representation (Kannappan and Krishnan 1977).

A third explanatory approach towards the development of participatory mechanisms concerns the nature of the power relations between the state, trade unions and employers. A strong and markedly repressive state (in historical terms) has been identified with the evolution of highly regulated and legally based participative machinery at plant level, as in Germany, France, the Netherlands and Luxembourg. Conversely, the less severe the restrictions placed on unions in their early stages, the more probable it was that, as in Britain, a powerful labour movement would ensure that plant-level representation would be based upon a single channel of trade union organisation, instead of statutory works council machinery (Sorge 1976). The existence of powerful employers' organisations, in the case of Germany, succeeded for a long period in keeping the shopfloor free from union activities in favour of the works council machinery (Leminsky 1980). On the other hand, where both the state and trade union movement are powerful but the employers' bodies correspondingly weak, there has been greater experimentation with a diversity of participative arrangements. In Israel, for instance, the existence of three major sectors in the economy (private, state and central Histadrut labour federation-operated) has weakened the position of the employers *vis-à-vis* the centralised trade union organisation. Participative arrangements include workers' committees, plant councils, productivity councils and in some Histadrut-owned cooperatives, a joint management system. A further variant is that of the United States where, because 'the role of government has been notably constrained and the density of unionisation has recently declined, the bulk of initiatives have been in the form of managerially inspired programmes of an *ad hoc* character' (Poole 1982: 196).

Broader political factors have also been adduced as contributory explanations. In Chile, it has been claimed that the establishment of a comprehensive system of industrial democracy was retarded not by technical considerations of economic performance, but by the threat it posed to the power of dominant socio-economic groups (Espinosa and Zimbalist 1978). As regards Italy, Caloia (1979) suggested that institutionalised schemes for participation, sanctioned by law, were less possible than elsewhere in Western Europe because of the large disparities in, and radically contraposed, political views of the various classes.

A related approach towards explaining the divergent evolution of either statutory or voluntary modes of participation at plant level is to look at differences in the particular historical circumstances and constraints which prevailed in various countries, at the time when the decisions to create such institutions were first made. Sorge (1976) points out that innovations in participative machinery in Western Europe are clustered around the same critical points in time, namely the aftermath of two world wars at a period of deep-seated changes in social values, followed by another subsequent burst of activity after the late 1960s.[6] According to his explanation, the strong repression of trade unionism by the state in the nineteenth century in much of continental Europe (notably France, Luxembourg, Austria and Germany) meant that, with a weakened, yet radicalised, union movement and recalcitrant employers, voluntary workplace institutions were subsequently more difficult to establish; if participatory mechanisms were to be introduced they would have to be on a statutory basis. They tended to emerge later – usually post-1945 – in conjunction with national crises when the position of employers was less strong and the state was attempting to integrate opposing forces by providing for works councils or committees. In contrast, where state repression of unionism had been relatively less severe (as in Britain, Scandinavia and Switzerland) voluntary institutions in the form of either contractually, or informally, recognised shop stewards and their committees became established at an earlier date, around the First World War.

Although this particular thesis is insightful it is, nevertheless, by no means all-embracing. Belgium is something of an exception to the pattern, since shop steward committees and statutory works councils became established there at roughly the same time. Germany is also a special case in that its works councils were instituted at an early date (1920) and also consisted, unusually (along with Austria), solely of employee representatives. This may be attributed to the late temporal location of German democracy, which occurred only after the First World War, and the resultant greater relative influence of the labour movement on state legislation than was the case in other comparable countries.

Empirical data

A comprehensive empirical study which systematically examines a number of possible determinants of formal participative arrangements across eleven Western European countries, together with Israel, has been carried out by an international research group (IDE 1981a). In an attempt to identify the forces to which 'participative structures', PS (i.e. the formal framework of participation within industrial relations), are a response, the research employs a combination of political, economic, social and related contextual factors which are assumed to operate jointly as determining influences. It is hypothesised, first, that an appropriate political background will facilitate the setting up of participative structures. The argument is that the development of industrial democracy measures is likely to follow, after a time lag, the achievement of political democracy. A second possible background variable relates to favourable economic conditions so that, other things being equal, the extent to which participative structures are introduced will depend upon the level of economic development (as measured by GNP). The rationale for this might be that the advanced technology which usually characterises well-developed economies may require the greater involvement of operatives so as to avoid costly mistakes. Or it could be that the richer the country then the more it can 'afford' participation – if this is seen as having certain accompanying costs in terms of possible efficiency loss – so that there would be less resistance to its introduction.

A third explanatory hypothesis concerns the extent of social differentiation in the countries concerned. The notion is that the distribution of GNP as well as its level is likely to be important, thereby distinguishing Nordic from 'Latin' European countries for instance. In this respect, we might expect countries with greater equality of incomes and less social stratification to be more favourably disposed towards participation. Lastly, there is a related argument in terms of dominant cultural (value-system) influences. A conjecture in the study is that participation will be more highly developed within a country if its industrial culture emphasises the value of cooperative norms between labour and employers, that is if the parties are regarded as having at least some interests in common rather than having totally divergent and irreconcilable interests.

Although it is suggested that these contextual variables will help determine the extent of prescribed employee participation, what the study emphasises is that they are only contingent, or facilitating, conditions which are not in themselves capable of bringing about participative arrangements. Instead, they can only promote, or alternatively frustrate, the attempts of the parties in industrial relations to introduce participative structures. More specifically, it is contended that a strong, well-organised and centralised trade union movement could exert pressure upon both employers and the government for the introduction of participatory mechanisms, either in the form of negotiated agreements or via legislation. Similarly, a strong centralised employers' body, although it is better able to resist participation should it so wish, is not likely to stand out against its introduction. Such an organisation will usually have a professionalised and more forward-looking orientation towards industrial relations and will foresee the potential gains to be secured from adopting a positive strategy. (These would include a greater ability to shape participatory structures in accordance with its own wishes, by becoming involved at an early stage.) As regards the role of government, it is anticipated that a left-of-centre government will be another favourable condition. Not only will it have a close affinity with the trade union movement, but measures promoting democratisation are also likely to be significant objectives of a socialist party in its own right.

As the IDE study points out, however, although these hypotheses are cast in the form of *a priori* arguments they were themselves formulated on the basis of the existing participation literature and preliminary, individual-country surveys. The empirical evidence therefore can hardly be expected to falsify any of the hypotheses, but it can indicate to what extent they may be considered generalised propositions across a preponderance of the twelve countries investigated. Each of the countries is given an overall relative ranking (from high to low) according to the degree of prescribed involvement of workers, or their representatives, in decision-making at various hierarchical levels of the enterprise. Yugoslavia is accorded first place, with Germany, Sweden and Norway also having a high standing. Holland and France occupy intermediate positions, with Belgium, Finland, Israel and Denmark being in the lower half of the ranking order. The two countries identified as having the weakest provisions for formalised worker participation are Italy and Britain. This ordering is, of course, only a very rough measure since it glosses over some quite important differences between individual systems of participation.[7]

In order to explain the rank ordering, subjective estimates are made of strength indicators (strong/average/weak) for the union and employer variables, together with more objective measures for some of the contextual variables. Gini-coefficients are employed as an indicator of income inequality, per capita GNP is a measure of economic wealth and – more questionably – strike rates are used to indicate the degree of cooperativeness of the industrial relations system. The findings provide broad support for the importance of an appropriate industrial relations structure in that a combination of strong union and employer organisations, along with a 'leftish' government, does seem to be conducive to the attainment of a high degree of prescribed participation (viz. the former Yugoslavia, Sweden, Norway and Germany). In contrast, there is a lower degree of prescribed participation where one or more of these requirements has generally not existed, such as in Israel and Britain (weak employers' body), and Italy (right-of-centre government).

Although the hypotheses relating to an appropriate industrial relations structure, assumed to be the critical conditioning variable, are reasonably well supported by the empirical evidence, the contextual variables appear to be less systematically related to the extensiveness of participative arrangements. Only economic growth and 'cooperativeness' of the industrial relations systems are (positively) related to participative structures. (Those countries with well-developed workers' participation have generally experienced a more rapid increase in living standards and a relatively peaceful industrial climate.) In contrast, the remaining indices for wealth, economic inequality and political democracy do not correspond at all well on an inter-country basis to the relative extent of prescribed worker-involvement in enterprise decision-making. These particular dimensions turn out to be, at best, much more random influences on participatory arrangements.

A subsequent (and partial) replication study, a decade on (IDE 1993: 25), includes the effects of changes in the macro-context upon participation – especially unemployment. It notes that a claim can be made 'that in principle where PS are largely underpinned by statutory safeguards, the potential for participation has been less undermined than where *de facto* involvement in decision making depends only on labour-market strength' – since unemployment is found to have a significantly negative (though weak) effect upon workers' influence.

OUTCOMES OF PARTICIPATION

The introduction of formal schemes for workers' participation does not in itself guarantee that their objective will, in practice, be realised since 'the process of participation is equally as important as the constitutional structure' (Loveridge 1980: 309). Also, as Strauss (1979) makes clear, the important consideration is not whether participation ever 'works' but rather under what conditions it will best function. It is therefore necessary to look at a number of what are termed 'contingency' conditions which have been shown to influence the *results* of participation in various countries. As we discuss below these include the strength of trade unions, enterprise size and hierarchical organisation, worker and management perceptions towards participation and a conducive external environment.

The effect of trade unions upon the outcomes of participation has been found to be significant in a number of individual-country studies. For the more limited forms of participation, as embodied for instance in joint consultation schemes, findings from both the USA and Britain indicate that consultation is likely to be perceived by employers as being most effective in establishments where unions either do not exist or else are weakly organised (Clarke *et al.* 1972). It would appear that, as a further Australian study points out, 'management usually regard such committees as a means of fostering employee motivation without infringing managerial prerogatives' (Lansbury 1978b: 77). In the case of statutory works councils, however, numerous studies indicate that participation is most effective in representing the interests of workers in those enterprises which are highly unionised. For one thing, union members are often more interested in participative bodies and want more influence in company decision-making than workers who are not unionised (IDE 1981b).

In Germany, a high degree of correlation has been found between unionisation and participation in works council elections and works meetings. Also, a union presence was found to be necessary since, without the protection of a union, workers in small firms might be victimised if they took the initiative to form a works council (Adams and Rummel 1977). Furthermore, although the works councils are not trade union bodies, since they are elected by all workers within an enterprise regardless of union membership, the distinction is often more apparent than real. Both in Germany and Austria more than 80 per cent of the works council members are active trade unionists. A close relationship is to be expected, since the union is the works councillors' principal source of legal and technical expertise, it provides them with training courses, and election to the works council may constitute the first step towards a union career.

In the Netherlands, a strong union presence for ensuring effective employee participation has also been found necessary. Participation could function well only if it was prepared to use means of power from time to time, which was possible only with sufficient means of support from trade unions (Looise 1989). Conversely, in Peru, the lack of unions within the worker-managed sector helped to undermine the effectiveness of participation (Berenbach 1979).

Although in many countries works councils may function in parallel with strong trade union entrenchment in the undertaking, especially where collective bargaining has traditionally taken place at the regional or industry level, nevertheless the simultaneous presence of works councils and shop stewards may lead to difficulties. In the Dutch system, for instance, although historically plant-level bargaining was not encouraged by the trade unions because of their weakness on the shopfloor, since the mid-1960s they have been establishing direct representation at plant level resembling in some respects the British shop steward system. The result has sometimes been the creation of strained relations between the works council members and shop stewards, since the union may fear that 'the works council weakens the union influence by usurping their functions; or when the works council is [apparently] too much on the side of management' (Andriessen 1976: 52). Similarly, German unions have in recent years attempted to increase their influence within the firm, particularly in the area of job regulation, by encouraging the election of shop stewards as a countervailing force to the works council. In this respect, Herding (1972: 330) has shown, in a comparison of the USA and Germany, that co-determination has been least effective in providing the equivalent of US shopfloor control, especially since grievance procedures remain under-developed, and in humanising immediate job conditions relating to physical effort, heat, safety and health conditions. As a result, he concludes that 'on the job itself management's discretion is hardly restricted'.

A second important contingency variable affecting the outcomes of participation relates to enterprise characteristics – including size, technology and, especially, hierarchical levels. In Germany, for instance, there is either minority or parity representation on supervisory boards of companies, dependent upon the type of industry and size of undertaking.[8] In that country, research findings suggest that participation is most effective in representing workers' interests in large organisations in which the management style is professional rather than paternal (Kissler 1989). Similarly, in Yugoslavia, workers in large enterprises were found to experience less sense of powerlessness than those in small organisations, although it is true that opportunities for individual involvement were generally improved in smaller enterprises (IDE 1981b). The influence of technology on participation, however, is somewhat more problematic. It has usually been assumed that increasing technological complexity will necessarily set limits to the feasibility of participation, at least at the shopfloor level. Yet the twelve-country IDE study (1981b) found little evidence of a close relationship between technology and the extent of actual participation – although automation did seem to be a significant obstacle to greater worker involvement. More recent international evidence, however, indicates that with the impact of new microelectronic technology, a smaller, more skilled and more highly motivated workforce is needed, with a correspondingly more participative approach to the management process. Participation will also be positively related to the growing integration of functions which technology permits in that 'the new worker meets fewer physical demands and acts as a monitor and facilitator rather than a maker and shaper of objects' (Cressey 1991: 9).

Of all the enterprise characteristics, there is little doubt that the strongest predictor of the distribution of influence – in the sense of capacity to affect decision outcomes – by various enterprise groups under participative arrangements is hierarchical level. Workers have the lowest amount of influence and top management the highest (IDE 1981b). In particular, it would appear that the more strategic the decision, such as capital investment programmes, the greater the concentration of influence in the hands of top management. Obradovic (1975; Obradovic and Bertsch 1979) shows that even with the Yugoslav system of workers' self-management in which the executive authority (management and staff) were supposed to implement decisions formulated by the policy authority (the workers' council and other organs of self-management), in practice deliberations within these councils were largely dominated by high-level managers and specialist, technical experts. Similar findings have emerged in relation to the Chinese 'workers congresses', established under a socialist tradition, which have become institutionalised there (Henley and Nyaw 1986) as well as in Poland.[9]

This domination by the firm's 'technocracy' in Yugoslav enterprises was especially apparent when issues such as sales policy, financial policy and market planning were debated. Thus workers' control at the top decision-making level does not appear to be a sufficient condition for overcoming inequalities created by a bureaucratic organisational structure and large differences in expertise (IDE 1981b). Nevertheless, it has been shown that Yugoslav workers could become highly involved in certain issues, such as income distribution where it involved ideological conflict with another enterprise group, when they considered it was within their interest and competence to do so. At the same time, they relinquished the more technical and business policy issues to those whom they saw as being most competent to make them (Comisso 1981). Evidence from Swedish companies also indicates that the law on codetermination has hardly affected the distribution of power therein and that, to an overwhelming degree, 'it is still owners and managements which formulate problems and identify possibilities . . . settle the alternatives and dominate the decision-making' (Berggren 1986: 107).

The importance of the particular subject area itself for the effectiveness of participation has been confirmed by other cross-national research. A three-country study of the Netherlands, Britain and Yugoslavia (DIO 1979) found that there was a relatively higher level of worker influence with respect to decisions related to personnel problems and working conditions. Danish experience with board-level representation (Westenholz 1979) also indicates that board members are likely to be more effective when the discussion concerns problems which are of direct interest to workers, such as wage and employment conditions. The influence of Dutch works councils would also appear to be greatest in the sphere of social and personnel issues (where a right of veto exists) whereas in other areas – production, technical, organisational and commercial – their influence has been limited or non-existent (Looise 1989). Similarly, in Germany, it has been concluded that 'the potential for works council intervention in managerial decision-making decreases the more closely it impinges on business policy' (Jacobi *et al.* 1992: 243).

The Biedenkopf Commission, in its evaluative study of codetermination in the German coal, iron and steel industries, also found that worker representatives on supervisory boards showed little inclination to want to influence the general business policies of their companies. Rather, they tended to defer to management representatives, particularly on matters such as investment and dividends. Finally, a comparative analysis of some producer cooperatives in France and Britain, set up in the 1970s, also confirms that 'worker directors tended to endorse managerial strategies instigated by experts, thus legitimating their control and authority and eradicating any opposition' (Bradley 1980: 165).

A third group of contingency variables concerns managers' and workers' subjective orientations, perceptions and attitudes towards participation. In Germany available data generally show a rather favourable perception of institutionalised codetermination by those directly concerned, in spite of much criticism of certain aspects of its implementation. Fürstenberg (1980) maintains, however, that its relative success was possible only because the employers' and management side became convinced that such a system provided an efficient sociotechnology for conflict management. Poole (1979) also stresses the importance of perceptions and attitudes, and suggests that the view purporting universal effects of participation, such as an assumed link between structural decentralisation and workers' satisfaction, regardless of differences in the subjective predispositions of the participants, is not tenable. Where workers regard their jobs in a markedly instrumental way they are unlikely to be concerned with control questions, and may not respond positively to participative arrangements. In the creation of the kibbutzim, however, the basic motivation was not economic but was part of a broad ideology which involved identification with the overall goals of the organisation. By contrast, empirical studies have shown that an economic motivation, certainly in joining the organisations, has been central in the plywood workers' co-operatives in the USA, and those at Mondragon in Spain (Rosner 1991). On an inter-country basis, the DIO (1979) research group reported that although in all three of its country studies (Britain, Yugoslavia and the Netherlands) workers became more satisfied with participation *per se* the more influence they had, especially because they felt that their capabilities and skills were being better utilised, there was nevertheless found to be a weaker relationship between the extent of their influence and their *general* satisfaction. An earlier cross-national study (Tannenbaum *et al.* 1974) compared the attitudes of workers in Yugoslav industry and the kibbutzim in Israel with those of workers in Italy, Austria and the USA. The Yugoslav and Israeli enterprises were seen by their employees as being relatively participative, and they reported higher levels of involvement than did their counterparts in Italy, Austria and the USA. However, differences in the extent of perceived participation cannot account for expressed differences in employee work satisfaction, trust, sense of responsibility or work motivation. Although kibbutz employees were found to be typically high in terms of these dimensions, Yugoslav workers were lower than those from less participative enterprises in the USA. The IDE study (1981b) also found that few relationships between participation and attitudes were generally stable across all twelve of its country samples. The type of participation seems to be an important factor, since research in Norway and Sweden suggests that while workers are likely to perceive that direct participation implies that employees have some degree of control, they are not so likely to see such implications in representative participation (Bartölke *et al.* 1982).

A further contingency condition relates to the influences of the external environment upon participation. No enterprise can remain autonomous from the influence of market forces and the effects of economic change. In particular, unemployment may impinge upon local processes of decision-making. In Sweden it was said that the state of codetermination has been affected more by the effects of economic recession, mergers and temporary dismissals of employees than by the new 1977 law (IDE 1981a). In western economies, it has been hypothesised by Marxists that the existence of an alien environment – including an economic system dominated by market relationships – inevitably implies inferior performance by producer-cooperative organisations in terms of efficiency, and their ultimate demise (Jones 1978). Although the validity of such a generalisation is questionable,[10] the demise of the workers' self-management system in the former Yugoslavia at the end of the 1980s has been attributed to a need to enhance managerial authority within the enterprise, as performance values came to be accorded greater emphasis in response to pressures in the economic environment to make the economy itself internationally competitive (Warner 1990). In some developing economies broader influences relating to an inhospitable environment have been adduced. Thus the failure of government-imposed participation in India has been partly attributed to a cultural and ideological climate of suspicion and distance between organised labour and management, reflected in an underdeveloped industrial relations system (Kannappan and Krishnan 1977). Similarly, research has shown that the disappointing results of the participative experiment in Peru

> must be examined partly in terms of the Peruvian culture, the evolution of industrial relations, the social structure and the distribution of power that prevailed in the past. Another country where social class lines are not drawn as sharply, where organised labour has been more fully involved in cooperative projects might [have been] able to avoid the negative results of the Peruvian model.
>
> (Whyte and Alberti 1977: 112)

PROFIT-SHARING AND EMPLOYEE SHAREHOLDING

The focus of this chapter has been upon the notion of workers' participation in decision-making and their involvement in the processes of control within the firm. However, profit-sharing and employee shareholding schemes (sometimes termed 'economic' democracy, in contrast to industrial democracy), although perhaps more marginal in this respect, may also be linked with policies on employee participation. The objective is to increase the sense of identity of employees with the companies in which they work, as well as providing an incentive to work harder, thereby improving their motivation and commitment towards enhancing organisational competitiveness. Kjellberg (1992) has noted that, in the case of Sweden, companies have introduced profit-sharing and convertible debenture schemes as a device for increasing employee commitment and for retaining staff in conditions of tight labour markets which still endured in that country. Similarly, since profit-sharing is frequently accompanied by information-sharing and enhanced communication, such financial participation may therefore increase and legitimate employee desires for increased participation in decision-making (Long and Warner 1987). Where, however, employee shareholding features as a weapon in the arsenal of the competent human-resource manager, it can impair a union's prospects since:

> Shareholding, apparently providing a personal financial stake, complements HRM attempts to establish an individual relationship between the company and its employees. Effective application of this strategy can

weaken the appeal of collectivism and even in the organised enterprise its tendency can be to marginalise the union.

(D'Art 1992: 290)

Poole (1989: 24) notes that the 1980s provided a 'period of spectacular advance' for employee financial participation schemes in a number of developed industrial countries. These include Britain, Sweden and the USA (typically in the latter via employee stock ownership plans in their own firms – ESOPs – which provide substantial tax advantages to firms) although, in contrast to extensive industrial democracy provisions, they were not introduced in Germany until more recently. Poole attributes this sort of clustering at particular periods, as with industrial democracy schemes, especially to common, supportive background conditions. In particular, positive support from governments and the legislature, as a facilitative if not determining factor, appears to have been a key influence in extending such schemes. In Britain, profit-related pay schemes (PRP) incorporating tax concessions were introduced in the 1986 Budget and now cover more than a million employees. As regards Germany, however, there has been a lack of government support in the form of fiscal encouragement by way of tax concessions, together with the complexity of German company law which also proved a restraining influence (Gurdon 1985, 1992). A theory of cross-national differences in the extent of employee financial participation based *inter alia* upon the existence of governmental and legislative support is therefore certainly sustainable, but requires further empirical assessment in order to corroborate it.

A good deal of work has, however, been done on the results of profit-sharing and share ownership schemes upon company economic and financial performance within a number of countries. For employee stock ownership schemes as well as profit-sharing in the USA, generally, though not invariably, there is evidence that the companies concerned are more profitable and more productive than their matched conventionally owned counterparts (Klein and Rosen 1986; Hanford and Grasso 1991). Yet the direction of causality is by no means clear, since it is possible that companies which are already successful introduce these kind of ownership plans, rather than employees being motivated to work harder. 'It is almost certainly the case that a company's pre-existing propensity to perform well is a major influence on company economic and financial performance rather than the introduction of the schemes themselves' (Poole and Jenkins 1990: 23). Moreover, the consequences of the schemes on financial performance will be affected by wider environmental influences, outside the control of those in the firms. A further study of the relationship between profit-sharing and productivity in the German metalworking industry found that it had a strong effect on productivity in those firms which utilised it (Fitzroy and Kraft 1987a), while in French, Italian and UK producer cooperatives profit-sharing was also generally found to have a positive effect on productivity in comparison with traditional firms (Estrin *et al.* 1987). For Japanese firms, it has been shown that the effect of introducing ESOPs is to increase productivity, on average, by almost 7 per cent (Jones and Kato 1993).

On the basis of the available empirical evidence Poole and Jenkins (1990) conclude, however, that the relationship between profit-sharing and share ownership schemes, and the economic and financial performance of companies, is complex. In general, the financial consequences would seem to be positive, although not necessarily substantial, and may operate mainly indirectly, via improved organisational identification and commitment on the part of workers, rather than directly upon their behaviour in the plant.

CONCLUSIONS

There is evidence that in the 1980s various forms of workers' participation experienced an upsurge in popularity and acceptance in Western Europe and North America – especially those which, unlike traditional adversarial collective bargaining as the central mechanism of participation, encourage greater collaboration within the enterprise and where the emphasis is on more direct types of participation (Long and Warner 1987). In this respect, as well as reflecting continuing social and technological changes, a major catalyst seems to have been the increasing competitive pressures upon firms and consequent need to secure more in the way of cooperation from their employees than simply compliance, in order to raise productivity, i.e. an increasing corporate support and initiative for participation (Drago and Heywood 1989).[11] Some observers would claim that 'the antagonistic relationship between management and unions is gradually being transformed into a symbiotic relationship in which cooperation is exchanged for participation in decision-making' (Windolf 1989: 4).

Although the cyclical, rather than evolutionary, approach to conceptualising trends in participation does recognise that the precipitating crisis for management could stem from productivity and cost competitiveness, as well as from labour challenge to managerial autonomy and control (Ramsay 1983), this perspective itself can be regarded as being perhaps too rhythmic and determinist to account for the markedly uneven advance of workers' participation schemes.[12] Poole (1989: 6) has therefore put forward the notion of 'favourable conjunctures' as an explanatory approach to organisational democracy, which also encompasses both workers' participation in decision-making and their financial participation. This

encapsulates the notion of an uneven, but advancing, pattern of participation which is dependent upon variations in environmental circumstances
and situations both between and within particular countries, as well as on
the strategies of the actors, in that 'international differences in practice . . .
are seen to reflect diverse cultural and ideological conditions; complexities
in the relationships of power between the state, employers and trade
unions; and distinctive legislative initiatives.'[13]

In assigning weights to the main explanatory propositions, the distribution of power in the industrial relations system is seen as especially
crucial to both the shaping of representative institutions and their operation. Where the state is dominant, highly formalised and regulated methods
of participation tend to occur, when management is powerful joint consultative machinery is likely to predominate and, if workers are the major
initiating agents, then producer cooperatives will frequently be forthcoming (Poole 1981, 1986b). Furthermore, the thesis also acknowledges
that specific forms of participation may advance or decline in distinctive
periods. For instance, historical evidence in Britain and the USA demon-
strates that producer (or worker) cooperatives have experienced discontinuous waves of formation, as a defensive reaction by labour to
periodic social and economic crises, such as to save or create jobs at times
of a slackening of economic activity, as in the UK, or to a loss of craft status
by workers as in the USA (Cornforth 1989).

In terms of the outcomes of employees' participation in decision-
making, cross-national evidence indicates that the results have been
limited. 'In general, the pattern is for management decision-making powers
to be left largely unimpaired by representative bodies and for no fundamental transformation of actual influence to take place' (Poole 1986b:
253). Thus, in Norway, Belgium and Holland it has been found that
workers' representatives on company boards and works councils have had
little success in influencing decisions (Wall and Lischeron 1977), and in
the German iron, steel and coal industries equal employee representation
on the boards of companies has not resulted in major changes in the nature
and substance of corporate decision-making. In Sweden, there is widespread scepticism about the usefulness of the codetermination law in ensuring employees' influence over crucial and strategic decisions when their
interests are fundamentally at odds with those of their employer, nor
evidently has it produced sufficient changes in working conditions on the
shopfloor to increase markedly job satisfaction (Haas 1983). In fact, in all
the countries investigated by the IDE group (1981b, 1993) the degree of
democratisation of decision-making processes within work organisations
appeared to be fairly low, with the one notable exception of Yugoslavia. In
that country, despite the discrepancies between formally prescribed

participation and its actual practical execution, enterprises did seem able to provide a more equal distribution of power and individual involvement in decision-making than those elsewhere. Generally, however, management was dominant in long-term strategic decisions and worker representative bodies had only limited influence, mainly confined to personnel and welfare issues.

Nevertheless, workers in many countries do appear to have obtained certain benefits from participative arrangements at the enterprise level, even though they apparently provide the individual worker with little sense of personal involvement. From the employees' standpoint it has been concluded that the greatest single improvement produced by the Swedish codetermination law is an increase in the flow of information (Hammarström 1987). Similarly, the main achievements of codetermination in the German coal and steel industries have been seen as the growing information potential and advance notice of enterprise change accorded to worker representatives, given the priority accorded to manpower planning under codetermination (Berghahn and Karsten 1987). This has meant that it has been possible to negotiate the substance, pace and conditions of economic reorganisation and technical change with a minimum of labour–management conflict and strikes (Adams and Rummel 1977).[14] Indeed, the Biedenkopf Commission was apparently more impressed with the pacifying effects which codetermination had on organised labour than with the sense of participation which it imparted to individual workers. Further evidence that formal participation as a mechanism of conflict resolution does contribute to the reduction of open industrial conflict is also available. In the Mondragon producer cooperatives, for instance, although conflict does undoubtedly exist there is a 'relative absence of a worker–management gulf' and only one strike has ever occurred within the group (Bradley and Gelb 1981).

Thus, as Eldridge *et al.* (1991: 143) have recently observed, the concept of participation or industrial democracy is important in shaping the whole industrial relations landscape regarding the boundaries of the authority of property and the limits imposed on the rights of labour, together with 'the questions of power that it raises, in its probing of the legitimate role of management, unions and workers within the state and enterprise, and in its potentiality for restructuring organizations'.

FURTHER READING

A useful and up-to-date, if somewhat factual, account of workers' participation in the EC and in twelve individual countries is contained in the special issue on the topic of the *Bulletin of Comparative Labour Relations*,

23, 1992. The German system is well analysed in Berghahn and Karsten (1987), while many of the issues raised in this chapter are dealt with in the contributions to the volumes of the *International Handbook of Participation in Organizations* (formerly *International Yearbook of Organizational Democracy*). A shorter, recent survey of employee participation schemes is Ramsay (1991).

8 Industrial relations in multinational enterprises

It is estimated that multinational enterprises (MNEs) control about half of the world's industrial capacity and two-thirds of its trade (Bendiner 1987). In 1980, some 350 firms, controlling 25,000 subsidiaries, accounted for 28 per cent of the Gross Domestic Product of the capitalist world. MNEs are thus a primary manifestation of the internationalisation of capital – 'the process which an increasingly integrated capitalist world economy has developed and by which capital has become ever more global in its operation' (Jenkins 1987: 11). The MNEs themselves are the predominant form of business organisation within international economic relations and they are 'among the most powerful economic institutions yet produced by the capitalist system' (Dunning 1981: 3). Within this overall pattern of activity, US-based multinationals continue to dominate international investment with US holdings abroad in 1979 accounting for half of the world's total multinational foreign assets (Little 1982). The relative importance of US-based enterprises has, however, been declining as a result of a recent trend towards greater diversification in the MNEs' countries of origin, including Japan, Germany and some other European nations, as well as some of the newly industrialising countries in South East Asia.

Although multinational concerns are by no means homogeneous, since they differ in aspects such as their size, type of technology utilised and the extent to which international production facilities are integrated, their key distinguishing features are subsumed in the following definitional characteristics: they produce or operate functionally in more than one country rather than merely selling abroad; their operations transverse national boundaries, often on a global scale; and they engage in foreign direct (rather than portfolio) investment. An additional criterion which is sometimes employed is that they have a ratio of foreign to total operations above some arbitrary percentage.

Enderwick (1982) proposes that one essential qualitative difference between national and multinational firms is the internalisation of previously external markets in the latter, and the consequent importance of intra-enterprise transactions within the MNE itself. Internalisation theory itself has been developed to provide an economic rationale for the existence of MNEs. It maintains that because of the transactions costs which arise as a result of conducting business in imperfect markets, it is more efficient (less expensive) for the firm to use its own internal structures rather than external market intermediaries, since this avoids the difficulties and uncertainties of, for instance, determining appropriate market prices for selling to independent firms.

THEORIES OF MNEs

There are a number of theories purporting to explain the primary impetus for the growth and extension of multinational firms which have been put forward. Two of the best-known general explanations relate first to the need to locate subsidiaries in foreign countries in order to overcome tariff barriers and import quotas which prevent competition via more traditional trading relationships. Second, there is the 'runaway' companies hypothesis whereby enterprises may invest abroad in order to secure the advantages of cheaper labour costs in the production process together with weaker unions or, as in Austria (Traxler 1992), the attractions of social peace. Trade unions in the USA would claim that the establishment by US companies of subsidiaries in Latin America, Asia, the Caribbean and Europe has brought about economic loss to US workers. In relation to this explanation, however, one difficulty is to account for the fact that many countries including the United States are both 'source' and 'host' countries to foreign investment at the same time. Also, there is the more obvious point that the level and rate of change of relative labour costs between countries may be misleading in terms of more crucial unit labour cost considerations, because of differences in productivity and output growth. Flanagan (1974) has suggested that the hypothesis may prove to be valid only for the limited case of some horizontal multinational investments in less developed countries, such as electronics in Taiwan or the clothing industry in Mexico. On this view, therefore, the primary motive for the extension of multinationals relates to economic variables other than labour costs.

In fact, a more sophisticated explanation holds that firms are encouraged to expand abroad and seek world-wide markets in order to exploit profitably some firm-specific advantage which they have managed to acquire. The advantage may take a number of possible forms such as product differentiation, managerial expertise, technological knowledge and marketing skills, or scale economies. Where knowledge is the firm-specific advantage, the MNE may exploit this property right by exporting to countries which do not impose substantial barriers to free trade, or by establishing subsidiaries in those which do.

One of the foremost theories of multinational growth within the manufacturing sector is the product-life-cycle model in which firms develop new products at home ('growth' stage) and then exploit them abroad, first by means of exporting and later by setting up subsidiaries to which the product, and ultimately process, technologies are transferred. Towards the 'maturity' stage of the cycle the product price tends to be driven down and profit margins decline as other firms begin to imitate the product, and exports then become displaced by the expanding, and lower-cost, foreign-based production ('decline' stage). In consequence, the firm's competitive strategy moves away from product technology where its control has been largely superseded towards new and superior process technology, as a defensive measure designed to reduce production costs. At the same time, it establishes its own subsidiaries in foreign markets which enables the elimination of non-competitive cost factors such as tariffs and transport charges, so that the firm itself becomes 'multinational'. Within its home-country base – although employment on the production side has declined – the enterprise then generates managerial capabilities and supporting services to supply world markets which often entail 'the development of large scale, high technology, conglomerate organisations with superior financial resources' (Kujawa 1979: 17).

A conceptual scheme relating to the behavioural aspects of the evolution of multinational companies has been advocated by Perlmutter (1969). He classifies MNEs in terms of their basic operating strategy which may be ethnocentric (home-country oriented), polycentric (host-country oriented), or geocentric (world-oriented):

> An ethnocentric strategy means that the top management . . . attempt to implement the values, policies and sentiments of the parent company regardless of environmental differences that affect foreign operations. A polycentric strategy, on the other hand, emphasises environmental differences and reflects a deliberate choice by the parent company to make foreign operations as local in identity as possible. The geocentric strategy reflects a truly global outlook; it recognises environmental differences but prescribes the inter-relationships with the external conditions on a purely functional basis without any preconceived notion of omniscience at home office or the foreign subsidiary.
>
> (Schöllhammer 1973: 21)

A fundamental premise of this classificatory approach is that an ethnocentric strategy is more liable to give rise to various forms of industrial relations conflict than either a polycentric or geocentric orientation. Other things being equal, the latter strategies help to promote greater organisational effectiveness.

INDUSTRIAL RELATIONS IMPLICATIONS

Having delineated some of the factors which account for the emergence and expansion of MNEs we may now consider their specific relationship to, and impact upon, industrial relations – in particular the ways in which they may impinge upon trade union and worker interests. In this respect, the major considerations derive from the perceived strength of the multinational (with power to act without reference to other interests) which operates as a transnational decision-making unit with internationally spread facilities and can thus marshal and mobilise resources across national boundaries. Unlike a national company whose management is an actor within a single industrial relations system, an MNE operates within a number of systems simultaneously. It can therefore be argued that multinationals represent a possible destabilising force within industrial relations, displacing the existing power balance and resulting in asymmetrical relationships between multinational managements, unions and even governments. 'The discretionary powers inherent in [MNEs'] supranational decision making structure potentially enable them to impose their will upon the local partners in the industrial relations systems in which they operate' (Bomers 1976: 2). It has also been claimed by Crouch (1982a) that the growth of multinational companies constitutes the most important challenge to the position which western trade unions have achieved within their own countries.

One particular implication of the product-life-cycle theory is that labour relations in overseas subsidiaries may be subject to a large degree of managerial control by the parent company as a result of transfers of product and process technologies. Managerial staffs seconded to the subsidiaries might attempt to 'carry-over' industrial relations policies which appertain in the home country, such as those relating to bargaining structures or union recognition. These may, however, be entirely inappropriate to the differing customs, practices and institutional framework found in the host country and could provoke industrial conflict.

In fact, the literature identifies a number of recurrent themes in which it is alleged that the nature and activities of MNEs may impinge adversely upon the interests of organised labour. Unions have typically viewed the multinational location of a firm's operations as an extension of the historical trend towards widening product markets. This development is seen as raising three major potential threats to trade union members and their organisations. The first relates to employment effects and the concern for job security, as a result of direct foreign investment displacing exports from the home country by producing abroad what could have been produced at home (as in the product-cycle model). In the United States, it is also claimed that multinational firms, as the main vehicle for transferring information, combine US capital and technology with cheap labour abroad and in the process erode US comparative advantage and damage labour interests (Hood and Young 1979). Furthermore, the possible job loss from long-term production transfers of existing MNE facilities to more favoured locations has also been of paramount concern and it is believed that multinational subsidiaries are more likely to disinvest and cease production than are home-based companies.

A second consideration is the undermining or weakening of union bargaining power in relation to that of management which arises particularly as a result of the broader financial base of the MNE. In the event, or threat, of a strike for instance at any one of its subsidiaries, the enterprise may be able to continue to meet its market commitments, maintain cash inflows and thus minimise the costs which the union is able to impose by means of production switching between its various locations. The ability to utilise what have been termed 'industrial relations scale economies' (Ulman 1974b) for strategic advantage and bargaining leverage is especially prevalent where the MNE has adopted a deliberate policy of dual, or multiple, sourcing (alternative supplies) of either products or components in different countries. Some observers would regard this capacity to continue to generate financial inflows in an environment external to a labour–management conflict as one important, distinguishing feature between multi- and uni-national companies (Kujawa 1980). The economic pressure which a nationally based union can exert upon an MNE is certainly less than would be the case if the company's operations were confined to one country. Within the multinational substantial financial resources and cross-subsidisation can be made available to any part of the organisation which is in conflict with a union, thus enhancing its ability to take a strike. In effect, the MNE typically has a greater range of options open to it and more staying power than a national company. Under certain conditions multinational location of production facilities, especially when combined with conglomerate diversification as between industries, may therefore give the employer the capacity to make the institutionalised collective bargaining system an ineffective method of resolving industrial disputes (Craypo 1975).

A related characteristic of the MNE which is also regarded as a threat to union bargaining power is the alleged remote locus of its decision-making, central authority. Unions claim (Levinson 1972) that they are being kept at arm's length and that local managements do not have the ultimate authority to respond to union initiatives, since the crucial industrial relations decisions are being made from outside the country in which a subsidiary is located. Bargaining and union penetration are made more difficult because of the inaccessibility of the decision-makers and the unions' inability to deal directly with those who make the final decisions on major labour issues. It is often difficult to define the point in the management structure at which to target union influence. Within the areas of corporate strategy and financial policy there is said to be a particular elusiveness, obscurity and lack of 'transparency' as to the real source of decision-making.

There is also likely to be a lack of hard financial information relating to the position of MNE subsidiaries which can be used for collective bargaining purposes since, 'when financial data are reported on a corporate-wide basis, unions are wholly dependent on whatever information the local subsidiary chooses to reveal' (Bomers 1976: 20). The financial performance of individual units may be further concealed because of the use of manipulative, intra-corporate 'transfer pricing' of goods and services between component parts of the organisation, at a higher or lower figure than for actual value received.[1] By this means, the multinational can allow profits to accrue at whichever national location it selects within the corporate structure, thereby distorting their real sources of origin. The shifting of income across national boundaries, with a view to the optimal exploitation of international differences, could be used not only as a means of reducing the overall tax liability of the enterprise but also to diminish trade union demands upon corporate revenue (Weinburg 1978). For all these reasons trade unions have experienced a sense of power loss from the expansion of MNE operations and wish to attempt to re-establish a measure of equilibrium.

Having identified the basic trade union concerns relating to possible job displacement, reduced bargaining power and a more remote locus of decision-making, it is necessary to examine the research findings from empirical studies of the interaction of MNEs upon industrial relations, particularly as between countries, in order to ascertain to what extent such claims appear to be substantiated. A careful examination of the evidence is required since the field is typified by much anecdotal evidence together with specific examples which, although they may be valid on an individual basis, might lack more general applicability.

EMPIRICAL EVIDENCE

The question of the employment effects of MNE activity is a complex one. To the extent that exports from the home country become replaced by sales from overseas subsidiaries, domestic employment opportunities would initially diminish. Nevertheless, such possible adverse effects from production displacement could be offset by positive employment influences. For instance, the location of production facilities abroad may enable the multinational to penetrate markets which otherwise would not be readily available to it. A net gain in employment may also result from the subsidiaries' demand for exports of capital goods, intermediate products or materials from the home country or, indirectly, from the expansion of white-collar employment as a result of the centralisation of management services at the parent headquarters. A number of studies have attempted to estimate, more specifically, the effects of foreign direct investment by US firms on the net number of US jobs thereby created or lost. Ulmer (1980) suggests that the findings are at least consistent with the hypothesis that, on balance, the growth of home-based MNEs has increased US employment. A further study of the employment impact of British, German and French MNE operations in Greece, Spain and Portugal, for the automobile, chemical and engineering industries (Buckley and Artisien 1988), found in some cases that exports were replaced by the direct investment – with a consequent reduction in home-country employment. In other instances, however, the increase in balancing exports (sub-assemblies, intermediate goods, technology flows) compensated for a fall in final goods exports and increased market penetration produced a zero impact on home employment. For industrialised market economies in general, it has been concluded that expansion of MNE activities has not been accompanied by a decrease in the volume of employment in home-country activities (ILO 1981a).

An examination of MNE industrial relations in Western Europe (ILO 1976) has instanced, however, a number of production and employment shifts in the food products industries which were intended to offset losses accruing from strikes. Also, there are well-known individual instances of company closure by US organisations and repatriation of capital following a prolonged strike, such as the textile engineering firm of Roberts–Arundel in Britain (Arnison 1970). There have also been a number of cases of precipitate plant or departmental shutdowns in Belgium, the Netherlands and France – but fewer in Germany where the works council system and worker representation on supervisory boards offer protection against this sort of arbitrary management action (ILO 1976). However, the evidence suggests that the possible job displacement which could occur from large-scale production switching to a more favoured location is limited. Technical-economic considerations, particularly in capital-intensive industries, are likely to reduce the propensity of companies to shift their production in this way. Three factors are identified as being significant in this respect. The high sunk costs in existing production facilities, together with the costs of liquidating large investments, provide effective constraints.

Once an investment has been made the enterprise may then be locked in, especially in the short run, although it could gradually disinvest over the longer term and run down its investment. In addition, a relatively low labour intensity restricts the incentive to move production to a lower wage location, while at the same time the greater capital intensity may enhance the ability of organised labour to effectively block potential production transfers (Bomers and Peterson 1977).

Temporary production switching in order to defeat a strike is more feasible, however, and the evidence suggests that this has occurred in the automobile industry (Kujawa 1971). It requires that the enterprise maintains some form of parallel production policy across a number of its locations as well as the existence of spare productive capacity, since if all plants are fully employed then production switching would prove costly. In the case of MNEs in Germany and the Netherlands, however, Bomers and Peterson (1977) found that such a practice was rare, partly as a consequence of union attempts to prevent it and because of subsidiary managements' concern for its possible adverse effects upon local labour relations. An additional constraint may derive from the high 'visibility' of multinationals and concern for their public image, which makes them sensitive to unfavourable public opinion. Further, the opportunities for production switching to defeat a strike are especially limited for vertically integrated MNEs, since the costs of duplicating processes are likely to prove exorbitant (Enderwick 1985).

As a further aspect of the conduct of MNEs in labour matters, we can examine the evidence concerning the locus of authority issue (parent/ subsidiary relationship) and the union claim of overcentralisation in decision-making. The propensity of corporate headquarters to intervene in subsidiaries' operations is partly dependent upon technological and organisational considerations. Intervention is more probable, for instance, if the subsidiary is a key plant, such as a single source of supply within a production system which is both technologically complex and highly integrated (Hamill 1984). Similarly, where investment in a given plant is very large because of the capital-intensive nature of its operations, the MNE is likely to exercise a greater degree of influence over the activities of a foreign subsidiary, including its industrial relations practices. As a result, multinational food companies located in Western Europe seem to have more decentralised policy-making than do automobile companies (ILO 1976).

A greater degree of local autonomy is also typical of long-established overseas subsidiaries which, with less well-developed international communications at the time of their founding, were encouraged to be more self-sufficient. This would be true in the case of British and Swedish parent companies, whereas with US multinationals established in more recent times high-speed communications were better developed. Thus the US subsidiaries became accustomed to maintaining closer contacts with the home country (Kassalow 1978a). Additionally, enterprises which are highly diversified in terms of product range and geographical markets served usually incorporate a multi-divisional organisational structure, which also encourages the decentralisation of functions such as industrial relations (Enderwick 1982).[2]

In fact, it is well established that the extent to which multinationals operate a relatively decentralised structure for managing the operations of their subsidiaries varies according to factors such as the structure of ownership (whether a fully integrated, or a holding, company) and the actual functional specialism involved. The allocation of investment funds, for instance, which has substantial effects on production and employment, is a strategic matter which is invariably controlled by central headquarters in the home country. In contrast, one of the most heavily decentralised, operational functions is industrial relations since inter-country cultural and legal differences make it a much more complex area than, say, production or marketing (Warner and Turner 1972). It is usually contended that the more marked are the differences between the customs or culture of the host country and those of the home country, the greater the need for decentralisation in industrial relations decision-making. A study of multinational operations in India, for instance, found that international companies enforce tight technical and financial control over subsidiaries, but allow purely local influences to determine the nature and form of their labour relations, even when foreign managers are retained in crucial positions (Banaji and Hensman 1990).

There is clear evidence, however, that within the industrial relations function itself significant differences also exist in the extent of parent company involvement, depending upon the national origin of the MNE. A number of studies (Roberts and May 1974; Bomers 1976; Hedlund 1981; Hamill 1984) indicate that US multinationals exercise greater centralised control over labour relations, whereas the subsidiaries of British companies are more decentralised. British multinational firms may give general policy advice to their subsidiaries but rarely become directly involved in collective bargaining issues or negotiating processes as such, believing that there should be minimum central interference on these matters. In contrast, Blake (1973) found a much greater readiness for the headquarters of US multinationals to become involved in their affiliates' industrial relations activities and to make them a more integral part of general corporate management. This was especially apparent in those areas of greatest potential conflict, such as collective bargaining negotiations and strike settlement. Studies of multinational operations in Canada, Brazil, Italy and

Nigeria (La Palombara and Blank 1976), and in Malaysia (Sim 1977) also found that US-based multinationals concentrate authority at corporate headquarters, with greater emphasis on formal management controls and a close reporting system. In contrast, for European-based MNEs, there was found to be a looser relationship between head office and local subsidiaries as well as a greater willingness to accept the judgement of local managers. In Italy during the 1980s, large companies such as Fiat and Olivetti consolidated a multi-divisional structure in which separate business sectors or sub-sectors were given operational autonomy within overall corporate strategic and financial control (Ferner and Hyman 1992b).

The reasons for this more pronounced emphasis in US multinationals on close and systematic managerial control may be partly related to the organisational structure of US firms. They display a greater tendency than European firms to operate rigidly hierarchical decision-making systems at the corporate level (Shetty 1979), particularly within the area of financial control, so as to ensure that profit planning targets are attained. European companies, on the other hand, tend to operate what is termed a 'collegial' decision-making system where there is collective responsibility among a top management team for the affairs of the enterprise – in contrast to the power embodied in the chief executive of a US firm. This European style of decision-making facilitates greater involvement by managements of foreign subsidiaries and therefore a higher degree of decentralisation and autonomy among the affiliates. European multinationals appear to prefer functional divisions, multiple reporting and more personalised headquarters–subsidiary relationships than do their US-based counterparts.

In addition to these differences in organisation, structure and processes, European-owned multinationals have dealt mainly with unions at industry (and sometimes plant) level and have had less well-developed company-based industrial relations policies and, possibly, less professionalised managements to implement them in comparison with US enterprises. Also, Roberts and May (1974), in a comparison of British and US multinationals, noted the greater tendency for US affiliates to be wholly-owned; whereas, with the more common British practice of joint ownership, by buying into an overseas company, it is usual to leave current local industrial relations practices undisturbed. With that type of arrangement, 'it is more likely that local patterns of industrial relations will be allowed to determine policy in this area of management responsibilities' (Roberts and May 1974: 407).

In those multinationals in which headquarters' control of important aspects of labour relations is extensive, a related question concerns the possibility of non-conforming behaviour by subsidiaries with the norms and industrial relations practices of their host countries, thereby provoking possible conflict. Research findings suggest that some MNEs initially attempted to export the policies characteristic of their home country, such as an unwillingness on the part of some US multinationals to permit their affiliates in Europe to join employers' associations or, in certain cases, to grant union recognition.

In a six-country study of MNE industrial relations in the food and metal industries of Western Europe (ILO 1976), few alleged problems were found in respect of lack of union recognition by foreign-based multinationals in France or Belgium. This was attributed to the universal practice in those two countries of large firms becoming members of their appropriate trade, or industry, employers' organisation – since union recognition is generally automatically accorded by these associations. Indeed, in Belgium, since the national or regional collective agreement can have a binding effect on all employers regardless of whether or not they are association members, some multinationals joined the employers' body in order to secure an influence on the negotiation of agreements affecting them. Also, in Germany, the extensive legal prescription of the structure and substance of industrial relations is an important constraining influence on the conduct and labour practices of multinationals, leaving them less room for manoeuvre and ensuring closer conformity with national practices in the host country. The greater legal prescription of industrial relations in Germany (and to a lesser extent in France) therefore means that in some ways multinational enterprises may constitute less distinctive problems to unions in those countries than in, say, Britain – despite the fact that their union membership densities are relatively lower. For Sweden, the strength of the employer and union federations and the primacy accorded to their joint regulation of industrial relations again makes it difficult for any large enterprise to hold out against employer association membership and conforming practices, which include union recognition.

There have been rather more problems, however, involving an initial, and occasionally continuing, refusal by MNEs to grant recognition in Britain and to some extent in the Netherlands. Some US companies, such as Kodak and IBM, attempted to carry over their home-country practices of opposition to union recognition, together with non-membership of employers' organisations. In the Italian subsidiaries of some foreign multinationals a trend towards direct employee involvement, by-passing the union, has also been observed (Ferner and Hyman 1992b), while in Spain MNE firms appear to have been in the vanguard of implementing individualistic approaches to industrial relations. They have led in the development of quality circles and of individualised payment systems, team-working and multiskilling (Lucio 1992).

Enderwick and Buckley (1983) and Buckley and Enderwick (1985) found evidence that in British manufacturing industry foreign-owned establishments had a somewhat higher probability than indigenous ones of having non-union manual employees, although a later study (based on a smaller sample) suggested that there was little difference between foreign and domestically owned enterprises in Britain in respect of union recognition (Purcell *et al.* 1987). Both studies, however, found that there was a greater preference on the part of foreign-owned firms for single-employer bargaining at either corporate, and more especially plant, level (together with non-membership of an employers' association) because of the advantage of the greater discretion which is permitted in labour utilisation, together with enhanced control over labour costs. Foreign-owned establishments showed a greater reluctance than British-owned plants to negotiate over recruitment, manning levels and changes in production methods, so that on matters of labour utilisation they asserted managerial prerogative – which, it is suggested, may go some way towards explaining their higher labour productivity. There was also evidence that they pursued more centralised and tightly controlled policies at corporate level in relation to industrial relations matters, which may lengthen and obfuscate bargaining processes, since wage bargaining in foreign-owned MNEs is likely to involve extensive upward consultation on the part of management.

In addition to the importance of employer association membership, as an intervening variable affecting the industrial relations conduct of multinationals and their assimilation of host-country practices, another important factor would appear to be the influence of the extent of the national product market. Because of the very large size of the US home market, for example, US overseas subsidiaries may represent only a relative minority of the parent MNE's business. Consequently, in proportion to their total sales 'where the overseas share is relatively small the home office may tend to regard overseas problems, including some labour problems, as a mere extension of home country operations and try to impose home country standards' (ILO 1976: 26). By way of contrast, however, for Dutch, Swedish, Swiss (and some British) multinationals, subsidiary operations abroad can represent the major part of their total business. Domestic sales of the two leading Swiss MNEs, for instance, amount in both cases to less than 4 per cent of their output – with the result that adaptation to host-country institutions and conditions may more easily be accepted than by US companies.

Gennard (1974) has pointed out, however, that certain multinational labour practices may be regarded as a positive and sometimes innovating – rather than adverse – influence upon host-country industrial relations. Within MNE subsidiaries located in Britain, he instances the development in the 1960s of productivity bargaining and measured-day-work schemes of wage payment to promote better labour utilisation. A comparative study by Takamiya (1981) of the operation of two Japanese television set factories located in Britain with similar British- and US-owned factories, broadly equivalent in size and technology (although not perfectly matched), found that the superior productivity performance of the Japanese plants could be attributed mainly to organisational factors carried over from the company's home base. Work practices and occupational categories were more flexible than in the British factory and there were fewer hierarchical as well as functional demarcations among workers. Since it was felt that the traditional British multi-union structure with its potential for demarcation difficulties would be detrimental to flexible work practices, one union (together with its white-collar section) was given organising rights for the entire workforce in the Japanese-owned plants, in contrast to the six unions which existed in the British factory. There was thus a partial introduction of some elements of Japanese-style union structure into the production units, although this factor should not be overrated (White and Trevor 1983).

Although the empirical evidence for Western European countries is limited and much of it based on general questionnaire survey techniques, Bomers and Peterson (1977) maintain that within the highly integrated and institutionalised industrial relations systems which typify those countries the potential for substantial negative effects from multinational activities is considerably constrained. For these authors, the critical, unresolved issue is somewhat different, namely the unilateral and supranational decision-making powers of the MNE itself. They recognise, however, that the discretionary powers of multinational companies and their potential for adverse industrial relations consequences could be considerably greater in other types of location. This might be the case in those countries with weak trade unions, a buyers' labour market and less well-entrenched industrial relations institutions and regulatory arrangements, as in many developing nations of the Third World which have been receptive to the inflow of foreign investment. In support of such a possibility Kassalow (1978a), in his three-country study of MNEs in Asia, found that in Malaysia there have been problems of resistance to union recognition, aided by restrictive government legislation designed to attract foreign investment (see Chapter 9). Once again, this was especially noticeable in the case of certain US companies which do not bargain with unions at home and have implemented a similar policy abroad. Yet equivalent problems do not seem to have arisen in Singapore where the unions' close relations with the ruling political party helped membership recruitment campaigns. In fact, in both countries – as well as in the Philippines – unions appear, on the whole, to have found it somewhat easier to organise and bargain with multinationals than with indigenously owned companies. The latter had less experience of dealing with unions, were more hostile towards them and had less systematically developed procedures for grievance handling.

STRIKE INCIDENCE

We have already noted that foreign-owned multinationals may have a greater potential for labour conflict than indigenous companies. This could occur either from the importing of 'alien' home-country practices into a different and unreceptive environment, or because of the remoteness of ultimate decision-taking, at too great a distance from the workforce concerned. On the other hand, it is generally conceded that wages and other economic benefits provided by MNEs usually compare very favourably with those of equivalent national firms. This may be a direct reflection of the fact that:

> for many [multinationals] the cost of a global division of labour is acute sensitivity to production disruption. Avoidance of such disruption may be one factor influencing the high wage policies and the use of financial inducements . . . to regulate labour relations.
>
> (Enderwick 1982: 37)

'Cross-border interdependency' of production within multinationals makes them particularly vulnerable to stoppages and there is evidence that in recent years some MNEs operating transnationally in Europe, such as Ford, have increased both the integration of their operations in the interests of economies of scale and reduced the levels of their inventory stocks because of cost considerations. Where such transnational sourcing patterns have been developed, so that a subsidiary in one country relies on another in a different country as a source of components, then as Robock and Simmonds (1989) have observed, industrial relations throughout the MNE becomes one of the key factors in operating a global production strategy. Furthermore, because of the vulnerability of MNEs with integrated operations to strike threats, a study of multinational management strategies in the European automobile industry found that manufacturers themselves use threats – namely to withhold future investment – in order to secure compliance with their needs and to put pressure on local bargainers (Mueller and Purcell 1992).

It is, however, an empirical question as to whether or not foreign-owned subsidiaries do experience more strike activity (used as a quantitative measure of conflict) than do equivalent domestic firms. The results of such comparisons might also influence the relative attractiveness of further multinational investment abroad. For the UK, Enderwick and Buckley (1982) found, as did an earlier study using a similar data base (Millward

1979), that foreign-owned plants in British manufacturing over the period 1971–3 (particularly US ones) had comparatively higher strike frequency and man-days lost than domestically owned plants. However, the adverse strike magnitude of foreign-owned, in relation to domestic, establishments was confined to the smaller bands of plant size.[3] As plant size increased above 1,000 employees, the overseas affiliates then appeared to have a much better comparative record in relation to indigenous plants within that size range. It may be that large foreign-owned plants, especially those with greater capital intensity and interrelated production processes, would face higher strike costs and that this encourages them to develop procedures for containing the conflict.

It is necessary, however, to note another important finding of this study that, as regards their relative strike-proneness, foreign-owned firms do not represent a homogeneous set. When strike frequency, after controlling for plant size, was subdivided by country groupings in terms of origins – USA, EEC or 'other' – it was found that multinationals with some home base other than the United States or EEC countries seem to experience a rather lower relative strike record at plant sizes below 1,000 employees, whereas above that size band their record rapidly deteriorates. It is suggested that this may be a consequence of their experience in operating plants typically of only a limited size in their home base, particularly where it is a small country such as Switzerland, together which the management difficulties which arise where the location of their (larger) overseas operations is in a markedly different social and cultural context. Yet the fact remains that, despite such qualifications, for most plant size ranges US firms experienced a somewhat higher strike rate than non-US firms and, when analysed by strike 'cause' (that is, the principal reasons given for striking), they also had a proportionately greater number of disputes over trade union questions and labour utilisation – manning levels, work allocation, etc. – especially in larger-sized plants. This 'supports the view that their higher productivity and the demands of operating a global division of labour may well be obtained at the price of proportionately more such disputes' (Enderwick and Buckley 1982: 318).

Similar investigations have been carried out for MNE subsidiaries located in Canada and Ireland. In their study of foreign ownership and strike activity in Canada, Cousineau *et al.* (1991: 619) argue that the probability of a strike may be increased when a third party is involved. This is because of the greater complexity of the ensuing negotiations and delay in the employers' reaction time, due to the increased quantity of information to be processed. Equally, however, the probability may be decreased, as a result of the greater cost of a strike in the case of subsidiaries of foreign countries which 'must, more so than other firms, appear to be good citizens [since] a strike may . . . be quickly interpreted as an attempt by a large and powerful foreign firm to exploit local workers'. Their findings suggest that foreign ownership actually has a statistically significant, negative influence upon strike activity in Canada – although this conclusion must be regarded as tentative since, not least, foreign firms are by no means a homogeneous grouping. Ng and Maki (1988) confined their Canadian empirical study to the effects on strike activity of US multinational subsidiaries. They found that, although decision-making authority for these enterprises is highly centralised at US headquarters, in terms of man-days lost US companies operating in Canada are no more likely to be involved in strikes than domestically owned firms.

In the case of Ireland, it was found that non-Irish companies operating there over the period 1960–84 have as a whole been more strike-prone than indigenous firms (Kelly and Brannick 1988). This was particularly the case for British companies after the 1960s. However, the explanation is felt to relate more to the economic pressures experienced by particular (often government grant-aided) companies, against the background of the change from a closed to a more open economy, than in factors such as adjustment difficulties of MNE subsidiaries to host-nation industrial relations traditions and practices.

In view of these somewhat disparate findings, it is apparent that further work remains to be done on this important question for particular countries, or groupings at a low level of aggregation, in order to clarify more fully the factors involved in relative strike-proneness as between home-based companies and the MNEs of different national origins.

TRADE UNION RESPONSE TO MNEs

The empirical evidence suggests that the relative bargaining power of labour in its dealings with MNEs is particularly disadvantaged as regards difficulties in obtaining information for bargaining purposes, together with the inaccessibility of higher management decision-making levels and the considerable delays introduced into the bargaining process by upward consultation requirements. Enderwick (1985) argues, however, that the frequent assertion that a multinational structure *per se* invariably places labour at a disadvantage has been too easily accepted, especially in the case of vertically integrated MNEs where labour may enjoy considerable bargaining leverage as a consequence of their interdependency. Nevertheless, it is true that a predominant view, particularly in the 1970s, was that the most effective long-term response by labour would involve some form of international union action in order to countervail the organisational structure and activities of MNEs and to redress the unions' own sense of power loss. Ultimately, this might result in the development of bargaining structures which are coextensive with the boundaries of the multinational itself, that is transnational, or global, collective bargaining.

As a means of facilitating coordinated action and the provision of mutual assistance, the unions have utilised the services of the International Trade Secretariats (ITSs) to which they are affiliated.[4] These represent one possible institutional form through which international collective bargaining structures might be developed. The sixteen ITSs, mostly Geneva-based, consist of individual unions from around the world grouped into more or less closely related industrial categories such as metals, transport, public services and chemicals (Windmuller 1980). Within any particular ITS, the major principle which therefore links the unions is their attachment to a specific industry, or industry groups, and their common problems. The Secretariats seek to advance the collective bargaining objectives of their member unions and are 'industrial' rather than 'global' internationals, unlike the World Federation of Trade Unions (WFTU) or the International Confederation of Free Trade Unions (ICFTU). The latter organisations are composed of national trade union federations (such as the TUC in Britain) rather than industrial unions, and both their orientation and mandate are primarily political rather than industrial. A further structural innovation on the part of the ITSs in the last two decades has been to establish 'world councils' for individual multinational enterprises, such as the auto-councils for each of the major European, American and Japanese automobile producers (Treckel 1972). Their purpose is to coordinate union bargaining approaches for specific multinationals and organise solidarity action where necessary, via regular meetings for the exchange of information and agreement on a common bargaining strategy.

Although international collective bargaining with MNEs may remain the long-term aim of organised labour, there are a number of more limited forms of international union reaction which have already taken place, sometimes on a regularised basis. The first is the collection, circulation and exchange of information regarding terms and conditions of employment in the various multinational subsidiaries as an aid to union bargaining strategy and as a basis from which to launch its initiatives. Also, as a result of improvements in the flow of information, the unions may then react more quickly and positively to any developing situation affecting industrial relations. A second type of response relates to international assistance given to a single union which comes into dispute with the subsidiary of an MNE. Although international sympathy strikes are infrequent, and may be limited in part by legal difficulties, nevertheless a number of instances of the imposition of a union boycott have occurred. Such action might prevent the switching of production between countries during a strike. Similarly, union pressure may be imposed at the parent company's home base to help secure objectives such as union recognition in less well-organised subsidiaries abroad.

A third, and more ambitious, union response relates to multiple negotiations with a multinational in several different countries simultaneously. This represents a preliminary attempt to create a unified bargaining strategy in that, although the size of the claims are not yet identical, the timing is coordinated so as to put greater pressure upon the MNE. In these cases, union coordination can prove effective only if existing collective agreements have common, or close, expiry dates to enable trade union pressure to be deployed on a consolidated basis. The first successful transnational coordinated bargaining on a significant scale occurred in 1969 with the French-owned St Gobain glass manufacturing company, and another well-publicised instance of coordinated union action took place at AKZO, a Dutch chemical firm, where an initial decision to close down a number of plants in the Netherlands, Belgium and Switzerland was ultimately reversed. However, doubts have been expressed as to whether, in the above two cases, international union assistance was a decisive influence upon the outcome, or a more peripheral factor (Northrup and Rowan 1979).

The final stage of union reaction would be fully integrated negotiations around common demands, designed to achieve parity and an upward harmonisation of terms and conditions throughout the constituent parts of the multinational. Direct international collective bargaining between the central management of an MNE and a trade union federation representing employees in several countries would then take place.

To date, however, the most developed form of international union cooperation has been the gathering and exchange of information, rather than more substantive strategic action. Similarly, although meetings between International Trade Secretariats and some multinationals have occurred, for the most part they have centred upon consultation and information exchange rather than bargaining. According to an extensive review of the documented evidence by Northrup and Rowan (1979), the only significant examples of actual international bargaining related to two (exceptional) industries, ocean transport and entertainment. Because of its strategically placed dockworkers' affiliates and the threat to boycott vessels, the International Transport Workers' Federation was able to secure direct negotiations with individual shipping companies and associations. Also, multinational collective bargaining became established in the European entertainment industry, setting performers' fees in radio and television, partly because of the international nature of its labour market (Miscimarra 1981).

OBSTACLES TO TRANSNATIONAL BARGAINING

In fact, the impediments to multinational unionism and transnational collective bargaining remain formidable. Not least has been determined management resistance, since generally the benefits of refusing to negotiate with unions on an international basis have far outweighed the costs that unions are able to impose. Managements may oppose multinational bargaining because they see it as a means of proliferating a further layer of bargaining, in addition to those which already exist. A development of this nature would not only impede flexibility, but also risk escalating the scope of industrial disputes and create another level of power capable of shutting down the entire enterprise. Also, union pressure to align pay and conditions to the higher levels prevailing throughout the multinational could result in significant cost increases (Roberts 1975). Furthermore, the labour utilisation practices of MNEs present a very real obstacle to the development of multinational bargaining since they result in both stratification and segmentation of the global labour force, for instance via a fragmented division of labour in assembly-line production industries (Enderwick 1984). Since collective bargaining structures in turn reflect managerial structure and strategies, it can therefore be claimed that multinational collective bargaining would only be forthcoming when management permitted its emergence.

Prospects for an internationalisation of industrial relations processes have also been limited because of difficulties within the labour movement. Although the ITSs regard themselves as a vehicle through which various national unions representing MNE employees can combine and coordinate their actions, so as to present a united front in bargaining, their power and influence have never been as great as their membership size (numbered in millions) would suggest. Rather, they are loosely knit federations in which the real sources of power reside in the affiliated, national unions rather than with the trade secretariats. Officials of member union organisations are reluctant to relinquish decision-making powers and authority to an international bargaining body, since their own constituents – whom it is their primary responsibility to represent – are nationally, not internationally, based. Because of disparities in conditions of production and wage levels across national boundaries there is, in fact, little coincidence of short-term economic interest between workers in different countries. As a result, trade unions seem more willing to commit themselves to long-term relationships with unions from other states where the potential cost of compliance or the degree of commitment is relatively small, as with routinised information exchange and consultation (Blake 1973).

International trade union collaboration is also made more difficult because of the plural and fragmented union structures and the divisions which these create in many European countries, in contrast with the US system of majority union rule and exclusive bargaining rights. Ideological and, to a lesser extent, religious differences both within and between national labour movements in Europe have presented barriers to effective joint union action. Not only may there be difficulties in securing full cooperation between union organisations, but also in mobilising rank-and-file support in concerted action against the multinationals, particularly where good wages and conditions prevail. In this respect:

> it is not easy to convince the average trade unionist that he or she is working for a multinational corporation and that it is in his or her long-term self interest to support fellow workers abroad who are encountering difficulties with the same employers.
>
> (Bomers 1976: 45)

For all these reasons, Haworth and Ramsay (1988) contend that the standard, union-based strategies for building countervailing organisation to match international capital are likely to be fragile under any conceivable circumstances. This is even more apparent at times of economic recession and rising unemployment, which tend to trigger reactions on the part of union movements of a protectionist and nationalist character. These take the form of demands for imposition of tariffs and quota restrictions on foreign production, so that the drive towards concerted, international union action becomes notably diminished and is no longer actively pursued. 'In a climate of uncertainty and decline, internationalism gives way to protectionism both for unions and for management' (Northrup *et al.* 1988).

Furthermore, there are fundamental environmental disparities among countries as regards varying legal provisions, and the extent to which they set the terms and conditions of employment rather than collective bargaining, together with differences in bargaining structures and industrial relations practices. All these present additional obstacles to the extension of bargaining across national boundaries. For instance, even the more limited objective of the realisation of common contract termination dates throughout the operations of a multinational is complicated by the variety of existing bargaining arrangements which, in a number of countries, incorporate not only national or multi-plant systems but also local-level bargaining with works councils (as in Germany) or shop steward committees (in Britain). In fact, for the terms of a negotiated settlement between an international union and an MNE to be similarly implemented on a global basis, it seems there would have to be a good deal more commonality in the economic, social and legal environments of the countries concerned than exists at present.

Blanpain (1977) maintains that because of the unions' weakness at the international level in collective bargaining they have been forced into lobbying and pressuring national governments to implement protective legislation to contain MNE activities, such as controls on the export of capital. At the international level, via intergovernmental agencies, they have also supported the establishment of guidelines to regulate the conduct of multinationals. In the last two decades, both the OECD and the ILO have drawn up codes of conduct for MNEs to observe in their industrial relations practices. The OECD guidelines encourage *inter alia* union recognition, labour relations practices which are consistent with those of the host nation and (limited) disclosure of information to employees. Although the observance of these guidelines is voluntary rather than mandatory, given the immense problems of ensuring their legal enforceability, government adoption of the guidelines creates an expectation of MNE compliance (Enderwick 1985). There is also evidence that they have had some limited impact upon industrial relations (Rojot 1985).

In view of the difficulties to which we have alluded, it may be that the best prospect for the future emergence of international industrial relations processes lies at the regional rather than the global level, particularly within the European Community (EC). In 1986 there were some 900 multinational corporate groups of enterprises with their headquarters in the EC which had more than 1,000 employees and subsidiaries in at least two member states. In addition, there were at least 280 multinationals with 1,000 or more employees in the EC which had their headquarters outside the Community (Sisson *et al.* 1992).

To the extent that the economic, social, legal and political similarities increase across countries, as with the intended harmonisation of policies within the EC, the instruments and procedures of industrial relations may also become more congruent. Furthermore, where multinational collective bargaining in Europe cannot be obtained directly, that is by convincing a sufficient number of employers to accept it, there is the possibility that it might be obtained indirectly, by imposing it on all firms through European Community statutes (Silvia 1991).

THE EUROPEAN DIMENSION

One of the expectations raised by the launching of the EC was that economic integration would lead to consultation, and eventually collective bargaining, between multinational managements and unions. Certainly, the development of cross-border collective bargaining within transnational companies was a key aim of the European Trade Union Confederation (ETUC)[5] since its establishment in 1973.

Such union–employer interactions could take one of two possible forms (Grahl and Teague 1991). The first is a horizontal (company) dimension in which transnational collective bargaining would emerge between multi-national corporations and European-based trade union industrial committees, such as the European Metalworkers Federation (EMF). Before 1986, however, only two agreements which involved workers and management in some form of extra-national dialogue had been concluded, between two French multinationals and regional trade union secretariats. The state-owned Thomson-Grand Public group (now Thomson Consumer Electronics), which was undergoing restructuring and took the view that the European dimension could facilitate a smooth introduction of changes needed in order to compete with Japan and South Korea in the consumer electronics sector, signed an agreement with the EMF (which was renewed in 1992) that created the first European works council for purposes of information and consultation. It was the first corporation in manufacturing industry to recognise an international union secretariat as an official representative of its workforce at the international level (Northrup et al. 1988). The food industry group BSN-Gervais Danone also concluded a written agreement with the IUF international trade union secretariat for the industry and its European organisation, establishing an international consultative committee. Although both these agreements are contractual arrangements, and appear to have been initiated by socialist-sympathetic managements, they eschew a bargaining relationship. Trade union representatives were given the right only to express opinions on the information supplied by management concerning the economic, industrial and restructuring activities of the companies and all matters relating to the determination of pay and conditions were explicitly excluded (Grahl and Teague 1991). Such agreements were, however, exceptional and by the end of 1990 they existed in only a small number of multinationals.

A second possible dimension to European-level collective bargaining is a vertical one, encompassing institutionalised discussion and dialogue between the confederations which represent employers and unions at Community level. A clear objective of European Community law has been to harmonise social legislation and policy among the member states and 'multinational union–management consultation may be considered a means to this end, on the one hand, and would be facilitated by such harmonisation, on the other' (Northrup et al. 1988: 528). A drive for compulsory MNE union–management consultation and formal information rights to workers, which would have increased their access to decision-makers at multinational levels within the firms, was undertaken by the supra-national policy initiative of the proposed Vredeling directive of 1980. The proposal foundered, however, under the weight of opposition by employer groups and the British government, among others, especially on the grounds that increased regulation of business in this way via

Community legislation would increase firms' costs and reduce their competitiveness with firms from non-member states. In addition, it was regarded by employers as the thin end of a wedge which would lead to full-blown international collective bargaining (Grahl and Teague 1991).

Despite the very limited progress made on both these fronts over virtually two decades towards the attainment of some form of European-level collective bargaining, interest in it was renewed once again within the context of the '1992 programme' for the completion of the Single European Market free of non-tariff barriers to trade which represents a fundamental 'recasting' of the Community, the first since the EEC itself was originally founded (Silvia 1991). Since, however, there were serious risks in the single internal market of social imbalance – including the potential for firms to exploit those areas of the EC with less restrictive labour laws, in the absence of a regulatory framework shared by all the member states (and possibly creating a pattern of competitive 'social dumping') – the EC proposed the creation of an accompanying Social Dimension. The Single Act also explicitly encourages a social dialogue between labour and management bodies at EC level, as a way of identifying areas of consensus. Ideally, the EC Commission would like the social dialogue to establish a series of informal conventions and norms which would regulate European labour markets. The Commission proposed that discussion at the European level between unions and employers should indirectly influence collective bargaining at member-state level, either by drawing up model agreements on specific issues, or by exploring new methods and policies to solve certain labour market and industrial relations problems (Grahl and Teague 1991).

A major objective of the single market is the restructuring of European businesses so as to increase their competitiveness in world markets. This entails the encouragement of larger and more powerful European multinational companies (Ramsay 1990). Employee implications of this transnationalisation of corporate structures were reflected in the emphasis in the Social Charter, which lays down minimum standards (although it does not have the force of law), on the need to develop information, consultation and participation – particularly in companies which have establishments in more than two member states. As Hall (1992: 550) has observed:

> The rationale for such an approach is that the transnationalisation of company organisation, ownership and control is resulting in an increasing proportion of employees within the Community being subject to transnational corporate decision-making under which key policy decisions affecting their establishments or undertaking are taken at head office or group level in a different country.

Since a gap exists between increasingly transnational corporate decision-making and the informative consultation rights of employees which are confined to the national level, new countervailing structures would therefore appear to be required.

Policy-making in this area was powerfully influenced by the precedent set by the committees of the French-based multinationals in the later 1980s. Thus in 1991, the EC Commission published a proposed directive which would require the establishment of European works councils in large transnational corporations operating within the EC where requested by employees or their representatives, or initiated by central management. In opting for a statutory works council as the vehicle for transnational information and consultation procedures, the directive reflects the model found in the majority of EC member states, rather than the more voluntarist approach inherent in the UK, Irish and Danish systems of industrial relations (Hall 1992). The European employers' confederation (UNICE) argued, however, that such a single legislative approach was unacceptable since it would be inflexible and incompatible with decentralised management structures, and would cut across the variety of information and consultation procedures introduced by companies to suit their own particular circumstances. In the UK employers also expressed opposition, on the grounds that European works councils could have the potential to become the vehicle for the development of European-level collective bargaining within MNEs.

The 1992 single market programme also stimulated renewed trade union interest in horizontal forms of European industrial relations. In Germany for instance, the unions attach great importance to agreements with transnational firms on the establishment of European works councils. These have already been concluded voluntarily with Volkswagen and Mannesmann, along with some of the large transnational firms in the chemicals sector (Jacobi *et al.* 1992). Similarly, the European Metalworkers Federation has signed agreements providing for formal information and consultation arrangements within a number of companies. These agreements, however, specifically exclude any rights to bargain at a European level and thus follow a 'continental' European industrial relations model in which a sharp distinction is drawn between negotiation and consultation. It is also suggested that there are some structural characteristics which make certain types of transnational enterprises themselves more likely to be willing to initiate management–union relations at European level. These include companies which have a single ownership and management structure within Europe, produce similar products and services in different locations (so that common labour relations problems may arise) and have strong business reasons, such as restructuring plans, to engage in a dialogue with unions (Marginson 1992).

FUTURE PROSPECTS

It would appear improbable that EC-wide collective bargaining at the vertical level will come to play a significant role in industrial relations in the near future, since national trade unions and employers' organisations would have to be prepared to transfer substantial amounts of authority to Community-level organisations. A major feature of the European Community, however, as regards industrial relations is the emergence of new actors such as the EC Commission and the European Parliament whose roles are essentially supra-national. They consciously strive to create convergence in industrial relations across the boundaries of member states, since the existing diversities militate against Community economic and social cohesion (Roberts 1992). Consequently, in certain areas common minimum standards seem likely to be laid down, while on other questions the development of a corpus of EC legislation will probably be capable of implying a convergence in the form of regulation, via legislation rather than collective bargaining, without implying a convergence in the content or the level for the area being regulated (Due *et al.* 1991).

At the horizontal level, some observers maintain that managements may well be able to resist pressure from trade unions for collective bargaining at the European group level, but information exchanges will almost certainly lead to claims being submitted that reflect practice in other member states. There is therefore likely to be a growing convergence in the conditions of employment, if not necessarily in pay levels, and a more general 'Europeanisation' of industrial relations (Sisson *et al.* 1992).

Future research in this whole area is also likely to pay increased attention to international joint ventures (which involve companies from two or more different countries), since their importance is growing relative to that of wholly-owned foreign subsidiaries. International joint ventures established by relatively large-sized parent companies, particularly in the manufacturing sector, have been increasingly stimulated by enhanced product market competition, with the integrated European market developments of the 1990s being an important specific instance. The available evidence suggests that these separate organisational entities are particularly difficult to manage. In the Airbus case in Europe, for instance, there were major problems in devising employee–management consultative arrangements that were acceptable both to the German and French workforces. Also, the study by Beaumont (1991) of a number of Anglo-German international joint ventures operating in Britain indicates that the geographical proximity of some of their locations (being sited very close to the other operations of their respective British parent companies) had the effect of making the British, rather than the German, parent company the dominant force in the area of industrial relations and human resource management practices. But a departure from the existing parent company practices, in the form of non-union recognition for instance, occurred where the new plants were located on greenfield sites and there was a strong emphasis on teamwork together with individual employee–organisational identification.

As Beaumont (1990) has also noted in the case of Britain, foreign-owned firms involve a considerable number of different countries of origin, and their potentially heterogeneous industrial relations policies and practices – as well as the nature and composition of their investment – need to be more fully reflected in the methodology and substantive content of future research studies of the influence of foreign ownership.

FURTHER READING

The most useful and comprehensive volume on the industrial relations and labour market effects of MNEs is Enderwick (1985). An empirical discussion of union collective bargaining attempts with multinationals is Northrup and Rowan (1979). The European Community dimension is examined in Northrup *et al.* (1988) and the special issue of the *British Journal of Industrial Relations*, 30, 4, 1992.

9 Industrial relations in developing countries

Developing, or Third World, societies – defined in terms of their (low to middle) per capita income levels,[1] together with growing social and political modernisation – are located predominantly in Africa, Asia (excluding Japan and the Middle East) and Latin America. Despite the generic, catch-all category of the term 'developing' countries, it is by no means easy to generalise about them with respect to their industrial relations. Within the Latin American region, for instance, Cordova (1980) distinguished four separate groups of countries. First, there are those such as Mexico and Venezuela whose industrial relations and collective bargaining practices are highly developed; a second group where the institutional framework of industrial relations, though similarly long-established, has been undergoing profound change (Argentina, Chile, Uruguay); third, there are those such as Ecuador and Honduras, in which collective labour relations are still very much in a formative stage with workers' and employers' organisations being relatively weak. A fourth single-country category is that of Brazil, where collective bargaining is of somewhat less importance and legal enactment has played a dominant role (partly in order to keep industrial relations under government control and direction). Bergquist (1986: 376) has emphasised in the case of Chile, Argentina, Venezuela and Colombia the importance in the historical process of organisation by workers in the predominant sector of (primary commodity) export production.[2] He notes 'how complex – and historically specific – [is] the relationship between export structure, labour movement formation, and national economic and political development'.

Likewise, for purposes of comparative analysis, in the African continent the countries of tropical Africa display a greater similarity of features than either North Africa, because of a different cultural development, or the settler countries of South Africa and pre-independence Rhodesia with different forms of industrialisation and political control. Furthermore, in examining African as opposed to Latin American industrial relations, a different weight has to be accorded to factors such as the colonial legacy, the associated racial stratification of employment and the post-independence Africanisation programme. Most of the Latin American republics acquired independence at a much earlier date and racial problems are less complex than those in Africa (Lucena 1980). Certainly, trade union development in Latin America was of a different order from that in Africa and Asia for much of its formative period in the late nineteenth century. The most important distinction is the effects of (later) colonial control in the latter two continents and therefore the inevitably large overlap between the economic and political activities of the labour movement (Busch 1983).

It is contended, however, that the experiences neither of western industrialised countries nor of less developed countries such as those in Africa are directly relevant to those in the newly industrialising countries (NICs) such as Singapore, South Korea, Taiwan and Hong Kong where there has been a drive to promote export-oriented industrialisation in the form of manufactured goods, instead of remaining heavily dependent upon primary production. Within this grouping however, there are also strong industrial relations differences among the various countries themselves. For the member states of the Associaiton of South East Asian Nations (ASEAN), Sharma (1985) has put forward a 'stages of labour' approach, whereby countries at different stages of structural transformation towards industrialisation have different types of requirements for capital accumulation – which determine the contrasting patterns of industrial relations that are found. Since governments in ASEAN countries have been concerned to maintain an industrial relations climate conducive to industrialisation, a framework of laws has been introduced aimed at restraining union power – especially in Singapore and Malaysia (Zappala and Lansbury 1990).

It has also been suggested that the single most important mechanism through which the level of development affects the employment relationship is that of the labour process. The reason is that

> capitalist industrial development effects changes on the labour process by increasing the social and technical division of labour and transforming both the type of technology people are working with and the concomitant ability of workers to exercise control over the pace and intensity of work.
>
> (Beresford and Kelly 1991: 87)

In South East Asian, African and Latin American countries there is therefore a very broad range of technologies and labour processes, from traditional agriculture and artisan craft to sophisticated industrial processes, which have led to a variety of patterns of industrial relations.

MAJOR CHARACTERISTICS

More generally, as Hyman (1979) has noted, it is often difficult to attempt to translate the perspectives of westernised industrial relations to the developing countries. For one thing, the proportion of the population which is engaged in formal wage-earning employment in the African states rarely amounts to more than 20 per cent and is sometimes less than 10 per cent of the economically active population, as in Nigeria where agriculture still provides nearly two-thirds of all occupations. In a few countries, such as Kenya and Zambia, the wage-earning proportion is notably higher (yet still less than one-third of the total labour force), probably a consequence of an earlier start as a wage economy under colonial rule. Among East African countries at the time of independence, Kenya had a larger industrial sector than either Uganda or Tanganyika due to the market provided by a larger immigrant population, a more developed infrastructure and access to the protected East African market for manufactured goods (Sandbrook 1975). Even in Kenya, however, in the 1970s less than 20 per cent of the labour force was employed in the 'modern' sector, including urban employment, large-scale farming and the public services, while the rest were absorbed in small-scale subsistence agriculture together with the rural and informal sectors. As a result 'the wage earners in the modern sector, where wage rates and conditions of employment are subject to collective bargaining, form a small minority of all those actively engaged in productive employment' (Henley 1978: 226). In the African countries, therefore, the purview of industrial relations in the usual sense of the term is very much of a minority interest to the country as a whole, although the wage-earning sectors themselves are of crucial significance to the economy and wage earners are a forceful interest group. Similarly, in India, the industrial relations framework is relevant principally to wage-earning labour in the urban and modern sector of the economy, covering no more than 3–4 per cent of the total labour force (Krishnan 1981).

Major features, therefore, of Third World industrial relations, as distinguished from those in the developed countries of the west, are a dualistic economic structure where a pre-capitalist economic system predominates alongside a small industrial sector, together with a segmented labour market where a sharp dualism exists both between modern and traditional manufacturing sectors and between small and large firms (Siddique 1989).

A consequence of the narrowness of the wage-earning base upon which the industrial relations system is typically built is the limited extent of trade unionism – in many developing countries accounting for less than 20 per cent of the economically active population (ILO 1985)[3] – for as Allen (1969: 290) has observed in relation to Africa:

Trade unionism is collective action by people who sell their labour power in order to protect and improve their living standards. The necessary condition for trade unionism, therefore, is the buying and selling of labour power on a significant scale, which in turn is the core element of industrialisation. But this in Africa has proceeded slowly.

Arrighi and Saul (1968), in fact, developed a 'labour aristocracy' thesis: that in African countries there is a privileged minority of urbanised, unionised wage-workers whose economic advantages have been secured not at the expense of the ruling élite but from the urban sub-proletariat, the peasant class in that part of the economy geared to subsistence agriculture, small-scale traders and the unemployed. In the ensuing debate which was generated, considerable scepticism has been expressed as to the plausibility and implications of this thesis, however, especially the assumption of a complementarity of economic interest between urbanised workers (particularly the skilled segment) and the professional and managerial groups. Similarly, in terms of its application to Latin America, few people were likely to credit 'labour aristocracy' status to, say, rioting car workers in Cordoba in 1968 and 1971, or industrial workers in Chile taking over their plants under the Allende government in the early 1970s (Carrière *et al.* 1989).

According to Nicol (1979), a background factor also generally missing in Africa has been an underpinning class-conscious proletariat. In this respect, he sees one difference between a country such as Uganda and some Western European countries as being that in the latter:

> trade unionism grew from the fertile soil of a class-conscious, exploited proletariat, dependent on wage-earning for survival. In Uganda these conditions have not existed and the trade union movement has had itself to foster the lateral class-consciousness previously obscured in the clan and tribal system [uniting workers across tribal, ethnic or caste divisions].
>
> (Nicol 1979: 303)

Since in African countries workers participate in a much wider social network, shared economic interest is at best likely to be a fragile basis for collective organisation (Henley 1989).

Again, unlike Europe in the nineteenth and early twentieth centuries, most of the unions in the newer African states have not been confronted to the same extent with major political deprivations, at least in terms of basic political voting and citizenship rights. Moreover, the major driving force of economic development in the new countries has been the state, in the absence of a growing bourgeoisie to provide capital accumulation – which helps to explain why in most African (and Asian) countries attempts have been made increasingly since independence to limit the unions to a more

restricted industrial role whereby their demands and activities are confined
to wages and conditions at the point of production (Pathy 1988), as opposed
to an earlier and broader political one. In some cases, state-controlled
unionism, or 'bureaucratic authoritarianism', has become dominant.

Yet
within the power structure faced by less developed countries, Haworth
(1991) emphasises the centrality of a political bargaining process and
political mobilisation of the bargaining parties, in marked contrast to the
procedural focus of industrial relations in, say, the UK. Although this
perspective may be overgeneralised, certainly in some of the Latin
American countries such as Peru[4] it has been shown that unions became
established in a client role (of dependency) with political parties which
offered them protection – and then used them in return, as electoral and
political agents in the struggles which centred around state power (Payne
1965). In India, too, both organisationally and ideologically the principal
wings of the labour movement have been political in nature, part of a
broader political movement with an implicit reconciliation of trade union
and political goals within one framework (Krishnan 1981). In the socialist
regimes of the Arab world (Syria, Iraq, Libya and Algeria), the role of
unions was redefined, so that they would no longer remain the counterparts
of management but were intended to become 'the leading vanguard in
economic and social development' and centres of 'revolutionary radiation'
(El-Sabbagh 1988).

As Lipset (1961) has noted, in comparing labour movements as between
economically developed, and developing, countries one would expect to
find the chief explanations of differences in production processes and
levels of technology, in the nature of class relationships and in political
structures. Undoubtedly, a number of factors within developing societies
may inhibit the emergence of trade unions and collective bargaining of the
western type, including a low degree of industrialisation, the high level of
illiteracy and lack of basic education, as well as instability of the workforce
and a lack of organisational resources.

A further prerequisite for the expansion of collective bargaining relates
to the organisation of undertakings as production units of a certain size,
since in medium- and large-scale undertakings 'the higher concentration of
the workforce and greater complexity of functions has inevitably resulted
in a need to lay down ground rules best adapted to the circumstances of
each undertaking' (Cordova 1980: 23). However, large production units are
by no means absent from the modern enclaves of developing economies,
since the character of late development brings with it the sudden appearance of large-scale industrial enterprises – often multinational subsidiaries
– which are conducive to the formation of enterprise-based unions
(Kassalow 1978b). In the case of Korea, the transformation of society from

agricultural to capitalist-industrial was so rapid that an occupational labour market with discrete jobs could not be established on a stable basis, and consequently occupational unions could not be organised. Furthermore, industrialisation there has progressed by means of heterogeneous oligopolistic enterprises, with the result that employment conditions were highly differentiated across the same industry – effectively precluding industry-wide trade unions. In these conditions, trade unions organised on an enterprise basis have been chosen as an easy and natural way of organising workers (Park 1992).

The role of transnational corporations themselves, as the major instrument of global capitalism, has recently been highlighted for developing countries by so-called New International Division of Labour (NIDL) theories. These place emphasis upon the concepts of the globalisation of production and upon a shift of labour-intensive manufacturing to the Third World where labour is cheap, that is to say export-oriented industrialisation (Southall 1988).[5] Such claims, however, should not be exaggerated since industrialisation in the Third World remains quite limited in extent and uneven in incidence. Furthermore, the NIDL perspective may overstate both the role of multinational capital and the autonomy which is frequently imputed to it, as well as the importance of export markets, in Third World industrialisation. Certainly, in Taiwan, South Korea and Singapore a major part has been played by domestic markets and by local private capital, in the regulation and direction of which the state has played a key role (Petras and Engbarth 1988). Also more latterly, in the case of Singapore, there has been a movement away from labour-intensive activities towards high-technology and high value-added activities which have involved a higher wages policy (Wilkinson 1986).

THE ROLE OF GOVERNMENT

One of the most distinctive features of developing countries concerns the centrality of the state, whereby in industrial relations matters the government has increasingly sought (varying degrees of) control over the trade union movement and its activities – not least, to protect the interests of foreign capital. The governments of these countries play a much more active and interventionist role in industrial relations than was traditionally the case in North America and some Western European countries (Schregle 1982). This role is strengthened by the fact that policies are guided by the requirements of national, growth-oriented development plans and the state itself is much more central to the development process. It may therefore have been largely inevitable, in many late-developing countries, that the functions of unions 'should be defined and re-defined according to new needs and roles' (Kassalow, 1978b:

8). For instance, in Zambia since independence, as Gertzel (1979) has shown, there has been progressive subordination of the trade unions to government, along with the extension of governmental regulation of labour–management relations. In French-speaking West Africa, 'efforts by governments to control all aspects of national life through single political parties and socio-economic development plans have narrowed the scope of industrial relations' (Martens 1979: 29).

In Malaysia, government policy has been similarly to subordinate the labour movement and 'guide' trade unionism to broader considerations of national economic development as defined by the ruling élite. A succession of anti-labour laws has been implemented, in part to facilitate the pursuit of a low wage strategy of national capital accumulation (Wad 1988). In both Singapore and South Korea, the primary actor in the industrial relations scene is the government itself. More generally, the scope for collective bargaining is restricted in most of the Third World because of the presence of a corporatist industrial relations framework (Siddique 1989).

Nevertheless, it does not follow as a result of these requirements that unions in the new African and Asian countries can be considered simply as 'administrative arms of the state' – although in a country such as Singapore, where since 1968 the assigned role of the labour movement has been to help preserve industrial peace and explain the ruling élite's policies and programmes to its members, they have come close to it. A similar situation also appertained in Taiwan until the mid-1980s (Kleingartner and Peng 1991). Equally, although they are certainly more restricted in their economic activities than their counterparts in western market economies, they have managed to perform some of the bargaining functions and pressure group activities usually regarded as essential for the functioning of an independent union role (Sandbrook and Cohen 1975). Gray (1980) argues that in Ghana, in particular, the bargaining achievements of the labour movement are significant and collective agreements have produced fundamental changes in the country's national wage structure. Some observers, such as Kassalow (1978b) view unions in developing countries as being 'intermediate forms' between the polar types of state-controlled unions on the one hand and sectional interest group representatives within a pluralist society on the other.

Governments in Third World countries maintain that industrial relations have a direct bearing upon the development process, since unions are viewed as largely consumptionist in function and would therefore impede the rate of capital investment (Mehta 1957; Deyo 1981). In addition, industrial conflict may adversely affect productivity and exports, particularly in fragile economies highly dependent upon perhaps a single primary commodity (countries such as Ghana and Zambia), or, as in Korea, reliant upon the production of labour-intensive manufactured goods targeted for export. Also, strikes are not likely to provide a climate which is conducive to the welfare of capital and the attracting of foreign investment, which have become identified with the 'national' interest. In the case of Ghana it has been stated that: 'Before 1957, labour unrest was a valuable tool in the struggle for independence; later it was perceived as a threat to domestic order, productivity and the willingness of foreign governments and companies to invest in Ghana' (Gray 1980: 179).

Similarly, a development plan (such as that in Kenya) which calls for an altered form of income distribution, or requires wage restraint in the interests of higher savings and investment, together with the achievement of greater competitiveness in international markets, has a greater probability of success if trade unions are supportive or at least acquiescent (Gladstone 1978). Therefore, in Kenya strike activity in practice became illegal, with disputes being subjected to compulsory arbitration. Also, the process of collective bargaining there can be considered trilateral – as opposed to bilateral in the pre-independence period – in that, as regards wage fixing, it has to satisfy the objectives of not only management and the union but the government. Indeed, in many Third World countries it has been said that strikes 'were considered a luxury that a developing society could not afford . . . thus industrial action and unfettered collective bargaining as traditional trade union instruments could no longer be countenanced' (Gladstone 1980: 56). In these countries, the predominant position of the government as the biggest single employer often employing more than half the total number of wage earners, in Ghana and in French West Africa for instance, gave the state an additional interest in regulating industrial relations processes and outcomes. According to Siddique (1989), the vast nationalised sector in most Third World countries is, in fact, the consequence of the state's attempt to substitute for the entrepreneur.

For all these reasons, it has become usual to delineate a certain 'duality' of trade union functions within developing nations – on the one hand defending and promoting the interests of their own members, yet at the same time (Mboya 1963) being required to contribute to the national development effort. However, the role of early trade unionism in these countries during the pre-independence era – particularly in Africa – was markedly different in character and requires some examination.

COLONIAL PERIOD

Given the very limited industrialisation during the colonial period in the first half of the present century, early and indigenous union organisations in British and French African territories tended to emerge mainly among groups of permanent employees (whose bargaining power was greater) including mineworkers, lower-grade civil servants and those within major public enterprises such as docks and railways. Reductions in real wages as a result of rising prices led to both spontaneous protests and embryonic growth of trade unions, which the colonial governments interpreted, especially for their own employees, as being politically subversive activities and rebellion. In consequence, 'the early history of African trade unions . . . became as much a reaction to imperial rule [to which workers attributed their grievances] as a reaction to working conditions' (Damachi *et al.* 1979: 3). In contrast to the position in nineteenth-century Europe, employers in Africa were both foreign and socially different and the main employer was the government. In Kenya the struggle against the employer necessarily involved the unions in political activities since the employers were also associated with the ruling power (Iwuji 1979). Ultimately, in that country, it became increasingly difficult to differentiate between trade union activities and African independence activities, although this was much less true of Ugandan unions whose part in the pre-independence struggle was peripheral rather than central. Similarly, in Singapore, Malaya and India, anti-colonialism seems to have been an important motivating factor for certain sectors of the labour movement. (In the absence of a significant number of skilled craftsmen in the early stages of industrial-isation, it is also not surprising – as Kilby (1967) has noted – that unions in Africa were initially organised on the basis of the place of employment, unlike the economically strong, craft-protective unionism found in nineteenth-century Britain and the USA.)

Although the colonial governments in Africa originally wished to ensure that the labour force lacked leverage and openly opposed the development of a trade union movement – fearing its political potential especially – over the course of time (particularly after the Second World War) government policy shifted significantly. It moved towards the foster-ing of trade unions patterned on the British or French models, albeit within a limited and well-controlled sphere of activity (Muir and Brown 1978). On the basis of his research in Tanzania, Bienefeld (1979) interprets the rapid expansion of trade unionism under government tutelage as an institutional response to changes which were occurring in the processes of colonial production. To meet world competitive pressures more efficient patterns of employment practices and labour utilisation were required. These included a more skilled, predictable and stable labour force, in place of the classical colonial pattern of part-time wage earning (the migrant labour system having been encouraged by the colonial authorities as the basis of a 'cheap labour' policy), which in turn required new forms of labour control: 'The new order required more regular, more settled, more productive labour compatible with greater degrees of mechanisation, with more complex labour processes, and with a demand for increased security of supply' (Bienefeld 1979: 564).

Again, in India, a policy of outright opposition to union recognition was revised to some extent in the modernised sector of the economy, because of the growing complexity of business organisation. 'The search for improved productivity led to the modernising of equipment, accentuated the shortage of skills and added to the responsibility for careful handling of costly machines' (Krishnan 1981: 242).

A further, and related, consideration in the African territories was increasing appreciation on the part of the colonial authorities of the benefits of institutionalising labour protest along trade union lines, as a mechanism of social control. They had come to learn that 'nothing was more inimical to their interests than spontaneous, guerrilla like actions of workers who were beyond their control and out of the hands of their own leaders' (Damachi *et al.* 1979: 6). Hence, the policy became one of encouraging union development while at the same time attempting to steer it in the direction of 'economistic' objectives and away from political involvement which could provide a serious threat to the colonial powers. The requirement was for union development to be narrow, sectional and therefore basically controllable.[6] Therefore, unlike the situation in Europe during the early period of industrialisation, where workers had a long and difficult struggle for recognition, in most African countries (though not all) the place of unions was more quickly recognised within a more compressed timeframe, to suit the administrative convenience of the colonial powers.

Similar considerations appear to have been paramount in some Asian countries as well. In Ceylon and Malaya, the objective was to foster 'responsible' unions which would assist the colonial administrators to maintain labour peace without becoming involved in political activities (Fong and Cheng 1978). In Singapore, after widespread and prolonged strikes during the late 1930s, both the colonial state and employers decided to take the lead to 'guide' unions, to ensure that they became constructive forces which could actually assist management in airing discontent and encouraging production (Rosa 1990).

An effort towards containing overt industrial conflict was also apparent in some of the Latin American countries. In Chile (and Argentina) the labour movement was politicised from the start, partly under the influence of European immigrants, with worker demands for improved wages and hours at the turn of the century escalating into calls for the abolition of capitalism and the establishment of a more egalitarian, socialist regime. In that country:

the creation of an institutionalised industrial relations system represented a response by governing elites to the conflict associated with increasing labour activities in the nineteenth and early twentieth centuries in order to preserve the capitalist system by institutionalising the peaceful resolution of industrial conflict.

(Loveman 1981: 93)

More generally in the Latin American region state regulation of industrial relations, as embodied in the labour codes which were promulgated during the inter-war period setting out detailed regulation of conditions of work and labour union activity, was based upon the assumption that labour relations were a manifestation of class struggle which, if not controlled, would have repercussions on society as a whole. The purpose of the codes was:

to coopt and assimilate labour . . . [which] had become politically dangerous [and] incorporate it into the state structure. It was a means of keeping the unions from launching radical challenges to the system; it helped keep them dependent, and tied to the state.

(Wiarda 1978: 14)

According to Cordova (1980), however, the codes were becoming obsolete and their capacity to set adequate standards has diminished over the course of time. This is one reason why collective bargaining has developed considerably in recent years, enabling changing conditions affecting labour to be dealt with more flexibly. In the Latin American countries, although industry-wide bargaining is common in Argentina and Brazil, there are nevertheless many enterprise unions. This, in itself, is a reflection not only of economic structure, in terms of the fragmentation and concentration of the labour force in a few large enterprises, but also, in part, of employer and state action. There was mistrust of national union organisations because of their potential for extensive politicisation and the possibility of their calling general strikes (Cella and Treu 1990).

POST-INDEPENDENCE PERIOD

Once the African and Asian territories had achieved independence from colonial rule a change took place in the attitude of government towards trade unions, which were soon accorded a new and more closely prescribed role. In a comparative study of industrial relations in Kenya and Malaysia, Henley (1980) discerns three parallel trends within the two countries. There has been continuity in labour policies from the colonial period in assigning a major role to the registrar of trade unions (who would regulate their formation and supervise their activities with a view to ensuring a compliant union movement), together with an industrial court as a form of compulsory or semi-compulsory arbitration to settle disputes. Second, there is a notable willingness on the part of government to subordinate the interests of labour to national economic development plans. Finally, he notes a weakening of the labour movements in both countries as a result of 'communalism', that is segmentation into socially isolated population groupings within an ethnically heterogeneous society.[7] Yet despite these similarities there is one important difference. In Kenya there were close links between the labour movement and a faction of the political leadership. These links facilitated a government policy of collaboration and incorporation of labour leaders into a web of state patronage (which was also to occur in Zambia), channelling the labour movement towards economistic objectives. In return for union agreement to limitations on the right to strike, for instance, the unions secured legislative institutional support in the form of a compulsory check-off system (deduction of union dues at source). The check-off was to prove very important for their stability and growth, since one of the most serious problems faced by unions in a developing country is inadequate financing. By contrast, in Malaysia, a government–union link never developed to the same extent, mainly as a result of the labour movement's early association with the Malayan Communist party. In the consequent absence of state patronage and incorporation of the labour movement the legal framework is much more elaborate and detailed.

In many of the post-colonial states (including Algeria and Egypt) a restructuring and consolidation of trade union organisations was also entailed. In Zambia, the government actively promoted a policy of one union for each industry. (As Turner (1992) has shown, the actions and policies of the state have also been the primary determinant of union growth in that country, for instance via enforcing the check-off system.) Kenya, however, is unusual in this respect in that the labour movement was remodelled towards industrial unionism[8] prior to independence. This was primarily a consequence of the accelerated development of the union movement and its early recognition by employers as a result of the important and influential role which it had played during the state of emergency at the time of the Mau Mau uprising in the 1950s.

Elsewhere, changes in trade union structure and a greater measure of centralisation also took place during the post-colonial period. In Ghana, in the immediate post-independence phase, the government wished to enlist the cooperation of the unions in accelerating the process of economic development and modernisation. But the fragmented and enterprise-oriented nature of existing trade unions was not conducive to the attainment of a high degree of governmental regulation and influence, and might also have threatened the development effort by exacerbating labour unrest via inter-union disputes. As a result, twenty-four industrial-type unions (later reduced to ten) were created by legislation from the existing eighty-five small and fragmented ones (Kraus 1979). Similarly, though at a later date, the labour movement in the Sudan – which had also been characterised by a preponderance of small, amorphous and unstable enterprise unions – was reconstructed in order to create bigger, and therefore more viable, unions. Between 1971 and 1974, the proportion of large unions (with more than 10,000 members) increased from 1 per cent to 30 per cent and small unions (with below 200 members), which had accounted for three-quarters of the total number of unions in 1971, had been eliminated three years later (Ali Taha 1982).

In Nigeria, also, there was a perceived need on the part of government and private employers to reorganise the multiplicity of unions on an industrial basis. The intention was to create more orderly and predictable collective bargaining structures, instead of negotiating with a relatively large number of atomised and splintered unions, characterised by factionalism and excessive competition, which could not fulfil the conditions of collective agreements. In the 1970s, therefore, 700–1,000 union organisations were reduced to forty-two national ones (Panford 1988; Fashoyin 1990).[9]

As well as reducing trade union multiplicity in the new African countries, a further government restructuring measure has been to attempt the creation of a strong and unified central union organisation – as in Nigeria in 1978, and subsequently taken over by the military administration a decade later – which would have extensive powers over its affiliates as well as close relations with the government or ruling party. The Ghana TUC was established by law as the single central organisation to which all unions had to affiliate, and in post-independence Zambia trade union power was centralised through the newly constituted Zambia Congress of Trade Unions (ZCTU). In Kenya, the Central Organisation of Trade Unions (COTU) has the appointment of its leader subjected to government ratification and a state official also sits on its governing council. All these government measures designed to unify, reorganise and rationalise trade unions gave governments a strong influence over union actions and behaviour and they made corporatist controls easier to achieve. The measures also had important implications for the collective bargaining process, which will now be considered.

COLLECTIVE BARGAINING

The creation of more effective unions as a result of the reduction in their multiplicity and clearer lines of industrial and sectoral demarcation, along with associated measures such as check-off arrangements (and in some countries an obligation upon employers to negotiate), have aided and promoted collective bargaining – although in many countries of Africa, Asia and Latin America it has gained only a weak foothold in the public sector (Fashoyin 1991). In Ghana, the guaranteed check-off also helped promote less conflictual union–management relations, since the control which the government maintained over certification of unions for bargaining purposes relieved employers of the obligation to deal with rival organisations claiming to represent their workers (Gray 1980). At the same time, it has to be recognised that the constraints placed upon trade union activities necessarily affect and restrict the free exercise of bargaining rights. In Kenya wage agreements made by independent collective bargaining – highly centralised at national level with little scope for workplace bargaining – have required the approval of the government-appointed Industrial Court. But one important difference in relation to wage determination as between the Anglophone and Francophone countries in Africa, reflecting their colonial heritage and transplantation of the metropolitan framework, is that in the latter countries (Senegal, Guinea, Benin, etc.) government-established minima set the benchmark for wages throughout the country and are of considerable importance. In consequence, 'the unions' role becomes not that of a bargaining adversary, but an institution trying to influence government action [and] wage setting is usually a process subject to political pressures and considerations' (Damachi *et al.* 1979: 12). By contrast, in the former British colonies such as Ghana there has been more extensive reliance upon voluntary collective bargaining for workers in the private sector. Exceptions exist, however, such as Nigeria where government-appointed commissions have been a major mechanism for fixing wages in the unionised sector – partly because of the actions of government itself which, by failing to fix the wages of its own employees by collective bargaining, undermined the bargaining potential within the private sector.[10]

Restrictions on strike activity, where – as in Zambia and Tanzania – the mandatory conciliation procedure makes legal strike action difficult if not impossible, also weakens the unions in their dealings with employers. 'In any confrontation with an employer workers soon find they are also engaging with the state' (Henley 1989: 296). Similar limitations on strikes apply in Singapore and, as an additional measure designed to attract foreign investment, the rights and prerogatives of management have been clearly asserted by means of legislation. This includes the setting of ceilings on fringe benefits and, as is also the case in Malaysia, restricting the scope of negotiable issues to exclude items such as employee transfer, dismissal, layoff and work assignments. Further recent legislation has provided employers with additional flexibility in work arrangements by removing various stipulations on minimum employment conditions (Wilkinson 1986).

The role of employers in industrial relations within African and Asian countries has been variable and may be differentiated partly on the basis of company size together with the relative importance of either indigenous or foreign-owned firms. In both Nigeria and Ghana, prior to independence, small firms were reluctant to recognise unions and engage in collective bargaining whereas the larger, expatriate firms (and more latterly MNEs) were more willing. Not only could such firms afford to pay relatively high wages, but they also found the process of collective bargaining the easiest and most efficient way of dealing with the complexities of their industrial relations (Kilby 1967). In Ghana, a further study found that although indigenous private employers were generally hostile to unions, preferring to deal with their own employees on a paternalist basis, most foreign private employers considered trade unionism to be an advantage since it was easier to deal with workers as an organised body than as individuals, so that the union functioned as 'the transmission belt between the employers and the workers' (Damachi 1976: 31). Nevertheless, foreign-owned firms were not always prepared to join together in employers' organisations since, in a country like Nigeria, the evidence suggests that they preferred to retain maximum individual autonomy in labour matters.

In many of these countries employers' organisations developed primarily in response to the growth of trade unions or, in Nigeria, as a result of government request. In that country, the restructuring of unions brought about a spate of responses to form employers' organisations, ostensibly as an equalising forum for employers to bargain with the larger unions, and a development which then led to the emergence of industry-wide bargaining in most industries (Fashoyin 1986). In Kenya, unions in their bargaining relationships confront well-organised employers combined into an association for industrial relations purposes, with a central national employers' federation (FKE) coordinating employer relations with unions and government. This body conducts negotiations on behalf of many of its members and represents them in almost all cases which come before the Industrial Court. It also provides general advice for its membership on labour relations matters and encourages collective bargaining to be conducted on an industry-wide basis. Finally, on the Asian continent, in India in those industries where employers are relatively well organised for industrial relations purposes, such as textile mills which employ the bulk of the industrial labour force, three distinct sub-categories of employers' associations may be distinguished. There are those which provide legal and other services and function as a common forum for discussion of mutual interests; second, associations which in addition to supplying advice and expertise for their members also provide a pool of personnel officers who act as trouble-shooters, and a third category of associations which actually negotiate with unions (Krishnan 1981).

SUMMARY

In this chapter we have shown that in Third World countries industrial relations need to be viewed within a political economy context, since one of the most salient features of industrial development is permeation by the state. In a number of developing countries governments have sought to influence both the role and structure of unions often by means of 'trade-offs' whereby, in return for conforming to the requirements of the development effort and limiting their independence of action, benefits such as a mandatory union shop and/or check-off arrangement would be granted. One result of this has been that in African and most Asian countries the labour movement is no longer committed to politics and parties to the extent that was evident around the time of independence although, in a country such as India, political factors have continued to be a major influence on strike activity, at least to the early 1980s (Bean and Holden 1992b). Also, in many of the newly independent states an important requirement has been that the trade union movement should not contribute a possible source of political opposition to the ruling élite.

In Kenya, the labour movement would appear to correspond most closely to a variant of 'business unionism' (emphasising economically/industrially oriented objectives) since this was all that remained feasible given the nature of the environment which it confronts. Even within this more limited area of operations further restrictions in the form of incomes policy requirements on union activities were also introduced, so that government control was extended from the political to the economic sphere. At the same time, the efficacy of these government measures remains open to question. Initial governmental efforts to reorganise, incorporate and limit the scope of union actions were challenged in Tanzania and to some extent in Ghana, and in French-speaking West Africa led to general strikes in the cases of Benin and Upper Volta. Although the extent of union independence and autonomy differs considerably within the African continent, even in those countries where government control is maximal and national union federations and individual union leaders[11] have been responsive to government requirements the rank and file at local level have not always been so accommodating. Grassroots militancy has persisted and strikes, although often technically illegal and therefore frequently of short duration, have still taken place to draw attention to sectional grievances. In Peru, the uninstitutionalised nature of employer–employee relations has also meant that (as in France) industrial conflicts transcend the demands of economism (Haworth 1991; Bean 1993).

A further consequence of extensive government influence and regulation relates to a certain reorientation of trade union functions in some of these countries. Where its collective bargaining role has been considerably diminished the union movement has sought to broaden its range of interests and define new functions. As an adjunct to their more usual activities trade unions in Ghana and Kenya began to operate their own business enterprises, such as consumer cooperatives and banking services. The objective was partly to become more directly involved in their countries' development efforts, but also to retain membership and subscriptions by continuing to provide a range of services. However, the most notable example is Singapore, where the central trade union body has created an extensive range of insurance, transport, dental and consumer cooperatives.

From a comparative perspective some observers such as Gray (1980) see certain similarities between the institutional development of organised labour and industrial relations in a Third World nation like Ghana and that in the United States. In both countries unions have become increasingly bureaucratic, they came to agree with employers on general areas of conflict resolution in industrial relations, and government legislation has been vital for union recognition and development. No doubt formal recognition of, and government support for, union organisation in African countries has strengthened the process of bureaucratisation both within unions and in the entire system of industrial relations (Damachi *et al.* 1979). Also, more generally across the Third World, Munck (1988) maintains that the western model of pluralism, based on an orderly resolution of conflict through institutionalised compromise, is increasingly being adopted – if only as an ideology. We have shown, however, that there are important and overriding differences between newly developing and western countries in their industrial relations practices, not least in the attempts of the trade unions in the former to remain viable, independent organisations – and sometimes even to survive.

Also, although there are many parallels between developing countries themselves in their industrial relations, consequent upon the drive towards industrialisation, it is important not to overstate the degree of homogeneity among them since the pattern is extremely diverse and there are significant differences and variety in Third World industrial relations systems. These reflect not only differential levels of attained development, but also appear to be rooted in the particular and specific historical circumstances of the various countries. Certainly, organisational forms cannot easily be separated from the total environment in which they operate and an examination of developing countries highlights, even more clearly than in industrialised western countries, the vital importance of the nature of the political economy and wider societal influences in shaping the salient features of industrial relations systems.

FURTHER READING

A useful recent and analytical survey is the article by Siddique (1989). On Third World industrial relations and economic development see Gladstone (1980) and Schregle (1982); on the NICs, the collection of studies by Southall (1988). The volume edited by Frenkel (1993) deals comparatively with unions in the Asia-Pacific region.

10 Industrial relations systems and economic outcomes

As we have shown in previous chapters, the industrial relations systems of particular countries differ, not only in their institutions and procedures, but also in their capacity for the containment and resolution of conflict. However, in order to round off the book, we also need to examine the question of whether different kinds of national industrial relations structures in developed market economies are associated with different types of economic outcome and performance (their substantive consequences), in addition to the comparative strike data which were considered in Chapter 6. These economic outcomes include growth and productivity, together with the effect which industrial relations may have on the macroeconomic variables of inflation and unemployment.

INDUSTRIAL RELATIONS 'MODELS'

In making comparisons between the industrial relations systems of various countries, it is sometimes claimed, or inferred, that one system is 'better' than another – with the added implication that a given country would be well advised to change or adapt its own system to a more advantageous form (Kassalow 1983, 1984). Particular countries which have been cast, historically, in such a 'model' role were Britain in the late nineteenth century,[1] Germany in the pre-First World War period, the United States from 1945 to 1960, Sweden in the 1960s, Germany again during the 1970s as the economic engine of Europe, and Japan in the 1980s. One prerequisite for the industrial relations arrangements of any one country to function as a model for others to attempt to emulate is a demonstrated capacity for high achievement or success within its own society, along one or more relevant lines such as rapid economic growth and the absence of serious industrial conflict (Windmuller 1963), i.e. as derived from specific and problematic policy issues. Thus Britain during the closing decades of the nineteenth century was at the height of its economic success and both the USA and

Sweden were at, or near, the zenith of their economic growth when their industrial relations systems attracted favourable comment and prescriptive relevance in the earlier post-Second World War period. In the case of Sweden, it was claimed that:

> [its] model can be viewed as a set of institutional arrangements and norms for managing distributive conflict consistently with the requirements of economic growth, given Sweden's small industrial, open economy on the one hand, and the distribution of power among the major actors in the political economy, on the other.
>
> (Martin 1987: 97)

In that country the system of economy-wide, centralised negotiations has been associated with continuously low unemployment, even in the mid-1980s when rates moved up to high levels in most industrialised countries, a very high standard of living, together with a very low level of industrial conflict since the 1930s. Indeed, prior to the last decade, Sweden had one of the lowest rates of overt industrial conflict in the world (see Table 10.1).

Table 10.1 Industrial disputes in five countries, 1953–89: working days lost per 1,000 persons employed in selected industries

	1953–62	*1962–71*	*1971–80*	*1980–9*
UK	300	412	1,132	740
USA	1,093	1,219	1,073	na*
Sweden	37	44	50	330
West Germany	69	56	92	50
Japan	440	222	200	20

Source: *Employment Gazette* (UK)
*Series changes.

The 'German model' of industrial relations is based upon four principles: a dual structure of interest representation whereby workers' representation at establishment level is separated from the collective bargaining system, extensive juridification, highly inclusive institutions of collective representation (which can make decisions in the name of the entire work-force with little formal obligation to seek endorsement), as well as relative centralisation of collective bargaining and coordinated policies of the bargaining parties at sectoral level (Jacobi *et al.* 1992). Furthermore, the codetermination arrangements at supervisory board and works council levels appear to have facilitated the introduction of change in the enterprise without major disruption. For much of the postwar period, Germany attained a high level of economic performance and competitiveness in the context of a substantial societal consensus, very low levels of industrial conflict and one of the best records among western countries for controlling inflation (Adams 1992b).

It is generally agreed that a critical element in the success of the German economy is the system of vocational training, also a 'dual' system, which blends general training in vocational schools with specific training in individual establishments.

The system creates opportunities for internal mobility and functional flexibility, reduces the significance of job demarcations, and avoids over-specialization. . . . From a macro perspective it encourages adaptability of qualifications and job content to changed structural conditions and guarantees a comparatively high standard of education for the national work force.

(Jacobi *et al.* 1992: 229)

In addition, the system helps to further cooperative industrial relations, since the homogeneity of the skill structure creates common values and orientations which are embodied in a craft ethos. 'This improves communications between different hierarchical levels, and conflicts of interest between management and labour become mediated by the cooperative culture of a craft community' (Lane 1990: 253).

During the past two decades the Japanese economy has experienced not only dramatic economic growth (at rates superior to those in western countries) but also full employment, low inflation, relatively low strike activity and a good deal of flexibility whereby 'companies have been known to completely change product lines and markets in remarkably short periods of time' (Adams 1992b: 14). Within firms, functional flexibility of employees is also high and has been facilitated by traditional enterprise-based training and enterprise unionism. Also, emphasis has been accorded to the organisational techniques of group work, continuous training and consultation to reach an internal consensus – directed towards the enhancement of productivity along with quality improvement. Had Japan's economy never taken off, and Japan remained a second- or third-rate power, then it is claimed that the supposedly unique practices of lifetime employment, seniority wages and enterprise unionism 'would be little more than objects of curiosity, the strange customs of a strange people' (Moore 1987: 140).

It is true, however, that these particular features of Japanese industrial relations also existed during the immediate post-Second World War period, at a time of less impressive economic performance together with high industrial conflict, and it is not obvious why their role should have changed. Batstone (1984) regards these factors as less than adequate as an explanation of a pattern of labour relations which permits peaceful and high economic growth. Instead, he points to determinants such as the degree of intra-plant mobility, which permits management a high level of flexibility in allocating labour (thereby being able to adjust rapidly to changing circumstances and idle working time), as well as weakening work group solidarity and any notions of 'job territory'.

At the same time, Kassalow (1983) has observed that a subsequent decline of interest in a country's industrial relations system as a possible model has generally coincided with some deterioration in that country's economic performance. Thus for example, during the late 1950s the US growth rate slackened and relative strike incidence increased. The 'Swedish model' has also recently been the subject of more critical scrutiny – consequent upon signs of crisis and disintegration appearing within it in the late 1970s and 1980s as the country experienced high inflation, current account deficits and (since 1974) declining productivity. Within Swedish manufacturing industry, productivity growth lagged behind that of a group of eleven important competitor countries in the periods 1974–7 and 1985–90, dropping from third place within this group in the 1960s to eighth in the 1970s and 1980s (Kjellberg 1992). In addition, the centralised collective bargaining system which was supported by employers in the 1950s as the best solution to the problems of the day came in more recent years to be regarded as too inflexible. It was unable to meet the need for adjusting pay levels to fit market conditions within an increasingly fragmented labour market in which skilled workers had become more difficult to recruit, and where firms in the exposed sector of the economy have had to restructure in order to remain competitive.

It is apparent, therefore, that over the years a succession of countries have been held up as universal models of industrial relations to be emulated by others. Yet in addition to the possible problems involved in making transplants as between countries (see Chapter 1),[2] it would seem unlikely that any one system offers great, permanent advantages over another. 'Rather, it appears that in a given era one country's system seems to provide more advantages, but in a subsequent period these positions are often reversed' (Kassalow 1984: 591). Hence, while corporatist systems of centralised decision-making (as in Scandinavia), for example, may have been effective in terms of macroeconomic crisis management in the stag-flation of the 1970s, they have perhaps been less successful in the restruc-turing tasks of the 1980s. These have required action at the level of the firm rather than the economy, with an accompanying emphasis on 'flexibility' to suit the specific needs of firms rather than the requirements of general, uniform regulation. They have also implied change, rapid adjustment and job losses (Crouch 1993).[3] In New Zealand, for instance, government attempts in the early 1990s to restructure industrial relations by freeing up the bargaining process, via increased flexibility in employment contracts, can be explained primarily by the failure of the previous highly centralised regime to maintain employment and incomes in the presence of increased competition in the product market and, after substantial deregulation, in the capital market (Brook Cowen 1993).

The view has also been expressed that the US industrial relations system has been more flexible than those in most of Europe (although less flexible than the Japanese system) in adjusting to change, due in part to more decentralised bargaining and a lower unionisation rate. The evidence for this relates to the greater decline in real wages and increase in employment in the USA since 1970, in contrast to the greater increase in long-term unemployment in Europe during the 1970s and 1980s (Marshall 1986).

LABOUR MARKET INSTITUTIONS AND ECONOMIC PERFORMANCE

Table 10.2 shows various measures of economic performance for a number of major countries over the past three decades. It is widely believed that a positive relationship exists between cooperative bargaining systems and economic performance, whereas there is a negative relationship between adversarial bargaining and a country's economic performance. Zeitlin (1990: 407) notes that, although the precise contribution of industrial relations to economic performance is exceedingly difficult to measure:

> Cooperative bargaining systems arguably link wage determination processes more closely to the demands of economic adjustment and provide a greater measure of flexibility in the usage of manpower within the enterprise. Both macro- and microstudies suggest that economies characterised by cooperative bargaining enjoy a better tradeoff between inflation and unemployment and adapt more easily to changing markets and technologies than do adversarial systems.

In the latter respect, it is claimed that where traditions are adversarial, as in most English-speaking countries, trade unions are more likely to oppose technological change than are their counterparts in countries with more recent traditions of social partnership, such as Germany, Austria and the Nordic countries (Lansbury and Bamber 1989). The empirical evidence would certainly indicate that in Germany, consistent with the cooperative nature of the industrial relations system, unions do not appear to have a negative impact on innovative activity (Schnabel and Wagner 1992). At the same time,

Table 10.2 Economic indicators for eleven countries, 1960–90

	Unemployment (as % of total labour force) average					Consumer price indices (year to year % changes) average					Growth of real GDP per capita (year to year % changes) average					Unit labour cost in manufacturing (year to year % changes) average		
	1960–67	1968–73	1974–79	1980–89	1960–90	1960–68	1968–73	1973–79	1979–90	1960–90	1960–68	1968–73	1973–79	1979–90	1960–90	1968–73	1973–79	1979–90
USA	5.0	4.6	6.7	7.0	6.0	2.0	5.0	8.5	5.5	5.1	3.1	2.0	1.4	1.6	2.0	3.2	8.2	2.1
Canada	4.8	5.4	7.2	9.2	6.9	2.4	4.6	9.2	6.3	5.5	3.6	4.1	2.9	1.8	2.9	3.3	9.8	5.4
Japan	1.3	1.2	1.9	2.5	1.8	5.7	7.1	9.9	2.6	5.6	9.1	7.1	2.5	3.5	5.3	6.8	7.4	0.3
Germany	0.8	0.8	3.4	6.7	3.4	2.7	4.6	4.7	2.9	3.5	3.1	4.1	2.5	1.7	2.6	7.1	5.0	3.3
UK	1.5	2.4	4.2	9.2	4.9	3.6	7.5	15.6	7.5	8.0	2.4	3.0	1.5	1.9	2.1	9.1	18.0	5.0
Belgium	2.1	2.3	5.7	10.9	6.0	2.8	4.9	8.4	4.7	4.9	3.9	5.3	2.1	2.1	3.1	4.0	7.5	1.0
Netherlands	0.7	1.5	4.9	na	na	3.6	6.9	7.2	2.8	4.6	3.5	3.7	1.9	1.2	2.4	5.8	5.8	0.6
Austria	2.0	1.4	1.7	3.3	2.3	3.5	5.2	6.3	3.8	4.5	3.6	5.4	3.0	2.1	3.2	5.5	5.3	1.5
Norway	1.0	na	1.8	3.0	na	3.9	6.9	8.7	7.9	6.8	3.6	3.3	4.4	2.2	3.2	5.8	11.1	6.2
Sweden	1.6	2.2	1.9	2.4	2.0	3.8	6.0	9.8	8.1	6.1	3.6	3.1	1.5	1.6	2.4	5.4	11.3	7.0
Australia	1.9	2.0	5.0	7.4	4.5	2.2	5.6	12.1	8.3	6.9	3.0	3.5	1.5	1.6	2.3	7.4	12.4	7.6

Source: OECD, Historical Statistics 1960–90

however, the evidence is by no means clear-cut, since in both Britain and Canada recent studies based on survey data (Daniel 1987; Betcherman 1991) indicate that unions there do not seem to inhibit the rate of technological change either. In the USA also, new techniques are adopted as rapidly in union settings as in non-union ones (Eaton and Voos 1989).

Similarly, there would seem to be no straightforward association between unionism and productivity, since unions may influence productivity in a number of positive and negative ways:

> On the positive side, unions can perform an important monitoring function for the employer, shock management into adopting best practice, promote a spirit of enterprise by enhancing communications between employer and employee. . . . On the negative side, unions may promote restrictive work practices, engage in costly industrial action, discourage investment in capital equipment and damage relations between employer and employee.
>
> (Nolan and Marginson 1990: 232)

In the latter respect, British studies have found that union limits on managerial discretion are more common in larger establishments than in smaller ones. This is consistent with the notion that large establishments are likely to have greater product market power, which enables them to 'afford' such restrictive practices (Wadhwani 1990).

There is evidence that in the USA – where unions have been linked to an adversarial industrial relations system – unionised firms, particularly via the provision of an information channel for enhancing communications between employers and employees by the mechanism of a 'collective voice', do tend to be more productive than their non-unionised counterparts (Freeman and Medoff 1984).[4] The empirical approach which is used here is to introduce the level of union density in estimating a production function, although this methodology does not permit a clear identification of the specific route through which any higher productivity effects may have occurred. In Britain by contrast, a union presence within a workplace or company seems, on balance, to be associated with lower labour productivity (Metcalf 1990). Also in Germany, despite the apparently favourable conditions for the existence of 'voice' effects, through the dual system of workers' representation by trade unions and works councils, various empirical studies have not been able to detect significant, net positive effects of these institutions on productivity (Schnabel 1991). In fact, one investigation of small- and medium-sized firms found a negative relationship between the existence of works councils and productivity (Fitzroy and Kraft 1987b). Although the results cannot necessarily be generalised to large firms, they may cast some doubt on the importance of the 'voice' mechanism. Similarly, a study of a large sample of manufacturing firms in Japan was unable to find any evidence that Japanese unions, by cooperating with management and exerting a 'collective voice', contributed to the achievement of higher productivity – on the contrary, their effect appeared to be substantially to reduce productivity (Brunello 1992).[5]

Further evidence from case studies in two plants in the Swedish and Australian automotive components industry (Lansbury *et al.* 1992) found that the higher productivity achieved by the Swedish plant in comparison with the Australian one appeared to be related not only to higher levels of investment in technology, but also to a greater emphasis on skills development and work organisation which emphasised teamwork and consultation. There was a high level of cooperation between workforce, unions and management in the Swedish case. By contrast, the Australian plant had low productivity and poor industrial relations.

More generally, however, it is quite possible that the effect of unions on economic performance is not homogeneous as between different types of predominant union organisation, such as craft or industrial. In this respect, a very influential study of collective action is that of Olson (1982), which examined the causes of differing economic growth rates among countries.

Olson's thesis

The essence of this theory concerns the activities of special-interest organisations for collective action, including trade unions. It is claimed that, on balance, these groupings reduce efficiency and slow down the adoption of new technologies, thereby impairing growth rates in the societies in which they operate.[6] A distinction is drawn, however, between what Olson terms 'encompassing' groupings, such as enterprise and industrial unions, whose membership represents a high proportion of the workforce (and of the wage bill) within the firms and industries in which they operate, and narrower craft organisations which control only a small percentage of the relevant employees. It is argued *inter alia* that the more embracing unions will have an interest in helping to make their firms and industries more productive and prosperous. This will be the case since it will promote the interests of their members who stand to secure a significant proportion of any resultant increase in total revenue, given that typically in labour-intensive industries two-thirds of the value added of each firm is devoted to the wage bill. In contrast, a narrow, special-interest craft union which, although it may determine work rules, controls only a small proportion of the total number of employees, would have little incentive to cooperate in raising efficiency – particularly since the amount of income to be redistributed to that union's members (only a fraction of the total gain) would be insufficient to compensate them for the costs borne in bringing about the change. Hence, it follows that enterprise and industrial unions will usually be more willing to agree to efficient work practices than craft unions. Similarly, at national level, peak organisations such as trade union confederations also seem likely to adopt a wider and more growth-oriented stance than that of the narrower associations of which they are composed.

On this line of argument, it is evident that an organised group which forms only a small part of the total society can gain by promoting its own interests. The reason is that it does not have to face any negative consequences arising from its actions, since they are general in impact, can therefore be externalised and are small enough so as not to matter. For example

a small work group that negotiates a rise in its pay that can be financed through price rises which in turn have no substantial effect on demand for the goods or services produced, need have no regard to the contribution thereby made to general inflation in the society at large.

(Crouch 1993: 9)

By contrast, once an organisation becomes sufficiently large and encompassing, its impact will be big enough to be discerned, and it will have to bear a significant fraction of the costs to society of pursuing its own interests in this way, i.e. it then has to internalise part of that externality. Thus, as unions become larger, the effect of nominal wages on the overall price-level increases and therefore the real wage gains of a given nominal wage increase is reduced. This tends to moderate wages as centralisation proceeds. In the case of Austria, for instance, it is contended that a 'cooperative bias' is built into unionism due, in large part, to the fact that representational monopoly and unity would make it almost impossible to externalise the costs (in terms of increased inflation and unemployment) of a conflict-oriented policy (Traxler 1992).

Some combination of centralisation in decision-making within (particularly trade union) organisations and wage bargaining arrangements, together with an indicator of social consensus, are usually included in the operational definition of (neo-) corporatism. It has therefore frequently been assumed that there is a monotonic relationship whereby the more corporatist an economy is, then the better its economic performance will be in bringing about lower real wages and unemployment.[7] In order to test this particular hypothesis a number of recent empirical studies have been undertaken, the results of which can now be assessed.

Corporatism and economic performance

Although inevitably somewhat judgemental, various rank orderings of countries have been made according to their degree of centralisation, in the absence of an actual measure of centralisation. One of the most frequently used rankings is that of Bruno and Sachs (1985) for seventeen countries. This is based on an index which incorporates the influence of central union organisations upon wage setting, as well as employer coordination and shopfloor power and – as a measure of consensus between labour and employers – the presence within firms of works councils. It was found that corporatist (strongly centralised) economies had superior macroeconomic performance in terms of overcoming problems of inflation and unemployment.

Newell and Symons (1987) view corporatism as a set of institutions whereby the interest organisations of labour and capital are brought together in a framework with the state, in which the aim is a high level of employment by limitation of wage demands. In their smaller sample of five countries, they conclude that corporatism results in a more powerful moderating influence of unemployment on wages, so that smaller increases in unemployment have been needed in order to produce a given downward adjustment of real wages. Consequently, highly corporatist economies such as Austria, some of the Nordic countries and Germany (on some definitions) seem to have been able to accommodate, at reduced employment cost, macroeconomic shocks in the 1970s and 1980s relative to experience elsewhere in Europe (Henley and Tsakalotos 1992). Cameron (1984) also concluded, from a study of eighteen countries from the mid-1960s to the early 1980s, that 'labour quiescence' – in the sense of infrequent strike activity and wage restraint (small increases in nominal and real earnings and prices) – was associated with the control of government by Social Democratic parties and, especially, with the structural conditions of corporatism *vis-à-vis* the labour movement and bargaining arrangements.

Yet, despite the apparently favourable experience of centralisation in reducing real wages and unemployment (via internalising the external effects of wage increases within large encompassing organisations) it has come to be recognised that a contrary view may also be valid. For countries with decentralised wage-setting institutions, it can be argued that wage increases will be restrained since competitive market forces are likely to play a larger role, thus enhancing real wage flexibility. In particular, decentralised bargaining may have important benefits by linking pay to localised economic conditions. It is also possible that in economies with centralised bargaining arrangements wage drift may be stronger, so that actual pay increases are more likely to exceed negotiated rates the more centralised the negotiation procedure (OECD 1988).

An implication of these contrasting arguments is that the relationship between the degree of centralisation and economic performance may be more complex, in that better macroeconomic performance may be associated with both most centralised, and least centralised, bargaining structures. By contrast, intermediate bargaining structures, such as those found in many continental European countries, including for instance Belgium and the Netherlands where industry-level bargaining prevails, might produce the worst outcomes – being associated with the greatest wage pressure and the highest levels of unemployment. Support for this hypothesis is provided by Calmfors and Driffill (1988). They show that for seventeen countries, grouped as between centralised, intermediate and decentralised economies over the period 1974–85, the intermediate grouping had the worst outcome. Although the classification of countries used in terms of their wage-setting has been subsequently criticised,[8] the findings indicate that, at either institutional extreme, both heavy centralisation (e.g. Austria and the Nordic countries) and far-reaching decentralisation (e.g. Canada, the US and Japan) are conducive to real wage restraint, whereas countries with intermediate degrees of centralisation perform less well. This would suggest, in diagrammatic form, the existence of a hump-shaped relationship between centralisation and real wages. Further, given an inverse relationship between labour demand and real wages, the employment performance (in terms of levels and changes) was found to be better in both centralised and decentralised economies than in those with intermediate centralisation, and the change in the Okun index (rate of unemployment plus rate of inflation) was also lower over the sample period. This conclusion, that economic performance appears better in countries which have either the most competitive decentralised labour markets, or the most highly centralised, encompassing institutions in the labour market, was further supported in subsequent work by Kendix and Olson (1990). A modification to the thesis, however, is that of Soskice (1990) who suggests that those countries with centralised bargaining, or with decentralised but *co-ordinated* industrial relations systems, will have a superior wage/ employment trade-off to other countries.

The conventional belief that, from the standpoint of macroeconomic performance, centralisation of wage bargaining is always preferable to decentralisation has, therefore, recently come under increasing challenge and needs to be qualified. Indeed, as the 1980s progressed, it became more difficult to perceive any relative superiority among the corporatist countries both in inflation performance and economic growth, although Austria, Norway and Sweden continued to provide far lower levels of unemployment than all low-corporatism countries (Crouch 1993).

A further aspect of (neo-) corporatism in relation to wage-setting behaviour is that its definition frequently includes the idea of institutionalised negotiation, collaboration and accord about wages and 'incomes policies' between labour confederations, central employer groupings and, often, representatives of the government. Such consensual incomes policies consist of the negotiated cooperation of unions, employers and government to coordinate and constrain wage increases (as well as, in some cases, prices and profits) within the context of a comprehensive macroeconomic programme. Marks (1986) has shown that, over the period 1964–80 across twelve countries, those societies in which consensual incomes policy was most consistently employed were able to maintain relatively low levels of unemployment (though apparently not inflation) and strike activity. More latterly, during the 1980s, econometric studies in Australia suggest that the 'Accord', as part of an economic strategy to reduce unemployment and inflation simultaneously, has delivered both nominal and real wage restraint, relative to levels which would otherwise have obtained, and has therefore improved macroeconomic outcomes. Some critics argue, however, that such wage restraint as has been achieved is due to other labour market forces rather than being a direct result of the Accord, and that in fact the Accord has impaired economic growth by inhibiting structural adjustments (Hancock and Isaac 1992).

IN CONCLUSION

In this chapter we have observed that the labour market performance of advanced industrialised countries exhibits marked cross-country divergences, and have sought to examine some of the implications for economic performance of different, national industrial relations institutions and wage bargaining structures. Yet, not only is the link between industrial relations and macroeconomic outcomes complex, but it is also apparent that countries with 'similar' institutions may still perform very differently. As Freeman (1988: 75) has emphasised, 'labour market structure is therefore only one element in understanding economic performance' and we should be wary of prescribing any particular set of institutional arrangements, within the broad spectrum of institutional relations and strategic choices available, as the simple key to success.

FURTHER READING

A book-length collection of detailed studies on industrial relations and economic performance in market economies is Brunetta and Dell'Aringa (1990), while a good account of the empirical literature for Britain is the article by Metcalf (1993), and for the United States Katz and Keefe (1992). On industrial relations 'models' see Kassalow (1983) and on the economic effects of unions in an international context, Blanchflower and Freeman (1992). Finally, MacDuffie and Krafcik's (1992) study of automobile plants in seventeen countries found that high performance firms had extensive training, multi-skilling and worker participation in problem solving and production decisions, as well as flexible technology.

Notes

1 INTRODUCTION: COMPARATIVE APPROACHES

1 'Those involved in industrial relations are embroiled in a never-ending struggle for domination and control, where different and various organisations seek to assert authority over those with which they react' (Dabscheck 1989: 177).

2 Dunlop wanted a less passive term than 'participants' and therefore used 'actors' in the sense of 'doers' or 'reagents'. Sociologists would regard this conceptualisation as being broadly equivalent to 'role-players'.

3 It can be argued that they are partly endogenous (internally determined) and interact with the industrial relations system, for example the parties' attempts to influence the pace of technological development and control market structure via the exercise of industrial and political power.

4 It is usual to distinguish between the 'substantive' rules of industrial relations which deal with wages, hours and working conditions and set the standards of employment, and 'procedural' devices for administering the substantive rules and for the peaceful settlement of industrial disputes.

5 'Which is why the firms which most closely approach Japanese counterparts in personnel practices are the élite firms – the Shells, the Unilevers, the IBMs and Hewlett-Packards – whose employees are least likely to better themselves by moving elsewhere' (Dore 1990: 441).

6 Some writers view comparative methodology in the social sciences as a (limited) counterpart to the controlled experiment in the natural sciences, enabling observation of differences made to the phenomenon under investigation by the varying circumstances in different countries (see Porter 1967).

7 Compare Marsh and Mannari (1981: 458): 'All too often "culture" or "values" are used as explanations when what is needed is better theory.'

8 In his study, culture is conceived as being the historically developed and learned pattern of beliefs, values and customs of a people.

9 For a discussion of the problems of separating industry and country effects in relation to strikes for instance, see Edwards (1977: 551–70).

10 Similarly, an international comparison of the extent of worker influence on management decision-making would not confine comparison of works councils in, say, Germany with similar formal institutional schemes for worker participation elsewhere. In the case of Britain, it would also investigate the role of shop steward organisation and, in the United States, the local union.

11 'Empiricism involves observation, classification and the evaluation of relations between observables' (Marsden 1982: 235). Critics would maintain that observation which is unguided by theory implies that what the empiricist sees depends on where he stands, so that his vision is partly obscured by his own preconceptions.

2 TRADE UNIONS

1 In France ... even if an agreement was signed by the unions, it was merely regarded as a temporary embodiment of the existing balance of power, and as a basis from which a new and more ambitious set of demands could immediately be unleashed.

(Gallie 1978: 255)

2 'Job control' includes control over access to the job (via such devices as union insistence upon seniority rights), its security and work content.

3 There were some important deviations, however, from the dominant Soviet model of trade unionism in countries such as Hungary and Yugoslavia, where there was greater economic and political decentralisation. In Poland, strikes were permitted by law in 1982. In other countries, such as Bulgaria, economic decision-making was excessively centralised and reforms had 'advanced with glacial slowness' (Jones 1992).

4 Although before the 1955 merger of the two central union organisations, the AFL and CIO, American unions were deeply split over a number of issues, including the political role of the unions.

5 Partly because of the long-established, high technical performance of industry German society has given priority to vocational training (as provided by industry) over theoretical training and general education, and there is also great respect among employers for craft skills and values.

6 In Germany, trainee engine drivers are recruited not from footplate occupations but more broadly from the skilled fitters or mechanics employed in railway workshops.

7 No new union can be registered if its members can 'conveniently belong' to an existing organisation.

8 Industrial power depends significantly upon the extent of union organisation (although it is by no means the only determinant) since, other things remaining equal, the greater the degree of unionisation 'the lower the substitutability of the relevant workforce, the greater its potential solidarity and the greater therefore its strike potential' (Wilkinson and Burkitt 1973: 114). For a broader, theoretical discussion of power relations see Lukes (1974), and Bacharach and Lawler (1981).

9 In 1954, the proportion of the French labour force employed in the service sector, 38 per cent (and 36 per cent as early as 1938), exceeded that in industry, 35.5 per cent – while agriculture still employed 26 per cent.

10 Such a provision was necessary since, where unions are divided between several central organisations, it is difficult to grant the same prerogatives to all unions on the same terms.

11 Using the technique of the 'dummy' variable (see Chapter 6).

12 Yet, at the same time, because ΔW is found to be significant the 'credit' effect still appears to be operative, i.e. the unions will still claim the credit for wage increases which have been secured because they make the case to the arbitration tribunals.

13 Since not all the benefits of union membership can be made selective – increased wages, for instance, may be secured by non-members – then workers may not be willing to join unions in order to obtain collective benefits that are available without their participation.

14 Due to the curbing of expansion of public employment because of the financial crisis of the state, along with a trend to shift public industries back to the private sector.

3 EMPLOYERS AND MANAGEMENTS

1 As Windmuller (1984: 8) expresses it: 'Employers' associations, by contrast with trade associations, specialise in representing the interests of their members mainly or exclusively in the labour area. In European terminology their chief concerns are the so-called "social" issues.'

2 In order to prevent those employers who did not recognise and negotiate with a union enjoying a labour cost advantage over their competitors who did. Thus in certain industries in the USA, multi-employer bargaining was initiated by employers faced with excess capacity and inelastic product demand.

3 A good illustration is the Engineering Employers' Federation in Britain: 'Historically, the principal function of the Federation has been to provide a defensive alliance of employers to meet actions of unions regarded as inimical to their interests, principally through the use of a nationally based "provision for avoiding disputes"' (Marsh *et al.* 1981: 9).

4 Edwards (1981) attributes this, in part, to the absence in the USA of a feudal tradition which required loyalty among employees. American employers had therefore to establish their legitimacy and secure their employees' undivided loyalty. They could tolerate no threat to the achievement of that objective.

5 In Germany, Italy and Japan the associations became absorbed into the political structures of fascist or military regimes.

6 By 1914 some 20 per cent of German manual workers were covered by collective agreements.

7 Gospel (1983) argues, however, that the impetus to plant-level bargaining about wages and conditions occurred because of competitive, product market factors. As the scope of markets became more international they were less amenable to (multi-employer) collusive arrangements.

8 The idea of management as a body of people with an independent source of power, as a distinct social group with a particular role, hinges, to a substantial degree, on the idea of the separation of ownership from control. In the absence of such a separation, management remains a cipher of the power of ownership of property.

(Eldridge *et al.* 1991: 49)

9 Sometimes replacing the (sub)contracting system of labour force management, as in the nineteenth-century British and US iron industries.

10 A further distinction is sometimes made between 'soft' and 'hard' HRM. 'Soft' HRM emphasises the human resource aspect and incorporates the view that there is an organisational payoff in terms of performance 'from a combination of HRM policies which emphasise consensualism and mutuality of management and employee interests' (Gunningle 1992: 6). By contrast, 'hard' HRM emphasises the management aspect, whereby the organisation's human

resources are seen as similar to any other resources and should be procured and managed in as cheap and effective a way as possible.

4 COLLECTIVE BARGAINING

1 In most European countries there has existed a formal distinction (greatly blurred in practice) between matters on which employer and union interests clearly differed and those on which it was assumed that they were broadly shared. Basically, conflictual matters – such as wage determination – were to be dealt with by collective bargaining carried on outside the enterprise itself. 'Common' interests, however, such as production and productivity issues, would be discussed internally via such bodies as works councils or joint consultation committees.

2 Because, for example, the negotiation of topics such as labour utilisation necessarily entails an erosion of management authority (Barbash 1977).

3 'A given percentage increase in wages translates itself into a higher percentage increase in unit labour costs in firms with lower proportions of capital to labour than in firms with higher proportions of capital to labour' (Ulman 1974a: 105).

4 The practice of 'whipsawing' by a union refers to the playing-off of one employer against another. The strategy is designed to obtain benefits from a number of employers by applying pressure initially on one, and then using the settlement as a base from which to obtain the same, or better, benefits elsewhere.

5 Order in Council PC 1003.

6 In 1974 within the private sector 64 per cent of all Japanese workers in establishments with 500 or more employees were union members, as against 9 per cent in establishments with less than 100 employees.

7 Thus, 'the stirring and spicing and baking process of industrialisation may have been the same [as elsewhere], but if you start off with a different cultural dough you end up with a different social cake' (Dore 1990: 375).

8 The weak position of trade unions at the workplace level has been attributed to the relatively late industrialisation of the country and slow development of the trade union movement, together with its division into separate federations – thereby making representation within firms difficult.

9 'By centralisation of structure is meant the extent to which trade unions and employer organisations are federated or joined into strong central bodies at the national level with substantial executive (and negotiating) powers capable for instance of negotiating with one another and dealing with government on behalf of their members' (Blyth 1979: 75).

10 A score of 3 indicates one dominating union confederation and one dominating private-sector employer organisation; 2 the existence of 2–5 union confederations and/or 2–5 central employer organisations; 1 is the absence of a central organisation on one, or both, sides of the labour market.

11 ILO (1985).

12 This finding at the cross-national level does not necessarily eliminate the possibility that bargaining structure might still be a significant determinant within the context of a single country's industrial relations system.

13 This is used as a proxy for the extent of union power.

5 THE ROLE OF THE STATE

1 Conciliation is a procedure whereby a third party brings union and employer representatives together, where negotiations have reached an impasse or broken down, to find their own solution. With mediation this role is more active, and the mediator may submit settlement proposals to them. In the case of arbitration the third party takes a decision which disposes of the dispute.
2 'One law for the lion and ox is oppression' (Clark 1971: 425).
3 In Sweden, for instance, the first modern unions were not founded until the late 1870s.
4 Schmidt (1972) maintains that historically in Sweden business interests have never been able to exert as much political and economic influence as they have in many other parts of Europe and in the USA. In the Swedish parliament it was farmers and small entrepreneurs who played the leading part until the Social Democrats came to power in 1932. Also, the multi-party constellation of power in the Swedish parliament produced by a proportional representative voting system meant that although repressive legislation was proposed it could not attract the necessary parliamentary support (Jackson and Sisson 1976).
5 This principle had been adopted by the American Federation of Labor since the 1880s to prevent disputes among its affiliated unions.
6 Including delineation of the appropriate bargaining unit, election of bargaining agents and the requirement upon employers to furnish necessary bargaining information and to bargain 'in good faith'.
7 Between 1965 and 1975, about 20 per cent of all new awards were 'consent' awards.
8 Walker (1976: 1) notes that, because of the distinctive feature of compulsory arbitration, the Australian industrial relations system was for long regarded by most other countries as 'an antipodean curiosity as exotic as the kangaroo or the boomerang'.
9 It has been observed (Thompson and Juris 1985: 400) that the US government did not need to take special action to attack organised labour, since a 'combination of less strict [law] enforcement, conservative macroeconomic policies, high unemployment, and the hostility of employers accomplished the same result'.
10 An earlier Conservative government had introduced the Industrial Relations Act (1971–4) whose intention was 'the replacement of collectivist *laissez-faire* in labour law with a comprehensive and strongly interventionist legal framework' (Lewis 1976: 12). The Act, nevertheless, failed to achieve its major objectives, since the trade unions actively and successfully resisted its operation and many employers failed to utilise its provisions. The legislation was repealed by a subsequent Labour government.
11 Although there is no obligation to reach an agreement and, unlike the USA, there is no requirement to bargain 'in good faith' (Goetschy and Rojot 1987).
12 However, the establishment of statutory Trade Boards (subsequently Wages Councils) in low-paid industries fulfilled some of the same functions. The Wages Councils are now (1993) to be abolished.
13 In Belgium, however, although the rights/interest distinction is made, it is of little practical consequence as either type of dispute may be settled by strike action.
14 Another branch of pluralist theory, however, maintains that the state is not simply a neutral actor, since it has identifiable interests of its own. Thus, from

this perspective, public policy is the result of a compromise between the objects of interest groups and the objects of the state itself (Adams 1992a).

15 He emphasises that the direct involvement of government in contemporary industrial relations requires legitimation, so as to avoid the charge of systematic bias in favour of capital – a function which is performed by the ideological identification of the interests of capital with the 'national' interest.

16 It is possible, however, for a corporatist system, once established, to survive the demise of a Social Democratic government, as happened in Germany and in Sweden (in the 1980s).

6 INDUSTRIAL CONFLICT AND STRIKES

1 Prior to 1981, the minimum threshold for the USA had been six workers. It is estimated that this change reduced the recorded number of working days lost by 30–40 per cent.

2 Korpi (1981) has shown, however, that official statistics greatly underestimated the number of (unofficial) stoppages in Sweden up to the 1970s.

3 In the case of Canada the explanation may relate to its high degree of integration with the US economy (which has lower concentration), and consequently with its labour movement in the form of bi-national unions, i.e. in this case the degree of concentration in the North American continent as a whole may be the decisive factor. Thompson (1987) in fact suggests that the high level of industrial conflict in Canada may be due to the existence of major multinational companies (and large international unions), resulting in strikes at individual production units which are incapable of inflicting major economic loss on the parent organisations. By contrast, Haiven (1990) points to deficiencies in the Canadian dispute resolution system which left untouched many of the main issues of contention on the frontier of control in the workplace.

4 The early development in nineteenth-century France of a centralised but wide-ranging state organisation seems to have been the major factor in explaining the important part played by public authority intervention in strikes (via the prefect, inspector of labour, or local deputy to the National Assembly) and the use by workers of political weapons for economic objectives (Sellier 1973).

5 Shorter and Tilly (1974) suggest that a strike wave exists when, in any given year, the number of strikes and strike participants exceeds by 50 per cent the average for the preceding five years.

6 'By "struggle" is meant . . . the behaviour that employers and workers use within work relations to influence the terms on which those relations are carried out' (Edwards 1986: 7).

7 This variable assumes a numerical value of 1 when the President belongs to the Democratic Party and 0 when he is a Republican.

8 Snyder's empirical results have been challenged by more recent studies which attempt to improve the specification of his equations. They suggest it may be that strike action is more, rather than less, sensitive to labour market conditions in uninstitutionalised settings, since under those conditions workers' ability to pursue industrial action is most directly dependent upon their market situation (Shalev 1983).

9 Also, the 'political' determinants of strikes may themselves be influenced by economic factors.

10 At the technical level, if simultaneous effects exist then estimating the model
    via the usual technique of ordinary-least-squares will result in biased and
    inconsistent coefficients.
11 The general emphasis on external influences in quantitative studies and neglect
    of the internal dynamics of the strike itself led Strauss (1982: 16) to comment:
    'It appears that few recent strike researchers have ever walked a picket line or
    even passed through one.'

7 WORKERS' PARTICIPATION IN DECISION-MAKING

1 The EC's Fifth Directive (as amended in 1983) would require the harmonisation of company law in each member state to provide for worker participation in the affairs of large companies.
2 Works councils have been widely established by legislation, including those in
   Belgium, France, Germany, Greece, Netherlands, Poland, Portugal and Spain
   as well as in a number of Latin American countries. In Denmark and Ireland
   they have been set up by agreement. The councils consist of workers only in
   Germany, Greece, India, Netherlands, Portugal, Poland and Spain. In Belgium,
   Denmark, France and Luxembourg there are also management representatives.
3 For a discussion of the relative merits of collective bargaining and some other
   representative forms of participation, see Ogden (1982).
4 Similarly, with respect to Austrian industrial relations, it is claimed that
   'conflict avoidance is an attitude, socioculturally based upon still prevailing
   authoritarian interaction patterns and founded upon a basic consensus of
   authorities, which thereby stabilises the status quo' (Fürstenberg 1982: 363).
5 He attributes the change in union attitudes to the new political background after
   the establishment of the democratic Weimar republic. For the German trade
   unions at that time, their
       sudden increase in influence over state legislation can be imagined to have
       had an effect on ideology, in that working through the legislative machinery
       seemed a hopeful and rational strategy under the circumstances, which also
       generated a closer attachment to the prevailing order of society compared to
       that under imperial rule.
                                                              (Sorge 1976: 288)
6 At a period of industrial upheaval and 'crisis' following upon the effects of a
   rapid rate of technical change, rationalisation and major structural problems in
   the economy.
7 For criticisms and an appraisal of the IDE study, see Teulings (1988).
8 A characteristic of joint stock companies under German law is the two-tier
   management structure, in the form of a policy-making supervisory board
   together with a management board. In the mining, iron and steel industries,
   parity of representation on the supervisory board between worker and share-
   holder representatives was introduced from the outset of codetermination.
   Elsewhere (since 1976) a parity system of workers' representation has applied
   in companies with more than 2,000 employees, whereas in smaller firms
   workers continue to elect only one-third of the supervisory board members.
   Even in the larger companies, however, in the event of deadlock, the chairman
   – who is generally appointed by the shareholders – has a decisive, casting vote.
9 These were also reported in an earlier study of Polish enterprises (Kolaja 1960).
   In the 1980s Polish workers had little influence on the self-management

organisation due to domination by both the economic administration and the Communist party (Jarosz and Kosak 1992).

10 In fact, some producer cooperatives in France and the USA have actually survived for more than fifty years, and a number appear to have outperformed capitalist firms in economic terms. In the Italian producer cooperatives, positive productivity effects from participation have also been observed.

11 Drago and Heywood (1989) suggest, however, that business opinion now views Japan, and not Sweden or Yugoslavia, as the ostensible mecca of participation, given Japan's weak labour movement and its use of participation to increase productivity but not workplace democracy *per se*. Long and Warner (1987) also see managerial desire for workers' participation as the prime variable, at least in the short run, mediating between forces for participation and its actual emergence. There is also some (limited) evidence that positive productivity effects are most marked in firms which involve their workers in decision-making (Cable 1988).

12 For criticism of the 'cycles of control' theory of participation, see Ackers *et al.* (1992).

13 Sorge (1976) also concludes that the causes of major international variations in institutional types of participation appear to be located, in part, 'in the wider political implications, value systems, beliefs and ideologies held by both trade unions and employers' organisations and the country at large'.

14 Other observers have attributed the smooth transition not directly to the codetermination mechanism but rather to the relative ease with which displaced workers could be resettled during a (former) period of high economic activity (ILO 1981b).

8 INDUSTRIAL RELATIONS IN MULTINATIONAL ENTERPRISES

1 For an analysis of transfer pricing practices see OECD (1979b). The reaction of one trade union body was to state, uncompromisingly, that 'transfer pricing is quite simply robbery' (Postal International Trade Secretariat, quoted in Weinburg 1978: 35). It can be argued, however, that the scope for transfer pricing practices has generally been exaggerated.

2 It is possible that, despite the formal management structure requiring a delegation of organisational responsibilities, there could still be quasi-control by group headquarters, since 'functional specialists [at head office], whose role was intended to by advisory, could gradually attract to themselves powers of decision-making in their areas' (OECD 1977: 10).

3 More generally in empirical investigations, size effects have been shown to have a major influence on many facets of industrial relations, including union recognition, bargaining arrangements and patterns of industrial conflict.

4 The ITSs were mostly established before 1914 in order to promote international trade union understanding and the exchange of experience at industry level. Until the growth of the multinationals, however, they played only a relatively minor role.

5 The ETUC is the largest umbrella organisation for national trade union confederations in Western Europe, comprising thirty-six confederations from twenty-one countries. It also has a number of industrial committees, such as the

European Metalworkers' Federation, which play a direct role in confronting the multinationals. Unions have, however, established their own horizontal contacts in the form of committees within individual multinationals (such as EMF committees in Philips, Ford and International Harvester) which, although they operate outside the formal company structure, exchange information among different European plants relating to wages and working conditions.

9 INDUSTRIAL RELATIONS IN DEVELOPING COUNTRIES

1 See World Bank, *World Development Report*, (1990). Indicators typically used to define 'newly industrialising countries' (NICs) include the level, or rate of growth, of manufactured exports.

2 All over Latin America, prior to the Second World War, attempts by workers to organise themselves met with virulent private and public repression as a result of the potential of workers' organisations to reduce capital accumulation and paralyse production in the most dynamic and important sector of the economy, as well as to impede the main generator of government revenues.

3 In countries such as Zimbabwe, where public servants are precluded from joining trade unions, there are further limitations to potential unionisable workers – given that the government is the single largest employer.

4 In Peru, the structure of the trade union movement has been oriented towards the 'political market' (in view of the weakness of the unions as economic bargainers) rather than, as in developed countries, towards labour and product markets.

5 According to these theories the result is the industrialisation of the global periphery, and the corresponding deindustrialisation of the advanced capitalist core.

6 As well as legitimising trade unions, legislation could be an important instrument of control – for instance by way of registration and deregistration provisions for particular unions.

7 In Zambia, by contrast, the organised labour movement – founded upon perceptions of common interest as industrial labour – appears to have been characterised for the most part by an absence of ethnic cleavages (Gertzel 1979).

8 Thereby also forestalling the possible growth of politicised general unions.

9 A contrasting development to such consolidated structures is the case of Malaysia. So anxious was the government to prevent a resurgence of communist influence and the use of unions for political action that the Trade Union Ordinance of 1959 limited the growth of widely drawn industrial unions (and horizontally based federations) by restricting union organisation to that of 'similar occupations or trades'. One consequence of limiting union size was the development of a multiplicity of 'peanut' unions, confined to organising the workers of a single employer (Henley 1980).

10 Kilby (1967) interprets the causes of the failure of collective bargaining in the public sector as including union leadership rivalries, status-conscious employer representatives and disagreements over the scope of bargaining.

11 Sandbrook (1975) maintains that where union leaders are dependent on financial and personal support from the rank and file they have pressed workers' demands on a militant basis.

10 INDUSTRIAL RELATIONS SYSTEMS AND ECONOMIC OUTCOMES

1   According to Fox (1985), even in the early 1950s Britain was still regarded as a model of 'industrial relations maturity', with a low incidence of working days lost by industrial disputes (although this was about to change).

2   In the case of Japan, Oliver and Wilkinson (1989) have also observed that the real issue is not simply whether or not particular elements of Japanese industrial relations practices can be transferred to a different socio-cultural environment, but also the extent to which, say, human resource practices 'fit' with other constituent parts of a company's total strategy, such as its manufacturing and marketing strategies – as is the case with successful Japanese companies in Britain.

3   Against this, however, it could be argued that neo-corporatist arrangements have given workers and their local representatives confidence that their co-operation in restructuring would not be accompanied by major unemployment.

4   Especially, it is claimed, the provision of 'voice' acts to reduce quitting and labour turnover.

5   Particularly by limiting managements' discretion in the allocation of workers, including transfers, promotions and redundancies.

6   Crouch (1993) points out that this study of the efficiency-inhibiting impact of the organisation of interests has been an important part of the intellectual case of the neo-liberal politics in the 1980s for breaking down organised groups, deregulation and the freeing of markets.

7   Corporatist structures may also be particularly effective in overcoming informational inefficiencies if a country is hit by economy-wide disturbances, such as the oil shocks of the 1970s (Heitger 1987).

8   Since even where economies are decentralised, wage-setting may still be co-ordinated across the economy, thereby helping to promote wage restraint (Soskice 1990).

Bibliography

Aaron, B. (ed.) (1971) *Labour Courts and Grievance Settlement in Western Europe*, Berkeley: University of California Press.

Ackers, P., Marchington, M., Wilkinson, A. and Goodman, J. (1992) 'The use of cycles? Explaining employee involvement in the 1990s', *Industrial Relations Journal* 23: 268–83.

Adams, R. J. (1975) *The Growth of White-Collar Unionism in Britain and Sweden. A Comparative Investigation*, Madison: University of Wisconsin Press.

—— (1981) 'A theory of employer attitudes and behaviour towards trade unions in western Europe and North America', in G. Dlugos and K. Weirermair (eds) *Management Under Differing Value Systems*, New York: de Gruyter.

—— (1983) Review, *Industrial and Labor Relations Review* 36: 310–11.

—— (1986) 'Two policy approaches to labour–management decision making at the level of the enterprise', in W. W. Craig Riddell (ed.) *Labour–Management Cooperation in Canada*, Toronto: University of Toronto Press.

—— (1989) 'North American industrial relations: divergent trends in Canada and the United States', *International Labour Review* 128: 46–64.

—— (1991) 'An international survey of courses in comparative industrial relations', in M. Bray (ed.) *Teaching Comparative Industrial Relations*, ACIRRT Monograph No. 2, Sydney, NSW: University of Sydney.

—— (1992a) 'The role of the state in industrial relations', in D. Lewin, O. Mitchell and P. Sherer (eds) *Research Frontiers in Industrial Relations and Human Resources*, Madison, Wis.: IRRA.

—— (1992b) 'Labour management, government relations and socioeconomic performance: lessons from the experience of Germany, Japan, Sweden and the United States', report prepared for the Canadian Labour Market and Productivity Centre.

—— (1993) 'Regulating unions and collective bargaining: a global, historical analysis of determinants and consequences', *Comparative Labor Law Journal* 14, 3: 272–301.

Adams, R. J. and Rummel, G. H. (1977) 'Workers' participation in management in West Germany: impact on the worker, the enterprise and the trade union', *Industrial Relations Journal* 8, 1: 4–23.

Ahiauzu, A. (1982) 'Cross-cultural study of job regulation at the workplace. A framework for analysis', Working Paper No. 234, University of Aston Management Centre.

Ahlén, K. (1989) 'Swedish collective bargaining under pressure: inter-union rivalry and incomes policies', *British Journal of Industrial Relations* 27: 330–46.

Albeda, W. (1971) 'Recent trends in collective bargaining in the Netherlands', *International Labour Review* 103: 247–68.

—— (1977) 'Changing industrial relations in the Netherlands', *Industrial Relations* 16: 133–44.

Ali Taha, A.R.E. (1982) 'Industrial relations in the Sudan', *Labour and Society* 7: 137–56.

Allen, G. C. (1981) 'Japan', in E. Owen Smith (ed.) *Trade Unions in the Developed Economies*, London: Croom Helm.

Allen, V.L. (1969) 'The study of African trade unionism', *Journal of Modern African Studies* 7: 289–307.

Andersen, S. S. (1988) *British and Norwegian Offshore Industrial Relations*, Avebury: Gower.

Andriessen, J. H. T. H. (1976) 'Developments in the Dutch industrial relations system', *Industrial Relations Journal* 7: 49–59.

Arnison, J. (1970) *The Million Pound Strike*, London: Lawrence & Wishart.

Arrighi, G. and Saul, J. S. (1968) 'Socialism and economic development in Tropical Africa', *Journal of Modern African Studies* 6: 141–69.

Ashenfelter, O. and Johnson, G. E. (1969) 'Bargaining theory, trade unions and industrial strike activity', *American Economic Review* 59: 35–49.

Bacharach, S. B. and Lawler, E. J. (1981) *Bargaining Power, Tactics and Outcomes*, San Francisco: Jossey-Bass.

Baglioni, G. (1989) 'Industrial relations in Europe in the 1980s', *Labour and Society* 14: 233–49.

—— (1991) 'Industrial relations in Europe in the 1980s', in G. Baglioni and C. Crouch (eds) *European Industrial Relations. The Challenge of Flexibility*, London: Sage.

Bain, G. S. and Clegg, H. A. (1974) 'A strategy for industrial relations research in Great Britain', *British Journal of Industrial Relations* 12: 91–113.

Bain, G. S. and Elsheikh, F. (1976) *Union Growth and the Business Cycle. An Econometric Analysis*, Oxford: Blackwell.

Bamber G. J. and Lansbury R. D. (eds) (1989) *New Technology: International Perspectives on Human Resources and Industrial Relations*, London: Unwin Hyman.

—— (1993) *International and Comparative Industrial Relations. A Study of Developed Market Economies*, London: Routledge.

Banaji, J. and Hensman, R. (1990) *Beyond Multinationalism: Management Policy and Bargaining Relationships in International Companies*, New Delhi: Sage.

Banks, J. A. (1974) *Trade Unionism*, London: Collier-MacMillan.

Barbash, J. (1977) 'Price and power in collective bargaining', *Journal of Economic Issues* 11.

—— (1979) 'Collective bargaining and the theory of conflict', *Relations Industrielles* 34: 646–57.

Barkin, S. (1980) 'European industrial relations: a resource for the reconstruction of the American system', *Relations Industrielles* 35: 439–45.

Barreto, J. (1992) 'Portugal: industrial relations under democracy', in A. Ferner and R. Hyman (eds) *Industrial Relations in the New Europe*, Oxford: Blackwell.

Bartölke, K., Eschweiler, W., Flechsenberger, D. and Tannenbaum, A. S. (1982) 'Workers' participation and the distribution of control as perceived by members of ten German companies', *Administrative Science Quarterly* 27: 380–97.

Batstone, E. V. (1984) *Working Order*, Oxford: Blackwell.
—— (1985) 'International variations in strike activity', *European Sociological Review* 1: 46–64.
Bean, R. (1987) 'International comparisons in the study of industrial relations', *Employee Relations* 9, 6: 3–8.
—— (1994) 'Industrial disputes in developing economies and DMEs: comparative profiles', *Comparative Labor Law Journal* 15, 1.
Bean, R. and Holden, K. (1989) 'Economic and political determinants of trade union growth in selected OECD countries: an update', *Journal of Industrial Relations* 31: 402–6.
—— (1992a) 'Cross-national differences in trade union membership in OECD countries', *Industrial Relations Journal* 23: 52–9.
—— (1992b) 'Determinants of strikes in India: a quantitative analysis', *Indian Journal of Industrial Relations* 28, 2: 161–8.
—— (1994) 'Union membership determinants in OECD countries: a survey', *International Journal of Manpower*.
Beaumont, P. B. (1987) *The Decline of Trade Union Organisation*, London: Croom Helm.
—— (1990) *Change in Industrial Relations. The Organisation and the Environment*, London: Routledge.
—— (1991) 'Human resource management and international joint venture: some evidence from Britain', *Human Resource Management Journal* 1: 90–101.
Beaumont, P. B. and Townley, B. (1987) 'Statutory recognition provisions: some lessons for Britain from abroad?', *Employee Relations* 9, 6: 9–12.
Beaumont, P. B., Thomson, A. W. J. and Gregory, M. B. (1980) 'Bargaining structure', *Management Decision* 18: 103–70.
Bendiner, B. (1987) *International Labour Affairs. The World Trade Unions and the Multinational Companies*, Oxford: Clarendon.
Berenbach, S. (1979) 'Peru's social property: limits to participation', *Industrial Relations* 18: 370–5.
Beresford, M. and Kelly, D. (1991) 'Industrial relations in ASEAN and other capitalist countries', in M. Bray (ed.) *Teaching Comparative Industrial Relations*, ACIRRT Monograph No. 2, Sydney, NSW: University of Sydney.
Berggren, C. (1986) 'Top management and co-determination in Swedish companies', *Economic and Industrial Democracy* 7: 99–108.
Berghahn, V. R. and Karsten, D. (1987) *Industrial Relations in West Germany*, Oxford: Berg.
Bergquist, C. (ed.) (1986) *Labor in Latin America. Comparative Essays on Chile, Argentina, Venezuela and Colombia*, Stanford, Calif.: Stanford University Press.
Betcherman, G. (1991) 'The effect of unions on the innovative behaviour of firms in Canada', *Industrial Relations Journal* 22: 142–51.
Bielasiak, J. (1989) 'Self-management and the politics of reform: Poland in the 1980s', *Economic and Industrial Democracy* 10: 282–309.
Bienefeld, D. A. (1979) 'Trade unions, the labour process and the Tanzanian state', *Journal of Modern African Studies* 17: 553–93.
Bird, D. (1991) 'International comparisons of industrial disputes in 1989 and 1990', *Employment Gazette* (UK) 99: 653–8.
Blain, N., Goodman, J. and Loewenberg, J. (1987) 'Mediation, conciliation and arbitration: an international comparison of Australia, Great Britain and the United States', *International Labour Review* 126: 179–98.

256   *Comparative industrial relations*

Blake, D. H. (1973) 'Cross-national cooperative strategies: union response to the MNCs', in K. P. Tudyka (ed.) *Multinational Corporations and Labour Unions*, Nijmegen: Sun.

Blanchflower, D. G. and Freeman, R. B. (1992) 'Unionism in the United States and other advanced OECD countries', *Industrial Relations* 31: 56–79.

Blanc-Jouvain, X. (1988) 'Trade union democracy and industrial relations: France', *Bulletin of Comparative Labour Relations* 17: 7–26.

Blanpain, R. (1974) 'The influence of labour on management decision-making: a comparative legal survey', *Industrial Law Journal* 3: 5–29.

—— (1977) 'The OECD guidelines for multinational enterprises', *Journal of the Royal Society of Arts* 126.

—— (1982) 'Belgium', in R. Blanpain (ed.) *International Encyclopaedia for Labour Law and Industrial Relations*, Deventer: Kluwer.

Blum, A. A. (ed.) (1981) *International Handbook of Industrial Relations. Contemporary Developments and Research*, London: Aldwych.

Blyth, C. A. (1979) 'The interaction between collective bargaining and government policies in selected member countries', in OECD, *Collective Bargaining and Government Policies*, Paris.

Bok, D. C. and Dunlop, J. T. (1970) *Labour and the American Community*, New York: Simon & Schuster.

Bomers, G. B. J. (1976) *Multinational Corporations and Industrial Relations. A Comparative Study of West Germany and the Netherlands*, Amsterdam: Van Gorcum.

Bomers, G. B. J. and Peterson R. B. (1977) 'Multinational corporations and industrial relations: the case of West Germany and the Netherlands', *British Journal of Industrial Relations* 15: 45–62.

Bradley, K. (1980) 'A comparative analysis of producer cooperatives: some theoretical and empirical implications', *British Journal of Industrial Relations* 18: 155–68.

Bradley, K. and Gelb, A. (1981) 'Motivation and control in the Mondragon experiment', *British Journal of Industrial Relations* 19: 211–31.

—— (1982) 'The replication and sustainability of the Mondragon experiment', *British Journal of Industrial Relations* 20: 20–33.

Brewster, C. (1992) 'Starting again: industrial relations in Czechoslovakia', *International Journal of Human Resource Management* 3: 555–74.

Brewster, C. and Bournois, F. (1991) 'Human resource management: a European perspective', *Personnel Review* 20, 6: 4–13.

Brewster, C. and Larsen, H. (1992) 'Human resource management in Europe: Evidence from ten countries', *International Journal of Human Resource Management* 3: 409–29.

Bridgford, J. (1990) 'French trade unions: crisis in the 1980s', *Industrial Relations Journal* 21: 126–35.

Brody, D. (1980) *Workers in Industrial America. Essays in the Twentieth-Century Struggle*, New York: Oxford University Press.

Bronstein, A. S. (1978) 'Collective bargaining in Latin America: problems and trends', *International Labour Review* 117.

Brook Cowen, P. J. (1993) 'Labor relations reform in New Zealand: the Employment Contracts Act and contractual freedom', *Journal of Labor Research* 14, 1: 69–83.

Brown, W. (ed.) (1981) *The Changing Contours of British Industrial Relations*, Oxford: Blackwell.

—— (1986) 'The changing role of trade unions in the management of labour', *British Journal of Industrial Relations* 24: 161–8.

Brunello, G. (1992) 'The effect of unions on firm performance in Japanese manufacturing', *Industrial and Labor Relations Review* 45: 471–87.

Brunetta, R. and Dell'Aringa, C. (eds) (1990) *Labour Relations and Economic Performance*, London: Macmillan.

Bruno, M. and Sachs, J. (1985) *Economics of Worldwide Stagflation*, Cambridge, Mass.: Harvard University Press.

Buckley P. J. and Artisien, P. (1988) 'Policy issues of intra-EC direct investment: British, French and German multinationals in Greece, Portugal and Spain, with special reference to employment effects', in J. Dunning and P. Robson (eds) *Multinationals and the European Community*, Oxford: Blackwell.

Buckley, P. J. and Enderwick, P. (1985) *The Industrial Relations Practices of Foreign-Owned Firms in Britain*, London: Macmillan.

Burawoy, M. (1983) 'Between the labour process and the state: the changing face of factory regimes under advanced capitalism', *American Sociological Review* 48: 587–605.

—— (1985) *The Politics of Production. Factory Regimes under Capitalism and Socialism*, London: Verso.

Busch, G. K. (1983) *The Political Role of International Trades Unions*, London: Macmillan.

Cable, J. (1988) 'Is profit-sharing participation? Evidence on alternative firm types from West Germany', *International Journal of Industrial Organization* 6: 121–37.

Calmfors, L. and Driffill, J. (1988) 'Bargaining structure, corporatism and macroeconomic performance', *Economic Policy* 6: 14–61.

Caloia, A. (1979) 'Industrial relations in Italy: problems and perspectives', *British Journal of Industrial Relations* 17: 259–67.

Cameron, D. (1984) 'Social democracy, corporatism, labour quiescence, and the representation of economic interest in advanced capitalist society', in J. H. Goldthorpe (ed.) *Order and Conflict in Contemporary Capitalism*, Oxford: Clarendon.

Carrière, J., Haworth, N. and Roddick, J. (1989) *The State, Industrial Relations and the Labour Movement in Latin America*, 1, London: Macmillan.

Cella, G. and Treu, T. (1990) 'National trade union movements', in R. Blanpain (ed.) *Comparative Labour Law and Industrial Relations in Industrialised Market Economies*, 2, 4th edn, Deventer: Kluwer.

Chamberlain, N. W. (1961) 'Determinants of collective bargaining structures', in A. R. Weber (ed.) *The Structure of Collective Bargaining. Problems and Perspectives*, Glencoe, Ill.: Free Press of Glencoe Inc.

Chang, C. and Sorrentino, C. (1991) 'Union membership statistics in 12 countries', *Monthly Labor Review* 114, 12: 46–53.

Cho, S. K. (1985) 'The labour process and capital mobility: the limits of the new international division of labor', *Politics and Society* 14: 185–222.

Clark, G. de N. (1971) 'Remedies for unfair dismissal: a European comparison', *International and Comparative Law Quarterly* 20: 397–432.

Clarke, R. O., Fatchett, D. J. and Roberts, B. C. (1972) *Workers' Participation in Management in Britain*, London: Heinemann.

Clegg, H. A. (1976) *Trade Unionism under Collective Bargaining. A Theory Based on Comparisons of Six Countries*, Oxford: Blackwell.

—— (1979) *The Changing System of Industrial Relations in Great Britain*, Oxford: Blackwell.

Cohn, S. and Eaton, A. (1989) 'Historical limits on neoclassical strike theories: evidence from French coal mining, 1890–1935', *Industrial and Labor Relations Review* 42, 4: 649–62.

Comisso, E. T. (1981) 'The logic of worker (non-)participation in Yugoslav self-management', *Review of Radical Political Economics* 13, 2: 11–22.

Cordova, E. (1980) 'Collective labour relations in Latin America. A reappraisal', *Labour and Society* 5: 227–42.

—— (1987) 'Social concertation in Latin America', *Labour and Society* 12: 410–23.

Cornforth, C. (1989) 'Worker cooperatives in the UK: temporary phenomenon or growing trend?', in C. J. Lammers and G. Széll (eds) *International Handbook of Participation in Organizations. 1, Organizational Democracy: Taking Stock*, Oxford: Oxford University Press.

Cousineau, J. M. and Lacroix, R. (1986) 'Imperfect information and strikes: an analysis of Canadian experience, 1967–1982', *Industrial and Labor Relations Review* 39, 3: 377–87.

Cousineau, J. M., Lacroix, R. and Vachon, D. (1991) 'Foreign ownership and strike activity in Canada', *Relations Industrielles* 46: 616–30.

Craypo, C. (1975) 'Collective bargaining in the conglomerate multinational firm: Litton's shutdown of Royal Typewriter', *Industrial and Labor Relations Review* 29: 3–25.

Creigh, S., Poland, A. and Wooden, M. (1984) *The Reasons for International Differences in Strike Activity*, Working Paper No. 61, National Institute of Labour Studies, Flinders University of South Australia.

Cressey, P. (1991) 'Trends in employee participation and new technology', in R. Russell and V. Rus (eds) *International Handbook of Participation in Organizations. 2, Ownership and Participation*, Oxford: Oxford University Press.

Crouch, C. (1978) 'The changing role of the state in industrial relations in Western Europe', in C. Crouch and A. Pizzorno (eds) *The Resurgence of Class Conflict in Western Europe since 1968. 2, Comparative Analyses*, New York: Holmes & Meier.

—— (1979) *The Politics of Industrial Relations*, London: Fontana.

—— (1982a) Review, *Industrial Relations Journal* 13,1: 77–8.

—— (1982b) *Trade Unions. The Logic of Collective Action*, London: Fontana:

—— (1991) 'United Kingdom: the rejection of compromise', in G. Baglioni and C. Crouch (eds) *European Industrial Relations. The Challenge of Flexibility*, London: Sage.

—— (1993) *Industrial Relations and European State Traditions*, Oxford: Clarendon.

Cupper L. and Hearn, J. M. (1981) 'Australia', in E. Owen Smith (ed.) *Trade Unions in Developed Economies*, London: Croom Helm.

Cziria, L. (1992) 'Collective forms of work organization in Czechoslovak economic practice', in G. Széll (ed.) *Labour Relations in Transition in Eastern Europe*, Berlin: de Gruyter.

Dabscheck, B. (1989) 'A survey of theories of industrial relations', in J. Barbash and K. Barbash (eds) *Theories and Concepts in Comparative Industrial Relations*, Columbia: University of South Carolina Press.

Dahrendorf, R. (1968) *Society and Democracy in Germany*, London: Weidenfeld & Nicolson.

Damachi, U. G. (1976) 'Government, employers and workers in Ghana: a study of the mutual perception of roles', *British Journal of Industrial Relations* 14: 26–34.

Damachi, U. G., Seibel, H. D. and Trachman, L. (eds) (1979) *Industrial Relations in Africa*, London: MacMillan.

Daniel, W. W. (1987) *Workplace Industrial Relations and Technical Change*, London: Francis Pinter.

D'Art, D. (1992) *Economic Democracy and Financial Participation. A Comparative Study*, London: Routledge.

Davis, H. B. (1941) 'The theory of union growth', *Quarterly Journal of Economics* 55: 611–37.

Deaton, D. R. and Beaumont, P. B. (1980) 'The determinants of bargaining structure: some large-scale survey evidence for Britain', *British Journal of Industrial Relations* 18: 202–16.

Deery, S. and De Cieri, H. (1991) 'Determinants of trade union membership in Australia', *British Journal of Industrial Relations* 29: 59–73.

Derber, M. (1976) 'Strategic factors in industrial relations systems. The metalworking industry', *Labour and Society* 1: 18–28.

——— (1984) 'Employers' associations in the United States', in J. P. Windmuller and A. Gladstone (eds) *Employers' Associations and Industrial Relations. A Comparative Study*, Oxford: Clarendon.

Despax, M. and Rojot, J. (1979) 'France', in R. Blanpain (ed.) *International Encyclopaedia for Labour Law and Industrial Relations*, Deventer: Kluwer.

Deyo, F. C. (1981) *Dependent Development and Industrial Order*, New York: Praeger.

DIO (Decisions in Organizations) (1979) 'Participative decision-making: a comparative study', *Industrial Relations* 18: 295–309.

Doeringer, P. B. (1981) 'Industrial relations research in international perspective', in P. B. Doeringer (ed.) *Industrial Relations in International Perspective. Essays on Research and Policy*, London: Macmillan.

Dølvik, J. E. and Stokland, D. (1992) 'Norway: the "Norwegian Model" in transition', in A. Ferner and R. Hyman (eds) *Industrial Relations in the New Europe*, Oxford: Blackwell.

Donovan, Lord (1968) Royal Commission on Trade Unions and Employers' Associations *Report*, Cmnd. 3623, London: HMSO.

Dore, R. (1990) *British Factory – Japanese Factory. The Origins of National Diversity in Industrial Relations*, Berkeley, Calif.: University of Los Angeles.

Drago, R. and Heywood, J. S. (1989) 'Support for worker participation', *Journal of Post-Keynesian Economics* 11: 522–30.

Drago, R. and Wooden, M. (1991) 'The determinants of participatory management', *British Journal of Industrial Relations* 29: 177–204.

Due, J., Madsen, J. S. and Jensen, C. S. (1991) 'The social dimension: convergence or diversification of IR in the Single European Market?', *Industrial Relations Journal* 22: 85–103.

Dunlop, J. T. (1958) *Industrial Relations Systems*, New York: Holt.

——— (1972) 'Political systems and industrial relations', *Bulletin of the International Institute for Labour Studies*, 9.

——— (1976) 'Structural changes in the American labor movement and industrial relations systems', in R. L. Rowan (ed.) *Readings in Labor Economics and Labor Relations*, Homewood, Ill.: Irwin.

—— (1978) 'Introduction', in J. T. Dunlop and W. Galenson (eds) *Labor in the Twentieth Century*, New York: Academic Press.

Dunning, J. H. (1981) *International Production and the Multinational Enterprise*, London: Allen & Unwin.

Eaton, A. E. and Voos, P. B. (1989) 'Unions and contemporary innovations in work organisation, compensation and employee participation' (mimeo), Washington, DC: Economic Policy Institute.

Edelstein, J. D. and Warner, M. (1975) *Comparative Union Democracy*, London: Allen & Unwin.

Edwards, P. K. (1977) 'A critique of the Kerr-Siegel hypothesis of strikes and the isolated mass', *Sociological Review* 25: 551–74.

—— (1978) 'Time-series regression models of strike activity: a reconsideration with American data', *British Journal of Industrial Relations* 16: 320–34.

—— (1981) *Strikes in the United States, 1881–1974*, Oxford: Blackwell.

—— (1986) *Conflict at Work. A Materialist Analysis of Workplace Relations*, Oxford: Blackwell.

—— (1992) 'Industrial conflict: theories and issues in recent research', *British Journal of Industrial Relations* 30: 361–404.

Edwards, P. K., Hall, M., Hyman, R., Marginson, P., Sisson, K., Waddington, J. and Winchester, D. (1992) 'Great Britain: still muddling through', in A Ferner and R. Hyman (eds), *Industrial Relations in the New Europe*, Oxford: Blackwell.

Edwards, R. (1979) *Contested Terrain. The Transformation of the Workplace in the Twentieth Century*, London: Heinemann.

Edwards, R., Garonna, P. and Tödtling, F. (eds) (1986) *Unions in Crisis and Beyond: Perspectives from Six Countries*, Dover, Mass.: Auburn House.

EJILB (Europe-Japan Institute for Law and Business) (1992) 'Employment practices of Japanese companies in Europe', *European Industrial Relations Review* 223, August, 18–22.

Elbaum, B. and Wilkinson, F. (1979) 'Industrial relations and uneven development: a comparative study of the American and British steel industries', *Cambridge Journal* 3: 275–303.

Eldridge, J. E. T. (1975) 'Panaceas and pragmatism in industrial relations', *Industrial Relations Journal* 6: 4–13.

Eldridge, J., Cressey, P. and MacInnes, J. (1991) *Industrial Sociology and Economic Crisis*, London: Harvester Wheatsheaf.

El-Sabbagh, Z. (1988) 'Role of labor unions in socialist regimes in the Arab world', *Indian Journal of Industrial Relations* 23: 346–59.

Elvander, N. (1974) 'The role of the state in the settlement of labor disputes in the Nordic countries: a comparative analysis', *European Journal of Political Research*, 2: 363–83.

Enderwick, P. (1982) 'Labour and the theory of the multinational corporation', *Industrial Relations Journal* 13, 2: 32–43.

—— (1984) 'The labour utilisation practices of multinationals and obstacles to multinational collective bargaining', *Journal of Industrial Relations* 26: 345–64.

—— (1985) *Multinational Business and Labour*, London: Croom Helm.

Enderwick, P. and Buckley, P. J. (1982) 'Strike activity and foreign ownership: an analysis of British manufacturing 1971–73', *British Journal of Industrial Relations* 20: 308–21.

—— (1983) 'Industrial relations practices in Britain: a comparative analysis of foreign and domestically-owned firms', *Labour and Society* 8: 315–32.

Espinosa, J. and Zimbalist, A. S. (1978) *Economic Democracy. Workers' Participation in Chilean Industry, 1970–73*, New York: Academic Press.

Estrin, S., Jones, D. C. and Svejnar, J. (1987) 'The productivity effects of worker participation: producer cooperatives in western economies', *Journal of Comparative Economics* 11: 40–61.

Evans, E. (1976) 'On some recent econometric models of strike frequency', *Industrial Relations Journal* 7, 3: 72–6.

Eyraud, F. and Tchobanian, R. (1985) 'The Auroux reforms and company-level industrial relations in France', *British Journal of Industrial Relations* 23: 241–59.

Fashoyin, T. (1980) *Industrial Relations in Nigeria*, London: Longman.

—— (1986) 'Management of industrial conflict in Africa: a comparative analysis of Kenya, Nigeria and Tanzania', in U. G. Damachi and H. B. Seibel (eds) *Management Problems in Africa*, London: Macmillan.

—— (1990) 'Nigerian labour and the military: towards exclusion?', *Labour, Capital and Society* 23: 12–37.

—— (1991) 'Recent trends in industrial relations research and theory in developing countries', in R. J. Adams (ed.) *Comparative Industrial Relations. Research and Theory*, London: Harper Collins Academic.

Ferner, A. (1991) 'Changing public sector industrial relations in Europe', IRRU, Warwick Papers in Industrial Relations, No. 37, Coventry: University of Warwick.

Ferner, A. and Hyman, R. (1992a) 'Introduction', in A. Ferner and R. Hyman (eds) *Industrial Relations in the New Europe*, Oxford: Blackwell.

—— (1992b) 'Italy: Between political exchange and micro-corporatism' in A. Ferner and R. Hyman (eds) *Industrial Relations in the New Europe*, Oxford: Blackwell.

—— (eds) (1992c) *Industrial Relations in the New Europe*, Oxford: Blackwell.

Fitzroy, F. and Kraft, K. (1987a) 'Cooperation, productivity and profit sharing', *Quarterly Journal of Economics* 102: 23–35.

—— (1987b) 'Efficiency and internal organization: works councils in West German firms', *Economica* 54: 493–504.

Flanagan, R. J. (1974) 'Introduction', in R. J. Flanagan and A. R. Weber (eds) *Bargaining Without Boundaries. The Multinational Corporation and International Labor Relations*, Chicago: University of Chicago Press.

Flanders, A. (1974) 'The tradition of voluntarism', *British Journal of Industrial Relations* 12: 352–70.

Fong, P. E. and Cheng, L. (1978) 'Changing patterns of industrial relations in Singapore', in E. M. Kassalow and U. G. Damachi (eds) *The Role of Trade Unions in Developing Societies*, Geneva: International Institute for Labour Studies.

Ford, G. W. (1980) 'Employers' associations: an introduction', in G. W. Ford, J. M. Hearn and R. D. Lansbury (eds) *Australian Labour Relations. Readings*, Melbourne: Macmillan.

Form, W. H. (1973) 'Job vs. political unionism. A cross-national comparison', *Industrial Relations* 12: 224–38.

Forsebäck, L. (1980) *Industrial Relations and Employment in Sweden*, Uppsala: Swedish Institute.

Fox, A. (1978) 'Corporatism and industrial democracy: the social origins of present forms and methods in Britain and Germany in industrial democracy. International views' (mimeo), Coventry: University of Warwick.

262   *Comparative industrial relations*

—— (1985) *History and Heritage. The Social Origins of the British Industrial Relations System*, London: Allen & Unwin.

Franzosi, R. (1985) Review, *Industrial and Labor Relations Review* 38: 454–5.

—— (1989a) 'One hundred years of strike statistics: methodological and theoretical issues in quantitative strike research', *Industrial and Labor Relations Review* 42: 348–62.

—— (1989b) 'Strike data in search of a theory: the Italian case in the postwar period', *Politics and Society* 17: 453–87.

Freeman, R. B. (1988) 'Labour market institutions and economic performance', *Economic Policy* 6: 64–80.

Freeman, R. B. and Medoff, J. L. (1984) *What Do Unions Do?*, New York: Basic Books.

Freeman, R. B. and Pelletier, J. (1990) 'The impact of industrial relations legislation on British union density', *British Journal of Industrial Relations* 28: 141–64.

Frenkel, S. J. (1990) 'Management strategy, labour relations and productivity in the state enterprise: a comparative workplace analysis', *Labour and Society* 15: 39–58.

—— (ed.) (1993) *Organized Labor in the Asia-Pacific Region. A Comparative Study of Trade Unionism in Nine Countries*, Ithaca, NY: Cornell International Industrial and Labor Relations Report No. 24.

Fulcher, J. (1988) 'On the explanation of industrial relations diversity: labour movements, employers and the state in Britain and Sweden', *British Journal of Industrial Relations* 26: 246–74.

—— (1991) *Labour Movements, Employers and the State. Conflict and Co-operation in Britain and Sweden*, Oxford: Clarendon.

Fürstenberg, F. (1980) 'Co-determination and its contribution to industrial democracy: a critical evaluation', IRRA, *Proceedings*, 33rd Annual Meeting: 185–90.

—— (1982) 'Conflict management in the Austrian system of social partnership', in G. B. J. Bomers and R. B. Peterson (eds) *Conflict Management and Industrial Relations*, Boston: Kluwer.

—— (1991) 'Structure and strategy in industrial relations', *Bulletin of Comparative Labour Relations* 21.

Galenson, W. (ed.) (1952) *Comparative Labor Movements*, New York: Prentice Hall.

Gallie, D. (1975) Review, *British Journal of Industrial Relations* 13: 285–6.

—— (1978) *In Search of the New Working Class. Automation and Social Integration within the Capitalist Enterprise*, Cambridge: Cambridge University Press.

Geary, D. (1981) *European Labour Protest, 1848–1939*, London: Croom Helm.

Gennard, J. (1974) 'The impact of foreign-owned subsidiaries on host country labour relations: the case of the United Kingdom', in R. J. Flanagan and A. R. Weber (eds) *Bargaining Without Boundaries: The Multinational Corporation and International Labor Relations*, Chicago: University of Chicago Press.

Gertzel, G. (1979) 'Industrial relations in Zambia to 1975', in U. G. Damachi, H. D. Seibel and L. Trachman (eds) *Industrial Relations in Africa*, London: Macmillan.

Giles, A. (1989) 'Industrial relations theory, the state and politics', in J. Barbash and K. Barbash (eds) *Theories and Concepts in Comparative Industrial Relations*, Columbia: University of South Carolina Press.

Gill, C. (1984) 'Industrial relations in Denmark: problems and perspectives', *Industrial Relations Journal* 15: 46–57.

Gill, J. (1969) 'One approach to the teaching of industrial relations', *British Journal of Industrial Relations* 7: 265–72.

Gladstone, A. (1978) 'Preface', in E. M. Kassalow and U. G. Damachi (eds) *The Role of Trade Unions in Developing Societies*, Geneva: International Institute for Labour Studies.

—— (1980) 'Trade unions, growth and development', *Labour and Society* 5: 49–68.

—— (1984) 'Employers' associations in comparative perspective: functions and activities', in J. P. Windmuller and A. Gladstone (eds) *Employers' Associations and Industrial Relations. A Comparative Study*, Oxford: Clarendon.

—— (1989) 'Introductory', in A. Gladstone, R. Lansbury, J. Stieber, T. Treu and M. Weiss (eds) *Current Issues in Labour Relations. An International Perspective*, Berlin: de Gruyter.

Goetschy, J. and Rojot, J. (1987) 'France', in G. J. Bamber and R. D. Lansbury (eds) *International and Comparative Industrial Relations. A Study of Developed Market Economies*, London: Allen & Unwin.

Goetschy, J. and Rozenblatt, P. (1992) 'France: the industrial relations system at a turning point?', in A. Ferner and R. Hyman (eds) *Industrial Relations in the New Europe*, Oxford: Blackwell.

Goldthorpe, J. H. (1984) 'The end of convergence: corporatist and dualist tendencies in modern western societies', in J. H. Goldthorpe (ed.) *Order and Conflict in Contemporary Capitalism. Studies in the Political Economy of Western European Nations*, Oxford: Clarendon.

Gospel, H. F. (1983) 'Managerial structures and strategies: an introduction', in H. F. Gospel and C. R. Littler (eds) *Managerial Strategies and Industrial Relations*, London: Heinemann.

Grahl, J. and Teague, P. (1991) 'European level collective bargaining. A new phase?', *Relations Industrielles* 46: 46–70.

Gray, P. S. (1980) 'Collective bargaining in Ghana', *Industrial Relations* 19: 175–91.

Griffin, L. J., Wallace, M. A. and Rubin, B. R. (1986) 'Capitalism and labor organization', *American Sociological Review* 51: 147–67.

Guest, D. E. (1987) 'Human resource management and industrial relations', *Journal of Management Studies* 24: 503–22.

Gunningle, P. (1992) 'Human resource management in Ireland', *Employee Relations* 14, 5: 5–22.

Günter, H. and Leminsky, G. (1978) 'The Federal Republic of Germany', in J. T. Dunlop and W. Galenson (eds) *Labor in the Twentieth Century*, New York: Academic Press.

Gurdon, M. A. (1985) 'Equity participation by employees: the growing debate in West Germany', *Industrial Relations* 24: 113–29.

—— (1992) 'The politics of property in the Federal Republic of Germany', *International Labour Review* 130: 595–611.

Haas, A. (1983) 'The aftermath of Sweden's co-determination law: workers' experiences in Gothenburg 1977–80', *Economic and Industrial Democracy* 4: 19–46.

Haimson, L. H. (1989) 'The historical setting in Russia and the West', in L. H. Haimson and C. Tilly (eds) *Strikes, Wars and Revolutions in an International Perspective. Strike Waves in the Late Nineteenth and Early Twentieth Centuries*, Cambridge: Cambridge University Press.

264   *Comparative industrial relations*

Haiven, L. (1990) 'Industrial conflict in Canada and Britain', *Employee Relations* 12: 14–18.

—— (1991) 'Past practice and custom and practice: adjustment and industrial conflict in North America and the United Kingdom', *Comparative Labor Law Journal* 12: 300–34.

Hall, M. (1992) 'Behind the European works councils directives: the European Commission's legislative strategy', *British Journal of Industrial Relations* 30: 547–66.

Hamill, J. (1984) 'Labour relations decision-making within multinational corporations', *Industrial Relations Journal* 15, 2: 30–4.

Hammarström, O. (1987) 'Swedish industrial relations', in G. J. Bamber and R. D. Lansbury (eds) *International and Comparative Industrial Relations. A Study of Developed Market Economies*, London: Allen & Unwin.

Hanami, T. (1979) *Labor Relations in Japan Today*, London: John Martin.

—— (1989) 'Co-operation and conflict in public sector labour relations in Japan', in A. Gladstone, R. Lansbury, J. Stieber, T. Treu and M. Weiss (eds) *Current Issues in Labour Relations. An International Perspective*, Berlin: de Gruyter.

Hancock, K. and Isaac, J. E. (1992) 'Australian experiments in wage policy', *British Journal of Industrial Relations* 30: 213–36.

Hanford, T. J. and Grasso, P. G. (1991) 'Participation and corporate performance in ESOP firms', in R. Russell and V. Rus (eds) *International Handbook of Participation in Organizations. 2, Ownership and Participation*, Oxford: Oxford University Press.

Hardy, C. (1985) 'Response to organizational closure: patterns of resistance and quiescence', *Industrial Relations Journal* 16: 16–24.

Hare, A. E. C. (1946) *Report on Industrial Relations in New Zealand*, Wellington: Victoria University College.

Hartman, H. (1975) 'Co-determination today and tomorrow', *British Journal of Industrial Relations* 13: 54–64.

Haworth, N. (1991) 'Teaching comparative industrial relations: a global perspective', in M. Bray (ed.) *Teaching Comparative Industrial Relations*, ACIRRT Monograph No. 2, Sydney, NSW: University of Sydney.

Haworth, N. and Ramsay, H. (1988) 'International capital and some dilemmas in industrial democracy', in R. Southall (ed.) *Trade Unions and the New Industrialization of the Third World*, London: Zed Books.

Haydu, J. (1988) 'Employers, unions and American exceptionalism: pre-World War I open shops in the machine trades in comparative perspective', *International Review of Social History* 33: 25–41.

Hedlund, G. (1981) 'Autonomy of subsidiaries and formalisation of headquarters-subsidiary relationships in Swedish MNCs', in L. Otterbeck (ed.) *The Management of Headquarters-Subsidiary Relationships in Multinational Corporations*, London: Gower.

Heitger, B. (1987) 'Corporatism, technological gaps and growth in OECD countries', *Weltwirtschaftliches Archiv* 123: 465–73.

Hendricks, W. E. and Kahn, L. M. (1982) 'The determinants of bargaining structure in U.S. manufacturing industries', *Industrial and Labor Relations Review* 35: 181–95.

Henley, A. and Tsakalotos, E. (1992) 'Corporatism and the European labour market after 1992', *British Journal of Industrial Relations* 30: 567–84.

Henley, J.S. (1978) 'Pluralism, underdevelopment and trade union power: evidence from Kenya', *British Journal of Industrial Relations* 16: 224–42.

—— (1980) 'The management of labour relations in industrialising market economies', *Industrial Relations Journal* 10, 3: 41–53.

—— (1989) 'African employment relationships and the future of trade unions', *British Journal of Industrial Relations* 24: 295–309.

Henley, J. S. and Nyaw, M. K. (1986) 'Introducing market forces into managerial decision making in Chinese industrial enterprises', *Journal of Management Studies* 23: 635–56.

Herding, R. (1972) *Job Control and Union Structure*, Rotterdam: Rotterdam University Press.

Herman, E. E. (1966) *Determination of the Appropriate Bargaining Unit by Labour Relations Boards in Canada*, Ottawa: Queen's Printer.

Héthy, L. (1991) 'Industrial relations in Eastern Europe: recent developments and trends', in R. J. Adams (ed.) *Comparative Industrial Relations. Contemporary Research and Theory*, London: Harper Collins Academic.

—— (1992) 'Hungary's changing labour relations system', in G. Széll (ed.) *Labour Relations in Transition in Eastern Europe*, Berlin: de Gruyter.

Hibbs, D. A. (1976) 'Industrial conflict in advanced industrial societies', *American Political Science Review* 70: 1033–58.

—— (1978) 'On the political economy of long-run trends in strike activity', *British Journal of Political Science* 8: 153–75.

Hill, S. and Thurley, K. (1974) 'Sociology and industrial relations', *British Journal of Industrial Relations* 12: 147–70.

Hince, K. and Vranken, M. (1991) 'A controversial reform of New Zealand labour law: the Employment Contracts Act 1991', *International Labour Review* 130: 475–93.

Hoffman, C. (1981) 'People's Republic of China', in A. A. Blum (ed.) *International Handbook of Industrial Relations*, London: Aldwych.

Hofstede, G. (1980) *Culture's Consequences. International Differences in Work-Related Values*, Beverly Hills, Calif.: Sage.

Holt, J. (1977) 'Trade unionism in the British and US steel industries, 1888–1912. A comparative study', *Labor History* 18: 5–35.

Homburg, H. (1983) 'Scientific management and personnel policy in modern German enterprise, 1918–1939: the case of Siemens', in H. F. Gospel and C. R. Littler (eds) *Managerial Strategies and Industrial Relations*, London: Heinemann.

Hood, N. and Young, S. (1979) *The Economics of Multinational Enterprise*, London: Longman.

Hotz-Hart, B. (1992) 'Switzerland: still as smooth as clockwork?', in A. Ferner and R. Hyman (eds) *Industrial Relations in the New Europe*, Oxford: Blackwell.

Howard, W. A. (1980) 'Australian trade unions in the context of union theory', in G. W. Ford, J. M. Hearn and R. D. Lansbury (eds) *Australian Labour Relations: Readings*, Melbourne: Macmillan.

Hughes, S. (1992) 'Living with the past: trade unionism in Hungary since political pluralism', *Industrial Relations Journal* 23: 293–303.

Hyman, R. (1975) *Industrial Relations. A Marxist Introduction*, London: Macmillan.

—— (1979) 'Third World strikes in perspective', *Development and Change* 10: 321–37.

—— (1982a) 'The concept of the public interest in industrial relations', in Lord Wedderburn and W. T. Murphy (eds) *Labour Law and the Community: Perspectives for the 1980s*, London: Institute of Advanced Legal Studies.

—— (1982b) Review Symposium, *Industrial Relations*, 21: 100–14.
—— (1983) 'Trade unions. Structure, policies and politics', in G. S. Bain (ed.) *Industrial Relations in Britain*, Oxford: Blackwell.
—— (1991) 'European unions: towards 2000', *Work, Employment and Society* 5: 621–39.
—— (1992) 'Trade unions and the disaggregation of the working class', in M. Regini (ed.) *The Future of Labour Movements*, London: Sage.
Hyman, R. and Streeck, W. (eds) (1988) *New Technology and Industrial Relations*, Oxford: Blackwell.
IDE Research Group (1981a) *European Industrial Relations*, Oxford: Clarendon.
—— (1981b) *Industrial Democracy in Europe*, Oxford: Clarendon.
—— (1993) *Industrial Democracy in Europe Revisited*, Oxford: Oxford University Press.
IILS (International Institute for Labour Studies) (1969) 'Strategic factors in industrial relations systems – a programme of international comparative industry studies', *Bulletin of the International Institute for Labour Studies* 6: 187–209.
ILO (International Labour Office) (1976) *Multinationals in Western Europe. The Industrial Relations Experience*, Geneva.
—— (1981a) *Employment Effects of Multinational Enterprises in Industrialised Countries*, Geneva.
—— (1981b) *Workers' Participation in Decisions Within Undertakings*, Geneva.
—— (1985) *World Labour Report 2*, Geneva.
Ingham, G. K. (1974) *Strikes and Industrial Conflict. Britain and Scandinavia*, London: Macmillan.
Isaac, J. E. (1973) 'Industrial relations', in R. I. Downing (ed.) *The Australian Economy: A Manual of Applied Economics*, London: Weidenfeld & Nicolson.
Iwuji, E. (1979) 'Industrial relations in Kenya', in U. G. Damachi, H. D. Seibel and L. Trachman (eds) *Industrial Relations in Africa*, London: Macmillan.
Jackson, M. P. (1982) *Trade Unions*, London: Longman.
—— (1987) *Industrial Conflict in Britain, USA and Australia*, Brighton: Wheatsheaf.
Jackson, P. and Sisson, K. (1976) 'Employers' confederations in Sweden and the UK and the significance of industrial infrastructure', *British Journal of Industrial Relations* 14: 306–23.
Jacobi, O. and Müller-Jentsch, W. (1991) 'West Germany: continuity and structural change', in G. Baglioni and C. Crouch (eds) *European Industrial Relations. The Challenge of Flexibility*, London: Sage.
Jacobi, O., Keller, B. and Müller-Jentsch, W. (1992) 'Germany: co-determining the future', in A. Ferner and R. Hyman (eds) *Industrial Relations in the New Europe*, Oxford: Blackwell.
Jacobs, A. (1986) 'Collective self-regulation', in B. Hepple (ed.) *The Making of Labour Law in Europe*, London: Mansell.
Jacobs, E., Orwell, S., Paterson, P. and Weitz, F. (1978) *The Approach to Industrial Change in Britain and Germany. A Comparative Study of Workplace Industrial Relations and Manpower Policies in British and West German Enterprises*, London: Anglo-German Foundation for the Study of Industrial Society.
Jacoby, S. (1979) 'Origins of internal labour markets in Japan', *Industrial Relations* 18: 184–96.
Jarosz, M. and Kosak, M. (1992) 'The role of self-management in Polish enterprises', in G. Széll (ed.) *Labour Relations in Transition in Eastern Europe*, Berlin: de Gruyter.

Jenkins, R. (1987) *Transnational Corporations and Uneven Development. The Internalization of Capital and the Third World*, London: Methuen.

Johnston, T. L. (1962) *Collective Bargaining in Sweden*, London: Allen & Unwin.

Jones, D. C. (1978) 'Producer-cooperatives in industrialised western economies: an overview', *Annals of Public and Cooperative Economy* 49: 149–61.

—— (1992) 'The transformation of labor unions in Eastern Europe: the case of Bulgaria', *Industrial and Labor Relations Review* 45: 452–70.

Jones, D. C. and Kato, T. (1993) 'Employee stock ownership plans and productivity in Japanese manufacturing firms', *British Journal of Industrial Relations* 31: 331–46.

Jürgens, U., Klinzing, L. and Turner, L. (1993) 'The transformation of industrial relations in Eastern Germany', *Industrial and Labor Relations Review* 46: 229–44.

Kahn-Freund, O. (1972) *Labour and the Law*, London: Stevens.

—— (1974) 'Uses and misuses of comparative law', *Modern Law Review* 37: 1–27.

—— (1979) *Labour Relations: Heritage and Adjustment*, Oxford: Oxford University Press.

—— (1981) *Labour Law and Politics in the Weimar Republic*, Oxford: Blackwell.

Kahn-Freund, O. and Hepple, B. (1972) *Laws Against Strikes*, London: Fabian Research Series.

Kannappan, S. and Krishnan, V. N. (1977) 'Participative management in India: Utopia or snare?', *Annals of the American Academy of Political and Social Science* 431: 95–102.

Karsh, B., Blain, N. and Nihei, Y. (1984) 'Airline pilot unions in Australia, Japan and the United States: a test of the cross-national convergence', *Journal of Industrial Relations* 26: 113–32.

Kassalow, E. M. (1968) 'The comparative labour field', *Bulletin of the International Institute for Labour Studies* 5: 92–107.

—— (1969) *Trade Unions and Industrial Relations. An International Comparison*, New York: Random House.

—— (1977) 'Industrial conflict and consensus in the United States and Western Europe: a comparative approach', IRRA *Proceedings*, 30th Annual Meeting: 113–22.

—— (1978a) 'Aspects of labour relations in multinational companies: an overview of three Asian countries', *International Labour Review* 117: 273–87.

—— (1978b) 'Introduction', in E. M. Kassalow and U. G. Damachi (eds) *The Role of Trade Unions in Developing Societies*, Geneva: International Institute for Labour Studies.

—— (1982) 'Industrial democracy and collective bargaining: a comparative view', *Labour and Society* 7: 209–29.

—— (1983) 'Japan as an industrial relations model', *Journal of Industrial Relations* 25: 201–19.

—— (1984) 'The future of American unionism: a comparative perspective', *Annals of the American Academy of Political and Social Science* 473: 52–63.

Katz, H. C. and Keefe, J. H. (1992) 'Collective bargaining and industrial relations outcomes: the causes and consequences of diversity', in D. Lewin, O. S. Mitchell and P. D. Sherer (eds) *Research Frontiers in Industrial Relations and Human Resources*, Madison, Wis.: IRRA.

Kaufman, B. E. (1982) 'The determinants of strikes in the United States, 1900–1977', *Industrial and Labor Relations Review* 35: 473–90.

Keller, B. K. (1991) 'The role of the state as corporate actor in industrial relations systems', in R. J. Adams (ed.) *Comparative Industrial Relations. Contemporary Research and Theory*, London: Harper Collins Academic.

Kelly, A. and Brannick, T. (1988) 'Explaining the strike proneness of British companies in Ireland', *British Journal of Industrial Relations* 26: 37–55.

Kendall, W. (1975) *The Labour Movement in Europe*, London: Allen Lane.

Kendix, M. and Olson, M. (1990) 'Changing unemployment rates in Europe and the USA: institutional structure and regional variation', in R. Brunetta and C. Dell' Aringa (eds) *Labour Relations and Economic Performance*, London: Macmillan.

Kerr, C., Dunlop J. T., Harbison, F. H. and Myers, C. A. (1962) *Industrialism and Industrial Man*, London: Heinemann.

—— (1971) 'Postscript to Industrialism and Industrial Man', *International Labour Review* 103: 519–40.

Kilby, P. (1967) 'Industrial relations and wage determination: failure of the Anglo-Saxon model', *Journal of Developing Areas* 1: 489–519.

—— (1973) 'Trade unionism in Nigeria 1938–66', in A. Sturmthal and J. G. Scoville (eds) *The International Labor Movement in Transition*, Urbana: University of Illinois Press.

Kissler, L. (1989) 'Co-determination research in the Federal Republic of Germany: a review', in C. J. Lammers and G. Széll (eds) *International Handbook of Participation in Organizations. 2, Organizational Democracy: Taking Stock*, Oxford: Oxford University Press.

Kjellberg, A. (1992) 'Sweden: can the model survive?', in A. Ferner and R. Hyman (eds) *Industrial Relations in the New Europe*, Oxford: Blackwell.

Klein, K. J. and Rosen, C. (1986) 'Employee stock ownership in the United States', in R. N. Stern and S. McCarthy (eds) *International Yearbook of Organizational Democracy. 3, The Organizational Practice of Democracy*, Chichester: Wiley.

Kleingartner, A. and Peng, S. (1991) 'Taiwan: an exploration of labour relations in transition', *British Journal of Industrial Relations* 29: 427–45.

Kobrin, S. J. (1976) 'Industrialisation and variation in social structure: an empirical test of the convergence hypothesis', IRRA 29th Annual Meeting, *Proceedings*: 177–85.

Kochan, T. A. (1980) *Collective Bargaining and Industrial Relations*, Homewood: Irwin.

Kochan, T. A. and McKersie, R. B. (1989) 'Future directions for American labor and human resources policy', *Relations Industrielles* 44: 224–48.

Kochan, T. A., McKersie, R. B. and Cappelli, P. (1984a) 'Strategic choice and industrial relations theory', *Industrial Relations* 23: 16–39.

Kochan, T. A., McKersie, R. B. and Katz, H. C. (1984b) 'US industrial relations in transition', IRRA 37th Annual Meeting, *Proceedings*: 261–76.

Koike, K. (1988) *Understanding Industrial Relations in Modern Japan*, London: Macmillan.

Kolaja, I. (1960) *A Polish Factory. A Case-Study of Workers' Participation in Decision Making*, Lexington: University of Kentucky Press.

Korpi, W. (1978a) *The Working Class in Welfare Capitalism. Work, Unions and Politics in Sweden*, London: Routlege & Kegan Paul.

—— (1978b) 'Workplace bargaining, the law and unofficial strikes: the case of Sweden', *British Journal of Industrial Relations* 16: 355–68.

—— (1980) 'Industrial relations and industrial conflict: the case of Sweden', in B. Martin and E. M. Kassalow (eds) *Labor Relations in Advanced Industrial Societies: Issues and Problems*, Washington, DC: Carnegie Endowment.

—— (1981) 'Sweden: conflict, power and politics in industrial relations', in P. Doeringer (ed.) *Industrial Relations in International Perspective. Essays on Research and Policy*, London: Macmillan.

Korpi, W. and Shalev, M. (1979) 'Strikes, industrial relations and class conflict in capitalist society', *British Journal of Sociology* 30: 164–87.

Kraus, J. (1979) 'The political economy of industrial relations in Ghana', in U. G. Damachi, H. D. Seibel and L. Trachman (eds) *Industrial Relations in Africa*, London: Macmillan.

Krishnan, V. N. (1981) 'India', in A. A. Blum (ed.) *International Handbook of Industrial Relations*, London: Aldwych.

Krislov, J. (1987) 'Are there industrial relations sub-models?', *Industrial Relations Journal* 18: 201–9.

Kritsantonis, N. D. (1992) 'Greece: from state authoritarianism to modernization', in A. Ferner and R. Hyman (eds) *Industrial Relations in the New Europe*, Oxford: Blackwell.

Kuisel, R. F. (1981) *Capitalism and the State in Modern France*, Cambridge: Cambridge University Press.

Kujawa, D. (1971) *International Labor Relations Management in the Automobile Industry: A Comparative Study of Chrysler, Ford and General Motors*, New York: Praeger.

—— (1979) 'The labor relations of United States multinationals abroad: comparative and prospective views', *Labour and Society* 4.

—— (1980) 'Labour relations of US multinationals abroad', in B. Martin and E. M. Kassalow (eds) *Labor Relations in Advanced Industrial Societies: Issues and Problems*', Washington, DC: Carnegie Endowment.

Kumar, P. and Dow, B. (1986) 'Econometric analysis of union membership growth in Canada, 1935–1981', *Relations Industrielles* 41: 236–55.

Lammers, C. J. and Széll, G. (eds) (1989) *International Handbook of Participation in Organizations. 1, Organizational Democracy: Taking Stock*, Oxford: Oxford University Press.

Lane, C. (1989) *Management and Labour in Europe. The Industrial Enterprise in Germany, Britain and France*, Aldershot: Edward Elgar.

—— (1990) 'Vocational training, employment relations and new production concepts in Germany: some lessons for Britain', *Industrial Relations Journal* 21: 247–59.

Lange, P. (1983) 'Politiche dei redditi e democrazia sindacale in Europa occidentale', *Stato e mercato* 9.

Lange, P., Ross, G. and Vannicelli, M. (1982) *Unions, Change and Crisis: French and Italian Union Strategy and the Political Economy, 1945–80*, London: Allen & Unwin.

Lansbury, R. D. (1978a) 'The return to arbitration. Recent trends in dispute settlement and wages policy in Australia', *International Labour Review* 117: 611–24.

—— (1978b) 'Industrial democracy under liberal capitalism: a comparison of trends in Australia, France and the USA', *Journal of Industrial Relations* 20: 431–45.

Lansbury, R. D. and Bamber, G. (1989) 'Technological change, industrial relations and human resource management', in G. J. Bamber and R. D. Lansbury (eds) *New Technology: International Perspectives on Human Resources and Industrial Relations*, London: Unwin Hyman.

Lansbury, R. D., Sandkull, B. and Hammarström, O. (1992) 'Industrial relations and productivity: evidence from Sweden and Australia', *Economic and Industrial Democracy* 13: 295–330.

La Palombara, J. and Blank, S. (1976) *Multinational Corporations and National Elites. A Study of Tensions*, New York: The Conference Board.

Lash, S. and Urry, J. (1987) *The End of Organized Capitalism*, Cambridge: Polity Press.

Lazonick, W. H. (1983) 'Technological change and the control of work: the development of capital–labour relations in US manufacturing industry', in H. F. Gospel and C. R. Littler (eds) *Managerial Strategies and Industrial Relations*, London: Heinemann.

Leminsky, G. (1980) 'Worker participation: the German experience', in B. Martin and E. M. Kassalow (eds) *Labor Relations in Advanced Industrial Societies: Issues and Problems*, Washington, DC: Carnegie Endowment.

Levine, S. B. (1958) *Industrial Relations in Postwar Japan*, Urbana: University of Illinois Press.

—— (1980) 'Changing strategies of unions and management: evaluation of four industrialised countries', *British Journal of Industrial Relations* 18: 70–81.

—— (1981) 'Japan', in A. A. Blum (ed.) *International Handbook of Industrial Relations*, London: Aldwych.

Levine, S. B. and Taira, K. (1980) 'Interpreting industrial conflict: the case of Japan', in B. Martin and E. M. Kassalow (eds) *Labour Relations in Advanced Industrial Societies: Issues and Problems*, Washington, DC: Carnegie Endowment.

Levinson, C. (1972) *International Trade Unionism*, London: Allen & Unwin.

Lewchuk, W. (1983) 'Fordism and British motor car employers, 1896–1932', in H. F. Gospel and C. R. Littler (eds) *Managerial Strategies and Industrial Relations*, London: Heinemann.

Lewin, D. (1978) 'The impact of unions on American business: evidence for an assessment', *Columbia Journal of World Business* 13, 4: 89–103.

Lewis, R. (1976) 'The historical development of labour law', *British Journal of Industrial Relations* 14: 1–17.

Lilja, K. (1992) 'Finland: no longer the Nordic exception', in A. Ferner and R. Hyman (eds) *Industrial Relations in the New Europe*, Oxford: Blackwell.

Lipset, S. M. (1961) 'Trade unions and social structure', *Industrial Relations* 1: 75–90.

—— (1977) 'Socialism in America', *Dialogue* 10, 4: 3–12.

Little, J. S. (1982) 'Multinational corporations and foreign investment: current trends and issues', *Annals of the American Academy of Political and Social Science* 460: 54–63.

Littler, C. R. (1982) *The Development of the Labour Process in Capitalist Societies. A Comparative Study of the Transformation of Work Organization in Britain, Japan and the USA*, London: Heinemann Educational Books.

Littler, C. R. and Lockett, M. (1983) 'The significance of trade unions in China', *Industrial Relations Journal* 14, 4: 31–42.

Littler, C. R. and Palmer, G. (1986) 'Communist and capitalist trade unionism: comparisons and contrasts', in A. Pravda and B. Ruble (eds) *Trade Unions in Communist States*, London: Allen & Unwin.

Livernash, E. R. (1963) 'The relation of power to the structure and process of collective bargaining', *Journal of Law and Economics* 6: 10–40.

Locke, R. M. (1992) 'The demise of the national union in Italy: lessons for comparative industrial relations theory', *Industrial and Labor Relations Review* 45: 229–49.

Lodge, G. and Henderson, K. (1979) 'United States of America', in B. C. Roberts (ed.) *Towards Industrial Democracy*, London: Croom Helm.

Long, R. J. and Warner, M. (1987) 'Organizations, participation and recession. An analysis of recent evidence', *Relations Industrielles* 42: 65–90.

Looise, J. C. (1989) 'The recent growth in employees' representation in the Netherlands: defying the times?', in C. J. Lammers and G. Széll (eds) *International Handbook of Participation in Organizations. 1, Organizational Democracy: Taking Stock*, Oxford: Oxford University Press.

Loveman, B. (1981) 'Chile', in A. A. Blum (ed.) *International Handbook of Industrial Relations*, London: Aldwych.

Loveridge, R. (1980) 'What is participation? A review of the literature and some methodological problems', *British Journal of Industrial Relations* 18: 297–317.

Lucena, H. (1980) 'Industrial relations in an enclave economy. The case of Venezuela', *Labour and Society* 5: 341–54.

Lucio, M. M. (1992) 'Spain: constructing institutions and actors', in A. Ferner and R. Hyman (eds) *Industrial Relations in the New Europe*, Oxford: Blackwell.

Lukes, S. (1974) *Power. A Radical View*, London: Macmillan.

MacDuffie, J. P. and Krafcik, J. (1992) 'Integrating technology and human resources for high performance manufacturing: evidence from the international auto industry', in T. A. Kochan and M. Useem (eds) *Transforming Organisations*, New York: Oxford University Press.

McKersie, R. B. (1987) 'The transformation of American industrial relations: the abridged story', *Journal of Management Studies* 24: 432–40.

McLoughlin, T. and Gourlay, S. (1992) 'Enterprise without unions: the management of employee relations in non-union firms', *Journal of Management Studies* 29: 669–91.

Mandel, E. (1980) *Long Waves in Capitalist Development*, Cambridge: Cambridge University Press.

Marginson, P. (1992) 'European integration and transnational management–union relations in the enterprise', *British Journal of Industrial Relations* 30: 529–46.

Marks, G. (1986) 'Neocorporatism and incomes policy in Western Europe and North America', *Comparative Politics* 18: 253–77.

Marsden, R. (1982) 'Industrial relations: a critique of empiricism', *Sociology* 16: 232–50.

Marsh, A., Hackman, M. and Miller, D. (1981) *Workplace Relations in the Engineering Industry in the UK and the Federal Republic of Germany*, London: Anglo-German Foundation for the Study of Industrial Society.

Marsh, R. M. and Mannari, H. (1981) 'Divergence and convergence in industrial organisations: the Japanese case', in G. Dlugos and H. Weiermair (eds) *Management Under Differing Value Systems*, New York: de Gruyter.

Marshall, R. (1986) 'America and Japan: industrial relations in a time of change', in S. M. Lipset (ed.) *Unions in Transition. Entering the Second Century*, San Francisco: ICS Press.

Martens, G. R. (1979) 'Industrial relations and trade unionism in French-speaking West Africa', in U. G. Damachi, H. D. Seibel and L. Trachman (eds) *Industrial Relations in Africa*, London: Macmillan.

Martin, A. (1987) 'The end of the "Swedish Model"? Recent developments in Swedish industrial relations', *Bulletin of Comparative Labour Relations* 16: 93–128.

Martin, R. M. (1975) *Trade Unions in Australia*, Melbourne: Penguin.

—— (1989) Trade Unionism. Purposes and Forms, Oxford: Clarendon.

Maurice, M. and Sellier, F. (1979) 'Societal analysis of industrial relations. A comparison between France and West Germany', British Journal of Industrial Relations 17: 322–36.

Mauro, M. J. (1982) 'Strikes as a result of imperfect information', Industrial and Labor Relations Review 34: 522–38.

Mboya, T. (1963) Freedom and After, London: Deutsch.

Mehta, A. (1957) 'The mediating role of trade unions in underdeveloped countries', Economic Development and Cultural Change 6: 16–23.

Meltz, N. M. (1991) 'Dunlop's Industrial Relations Systems after three decades', in R. J. Adams (ed.) Comparative Industrial Relations. Contemporary Research and Theory, London: Harper Collins Academic.

Metcalf, D. (1990) 'Trade unions and economic performance: the British evidence', in R. Brunetta and C. Dell'Aringa (eds) Labour Relations and Economic Performance, London: Macmillan.

—— (1993) 'Industrial relations and economic performance', British Journal of Industrial Relations 31: 255–83.

Meyers, F. (1967) 'The study of foreign labor and industrial relations', in S. Barkin (ed.) International Labor, New York: Harper & Row.

—— (1981) 'France', in A. A. Blum (ed.) International Handbook of Industrial Relations, London: Aldwych.

Michel, J. (1990) 'Industrial relations in the French coal mining industry from the late nineteenth century to the 1970s', in G. D. Feldman and K. Tenfelde (eds) Workers, Owners and Politics in Coal Mining. An International Comparison of Industrial Relations, Oxford: Berg.

Miliband, R. (1969) The State in Capitalist Society, London: Weidenfeld & Nicolson.

Millard, F. (1987) 'Trade unions and economic crisis in Poland', in W. Brierley (ed.) Trade Unions and the Economic Crisis of the 1980s, Aldershot: Gower.

Miller, R. (1987) 'The mid-life crisis of the American labour movement', Industrial Relations Journal 18: 159–70.

Millward, N. (1979) 'Research note: the strike record of foreign-owned manufacturing plants in Great Britain', British Journal of Industrial Relations 17: 99–104.

Miscimarra, P. A. (1981) 'The entertainment industry: inroads in multinational collective bargaining', British Journal of Industrial Relations 19: 49–65.

Moore, J. B. (1987) 'Japanese industrial relations', Labour and Industry 1: 140–56.

Mueller, F. and Purcell, J. (1992) 'The Europeanization of manufacturing and the decentralization of bargaining: multinational management strategies in the European automobile industry', International Journal of Human Resource Management 3: 15–31.

Muir, J. D. and Brown, J. L. (1978) 'The changing role of government in collective bargaining', in E. M. Kassalow and U. G. Damachi (eds) The Role of Trade Unions in Developing Societies, Geneva: International Institute for Labour Studies.

Müller-Jentsch, W. (1985) 'Trade unions as intermediary organizations', Economic and Industrial Democracy 6: 3–32.

Munck, R. (1988) The New International Labour Studies: An Introduction, London: Zed Books.

Newell, A. and Symons, J. V. (1987) 'Corporatism, laissez-faire and the rise in unemployment', European Economic Review 31: 567–614.

Ng, I. (1987) 'The economic and political determinants of trade union growth in selected OECD countries', *Journal of Industrial Relations* 29: 233–42.

Ng, I. and Maki, D. (1988) 'Strike activity of US institutions in Canada', *British Journal of Industrial Relations* 26: 63–73.

Nicol, B. (1979) 'Industrial relations in Uganda', in U. G. Damachi, H. B. Seibel and L. Trachman (eds) *Industrial Relations in Africa*, London: Macmillan.

Niland, J. (1978) *Collective Bargaining and Compulsory Arbitration in Australia*, Sydney: University of New South Wales.

Nolan, P. and Marginson, P. (1990) 'Skating on thin ice? David Metcalf on trade unions and productivity', *British Journal of Industrial Relations* 28: 227–47.

Northrup, H. R. and Rowan, R. L. (1979) *Multinational Collective Bargaining Attempts. The Record, the Cases and the Prospects*, Philadelphia: University of Pennsylvania.

Northrup, H. R., Campbell, D. C. and Slowinsky, B. J. (1988) 'Multinational union–management consultation in Europe: resurgence in the 1980s?', *International Labour Review* 127: 525–43.

Obradovic, J. (1975) 'Workers' participation: who participates?', *Industrial Relations* 14: 32–44.

Obradovic, J. and Bertsch, G. K. (1979) 'Participation and influence in Yugoslav self-management', *Industrial Relations* 18: 322–9.

OECD (1977) *The Industrial Relations and Employment Impacts of Multinational Enterprises. An Inquiry into the Issues*, Paris.

—— (1979a) *Wage Policies and Collective Bargaining Developments in Finland, Ireland and Norway*, Paris.

—— (1979b) *Transfer Pricing and Multinational Enterprises*, Paris.

—— (1988) 'The structure of collective bargaining, unemployment and inflation', *Economic Outlook*, June: 34–5.

—— (1993) 'Preventing and resolving industrial conflict', Occasional Papers No. 11, Paris.

Oechslin, J. J. (1972) 'Employers' organisations in France', *International Labour Review* 106: 391–413.

Ogden, S. G. (1982) 'Trade unions, industrial democracy and collective bargaining', *Sociology* 16: 544–63.

Okamoto, H. (1979) 'Japan', in B. C. Roberts (ed.) *Towards Industrial Democracy. Europe, Japan and the United States*, London: Croom Helm.

Okayama, R. (1983) 'Japanese employer labour policy. The heavy engineering industry 1900–1930', in H. F. Gospel and C. R. Littler (eds) *Managerial Strategies and Industrial Relations*, London: Heinemann.

Okochi, K., Karsh, B. and Levine, S. B. (1973) *Workers and Employers in Japan. The Japanese Employment Relations System*, Tokyo: University of Tokyo Press.

Oliver, N. and Wilkinson, B. (1989) 'Japanese manufacturing techniques and personnel and industrial relations practice in Britain: evidence and implications', *British Journal of Industrial Relations* 27: 73–91.

Olson, M. (1982) *The Rise and Decline of Nations. Economic Growth, Stagflation and Social Rigidities*, New Haven: Yale University Press.

Omaji, P. O. (1993) 'The state and industrial relations: background to the adoption of compulsory arbitration law in Australia', *British Journal of Industrial Relations* 31: 37–55.

Ozaki, M. (1987) 'Labour relations in the public service: labour disputes and their settlement', *International Labour Review* 126: 405–22.

Paldam, M. and Pederson, P. J. (1982) 'The macroeconomic strike model: a study of seventeen countries, 1948–1975', *Industrial and Labor Relations Review* 35: 504–21.

—— (1984) 'The large pattern of industrial conflict – a comparative study of 18 countries 1919–79', *International Journal of Social Economics* 11, 5: 3–28.

Panford, K. (1988) 'State–trade union relations: the dilemmas of single trade union systems in Ghana and Nigeria', *Labour and Society* 13: 37–53.

Panitch, L. (1977) 'The development of corporatism in liberal democracies', *Comparative Political Studies* 10: 61–90.

—— (1980) 'Recent theorizations of corporatism', *British Journal of Sociology* 31: 159–87.

Park, D. (1992) 'Industrial relations in Korea', *International Journal of Human Resource Management* 3: 105–23.

Pathy, J. (1988) 'Structure of the Indian working class and conventional unionism', in R. Southall (ed.) *Labour and Unions in Asia and Africa. Contemporary Issues*, London: Macmillan.

Payne, J. (1965) *Labour and Politics in Peru*, New Haven: Yale University Press.

Peetz, D. (1990) 'Declining union density', *Journal of Industrial Relations* 32: 197–223.

Pellegrini, C. (1987) 'Italy', in G. J. Bamber and R. D. Lansbury (eds) *International and Comparative Industrial Relations. A Study of Developed Market Economies*, London: Allen & Unwin.

Perlmutter, H. V. (1969) 'The tortuous evolution of the multinational corporation', *Columbia Journal of World Business* 4, 1: 9–18.

Peterson, R. B. (1986) 'Research design issues in comparative industrial relations', IRRA 39th Annual Meeting, *Proceedings*: 244–51.

Petras, J. and Engbarth, D. (1988) 'Third World industrialization and trade union struggles', in R. Southall (ed.) *Trade Unions and the New Industrialization of the Third World*, London: Zed Books.

Phelps Brown, E. H. (1959) *The Growth of British Industrial Relations. A Study from the Standpoint of 1906–14*, London: Macmillan.

—— (1983) *The Origins of Trade Union Power*, Oxford: Clarendon.

Piore, M. J. and Sabel, C. (1984) *The Second Industrial Divide*, New York: Basic Books.

Pizzorno, A. (1978) 'Political exchange and collective identity in industrial conflict', in C. Crouch and A. Pizzorno (eds) *The Resurgence of Class Conflict in Western Europe since 1969. 2, Comparative Analyses*, New York: Holmes & Meier.

Plowman, D. (1980) 'Employer associations: challenges and responses', in G. W. Ford, J. M. Hearn and R. D. Lansbury (eds) *Australian Labour Relations: Readings*, Melbourne: Macmillan.

—— (1987) 'The study of employer associations', Paper presented to the 4th AIRAANZ Conference, Massey University, New Zealand.

—— (1988) 'Employer associations and bargaining structures: an Australian perspective', *British Journal of Industrial Relations* 26: 371–96.

Poole, M. (1979) 'Industrial democracy: a comparative analysis', *Industrial Relations* 18: 262–72.

—— (1980) 'Managerial strategies and industrial relations', in M. Poole and R. Mansfield (eds) *Managerial Roles in Industrial Relations*, London: Gower.

—— (1981) 'Industrial democracy in comparative perspective', in R. Mansfield and M. Poole (eds) *International Perspectives on Management and Organizations*, Aldershot: Gower.

—— (1982) 'Theories of industrial democracy: the emerging synthesis', *Sociological Review* 30: 181–207.

—— (1986a) *Industrial Relations. Origins and Patterns of National Diversity*, London: Routledge & Kegan Paul.

—— (1986b) 'Participation through representation: a review of constraints and conflicting pressures', in R. N. Stern and S. McCarthy, *International Yearbook of Organizational Democracy. 3, The Organizational Practice of Democracy*, Chichester: Wiley.

—— (1989) *The Origins of Economic Democracy. Profit-Sharing and Employee-Shareholding Schemes*, London: Routledge.

—— (1990) 'Human resource management in an international perspective', *International Journal of Human Resource Management* 1: 1–15.

Poole, M. and Jenkins, G. (1990) *The Impact of Economic Democracy. Profit Sharing and Employee Shareholding Schemes*, London: Routledge.

Porter, J. (1967) 'Some observations on comparative studies', *Bulletin of the International Institute for Labour Studies* 3: 82–104.

Pravda, A. (1983) 'Trade unions in East European communist systems: towards corporatism', *International Political Science Review* 4: 241–60.

Price, R. (1991) 'The comparative analysis of union growth', in R. Adams (ed.) *Comparative Industrial Relations: Contemporary Research and Theory*, London: Harper Collins.

Purcell, J., Marginson, P., Edwards, P. and Sisson, K. (1987) 'The industrial relations practices of multi-plant foreign owned firms', *Industrial Relations Journal* 18: 130–8.

Puységur, S. J. (1951) 'Employers' associations in Europe and North America', *International Labour Review* 63: 507–36.

Ramsay, H. (1977) 'Cycles of control: worker participation and historical perspectives', *Sociology* 11: 481–506.

—— (1983) 'Evolution or cycle? Worker participation in the 1970s and 1980s', in C. Crouch and F. A. Heller (eds) *International Yearbook of Organizational Democracy. 1, Organizational Democracy and Political Processes*, Chichester: Wiley.

—— (1990) '1992 – the year of the multinational? Corporate behaviour, industrial restructuring and labour in the single market', IRRU, Warwick Papers in Industrial Relations 35, Coventry, University of Warwick.

—— (1991) 'Reinventing the wheel? A review of the development and performance of employee involvement', *Human Resource Management Journal* 1, 4: 1–22.

Rees, A. (1952) 'Industrial conflict and business fluctuations', *Journal of Political Economy* 60: 371–82.

Reynaud, J. D. (1975) 'Trade unions and political parties in France: some recent trends', *Industrial and Labor Relations Review* 28: 208–25.

Reynolds, L. G. (1978) *Labor Economics and Labor Relations*, Englewood Cliffs, NJ: Prentice Hall.

Riddell, D. S. (1968) 'Social self-government. The background of theory and practice in Yugoslav socialism', *British Journal of Sociology* 19: 47–75.

Rimlinger, G. (1977) 'Labor and the government: a comparative historical perspective', *Journal of Economic History* 37: 210–25.

Roberts, B. C. and May, J. (1974) 'The response of multinational enterprises to international trade union pressure', *British Journal of Industrial Relations* 12: 403–16.

276   *Comparative industrial relations*

Roberts, I. L. (1975) 'Industrial relations and the European Community', *Industrial Relations Journal* 6, 2: 23–35.
—— (1992) 'Industrial relations and the European Community', *Industrial Relations Journal* 23: 3–13.
Robertson, D. (1990) 'Transaction-cost economics and cross-national patterns of industrial conflict', *American Journal of Political Science* 34: 153–89.
Robock, S. H. and Simmonds, K. (1989) *International Business and Multinational Enterprises*, Homewood, Ill.: Irwin.
Roche, W. K. (1986) 'Systems analysis and industrial relations', *Economic and Industrial Democracy* 7: 3–28.
Rojot, J. (1985) 'The 1984 revision of the OECD guidelines for multinational enterprises', *British Journal of Industrial Relations* 23: 380–97.
Rosa, L. (1990) 'The Singapore state and trade union incorporation', *Journal of Contemporary Asia* 20: 487–508.
Rose, M. (1983) Review, *British Journal of Industrial Relations* 21: 134–35.
Rosen, S. (1975) 'The United States', in S. Barkin (ed.) *Worker Militancy and its Consequences, 1965–75*, New York: Praeger.
Rosner, M. (1991) 'Ownership, participation and work reconstruction in the Kibbutz: a comparative perspective' in R. Russell and V. Rus (eds) *International Handbook of Participation in Organizations. 2, Ownership and Participation*, Oxford: Oxford University Press.
Ross, A. M. and Hartman, P. T. (1960) *Changing Patterns of Industrial Conflict*, New York: Wiley.
Roth, H. (1974) 'Trade unions', in J. M. Howells, N. S. Woods and F. J. L. Young (eds) *Labour and Industrial Relations in New Zealand*, Carlton, Victoria: Pitman.
Rothstein, B. (1990) 'Marxism, institutional analysis, and working-class power: the Swedish case', *Politics and Society* 18: 317–46.
Ruble, B. A. (1979) 'Dual functioning trade unions in the U.S.S.R.', *British Journal of Industrial Relations* 17: 235–41.
Sadowski, D. and Jacobi, O. (eds) (1991) *Employers' Associations in Europe. Policy and Organisation*, Baden Baden: Nomos Verglagsgesellschaft.
Sakoh, K. (1990) 'Economic implications of enterprise unions', *Journal of Labor Research* 11: 257–67.
Sandbrook, R. (1975) *Proletarians and African Capitalism. The Kenyan Case 1962–70*, Cambridge: Cambridge University Press.
Sandbrook, R. and Cohen, R. (1975) *The Development of an African Working Class*, London: Longman.
Schmidt, F. (1972) 'Industrial action: the role of trade unions and employers' associations', in B. Aaron and K. W. Wedderburn (eds) *Industrial Conflict. A Comparative Legal Survey*, London: Longman.
Schnabel, C. (1987) 'Trade union growth and decline in the Federal Republic of Germany', *Empirical Economics* 12: 107–27.
—— (1991) 'Trade unions and productivity: the German evidence', *British Journal of Industrial Relations* 29: 15–24.
Schnabel, C. and Wagner, J. (1992) 'Unions and innovative activity in Germany', *Journal of Labor Research* 13: 393–406.
Schöllhammer, H. (1973) 'Strategies and methodologies in international business and comparative management research', *Management International Review* 13, 6: 17–32.

Schregle, J. (1976) 'Workers' participation in decisions within undertakings', *International Labour Review* 113: 1–16.

—— (1978) 'Co-determination in the Federal Republic of Germany: a comparative view', *International Labour Review* 117: 81–98.

—— (1981) 'Comparative industrial relations: pitfalls and potential', *International Labour Review* 120: 15–30.

—— (1982) *Negotiating Development: Labour Relations in Southern Asia*, Geneva: ILO.

—— (1987) 'Workers' participation in the Federal Republic of Germany in an international perspective', *International Labour Review* 126: 317–27.

Screpanti, E. (1987) 'Long cycles in strike activity: an empirical investigation', *British Journal of Industrial Relations* 25: 99–124.

Seglow, P., Streeck, W. and Wallace, P. (1982) *Rail Unions in Britain and West Germany. A Study of their Structure and Policies*, London: Policy Studies Institute.

Segrestin, D. (1991) 'Recent changes in France', in G. Baglioni and C. Crouch (eds), *European Industrial Relations. The Challenge of Flexibility*, London: Sage.

Sellier, F. (1973) 'The French workers' movement and political unionism', in A. Sturmthal and J. G. Scoville (eds) *The International Labor Movement in Transition*, Urbana: University of Illinois Press.

—— (1978) 'France', in J. T. Dunlop and W. Galenson (eds) *Labor in the Twentieth Century*, New York: Academic Press.

Sellier, F. and Silvestre, J. J. (1986) 'Unions' policies in the economic crisis in France', in R. Edwards, P. Garonna and F. Tödling (eds) *Unions in Crisis and Beyond. Perspectives from Six Countries*, Dover, Mass.: Auburn House.

Sewell, W. H. (1977) 'Comment', *Journal of Economic History* 37: 226–9.

Shalev, M. (1980a) 'Industrial relations theory and the comparative study of industrial relations and industrial conflict', *British Journal of Industrial Relations* 18: 26–43.

—— (1980b) 'Trade unions and economic analysis: the case of industrial conflict', *Journal of Labor Research* 1: 133–74

—— (1981) 'Theoretical dilemmas and value analysis in comparative industrial relations', in G. Dlugos and K. Weiermair (eds) *Management Under Differing Value Systems*, New York: de Gruyter.

—— (1983) 'Strikes and the crisis: industrial conflict and unemployment in the western nations', *Economic and Industrial Democracy* 4: 417–60.

—— (1992) 'The resurgence of labour quiescence', in M. Regini (ed.) *The Future of Labour Movements*, London: Sage.

Shalev, M. and Korpi, W. (1980) 'Working-class mobilization and American exceptionalism', *Economic and Industrial Democracy* 1: 31–61.

Sharma, B. (1985) *Aspects of Industrial Relations in ASEAN*, Singapore: Institute of Southeast Asian Studies.

Shetty, Y. (1979) 'European and American styles of managing the multinational corporation', *Management International Review* 19, 3: 39–48.

Shirai, T. (1983) 'A theory of enterprise unionism', in T. Shirai (ed.) *Contemporary Industrial Relations in Japan*, Madison: University of Wisconsin Press.

Shirai, T. and Shimada, H. (1978) 'Japan', in J. T. Dunlop and W. Galenson (eds) *Labor in the Twentieth Century*, New York: Academic Press.

Shirom, A. and Jacobsen, D. (1975) 'The structure and function of Israeli employers' associations', *Relations Industrielles* 30: 452–74.

Shirom, A., Peterson, R. B. and Tracy, L. N. (1992) 'Problem solving in labour negotiations: a comparative study of the United States, Israel and New Zealand', *International Journal of Human Resource Management* 3: 59–69.

Shorter, E. and Tilly, C. (1974) *Strikes in France 1830–1968*, Cambridge: Cambridge University Press.

Siddique, S. A. (1989) 'Industrial relations in a Third World setting: a possible model', *Journal of Industrial Relations* 31: 385–401.

Silvia, S. J. (1991) 'The Social Charter of the European Community: a defeat for European labour', *Industrial and Labor Relations Review* 44: 626–43.

Sim, A. B. (1977) 'Decentralized management of subsidiaries and their performance', *Management International Review* 17, 2: 45–51.

Sisson, K. (1987) *The Management of Collective Bargaining. An International Comparison*, Oxford: Blackwell.

—— (1990) 'Employers' organisations and industrial relations. The significance of the strategies of large companies', Paper presented at the First Conference of the International Network of Research Institutions. Industrial Relations in the European Community, Trier.

Sisson, K., Waddington, J. and Whitston, C. (1992) 'The structure of capital in the European Community: the size of companies and the implications for industrial relations', IRRU, Warwick Papers in Industrial Relations No. 38, Coventry: University of Warwick.

Skeels, J. W. (1982) 'The economic and organizational basis of early United States strikes, 1900–48', *Industrial and Labor Relations Review* 35: 491–503.

Slack, E. (1980) 'Plant-level bargaining in France', *Industrial Relations Journal*, 11, 4: 27–38.

Slomp, H. (1990) *Labour Relations in Europe. A History of Issues and Development*, New York: Greenwood Press.

Smith, D. F. and Turkington, D. J. (1981) 'Testing a behavioural theory of bargaining: an international comparative study', *British Journal of Industrial Relations* 19: 361–9.

Snyder, D. (1975) 'Institutional setting and industrial conflict: comparative analyses of France, Italy and the United States', *American Sociological Review* 40: 259–78.

Sorge, A. (1976) 'The evolution of industrial democracy in the countries of the European Community', *British Journal of Industrial Relations* 14: 274–94.

Sorge, A. and Warner, M. (1980) 'The context of industrial relations in Great Britain and West Germany', *Industrial Relations Journal* 11: 41–9.

Soskice, D. (1990) 'Wage determination: the changing role of institutions in advanced industrialized countries', *Oxford Review of Economic Policy* 6, 4: 36–61.

Southall, R. (1988) 'Introduction', in R. Southall (ed.) *Trade Unions and the New Industrialization of the Third World*, London: Zed Books.

Stephens, E. H. (1980) *The Politics of Workers' Participation. The Peruvian Approach in Comparative Perspective*, New York: Academic Press.

Stephens, J. D. (1979) *The Transition from Capitalism to Socialism*, London: Macmillan.

Stone, K. (1974) 'The origins of job structures in the steel industry', *Review of Radical Political Economics* 6.

Storey, J. and Sisson, K. (1990) 'Limits to transformation: human resource management in the British context', *Industrial Relations Journal* 21: 60–5.

Strauss, G. (1979) 'Workers' participation: symposium introduction', *Industrial Relations* 18: 247–61.

—— (1982) 'Bridging the gap between industrial relations and conflict management', in G. B. J. Bomers and R. B. Peterson (eds) *Conflict Management and Industrial Relations*, Boston: Kluwer.

Strauss, G., Gallagher, D. G. and Fiorito, J. (eds) (1991) *The State of the Unions*, Madison, Wis.: IRRA.

Streeck, W. (1981) 'Qualitative demands and the neo-corporatist manageability of industrial relations', *British Journal of Industrial Relations* 19: 149–69.

—— (1987) 'The uncertainties of management in the management of uncertainty: employers, labor relations and industrial adjustment in the 1980s', *Work, Employment and Society* 1: 281–308.

—— (1988) 'Industrial relations in West Germany, 1980–1987', *Labour* 2: 3–44.

Strinati, D. (1982) *Capitalism, the State and Industrial Relations*, London: Croom Helm.

Sturmthal, A. (1958) 'The labor movement abroad', in N. W. Chamberlain (ed.) *A Decade of Industrial Relations Research 1946–1956*, New York: Harper.

Summers, C. (1991) 'Patterns of dispute resolution: lessons from four continents', *Comparative Labor Law Journal* 12: 165–77.

Szul, R. (1986) 'Workers' self-management in Poland', *Economic Analysis and Workers' Management* 20: 169–93.

Taft, P. and Ross, P. (1979) 'American labour violence: its causes, character and outcome', in H. D. Graham and T. R. Gurr (eds) *Violence in America: Historical and Comparative Perspectives*, Beverly Hills, Calif.: Sage.

Taira, K. (1973) 'Labor markets, unions and employers in inter-war Japan', in A. Sturmthal and J. G. Scoville (eds) *The International Labor Movement in Transition*, Urbana: University of Illinois Press.

Takamiya, M. (1981) 'Japanese multinationals in Europe: internal operations and their public policy implications', *Columbia Journal of World Business* 16, 2: 5–17.

Tannenbaum, A. S., Kavić, B., Rosner, M., Vianello, M. and Wesier, G. (1974) *Hierarchy in Organizations*, San Francisco: Jossey-Bass.

Teulings, A. W. M. (1988) 'The comparative analysis of systems of industrial democracy in Europe', *International Journal of Sociology and Social Policy* 8, 1: 32–52.

Thomas, H. and Logan, C. (1982) *Mondragon. An Economic Analysis*, London: Allen & Unwin.

Thompson, M. (1987) 'Canada', in G. J. Bamber and R. D. Lansbury (eds) *International and Comparative Industrial Relations. A Study of Developed Market Economies*, London: Allen & Unwin.

Thompson, M. and Juris, H. A. (1985) 'The response of industrial relations to economic change', in H. Juris, M. Thompson and W. Daniels (eds) *Industrial Relations in a Decade of Economic Change*, Madison, Wis.: IRRA.

Thompson, M. and Roxborough, I. (1982) 'Union elections and democracy in Mexico: a comparative perspective', *British Journal of Industrial Relations* 20: 201–17.

Thomson, A. W. J. (1981) 'The United States of America', in E. Owen Smith (ed.) *Trade Unions in the Developed Economies*, London: Croom Helm.

Thurley, K. and Wood, S. (eds) (1983) *Industrial Relations and Management Strategy*, Cambridge: Cambridge University Press.

Tolliday, S. and Zeitlin, J. (1991a) 'Employers and industrial relations: between theory and history', in S. Tolliday and J. Zeitlin (eds) *The Power to Manage? Employers and Industrial Relations in Comparative-Historical Perspective*, London: Routledge.

—— (1991b) *The Power to Manage? Employers and Industrial Relations in Comparative-Historical Perspective*, London: Routledge.

Traxler, F. (1992) 'Austria: still the country of corporatism', in A. Ferner and R. Hyman (eds) *Industrial Relations in the New Europe*, Oxford: Blackwell.

Treckel, K. F. (1972) 'The world auto councils and collective bargaining', *Industrial Relations* 11: 72–9.

Treu, T. (1981) 'Italy', in R. Blanpain (ed.) *International Encyclopaedia for Labour Law and Industrial Relations*, Deventer: Kluwer.

—— (1987a) 'Centralization and decentralization in collective bargaining', *Labour* 1: 147–75.

—— (1987b) 'Ten years of social concertation in Italy', *Labour and Society* 12: 355–66.

—— (1988) 'Italy. Trade union democracy and industrial relations', *Bulletin of Comparative Labour Relations* 18: 51–4.

—— (1989) 'Industrial relations, tripartism and concerted action: where do we stand?', *International Journal of Comparative Law and Industrial Relations* 5: 143–55.

Troy, L. (1986) 'The rise and fall of American unions: the labor movement from FDR to RR', in S. M. Lipset (ed.) *Unions in Transition: Entering the Second Century*, San Francisco: ICS Press.

—— (1990) 'Is the US unique in the decline of private sector unionism?', *Journal of Labor Research* 11: 111–43.

Turner, L. (1991) *Democracy at Work: Changing World Markets and the Future of Labor Unions*, Ithaca, NY: Cornell University Press.

Turner, T. (1992) 'The determinants of union growth in Zambia since independence', *Employee Relations* 14, 2: 55–67.

Ulman, L. (1974a) 'Connective and competitive bargaining', *Scottish Journal of Political Economy* 21: 97–109.

—— (1974b) 'The rise of the international union', in R. J. Flanagan and A. R. Weber (eds) *Bargaining Without Boundaries. The Multinational Corporation and International Labor Relations*, Chicago: University of Chicago Press.

—— (1990) 'Labor market analysis and concerted behaviour', *Industrial Relations* 29: 281–99.

Ulmer, M. J. (1980) 'Multinational corporations and Third World capitalism', *Journal of Economic Issues*, 14: 453–71.

van de Vall, M. (1970) *Labor Organization. A Macro- and Micro-Sociological Analysis on a Comparative Basis*, Cambridge: Cambridge University Press.

van Voorden, W. (1984) 'Employers' associations in the Netherlands', in J. P. Windmuller and A. Gladstone (eds) *Employers' Associations and Industrial Relations. A Comparative Study*, Oxford: Clarendon.

Vilrokx, J. and Leemput, J. (1992) 'Belgium: a new stability in industrial relations?', in A. Ferner and R. Hyman (eds) *Industrial Relations in the New Europe*, Oxford: Blackwell.

Visser, J. (1987) 'In search of inclusive unionism. A comparative analysis', Ph.D. thesis, University of Amsterdam.

—— (1988) 'Trade unionism in Western Europe', *Labour and Society* 13: 125–82.

—— (1991) 'Trends in trade union membership', *OECD Employment Outlook*, July.

—— (1992a) 'The Netherlands: the end of an era and the end of a system', in A. Ferner and R. Hyman (eds) *Industrial Relations in the New Europe*, Oxford: Blackwell.

—— (1992b) 'The strength of union movements in advanced capital democracies:

social and organizational variations', in M. Regini (ed.) *The Future of Labour Movements*, London: Sage.

von Beyme, K. (1980) *Challenge to Power. Trade Unions and Industrial Relations in Capitalist Countries*, London: Sage.

Wad, P. (1988) 'The Japanization of the Malaysian trade union movement', in R. Southall (ed.) *Trade Unions and the New Industrialization of the Third World*, London: Zed Books.

Wadhwani, S. (1990) 'The effects of unions on productivity growth, investment and employment', *British Journal of Industrial Relations* 28: 371–85.

Walker, K. F. (1967) 'The comparative study of industrial relations', *Bulletin of the International Institute for Labour Studies* 3: 105–32.

—— (1970) *Australian Industrial Relations Systems*, Cambridge, Mass.: Harvard University Press.

—— (1974) 'Workers' participation in management: problems, practice and prospects', *Bulletin of the International Institute for Labour Studies* 12: 3–35.

—— (1976) 'Compulsory arbitration in Australia', in J. Loewenberg (ed.) *Compulsory Arbitration. An International Comparison*, Lexington, Mass.: Lexington Books.

Wall, T. D. and Lischeron, J. A. (1977) *Worker Participation. A Critique of the Literature and Some Fresh Evidence*, London: McGraw Hill.

Wallerstein, M. (1989) 'Union organization in advanced industrial democracies', *American Political Science Review* 83: 481–501.

Walsh, P. and Wetzel, K. (1993) 'Preparing for privatisation: corporate strategy and industrial relations in New Zealand's state-owned enterprises', *British Journal of Industrial Relations* 31: 57–74.

Warner, M. (1990) 'Yugoslav "self-management" and industrial relations in transition', *Industrial Relations Journal* 21: 209–20.

—— (1991) 'Labour–management relations in the People's Republic of China: the role of the trade unions', *International Journal of Human Resource Management* 2: 205–20.

Warner, M. and Turner, L. (1972) 'Trade unions and the multinational firm', *Journal of Industrial Relations* 14: 143–70.

Waters, M. (1982) *Strikes in Australia*, Sydney: Allen & Unwin.

Weber, A. R. (1963) 'The structure of collective bargaining and bargaining power: foreign experiences', *Journal of Law and Economics* 6: 79–151.

—— (1974) 'Bargaining without boundaries: industrial relations and the multinational firm', in R. J. Flanagan and A. R. Weber (eds) *Bargaining Without Boundaries. The Multinational Corporation and International Labor Relations*, Chicago: University of Chicago Press.

Wedderburn, D. (1974) 'Perspectives on Sweden', *Personnel Management* 6, 5: 31–4.

Wedderburn, Lord (1983) 'Otto Kahn-Freund and British labour law', in Lord Wedderburn, R. Lewis and J. Clark (eds) *Labour Law and Industrial Relations: Building on Kahn-Freund*, Oxford: Clarendon.

—— (1988) 'Trade union democracy and industrial relations. United Kingdom', *Bulletin of Comparative Labour Relations* 17: 107–44.

—— (1989) 'Freedom of association and philosophies of labour law', *Industrial Law Journal* 18: 1–38.

Weinburg, P. J. (1978) *European Labor and Multinationals*, New York: Praeger.

Wells, D. (1993) 'Are strong unions compatible with the new model of human resource management?', *Relations Industrielles* 48: 56–84.

Westenholz, A. (1979) 'Workers' participation in Denmark', *Industrial Relations* 18: 376–80.

Wheeler, H. (1987) 'Management–labour relations in the USA', in G. J. Bamber and R. D. Lansbury (eds) *International and Comparative Industrial Relations. A Study of Developed Market Economies*, London: Allen & Unwin.

White, M. and Trevor, M. (1983) *Under Japanese Management. The Experience of British Workers*, London: Heinemann.

Whyte, W. F. and Alberti, G. (1977) 'The industrial community in Peru', *Annals of the American Academy of Political and Social Science* 431: 103–12.

Wiarda, H. J. (1978) 'Corporative origins of the Iberian and Latin American labor relations systems', *Studies in Comparative International Development*, 13.

Wilkinson, B. (1986) 'Human resources in Singapore's second industrial revolution', *Industrial Relations Journal* 17, 2: 99–114.

Wilkinson, R. and Burkitt, B. (1973) 'Wage determination and trade unions', *Scottish Journal of Political Economy* 20: 107–21.

Willman, P. (1983) *Bargaining for Change. A Comparison of the UK and USA*, Occasional Paper No. 2, Industrial Relations Group, University of Durham.

Windmuller, J. P. (1963) 'Model industrial relations systems', IRRA 16th Annual Meeting, *Proceedings*: 60–75.

—— (1967) 'Employers and employers' associations in the Netherlands industrial relations system', *Relations Industrielles* 22: 47–72.

—— (1974) 'European labor and politics: a symposium, II', *Industrial and Labor Relations Review* 28: 203–7.

—— (1977) 'Industrial democracy and industrial relations', *Annals of the American Academy of Political and Social Science* 431: 22–31.

—— (1980) *The International Trade Union Movement*, Deventer: Kluwer.

—— (1981) 'Concentration trends in union structure: an international comparison', *Industrial and Labor Relations Review* 35: 43–57.

—— (1984) 'Employers' associations in comparative perspective. Organisation, structure, administration', in J. P. Windmuller and A. Gladstone (eds) *Employers' Associations and Industrial Relations. A Comparative Study*, Oxford: Clarendon.

—— (1987) *Collective Bargaining in Industrialised Market Economies: A Reappraisal*, Geneva: ILO.

Windmuller, J. P. and Gladstone, A. (eds) (1984) *Employers' Associations and Industrial Relations. A Comparative Study*, Oxford: Clarendon.

Windolf, P. (1989) 'Productivity coalitions and the future of corporatism. A comparative view on Western European industrial relations', *Industrial Relations* 28: 1–20.

World Bank (1990) *World Development Report*, New York: Oxford University Press.

Yarmie, A. H. (1980) 'Employers' organisations in mid-Victorian England', *International Review of Social History* 25: 209–35.

Zappala, J. and Lansbury, R. (1990) 'Recent industrial relations trends in the Republic of Korea', *Labour and Industry* 3: 235–57.

Zeffane, R. (1981) 'Participative management in Algeria', in R. Mansfield and M. Poole (eds) *International Perspectives on Management and Organization*, Aldershot: Gower.

Zeitlin, J. (1983) 'The labour strategies of British engineering employers, 1890–1922', in H. F. Gospel and C. R. Littler (eds) *Managerial Strategies and Industrial Relations*, London: Heinemann.

—— (1987) 'From labour history to the history of industrial relations', *Economic History Review* 40: 159–84.

—— (1990) 'The triumph of adversarial bargaining: industrial relations in British engineering, 1880–1939', *Politics and Society* 18: 405–26.

Author index

Silvia, S.J. 207, 209
Sim, A.B. 196
Simmonds, K. 200
Sisson, K. 51, 143; collective
bargaining 75, 82; employers 56,
57, 60, 61, 62–3, 64, 70;
government 58; MNEs 207,
211
Skeels, J.W. 157
Slomp, H. 30
Smith, D.F. 79
Snyder, D. 153–7
Sorge, A. 10, 13, 168, 171, 172
Sorrentino, C. 38
Soskice, D. 241
Southall, R. 218
Stephens, E.H. 166
Stephens, J.D. 43
Stokland, D. 92, 163
Stone, K. 67
Storey, J. 70
Strauss, G. 164, 166, 175–6
Streeck, W. 3, 4, 10, 30, 139;
collective bargaining 77, 91;
employers 69
Strinati, D. 113, 128
Sturmthal, A. 4
Summers, C. 130
Symons, J.V. 240
Széll, G. 160
Szul, R. 166

Taft, P. 59
Taira, K. 54, 56, 68, 130
Takamiya, M. 199
Tannenbaum, A.S. 180
Tchobanian, R. 76
Teague, P. 207, 208, 209
Thomas, H. 168
Thompson, M. 37
Thomson, A.W.J. 60
Thurley, K. 9, 10, 68
Tilly, C. 102, 132, 145–7, 154
Tolliday, S. 52
Townley, B. 7
Traxler, F. 21, 34, 164, 188, 239
Treckel, K.F. 203
Treu, T. 125, 127, 223; collective
bargaining 81, 82, 90, 96, 101;
trade unions 31, 37, 49

Trevor, M. 199
Troy, L. 22, 40
Tsakalotos, E. 240
Turkington, D.J. 79
Turner, L. 49, 195
Turner, T. 224

Ulman, L. 19, 54, 191
Ulmer, M.J. 193
Urry, J. 90, 127

Van de Vall, M. 22
Van Voorden, W. 56
Vilrokx, J. 118
Visser, J. 20, 34, 46, 49, 64, 76, 91
Von Beyme, K. 13, 30, 35, 131, 132,
136, 143–4
Voos, P.B. 237
Vranken, M. 117

Wad, P. 219
Wadhwani, S. 237
Wagner, J. 235
Walker, K.F. 8, 13, 111, 113, 161
Wall, T.D. 184
Wallerstein, M. 43
Walsh, P. 118
Warner, M. 10, 25, 36, 160, 163, 181,
183
Waters, M. 143
Weber, A.R. 16, 88
Wedderburn, D. 6
Wedderburn, Lord 106, 118
Weinburg, P.J. 192
Wells, D. 70
Westenholz, A. 179
Wetzel, K. 118
Wheeler, H. 115
White, M. 199
Whyte, W.F. 181
Wiarda, H.J. 223
Wilkinson, B. 218, 227
Wilkinson, F. 97–8
Willman, P. 170
Windmuller, J.P. 6, 169, 203, 231;
collective bargaining 74, 76, 78, 80,
84, 89; employers 52, 56, 60; trade
unions 19–20, 31, 34, 81, 83
Windolf, P. 91, 127, 183
Wood, S. 68

Subject index

adversarial bargaining 75
Africa 213–14, 215, 226, 228;
  colonies 6–7, 221, 222; trade unions
  215–16, 216–17; *see also under*
  individual countries
Airbus 211
AKZO 204
Algeria 165, 166
Arab states 217
arbitration 102, 122, 247; Australia 60,
  77, 103–4 (government role
  111–14; trade unions 33, 46,
  115–16)
Argentina 213, 222, 223
Association of South East Asian
  Nations (ASEAN) 214
attitudes towards participation 179–80
Australia 11, 114, 161, 238; Accord
  89, 242; arbitration see arbitration;
  bargaining coverage 78; CAI 62;
  economic indicators 236; employers
  53–4, 56–7, 62; strikes 134, 135,
  143; trade unions 19, 32–3, 38, 46,
  47, 78
Austria 133, 148, 188, 240, 249;
  concertation 126; economic
  indicators 236; employers 53;
  participation 34, 164, 176, 180;
  trade unions 21, 34, 171, 176, 239
autonomous work groups 162–3

bargained corporatism 126
Basque nationalism 168
Belgium 118; collective bargaining 77;
  MNEs 193, 197; participation
  172–3, 174, 184; strikes 134, 136

Benin 226, 228
Brazil 213, 223
brigade system 166
Britain: collective bargaining 76, 78,
  91, 97–9 (industry level 80–1,
  81–2, 82–3); economic indicators
  236; employers 51, 59 (associations
  54, 60–1; bargaining 62–3, 63–4;
  management strategies 65–6, 67,
  70–1); Engineering Employers'
  Federation 245; government 103,
  126, 128–9 (collective bargaining
  104, 105–7, 117–18; dispute
  settlement 112, 122; employment
  terms 119–20); Industrial Relations
  Act (1971) 6, 247; industrial
  relations system 11, 231–2, 237,
  252; MNEs 194, 195, 196 (joint
  ventures 211–12; strikes 200–1;
  union recognition 196, 197; work
  practices 198–9); oil-rig unions 12;
  participation 162, 163, 168, 170–1,
  171, 174, 175, 184 (outcomes 179,
  180; profit-sharing 182, 183;
  quality circles 163); single-union
  agreement 7; strikes 134, 135, 136,
  150–1, 232 (institutionalisation
  theory 141, 142, 142–3); territories
  in Africa 6–7; TGWU 36; trade
  unions 19, 21, 25–6, 29, 44 (density
  38, 42, 78; internal democracy 36,
  37; labour movement 26; workplace
  organisation 34–5); Wages
  Councils 247
BSN-Gervais Danone 208
building industry 14–15, 52–3, 61